Mindful LIVING

Workbook and Journal for Life Transformation

ANGELA M. DAY

AuthorHouse™
1663 Liberty Drive
Bloomington, IN 47403
www.authorhouse.com
Phone: 1-800-839-8640

© 2013 Angela M. Day. All rights reserved.

No part of this book may be reproduced, stored in a retrieval system, or transmitted by any means without the written permission of the author.

Published by AuthorHouse   04/03/2013

ISBN: 978-1-4817-3096-9 (sc)
ISBN: 978-1-4817-3097-6 (e)

Library of Congress Control Number: 2013905698

Because of the dynamic nature of the Internet, any web addresses or links contained in this book may have changed since publication and may no longer be valid. The views expressed in this work are solely those of the author and do not necessarily reflect the views of the publisher, and the publisher hereby disclaims any responsibility for them.

Contents

Introduction x

How to use this book xi

Chapter 1: Who Am I? 1
    I am content 2
    I am proud of myself 4
    I am successful 6
    I am likeable and loveable 8

Chapter 2: What am I looking for? 11
    I look for others to show me love, appreciation, support and kindness 12
    I look for ways to show love, appreciation, support and kindness 14
    I look for ways to help others and pay it forward 16
    I look for opportunities to give my undivided attention 18
    I look for ways to make things better 20
    I look for joy, happiness, fun and laughter 22

Chapter 3: What am I doing? 25
    I am smiling 26
    I am praying or meditating 28
    I am inspired 30
    I am listening to and acting on intuition 32
    I am physically active 34
    I am honest 36
    I am taking care of myself 38

Chapter 4: Where am I going? 41
    I have purpose 42
    I have intention 44
    I have goals 46
    I have vision 50

Chapter 5: Why do I deserve a wonderful life? 53
    I am grateful 54
    I am looking forward 56

Daily Journal (Mindful Living Worksheets) 59

"It's the parents' job to screw up their children as much as possible, and the kids' job is to fix themselves."—Larry C. Day

This book is dedicated . . .

To all of my parents who did their job exceptionally well. I sincerely appreciate each one of you. And now, I have done my job. *Exceptionally well.*

And to David and Devon. We have all done our job exceptionally well. You both have the brains, the courage, the heart and the strength to do yours. *Exceptionally well.*

Acknowledgements

I would like to thank the Creative Spark writing group for your loving support and feedback. Becky Kiper, thank you for your friendship, helping me through terror barriers and jumping on this train without a moment's hesitation. Elizabeth Parker, I greatly appreciate your professional and proficient copy editing and for lighting my path when I couldn't see the way. Thank you, Vance Davis of Hammerhead Designs, for your patience with two silly women on a cold February evening; your picture makes me smile and laugh every time I see it! And, a special thanks to you, Tim, for being my guinea pig and your consistent faith in this book.

Every one of you came forward and offered your assistance with no expectation of compensation. Not one of you asked, "What's in it for me?" I am so deeply grateful to all of you and I know that your kindness will be returned in ways that are much bigger than I could ever repay.

Thank you.

Dear Reader,

You are invited to join the Like Minded Community!

The Like Minded Community is an online network of people who come together to give and receive positive support and encouragement. It is a place for people to meet **live and face-to-face** for collaborative discussions.

The Like Minded Community is NOT another social network.

Weekly meetings are held in small Empowerment Groups so that you can develop more personal relationships and truly get to know the other people you're working with.

Joining the Like Minded Community and working with your Empowerment Group will:
- jump-start your personal growth.
- help you stay focused on your priorities.
- present new perspectives from people who want to help you succeed.
- provide motivation to work toward your goals.
- help you work through your personal challenges.
- build relationships with others who share a similar drive.

As a member of the Like Minded Community you work directly with a group of four other people. Each week your Empowerment Group meets virtually via video conferencing to talk about and work through one section of *Mindful Living*. During each meeting you discuss a *Mindful Living* section using a suggested agenda and topic questions.

The members of your Empowerment Group change every 6 months, giving you the opportunity to meet new like minded people and get different perspectives from all over the world.

To join the Like Minded Community or to view a calendar of events for workshops and book signings, please visit www.MindfulLivingTransformation.com.

I look forward to meeting you, either virtually or in person!

Sincerely,

Angela Day

Introduction

One of the most important things in my life is being committed to personal growth and development.

For many years I have read books, attended seminars and workshops, listened to audio programs and participated in groups with the focus of improving myself and my life. And it's worked! But throughout my journey, I have been overwhelmed with suggestions of what I should do *every day* to make the changes I desired.

I agreed with most of the suggestions and saw the value in daily practice, but if I tried to incorporate everything I had learned into each day, I'd never be able to do anything else. Meditate for an hour three times a day, journal about everything that you do throughout the day, work out at the gym for an hour every day. Who has time for just those three things on a daily basis? I know I certainly don't!

So, in order to organize and streamline my efforts, I developed a daily worksheet and checklist.

Every night before I go to sleep, I take about 15-20 minutes to complete the worksheet. It basically serves as a bullet-point journal. It is a list of everything I want to incorporate into my daily life and a measure of how successful I am each day.

Since I began using this worksheet, I live each day more present and engaged in my life.

Each item on the list becomes something I look for or make a point of doing throughout the day. I see the world as a better place because I'm looking for the good. I make the world a better place because I'm *doing* more good.

I offer this Mindful Living Worksheet to you in hope that you will also discover wonderful things about yourself, see the world as a beautiful canvas full of opportunity and create the life you dream of living. This book explains each item on the Mindful Living Worksheet and offers an exercise to help get you started.

In these pages you will find hard work, confidence and empowerment. But most of all you will find a simple guide to loving your life every day.

How to use this book

I recommend completing the Mindful Living Worksheet daily, even as you are reading and working through the book and exercises.

You will probably not be able to check off every item, but in completing the ones you can you get in the habit of using the worksheet and looking for or doing these things throughout the day.

Please remember that the purpose of this program is to help you improve. I encourage you to celebrate the items that are easier for you and to be patient with yourself as you work toward the items that are more challenging. Ultimately, the challenging items will offer a path to more personal growth and improvement.

This program and the positive changes you will experience are based on repetition and building momentum. Completing a Mindful Living Worksheet every day is vital and only takes approximately 10 to 20 minutes. If you want to live a wonderful life it will take a commitment to continue using the Mindful Living Worksheet long after you've read this book and completed the exercises.

Becoming the person you want to be and living the life you want to live is not a race or a competition. It will not happen overnight. After you have been using the Mindful Living Worksheet for several weeks, read back through your entries and look for progress you've made.

Like life, these exercises are not about perfection, only progress.

Knowing yourself is
the beginning of all wisdom.

—**Aristotle**

Chapter 1

Who Am I?

I AM CONTENT

In a society that glorifies 'more, faster, better', finding things that you are content with can seem difficult. You might be happy with the latest technology you've purchased until you find a new item that does more, goes faster or looks better.

Wanting more, faster and better is a symptom of being caught up in a materialistic culture. It can leave you feeling unfulfilled and exhausted from trying to reach a bar that is always being moved out of reach.

The way to break out of this cycle is to look for things that you are content with. You might be content with your level of education, one or more of your relationships, or something as simple as reading a book or listening to music.

> Quick Tip: What does the word 'content' mean to you? For the purpose of this exercise, I encourage you to view contentment as something you're satisfied, comfortable and happy with *today*. You may work toward something different in the future, but just for today, it's good enough.

Take a look at the different areas of your life. Are you content in your job, your home, your hobbies? How about your relationships? Not just a romantic relationship with a significant other, but with your family, friends, co-workers, neighbors, etc. Is there a place where you like to go that you feel peaceful and content? What activities do you like to participate in that you are content with?

Exercise

On the opposite page, make a list of everything you are content with in your life. Write down anything that you deem 'good enough' just as it is. This is a brain-storming session to start thinking about being content.

Mindful Living Worksheet

The first item on your Mindful Living Worksheet is "I am content with . . .". Fill in this blank with something from your day that you see no need to change or improve. Check this item off of your worksheet each day that you find something you're content with—at least for today.

I am content with . . .

My Relationships (family, friends, neighbors, co-workers): _____
_____
_____

My Personality Traits (compassionate, grounded, confident, loving): _____
_____
_____

My Skills (fixing things, typing, leadership abilities, sales): _____
_____
_____

My Physical Body (eyes, strong hands, hair, skin, smile): _____
_____
_____

My Experiences (education/knowledge, travel): _____
_____
_____

My Work (job, career, volunteering, source of income): _____
_____
_____

My Hobbies (cooking, scuba diving, singing, target shooting, kayaking, dancing): _____
_____
_____

My Environment (home, office, room): _____
_____
_____

My Material Possessions (clothes, car, tools, electronics): _____
_____
_____

I AM PROUD OF MYSELF

Self-esteem is influenced by two things: what you think about yourself and what you believe others think about you. These two factors fluctuate so sometimes your self-esteem is based more on your own opinion, and other times it's based more on the opinion of others.

Both of these ingredients make up your self-esteem, but you only have control over one: what you think about yourself.

So, what *do* you think about yourself? Do you like yourself? Do you think you're a good person? Do you think you're valuable? No matter how you answered these questions, there is an easy way to improve your self-esteem— give yourself credit for positive accomplishments and attributes.

> Quick Tip: There is a simple formula for feeling like a super-hero. First, be completely honest (discussed in more detail on page 36). Second, do things that you're proud of and give yourself credit for them every day. If you practice either of these, your confidence and self-esteem will improve. If you focus on both of these every day, you will soar!

Exercise

On the next page, make a list of everything you are proud of. This can be anything in your entire life that you consider a success. Write down all of your accomplishments, both large and small. Do you make a mean lasagna? Did you graduate high school? Get a job or a promotion? Take care of your children, sibling, parent or other family member? Learn how to swim? Complete a training program? Reach a personal goal? Give yourself credit for all of your successes!

Also, start paying attention to your self-talk. Really listen to the thoughts that run through your mind during the day. If you catch your self-talk being negative or condescending, change what you are thinking to your accomplishments. Choose one thing you're proud of and remember how wonderful it felt! Or, see how many successes you can count in your mind. You can also read over the list you've made here in your workbook and look back at previous entries on your Mindful Living Worksheet of things you're proud of.

Mindful Living Worksheet

Complete this item on your Mindful Living Worksheet by writing something you're proud of that happened today or that was relevant today.

Mindful Living

I am proud of . . .
(Relationships, Personality Traits, Skills, Physical Body, Experiences, Work, Hobbies, Environment, Material Possessions)

Accomplishment: I am proud of this because:

I AM SUCCESSFUL

You have now identified some things you're proud of. Congratulations! You've listed lifetime accomplishments and included daily accomplishments on your Mindful Living Worksheet.

We're going to take these one step further and create ways to energize yourself with success.

Exercise

Choose one or more of the projects below to organize your accomplishments. When choosing the success projects you want to create, keep in mind that some are more portable than others. Choose the projects that are most realistic to incorporate into your lifestyle. Plan to spend about 15 minutes each day looking at or listening to your successes.

Success Board: Gather pictures representing things you have accomplished. These can be photographs, copies of certificates or diplomas, ticket stubs and brochures. If you don't have these items, use the internet and print pictures that represent your successes. You may even want to include hand-drawn pictures, cards or notes that were given to you by people you love. (Having good, positive, supportive relationships is definitely an accomplishment to celebrate!) Then, tape or glue the pictures to a large piece of poster board, cardboard or display board. You could also use a bulletin board or your refrigerator.

Success Box: Collect pictures and items as described above and put them in a box. Paint and/or decorate the box any way that appeals to you.

Success Book: Collect pictures as described above. Put your pictures in a photo album where the plastic cover of the pages peal back so you can arrange the things you want anywhere on the page. If you scrapbook, create a book specifically of your accomplishments.

Success Photo Album: Collect pictures and items as described above. Take a close-up picture of each one with your cell phone. If possible, store these in a separate folder or album on your phone for easy access.

Success Slide Show: Scan or take a picture of your success items and upload them to a folder on your computer. Use them to create a slide show or to rotate as the background of your desktop.

Success Art: If you paint, sculpt or build models, create pieces that depict your successes.

Success Track: Collect pictures and items as described above. Make a voice recording describing the experience of each picture and item. Talk in detail about how wonderful it felt to be in that moment and to have that experience. Elaborate on as many details as you possibly can, especially the senses. What did you hear, smell, see, taste and feel (physically and emotionally)? Save the recording on your computer, tablet or cell phone so that you can listen to it on a regular basis.

Mindful Living Worksheet

Spend at least 15 minutes every day looking at or listening to your successes. When you do, check this item off of the Mindful Living Worksheet. The wonderful feeling you get when remembering your successes will be fuel for even more accomplishments and will give you an amazing boost in self-confidence and motivation!

Mindful Living

I will create a . . .

- ☐ Success Board
- ☐ Success Box
- ☐ Success Book/Scrapbook
- ☐ Success Photo Album (cell phone)
- ☐ Success Slide Show
- ☐ Success Art
- ☐ Success Track
- ☐ Other: _____

I will review my success project . . .

- ☐ When I wake up in the morning
- ☐ Before I go to sleep at night
- ☐ On my lunch break
- ☐ When I'm driving (Success Track)
- ☐ While I eat breakfast/lunch/dinner
- ☐ While I'm waiting for: _____
- ☐ Other: _____

I AM LIKEABLE AND LOVEABLE

Say these statements out loud: "I like who I am." "I love myself!"

How difficult was that for you to say?

What if someone asked, "Why should I like you?" or "Why should I love you?" Could you answer them with multiple reasons? By the end of this exercise you will be able to do just that.

Everyone wants to be liked and loved. Unfortunately, many of us don't like ourselves; so how could anyone else love us? Even if someone else says they like you or shows you love, if you don't believe you're likeable/loveable, then they must be lying.

It is now time to prove that you are likeable and loveable. And yes, it starts with yourself.

Exercise

Make a list of everything you like about yourself. It can be personality traits like, "I am funny. I am kind. I am considerate. I am hard-working." It can be things that you're good at like, "I am good at dancing. I am good at math. I am good at showing people I care about them." Think of things you're committed to like, "I am committed to personal growth and development. I am committed to providing for my family. I am committed to leading by example." Also include physical traits like, "I have beautiful eyes. I have strong hands. I have thick hair."

List everything you can possibly think of. This is not a time to be modest and no one else's opinion matters. Only yours.

> Quick Tip: Try to come up with 101 things you like about yourself. If you can only find 5 or 10, that's okay. You can always add to this list and I hope you do!

Mindful Living Worksheet

The next item on the Mindful Living Worksheet is, "I love myself because . . ." Each day you will find things to love about you because of what you do. For example, if you hold a door open for someone this proves that you are kind and considerate. So, you would write on your worksheet, "I am kind and considerate." If you call a friend who has been sick to see how they're feeling, you would write, "I show my friends I love them and care about them." That's something to love about yourself!

You might notice that this is the only item on the Mindful Living Worksheet that has two check boxes. The first check box is for writing something you love about yourself based on something that happened today.

The second task is to read the things you've written in this box for the last 5 to 10 days. Looking back at the things you've written will show that you have so many reasons to love yourself. After all, each entry wasn't just an idea. You took action to *prove* that attribute is true. Check the second box showing that you have reviewed the things you love about yourself from the last week or two.

Mindful Living

I like and love myself because . . .
(Include personality traits, physical traits, skills, things you're good at, and things you're committed to.)

1. _____	35. _____	69. _____
2. _____	36. _____	70. _____
3. _____	37. _____	71. _____
4. _____	38. _____	72. _____
5. _____	39. _____	73. _____
6. _____	40. _____	74. _____
7. _____	41. _____	75. _____
8. _____	42. _____	76. _____
9. _____	43. _____	77. _____
10. _____	44. _____	78. _____
11. _____	45. _____	79. _____
12. _____	46. _____	80. _____
13. _____	47. _____	81. _____
14. _____	48. _____	82. _____
15. _____	49. _____	83. _____
16. _____	50. _____	84. _____
17. _____	51. _____	85. _____
18. _____	52. _____	86. _____
19. _____	53. _____	87. _____
20. _____	54. _____	88. _____
21. _____	55. _____	89. _____
22. _____	56. _____	90. _____
23. _____	57. _____	91. _____
24. _____	58. _____	92. _____
25. _____	59. _____	93. _____
26. _____	60. _____	94. _____
27. _____	61. _____	95. _____
28. _____	62. _____	96. _____
29. _____	63. _____	97. _____
30. _____	64. _____	98. _____
31. _____	65. _____	99. _____
32. _____	66. _____	100. _____
33. _____	67. _____	101. _____
34. _____	68. _____	

How you look at it
is pretty much how you'll see it.

—Rasheed Ogunlaru

CHAPTER 2

What am I looking for?

I LOOK FOR OTHERS TO SHOW ME LOVE, APPRECIATION, SUPPORT AND KINDNESS

Everyone wants love, support, appreciation and kindness from other people. It's human nature.

But we can't control other people's behavior, so we can't *make* other people love, support and appreciate us or show us kindness. So how do you get these basic needs met when you can't force others to do what you want?

The solution is simple and has three steps. First, you have to believe you deserve kindness and are worthy of being loved, supported and appreciated. (You have been working toward this first step by completing the previous exercise and filling in the "I love myself because . . ." section of your Mindful Living Worksheet.) Second, you have to be open to receiving these gifts. Third, you have to *be* loving, supportive, appreciative and kind. In this section, we're going to focus on the second step.

If you feel that others are not treating you with love, support, appreciation and kindness, you have blinders on. You are not open to receiving these gifts and are not paying attention when they are offered to you.

Has anyone recently let you into traffic or smiled at you? That was a complete stranger being kind to you.

Has anyone said, "Thank you" for any reason? They were showing appreciation.

Has anyone helped you in any way, offered a word of encouragement or just listened to you? They were giving you support.

Has anyone told you they love you or care about you, given you their time and attention, done something they knew you would like, or given you a gift? They were showing love.

Exercise

Make a list on the opposite page of every time someone has shown you love, support appreciation and kindness. List any gesture, both large and small that you can think of from any time in your life.

> Quick Tip: If you want more love, support, appreciation and kindness, look for and be grateful when these are offered to you. Don't ignore that smile. Don't take it for granted when a friend listens to your concerns. Pay attention to what people are really doing and value what they're giving you. Also realize that when someone does any of these for you, it is PROOF that you are worth it and deserve it, which goes back to the first step in bringing more of this into your life.

Mindful Living Worksheet

Make a point to go through the day looking for instances where people are loving, supportive, thankful and kind to you. When you see these things happen, write them down on your Mindful Living Worksheet. When you list at least four examples, check off this item.

Get ready to be pleasantly surprised at how much love, support, appreciation and kindness are coming to you!

Mindful Living

Fill in the information below. Include experiences with immediate and extended family, friends, co-workers, neighbors or complete strangers.

Name or Stranger

_____ showed me ☐ love ☐ support ☐ appreciation ☐ kindness when they
_____

_____ showed me ☐ love ☐ support ☐ appreciation ☐ kindness when they
_____

_____ showed me ☐ love ☐ support ☐ appreciation ☐ kindness when they
_____

_____ showed me ☐ love ☐ support ☐ appreciation ☐ kindness when they
_____

_____ showed me ☐ love ☐ support ☐ appreciation ☐ kindness when they
_____

_____ showed me ☐ love ☐ support ☐ appreciation ☐ kindness when they
_____

_____ showed me ☐ love ☐ support ☐ appreciation ☐ kindness when they
_____

_____ showed me ☐ love ☐ support ☐ appreciation ☐ kindness when they
_____

_____ showed me ☐ love ☐ support ☐ appreciation ☐ kindness when they
_____

_____ showed me ☐ love ☐ support ☐ appreciation ☐ kindness when they
_____

I LOOK FOR WAYS TO SHOW LOVE, APPRECIATION, SUPPORT AND KINDNESS

In the last section on love, support, appreciation and kindness, we looked at the three steps needed to bring more of these qualities into your life.

The first step is to believe that you are worthy of kindness, being loved, supported and appreciated. You have already begun this process by completing the 'I love Myself' and 'I'm proud of Myself' activities on pages 9 and 5. Each day you wrote something in these sections on the Mindful Living Worksheet you reinforced that you deserve all of these wonderful gifts.

The second step is to be open to receiving love, support appreciation and kindness. You started this process by completing the activities on page 13. You then practiced receiving each day that you wrote something in the 'Love, support, appreciation and kindness for me' section of your Mindful Living Worksheet.

It is now time to master the third step, which is to *be* loving, supportive, appreciative and kind to other people.

Exercise

Use the opposite page to list any time that you have been loving, supportive, appreciative and kind at any point in your life. Write a brief note about the situation, what you did and who it was for.

> Quick Tip: Loving, supportive, appreciative and kind actions are definitely a gift to someone else. But, they are also a gift to yourself. In the past, if you were giving out of expectation or obligation, you probably didn't feel much. You may have been resentful or even angry. But if your actions were true gifts because they were your choice, you probably felt a strong emotion of love or joy. Give this gift to yourself as often as possible by being loving, supportive, appreciative and kind to others!
>
> People are more inclined to be loving, supportive, appreciative and kind when you're acting this way toward them. They, in turn, act this way toward you and to others they interact with. So, a whole cycle of generating love, support, appreciation and kindness is created by each action you take.

Mindful Living Worksheet

Write down ways you show love, support, thanks and kindness every day on your Mindful Living Worksheet. Every day you list at least four actions you've taken, check this item off of your worksheet.

Mindful Living

Fill in the information below. Include experiences with immediate and extended family, friends, co-workers, neighbors or complete strangers.

I showed _____ (name or stranger) ☐ love ☐ support ☐ appreciation ☐ kindness when I
_____

I showed _____ (name or stranger) ☐ love ☐ support ☐ appreciation ☐ kindness when I
_____

I showed _____ (name or stranger) ☐ love ☐ support ☐ appreciation ☐ kindness when I
_____

I showed _____ (name or stranger) ☐ love ☐ support ☐ appreciation ☐ kindness when I
_____

I showed _____ (name or stranger) ☐ love ☐ support ☐ appreciation ☐ kindness when I
_____

I showed _____ (name or stranger) ☐ love ☐ support ☐ appreciation ☐ kindness when I
_____

I showed _____ (name or stranger) ☐ love ☐ support ☐ appreciation ☐ kindness when I
_____

I showed _____ (name or stranger) ☐ love ☐ support ☐ appreciation ☐ kindness when I
_____

I showed _____ (name or stranger) ☐ love ☐ support ☐ appreciation ☐ kindness when I
_____

I showed _____ (name or stranger) ☐ love ☐ support ☐ appreciation ☐ kindness when I
_____

I LOOK FOR WAYS TO HELP OTHERS AND PAY IT FORWARD

You have learned that you have the opportunity to make the world a better place every day. In the last section, you put love, appreciation, support and kindness into action.

We're going one step further and adding good deeds, selfless acts and acts of random kindness. The difference between these two items is that you are now looking for ways to help people you don't even know—complete strangers.

You are probably doing these types of things and just not giving yourself credit for the good you're bringing to other people. This includes letting another car into traffic, being patient and understanding when a customer service representative puts you on hold or letting someone go in front of you in the check-out line at the grocery store.

Exercise

As you go through your day, look for things you can do for random strangers. Here are some suggestions to help get you started:

- If you drive on a toll road, pay for the person behind you.
- Pick up trash as you walk around the neighborhood for exercise.
- Take a meal or dessert to your local police or fire station.
- Donate blood.
- Give someone a sincere compliment.
- Buy small bottles of bubbles and hand them out to children at a park (then sit back and soak up the joy that will ensue).
- Take gently-worn clothing, furniture or household items to a charity like Good Will.
- Register as an organ donor when you get your driver's license renewed.
- If you play a portable instrument, take it to a park and give an impromptu concert (no tips, or it doesn't count as a selfless act!).
- Stop to help someone on the side of the road with car problems.
- Smile at someone who looks like they're having a bad day or may be shy.
- Do you know of a place where the homeless congregate? Order pizza and have it delivered there.
- Read poetry or just talk with nursing home residents.
- Offer a ride to someone walking down the street with grocery bags.
- Write a letter or send a gift box to someone serving in the military overseas.

Write down things that you've done in the past that would qualify as good deeds or selfless acts. There's no time frame, so include anything you've ever done.

Make a list of things you would be willing to try. This could be from my suggestions or ideas you come up with on your own. Keep in mind that you have unique talents and resources! How can you share these with the world?

Mindful Living Worksheet

Each day that you are able to find some way to do a good deed, check this item off of the Mindful Living Worksheet. Remember that no act of kindness is too large or too small.

I have done good deeds, acted selflessly and participated in acts of random kindness by . . .

_____

_____

_____

_____

_____

_____

_____

_____

_____

I am willing to try the following good deeds, selfless acts and acts of random kindness . . .

_____

_____

_____

_____

_____

_____

_____

_____

_____

I LOOK FOR OPPORTUNITIES TO GIVE MY UNDIVIDED ATTENTION

I once heard that the greatest gift you can give someone is your undivided attention. I believe this is true.

When I think back over my life, I realize that I felt the happiest and most loved when people I cared about were spending time with me—grandparents, parents, extended family, friends, my own children. It's time to pay those gifts forward.

Giving someone your undivided attention means doing more than being in the same room together. Remember, this is a gift to them. Think about what they enjoy doing and do it with them. Read a book together, try playing a video game, catch up over a cup of coffee or tea, play cards, invite them over for dinner. You don't have to come up with an elaborate plan to entertain them. In fact, what you do is mostly irrelevant as long as you're making their preferences the priority. Look for random opportunities and you might be surprised at how much time you can 'find' to connect.

The simplest and most effective way to create quality time is to start a conversation *without an agenda*. Give them the opportunity to talk about anything they choose. Be engaged and participate in the discussion, but the most important thing to do is listen.

When people you care about are too far away to see in person on a regular basis, these conversations become even more important. Take time to talk with them on the phone, online via social networking sites or video chats.

> Quick Tip: In the fast-paced world we live in, making time to completely devote to someone else may be a challenge. But, even if it's only for 10-15 minutes each day, it will make a difference. The gift of your focused attention is something they will probably remember for the rest of their lives. Plus, you get the benefit of having deeper, more connected relationships that add so much joy to your life.

Exercise

On the opposite page, make a list of the people you want to give the gift of your time and attention. Then, jot down a few ideas of what you could do with each person that they would enjoy.

Mindful Living Worksheet

Check this off on your Mindful Living Worksheet every day that you find a way to give someone else your undivided attention.

Mindful Living

I will give my undivided time and attention to (name of person): _____
I can do this by: 1. _____
                     2. _____
                     3. _____
                     4. _____

I will give my undivided time and attention to (name of person): _____
I can do this by: 1. _____
                     2. _____
                     3. _____
                     4. _____

I will give my undivided time and attention to (name of person): _____
I can do this by: 1. _____
                     2. _____
                     3. _____
                     4. _____

I will give my undivided time and attention to (name of person): _____
I can do this by: 1. _____
                     2. _____
                     3. _____
                     4. _____

I will give my undivided time and attention to (name of person): _____
I can do this by: 1. _____
                     2. _____
                     3. _____
                     4. _____

I LOOK FOR WAYS TO MAKE THINGS BETTER

Have you ever noticed how much time you and other people spend complaining? Complaining only adds more negative energy to a situation and can be a difficult habit to break. Try this as your new standard: "Don't complain about something unless you're willing to DO something about it."

Some people see complaining as a good way to vent their problems in order to make them feel better about themselves. While it is important to acknowledge your emotions, complaining doesn't actually produce any positive change. Complaining to other people just spreads the misery, turning their thoughts and energy negative, too. If you feel venting is absolutely necessary, do yourself and the people in your life a favor, give yourself a time limit of 5 minutes then move on.

When you're ready to feel better long-term, refocus your thoughts on what you can do to improve the situation. This doesn't mean you have to figure out how to solve the entire problem. Just brainstorm anything that you could do to make things better. Then choose the idea that you like the best, feel the most comfortable with or will make the most positive impact.

Exercise

If you're having a conflict with a friend, family member or co-worker these might be some ideas you develop to improve the situation:

- Ask to schedule some time to talk. Agree to have 5 minutes each to explain, uninterrupted, the problem from each person's perspective. (Let them go first.) Then, have 5 minutes for each of you to respond to what the other person says. Establish that the goal is not necessarily to solve the problem, but to understand each other better.
- Do something nice for them without expecting thanks or acknowledgement.
- Find something positive to sincerely compliment them on.
- Smile at them.
- Hug them, even if you're still upset.
- Tell them something you appreciate about them or that they do.

There will always be problems in life; this is how we grow and learn. This daily exercise will help you become empowered by taking responsibility for what you CAN do and what you DO have control over—your thoughts and actions. Remember, first change your thoughts (from complaints to improvement ideas), then take action to make things better.

> Quick Tip: Problems will not resolve overnight. But with your dedication and consistency, they will improve. Most importantly, you will gain confidence in your ability to positively impact any situation.

Mindful Living Worksheet

Check this item off on your Mindful Living Worksheet each day that you take action to make things better.

I have made things better in the past . . .

Situation: _____
What I did: _____

Situation: _____
What I did: _____

Situation: _____
What I did: _____

Situation: _____
What I did: _____

I can make these situations better now . . .

Situation: _____
What I can do now: 1. _____
2. _____
3. _____
4. _____

Situation: _____
What I can do now: 1. _____
2. _____
3. _____
4. _____

Situation: _____
What I can do now: 1. _____
2. _____
3. _____
4. _____

Situation: _____
What I can do now: 1. _____
2. _____
3. _____
4. _____

I LOOK FOR JOY, HAPPINESS, FUN AND LAUGHTER

Do you remember how excited you were as a child when it was time for the annual Easter Egg Hunt? Think about the exhilaration you felt as you searched for those brightly colored eggs. Or maybe you liked to play Hide and Seek and loved finding your friends, no matter how well they hid from you.

You have the opportunity to experience that excitement every day. Only now you'll be searching for joy, happiness, fun and laughter!

Exercise

What brings you joy? Do you find joy in watching the sunrise, picking flowers or playing with a baby? What makes you happy? Having dinner with your friends or family, curling your toes in the sand, blowing bubbles? Make a list on the next page of the things that really bring you joy and happiness.

What activities do you consider to be fun? Write these down, too.

Has it been a while since you had fun? If you have difficulty creating your "Fun List", think back to when you were a child and what your favorite things were. Did you love riding go-carts, sledding in the snow, building sand castles? What were your favorite games; tag, frisbee, ping-pong, foosball, board games, card games? All of these can be fun now, too!

How fun would it be to invite your friends and/or family to a water-gun fight at a pool or in the back yard? If it's too cold for outside activities, it could be a Nerf-gun battle with foam darts. BYOG—bring your own gun! You could also put together a scavenger hunt at the mall, have a water balloon toss competition or play air-hockey at the local bowling alley.

Think about things you've done or would like to try as an adult. Have you tried singing karaoke, played bingo? You can wear fun, too! Do you have a hat or novelty t-shirt that makes you feel fun? If you loved glitter as a child, try some sparkling nail polish or make-up.

If you've done any of these and think they're fun, add them to the list on the next page. If you haven't tried these, or have other ideas you think would be fun, include them, too!

What makes you laugh? If you have a favorite TV show, movie or video clip that you find hilarious, put it on your laughter list. Do comedy clubs or improv shows crack you up? Even if it's as simple as trading jokes with a friend via phone, text or email, if it makes you laugh, it counts!

Use this list to start bringing joy, happiness, fun and laughter into your life. Plan to incorporate these into your day or sprinkle them throughout your week. Make a point of creating more, but also start looking for them in unexpected places. This is where it gets exciting! The surprise of finding joy, happiness, fun and laughter in strange places makes it even sweeter!

Mindful Living Worksheet

Every day that you experience joy, happiness, fun and laughter write down how or where you found them on your Mindful Living Worksheet. Happy hunting!

Mindful Living

My Joy, Happiness, Fun and Laughter Lists

Joy and Happiness	FUN!	Laughter

What one does is what counts.
Not what one had the intention of doing.

—Pablo Picasso

Chapter 3

What am I doing?

I AM SMILING

Everyone knows that when you're happy you smile. But did you know that when you smile you get happy? It actually works both ways!

Smiling for no particular reason programs your brain in reverse. You're tricking yourself into thinking, "I'm smiling, so I must be happy." And then you are!

If you're feeling down or sluggish, smiling is a great way to almost instantly improve your mood.

> Quick Tip: We're not talking about a half-hearted tilting-the-corners-of-your-mouth-up smile. This is the full-on ear-to-ear grin that even crinkles your eyes!

You may not have thought much about smiling before, but here are a few things to keep in mind:

- Smiling is free! People spend a lot of money on things they hope will make them happier—vitamins, aromatherapy, prescriptions, etc. But smiling doesn't cost anything!
- Smiling is almost effortless! You don't have to work up a sweat or raise your heartrate.
- You can smile anywhere and anytime! There's nothing to add to your schedule or go out of your way for.
- Smiling is contagious! You may be uncomfortable at the thought of other people seeing you smile from ear-to-ear. But, they don't know you're only practicing! If someone asks why you're smiling, tell them you're just happy. Or, you could say, "I'm just trying to see how many other people I can get to smile." (What would happen to our world if everyone had this goal?)
- Smiling improves your appearance. People who smile are more often described as 'beautiful' or 'attractive'. Most of us spend time, money and energy to look good, so why not do something as simple as smiling!

Exercise

I recommend smiling this way for five minutes. Use a clock or timer. Don't be surprised if it's a little harder than you expect at first. How do you feel afterward?

Try smiling for as long as you can and for no specific reason at least once a day. However, if you're stressed or depressed you may need a little more. Try these suggestions to use smiling to help you through it:

- Think of something that makes you happy while you smile—a great vacation; spending time with your family, friends or pet; singing; dancing or cooking.
- See if you can work your way up to smiling for 10, 15 or even 20 minutes. The more you smile, the better you'll feel. So if you're feeling really bad, keep smiling until you notice your mood lighten. Even if it only helps you feel slightly better, it's an improvement!
- Smile at yourself in the mirror. Look into your eyes as you smile so big it hurts! Try smiling for thirty seconds when you're washing your hands after you use the restroom. If you're really serious about feeling better, tell yourself, "I love you."

Use checklist below to plan your smiling time. Try combinations of these until you find something that works for you.

Mindful Living Worksheet

Write down how long you smiled today. If it's more than 5 minutes, check it off!

I am going to smile . . .

(Choose one or more)

- ☐ During one full song on the radio
- ☐ While I'm praying or meditating
- ☐ When I'm preparing a meal
- ☐ Looking at myself in the mirror every time I wash my hands
- ☐ For an entire commercial break during each TV show I watch
- ☐ When I first wake up in the morning
- ☐ When I'm going to sleep at night
- ☐ The entire time I'm in the shower
- ☐ While I'm driving
- ☐ For one full commercial during each commercial break when I watch TV
- ☐ When I'm washing my face, putting on make-up and/or fixing my hair
- ☐ While I'm talking on the phone
- ☐ The entire time I'm waiting at red-lights or stop signs
- ☐ While I'm reviewing my success project(s)
- ☐ While I'm reviewing my vision project(s)
- ☐ When I'm exercising
- ☐ Every time I wash my hands
- ☐ Other: _____

I AM PRAYING OR MEDITATING

If you aren't nurturing your spirit, this is the time to start. Begin by determining when you will incorporate prayer or meditation into your day and formulate your plan on the opposite page. Then, take a few minutes to think about what you want to pray for or meditate on. Write these down as well. You may decide to pray, meditate or create some combination of both.

Your religious or spiritual beliefs will probably determine the way you choose to pray. There is no right or wrong way to do this. What is important is that you are taking the time to connect to what you consider your higher power.

The goal of meditation is to calm or focus the mind. During meditation, there will be mundane thoughts that invade the peace you're trying to find. If you focus on these unwanted thoughts, they only get stronger and become more distracting. Instead, let these thoughts float away like clouds.

> Quick Tip: There are so many different ways to meditate and, like prayer, it is only important to find what is comfortable for you.

Exercise

Below are some simple meditation techniques. For each meditation, sit upright or lay with your spine straight and close your eyes. (If you fall asleep when lying down, try sitting.)

Breathing: Focus on the sensation of your breath coming in and going out of your nose and mouth. Breathe deeply and feel the air travel down through your throat and deep into your abdomen. Let your stomach expand completely as you inhale. Regulate your breathing so that it is slower and quieter than normal. Count the seconds or heartbeats of your in and out breaths and try to make them even. (Advanced – When you inhale, imagine breathing in love, joy and happiness. As you exhale, imagine sending love, joy and happiness out to the world.)

Goal Visualization: Create a picture of something you want in your mind. This could be a tangible object, such as a new car, or an intangible object, such as a loving relationship. Build the image like a scene in a movie, complete with as many details as you can incorporate. Include yourself in the image and notice your actions and how wonderful it feels to be living this perfect scenario. (Advanced – Include elements of all five senses. What do you see, touch, taste, smell and hear?)

Grounding: When you feel scattered or stressed, try this meditation. Visualize yourself becoming a tree. Imagine your legs and feet becoming thick roots that reach deep into the earth, giving you a solid foundation. Your body becomes a strong trunk and your arms are branches reaching up to the sky. Feel your leaves dancing in the wind. Feel the sunlight warming your bark. Feel the rocks, soil and water that your roots are gathering nutrition from. (Advanced – Let any problems or negativity be swept away from you by the wind, or pushed down through your roots to be recycled by the earth.)

Guided Meditation: There are a wide variety of CDs, DVDs, online tracts and videos of guided meditations. With this type of meditation, you listen to someone's voice as they describe a scene or scenario for you to focus on. You can also develop your own guided meditation by recording yourself talking or reading a prepared narrative.

As you begin meditating, you may only be able to hold your focus for a few seconds. Don't give up! The more time you spend in meditation, the longer you will be able to do it and the more comfortable it will become.

Mindful Living Worksheet

Each day that you spend time in prayer or meditation, check this off of your Mindful Living Worksheet. Include how many minutes you are able to keep your focus so that you can track your progress.

I will pray or meditate . . .

(Choose one or more)

- ☐ When I'm preparing a meal
- ☐ For an entire commercial break during each TV show I watch
- ☐ When I first wake up in the morning
- ☐ Before I go to sleep at night
- ☐ The entire time I'm in the shower
- ☐ While I'm driving
- ☐ For one full commercial during each commercial break when I watch TV
- ☐ When I'm washing my face, putting on make-up and/or fixing my hair
- ☐ While I'm waiting at red-lights or stop signs
- ☐ When I'm exercising
- ☐ Every time I wash my hands
- ☐ Other: _____

This is how I will pray or meditate:
_____

These are the things I will pray about or meditate on:

_____   _____

_____   _____

_____   _____

_____   _____

I AM INSPIRED

In high school, one of my teachers had a sign in her room that read, "Garbage In = Garbage Out". It took years for me to really understand the wisdom in these words.

Every day you are inundated with negativity, crisis, and conflict. You're bombarded with disturbing images and stories from t.v., radio, movies, advertisements and internet content. It's not surprising that it's so difficult to feel happy, peaceful and enthusiastic when you're immersed in this type of environment.

Whether you realize it or not, all of the garbage you're ingesting effects so many things in life—how you feel about yourself, how you interact with other people and what you're contributing to the world. If you're taking in a lot of garbage, you're probably going to feel like garbage, have garbage for relationships and produce garbage, too.

It just isn't realistic to think we can go through life with blinders on to block out all of the negativity and conflict in the world. And you probably don't want to sacrifice your favorite horror movies or newscast. There is a healthy alternative.

Exercise

Take a good look at what kind of garbage you have coming into your life and how much time and attention you give it. List these sources on the opposite page. Write down anything from violent video or on-line games to friends and relatives that constantly criticize and complain. Make a note of how much time you spend doing this on a daily basis. Determine if there is any source(s) that you want to cut down or eliminate.

Now, brainstorm ways you can bring inspiration into your life. Here are some suggestions:

- Read books that are positive, encouraging and nurture your soul.
- Listen to uplifting music.
- Watch meaningful movies.
- Join a spiritual group, blog, chat group or the Like Minded Community.
- Listen to audio books on self-improvement.
- Search for and watch online videos that cultivate positivity.

For each garbage item, try to find at least one source of inspiration. The goal of this exercise is simply to balance what you're focusing on and maybe tip the scale—even just a little bit—toward inspiration.

Mindful Living Worksheet

Check off this item on your Mindful Living Worksheet each day that you spend at least 15 minutes engaged in an inspiring activity. Refer back to the list you've made on the opposite page until you get in the habit of incorporating these regularly.

Mindful Living

Garbage Inventory

Type of Garbage: _____
I spend _____ per ☐ day ☐ week ☐ month ingesting this garbage.
I want to ☐ continue with this activity ☐ spend less time on this activity ☐ eliminate this activity.
Inspiration to balance or replace this garbage: _____

Type of Garbage: _____
I spend _____ per ☐ day ☐ week ☐ month ingesting this garbage.
I want to ☐ continue with this activity ☐ spend less time on this activity ☐ eliminate this activity.
Inspiration to balance or replace this garbage: _____

Type of Garbage: _____
I spend _____ per ☐ day ☐ week ☐ month ingesting this garbage.
I want to ☐ continue with this activity ☐ spend less time on this activity ☐ eliminate this activity.
Inspiration to balance or replace this garbage: _____

Type of Garbage: _____
I spend _____ per ☐ day ☐ week ☐ month ingesting this garbage.
I want to ☐ continue with this activity ☐ spend less time on this activity ☐ eliminate this activity.
Inspiration to balance or replace this garbage: _____

Type of Garbage: _____
I spend _____ per ☐ day ☐ week ☐ month ingesting this garbage.
I want to ☐ continue with this activity ☐ spend less time on this activity ☐ eliminate this activity.
Inspiration to balance or replace this garbage: _____

Type of Garbage: _____
I spend _____ per ☐ day ☐ week ☐ month ingesting this garbage.
I want to ☐ continue with this activity ☐ spend less time on this activity ☐ eliminate this activity.
Inspiration to balance or replace this garbage: _____

Type of Garbage: _____
I spend _____ per ☐ day ☐ week ☐ month ingesting this garbage.
I want to ☐ continue with this activity ☐ spend less time on this activity ☐ eliminate this activity.
Inspiration to balance or replace this garbage: _____

I AM LISTENING TO AND ACTING ON INTUITION

Just as we process information through our five physical senses, we constantly receive information through our intuition. Your intuition is simply another function that you perform all of the time, like breathing or blinking. The only difference is that these physical functions are much easier to understand and control.

Intuition happens when your sub-conscious mind, higher-self or higher power communicates with you. As communication, intuition takes on many forms. The form depends on what your rational mind is most comfortable accepting.

Here are some types of intuition that you may experience:

- Having profound, meaningful dreams.
- Physical sensations such as a tightening in your stomach (a "gut reaction"), tingling or even a random fleeting sensation in your body.
- The simple but unexplainable knowing of what is going to happen or what to do.
- Hearing words that are somehow different than the normal chatter or self-talk in your mind.
- An emotional response like crying with joy when something feels right.
- Seeing a picture of something in your mind; almost as a memory, but nothing you've experienced before.
- Emotions that don't seem logical, such as a feeling of peace during a difficult situation or a sense of fear and panic when nothing seems to be wrong.

These are all ways intuition is trying to tell you something.

Exercise

Which of these have you experienced? Draw an asterisk (*) next to the intuition type listed above that has happened to you. Which type of intuition is most prominent for you? Write this down on the next page.

How in-tune with your intuition are you? Do you listen to intuition on a regular basis or have there been a few times in your life when following your intuition really paid off? Take a few minutes to jot these down.

Intuition is like a non-physical muscle; the more you use it, the stronger it gets. Be open to receiving the message your intuition is trying to send you. You have already identified the way(s) intuition tries to communicate. Simply remind yourself to be aware when these happen to you. Then, when you receive the message from your intuition, act on it! Taking action completes the communication cycle with your intuition.

Mindful Living Worksheet

The Mindful Living Worksheet will help remind you to practice listening to and acting on your intuition. Write down anything intuitive that happens during your day, even small messages or acts that seem insignificant. You will be surprised at how they build up and lead to monumental positive changes.

The types of intuition I most often experience are:

_____
_____
_____

These are experiences where my intuition was very strong and it paid off to listen:

_____
_____
_____
_____
_____
_____
_____
_____
_____
_____
_____
_____
_____
_____
_____
_____
_____

I AM PHYSICALLY ACTIVE

I'm sure you've heard many of the benefits of exercise: better health, reduced stress, improved mood, etc. If you're not getting enough exercise, another lecture on why you should make it a priority probably isn't productive. Instead, let's focus on how to incorporate exercise into your busy life without making it a dreaded chore.

What types of physical activities are you already doing? Give yourself credit for the exercise you get from yard work, carrying laundry up and down stairs or playing tag with the kids in the back yard. Also, think about work-related exercise like hiking through airports, lifting or carrying boxes or equipment and generally being on your feet all day.

What types of physical activities do you enjoy doing? Do you like to golf, swim or dance? How about skiing, yoga or volleyball? The more you enjoy an activity, the more likely you are to do it on a regular basis. Make a list of these and include things you already like and things you haven't tried but think you might enjoy.

If coming up with a strict set of exercises that you're going to do at the gym 4-5 times a week works for you, great! But if you've tried that type of program before and it didn't last, it's time to get creative! Here are some ideas to get you started on a plan that is realistic:

- Take the stairs instead of the elevator.
- Park at the far end of the parking lot when you go into a store or building.
- Go for a walk for 5 minutes. Then, increase the time by 1 minute every day until you work up to an hour.
- Do exercises during commercial breaks of your favorite t.v. shows. Try doing as many jumping jacks as you can during the first commercial set. Then as many crunches as you can for the next set. Also try squats, push-ups, lunges, jumping rope or jogging in place. If you can only do 3 crunches or jog in place for 15 seconds at a time, that's okay! You have to start somewhere!
- Pack an exercise band in your purse or briefcase and use it in your car or at your desk when no one's around.
- When you go to the restroom, do push-ups using the counter before you wash your hands. Do as many push-ups as you can once or twice every day or every time you go to the bathroom. You can also do this leaning against your desk at work or the kitchen counter while you're lunch is heating up.
- Every time you go up or down the stairs at home, make an extra trip.
- Ask a friend to be your work-out buddy over the phone. Use a headset and talk to each other while you're walking, jogging, biking, etc. The exercise is so much more enjoyable if you have something to take you mind off the 'work'. It's also a great way to keep up with friends or family who live far away from you. Plus, if you have someone you care about offering support and encouragement, you'll feel twice as good when you're done. Don't forget to be their cheerleader, too!

Exercise

Write down your personal strategy and implement it today. Even if it's something small, it's worth doing. Yes, there are many benefits to exercising, but the most wonderful may be the sense of accomplishment you feel from doing something (anything!) as opposed to nothing.

> Quick Tip: Whatever you choose to do, you will find that you get better at it over time. You will be able and you will want to do more or go longer with consistency. Celebrate your progress!

Mindful Living Checklist

Check this item off of the Mindful Living Worksheet and note how many minutes of physical activity you got in the day. Have fun and see how creative you can be in finding ways to be active.

I am currently engaged in these physical activities on a regular basis:

_____
_____
_____
_____
_____

I enjoy these physical activities:

_____
_____
_____
_____
_____

I think I would enjoy these physical activities:

_____
_____
_____
_____
_____

My strategy to be physically active is to:

_____
_____
_____
_____

I AM HONEST

Please fill in the blanks below with the percentage of time that you agree with each statement.

_____ I have true confidence.
_____ I ask for what I need.
_____ I feel empowered.
_____ I have healthy relationships.

_____ Total Divided by 4 = _____%

This final score shows the percentage of time that you are honest.

You might think your honesty is important to other people in your life. While this is true, your level of honesty affects yourself more than anyone else.

Being honest requires you to be vulnerable to other people who may not like what you have to say and may very well reject you. If you aren't being honest, they're having a relationship with someone who doesn't really exist, anyway. Whether it's a friend, boss, or significant other, you are only setting yourself up for a miserable relationship that will ultimately end in disaster unless you make the truth a priority. If you are honest and do get rejected, it is much better to know as early as possible. It takes an incredible amount of energy to pretend to be something you're not, especially on an on-going basis. Being true to yourself will increase the peace, joy and happiness in your life, no matter who is around.

> Quick Tip: Being honest builds confidence and empowers you to be authentic. When you accept yourself fully, including all your flaws and imperfections, you maximize your personal power by speaking your truth.

For just a moment, think about shouting to the world, "This is who I am! This is what I think! I'm not perfect, but I AM wonderful and I'm not afraid to show it!" If you're alone, try it out loud a few times. Now, say it like you really mean it. Louder! How does that make you feel: empowered, scared, invincible, free? What would it feel like to go through life truly believing this statement? I hope you want to find out.

Exercise

Take a few minutes to think of things you've recently lied about and make a list on the next page. Make sure to include those little white lies and lying by omission. Then determine why you felt it was necessary to lie. Look for themes and the common reasons you're not comfortable telling the truth. Are you trying to make other people feel better about themselves or a situation? Are you concerned that you won't be liked if others knew of the mistakes you've made or how you really feel? Do you lie or exaggerate to make yourself look or feel better? Make a list of these, too.

Whatever the reasons, you can be assured they are not necessary or healthy for you.

When you lie you are saying, "I don't have enough confidence in myself because the truth will cause other people to reject me." Or, "I'm not good enough as I am and I have to trick others into thinking I'm valuable, competent or worthy."

Mindful Living Worksheet

So, how do you increase your honesty (confidence, getting your needs met, personal power and healthy relationships)? One day at a time. Make a commitment to be completely honest every day. Even small and white-lies are off limits. Every day that you are totally honest, check this item off on your checklist.

Are you going to be 100% honest every day? No, probably not; and that's okay. When you find yourself telling a lie, pay attention to the real reasons you don't want the truth to come out. This will give you some valuable information.

As you practice being honest, the lies you do tell will start to jump out at you more. The most important thing to remember is that you are becoming more honest. After a few weeks, look back over the Mindful Living Worksheets you've completed and see if you're able to check this item more often as time goes on.

I have recently lied about . . .

Lie: _____
I lied because: _____
I would like to say or express: _____
_____

Lie: _____
I lied because: _____
I would like to say or express: _____
_____

Lie: _____
I lied because: _____
I would like to say or express: _____
_____

Lie: _____
I lied because: _____
I would like to say or express: _____
_____

Common reasons I haven't felt comfortable being honest: _____
_____
_____
_____

I AM TAKING CARE OF MYSELF

What have you done for *you* lately? When was the last time you did something just to take care of yourself? What did you do?

It's easy to get caught up in a hectic daily routine. With so much to do, we have to prioritize our activities. Too often taking care of ourselves falls to the bottom of the list and gets put off day after day.

Some people, especially caretakers, don't feel they're as important as others and put other people's wants and needs before their own. This pattern is unhealthy and it also fuels co-dependent relationships. If you enjoy helping or taking care of others, do everyone a favor and work toward taking care of yourself, too. The more mentally, spiritually, physically and emotionally healthy you are, the more good you can bring other people.

Exercise

Make a list on the opposite page of anything you're already doing to take care of yourself. You can start with reading this book and completing the activities. What else do you already do? Do you pray or meditate, eat healthy foods, go for walks, talk to friends, go to church?

Next, think about things you could do to take care of yourself and make a list of all of these. You could include relaxing in a bubble bath, scheduling a medical or dental check-up, taking yourself out for a healthy lunch, listening to your favorite music, planning a vacation or cooking your favorite meal.

Imagine living in a perfect world and write down what you would do for yourself. Then, go back and put an asterisk (*) by the top five ideas that you want to do in the next week.

> Quick Tip: In a perfect world we would all have enough money to do anything we want. But, don't let money be an obstacle to taking care of yourself. If a gym membership is too expensive, start a walking club with a friend or group of friends. If spa services aren't in the budget, give yourself a facial with an exfoliating scrub from the grocery store and ask your spouse for a massage. Get creative and enjoy!

Mindful Living Worksheet

Every day that you find a way to take care of yourself, check this off of your Mindful Living Worksheet. See how many of your new ideas you can indulge in over the next month.

I already take care of myself by . . .

_____

_____

_____

_____

_____

_____

_____

_____

_____

I could take care of myself by . . .

_____

_____

_____

_____

_____

_____

_____

_____

_____

_____

_____

_____

_____

If one advances confidently in the direction of his dreams, and endeavors to live the life that he has imagined, he will meet with a success unexpected in common hours.

—Henry David Thoreau

CHAPTER 4

Where am I going?

I HAVE PURPOSE

For many years I felt that I had no direction and that I was drifting aimlessly from one thing to another. I had been to seminars, workshops, and read many books that talked about living on purpose. I wanted purpose. But, 'purpose' seemed like a very elusive thing that I was constantly looking for and didn't have any idea of where or how to find it. Then I came across someone who gave me the keys to purpose.

First, you don't have to search for purpose; it's right in front of you. In fact, it's probably what you're already doing. Second, you will recognize purpose by the passion you feel when you're engaged in it.

Exercise

If you haven't already identified your purpose, now is the time to do it. We're going to start with passion. Make a list on the opposite page of 10 things you're passionate about. These are the things you do, or want to do, regardless of if anyone ever knew about it or compensated you for it. What are activities that just thinking about them makes you want to drop what you're doing and indulge in? If you have more than 10 things you feel this way about, write them all down and then choose the 10 that are the most exciting to you. If you can only think of a few things that you feel this way about, then you've narrowed it down and it will be more obvious. These are the 'what' of your purpose.

Next, let's figure out why you enjoy this. Is there some benefit that you get from your passion, or do you feel strongly about sharing it with others? If you love gardening, it might be because you feel peaceful and happy when you're working in the soil. Or, because you enjoy the sense of accomplishment when your beautiful flowers bloom or you take a bite of the delicious food you've grown. Your passion could also be in teaching others how to garden, making the world a more beautiful place by sharing your flowers or feeding those who don't have enough to eat. You may have multiple reasons you love what you do. Write them down now. This is the 'why' of your purpose.

If you have many activities that you enjoy, look for a common theme in all or most of them. This may give you a hint as to your 'why'. If your passions include painting, dancing and cooking your purpose may be about creatively expressing yourself. If your passions are teaching and volunteering your 'why' may be helping other people.

Now, we're going to put your 'what' and 'why' together to develop your purpose. Try this formula: My purpose is to (insert 'why' here) by (insert 'what' here).

Using the examples above, this might read:
"My purpose is to creatively express myself by painting, dancing and cooking."
"My purpose is to feed people who don't have enough to eat by teaching them to grow their own food."
"My purpose is to inspire children to be physically active through dance."
"My purpose is to make the world a more beautiful place by growing and sharing flowers."

> Quick Tip: It's unlikely that all of your 'whats' will be incorporated into your purpose. There are some things that will just be hobbies that you enjoy. Pay attention to your passion and your intuition to find your true purpose.

Mindful Living

Mindful Living Worksheet

Now that you have identified your specific purpose, keep it at the forefront of your mind and take actions toward it. Each day, read, recite or listen to a self-made recording of your purpose at least three times and check this item off of your Mindful Living Worksheet.

WHAT	**WHY**
I am passionate about . . .	because . . .
_____	_____
_____	_____
_____	_____
_____	_____
_____	_____
_____	_____
_____	_____
_____	_____
_____	_____
_____	_____
Common themes of WHAT I'm passionate about	Common themes as to WHY I'm passionate
_____	_____
_____	_____
_____	_____

My purpose is to (insert WHY here—common themes or things you feel most strongly about) _____

_____

by (insert WHAT here—common themes or what you feel most strongly about) _____

_____

I HAVE INTENTION

Developing intentions is the next step in creating an internal compass that, along with your purpose, will give you direction to live the life of your dreams.

Exercise

To formulate intentions, first list what is most important to you on the opposite page. Then, use this priority list to define your intentions. For example, you may list that your family is a top priority. Think about what you want to continue or improve, like spending more quality time together, having better communication, or simply having closer relationships.

Then, write your intentions so they're stated in a positive, ongoing manner like these examples:

- I intend to spend quality time with my family.
- I encourage effective communication and set a good example for my family.
- I look for and act on things that deepen and improve my family relationships.

You can also combine these if you have multiple intentions on the same topic: I intend to spend quality time with my family, encourage effective communication and deepen our relationships.

Use this process to develop an intention for each item on your priority list. You may have just one intention or a list of many, depending on the number of things you listed as important to you. Developing between 3 and 6 intentions is ideal!

Once you are satisfied that your intentions accurately represent your priorities, write them down on the next page. Also, place them in various locations that you will see throughout the day. Tape them to your bathroom mirror or the sun visor in your car. Carry them in your purse or wallet.

Mindful Living Worksheet

Make a point to read your intentions out loud at least three times every day. Use a strong, confident voice as you read. Take a moment to really feel empowered to take action toward each intention.

Each day that you review your intentions and read them out loud, check this item off of the Mindful Living Worksheet.

> Quick Tip: Use your purpose and intentions as a measuring stick when making decisions. Compare your choices or possible actions to your purpose and intentions, then choose the option that is most in line. Your purpose and intentions become a compass that will guide you in the right direction by keeping you focused on what is most important to you.

Mindful Living

My Priorities:

_____
_____
_____
_____
_____
_____
_____

My Intentions:

1. _____
_____
_____

2. _____
_____
_____

3. _____
_____
_____

4. _____
_____
_____

5. _____
_____
_____

6. _____
_____
_____

I HAVE GOALS

Goals are experiences you want to have but don't necessarily relate to your purpose or intentions. For example, your *purpose* may be to give children a better future by teaching them to read. But you may also love baseball and would like to see a baseball game in every major league stadium. This will be perfect for your goal list!

Exercise

Follow these guidelines for goal setting:

— Write your goals as if you have already achieved them.
    Initial thought: "I want to get a job."
    Revised goal: "I am a successful IT professional."

— Be specific enough that you feel good about your goals, but not too specific that you limit how they can come into your life.
    Initial thought: "I want to lose 25lbs before my vacation in two months."
    Revised goal: "I am at my ideal weight of ____lbs and I feel healthy, confident and strong."

— Include sensory details about your goal.
    Initial thought: "I want a new car."
    Revised goal: "I love the smell of my new car and how comfortable the leather seats are!"

— Set a specific time frame in which you intend to reach the goal.
    Initial thought: "I want to go on vacation."
    Revised goal: "I am vacationing in the Bahamas by September 15th."

Think of what you want to accomplish in the different areas of your life: health, finances, relationships, your home, material possessions, hobbies, spirituality, education, travel, career, appearance, etc.

Quick Tip: See if you can develop 101 goals. If not, keep working toward that number.

Once you have listed as many goals as you can think of, go back and put an asterisk (*) next to the four that are your top priorities. For each of these goals, develop a step-by-step action plan. For instance, if your goal is to be a successful IT professional, your action plan might look like this:
  1. Determine your ideal job and research the qualifying credentials needed.
  2. Complete an educational training program or ask someone to teach you new skills.
  3. Write your resume, ask someone to help you write it or find a job-assistance program that offers this service.

Take your action plan as far as you can for each of your four priority goals. If you cannot see a way to get from the steps you know about now to your ultimate goal, that's okay. *Simply start the process by taking the first action.* By the time you work your way through the tasks that you can anticipate now, you will have a different perspective and additional information. Then, you will be able to see the next logical step(s) to take. The path will unfold as you continue the journey.

Mindful Living Worksheet

When it comes to your purpose, intentions and goals, celebrate each and every accomplishment that indicates progress—no matter how small. Write any action steps that you take on the Mindful Living Worksheet under the "Steps Toward Goals, Intentions and Purpose" section.

My Goals

1. _____
2. _____
3. _____
4. _____
5. _____
6. _____
7. _____
8. _____
9. _____
10. _____
11. _____
12. _____
13. _____
14. _____
15. _____
16. _____
17. _____
18. _____
19. _____
20. _____
21. _____
22. _____
23. _____
24. _____
25. _____
26. _____
27. _____
28. _____
29. _____
30. _____
31. _____
32. _____
33. _____
34. _____
35. _____
36. _____
37. _____
38. _____
39. _____
40. _____
41. _____
42. _____
43. _____
44. _____
45. _____
46. _____
47. _____
48. _____
49. _____
50. _____
51. _____
52. _____
53. _____
54. _____
55. _____
56. _____
57. _____
58. _____
59. _____
60. _____
61. _____
62. _____
63. _____
64. _____
65. _____
66. _____
67. _____
68. _____
69. _____
70. _____
71. _____
72. _____
73. _____
74. _____
75. _____
76. _____
77. _____
78. _____
79. _____
80. _____
81. _____
82. _____
83. _____
84. _____
85. _____
86. _____
87. _____
88. _____
89. _____
90. _____
91. _____
92. _____
93. _____
94. _____
95. _____
96. _____
97. _____
98. _____
99. _____
100. _____
101. _____

Angela M. Day

Priority Goal: _____

Action Steps: 1. _____ ☐
2. _____ ☐
3. _____ ☐
4. _____ ☐
5. _____ ☐
6. _____ ☐
7. _____ ☐
8. _____ ☐
9. _____ ☐
10. _____ ☐
11. _____ ☐
12. _____ ☐

Priority Goal: _____

Action Steps: 1. _____ ☐
2. _____ ☐
3. _____ ☐
4. _____ ☐
5. _____ ☐
6. _____ ☐
7. _____ ☐
8. _____ ☐
9. _____ ☐
10. _____ ☐
11. _____ ☐
12. _____ ☐

Mindful Living

Priority Goal: _____

Action Steps: 1. _____ ☐
2. _____ ☐
3. _____ ☐
4. _____ ☐
5. _____ ☐
6. _____ ☐
7. _____ ☐
8. _____ ☐
9. _____ ☐
10. _____ ☐
11. _____ ☐
12. _____ ☐

Priority Goal: _____

Action Steps: 1. _____ ☐
2. _____ ☐
3. _____ ☐
4. _____ ☐
5. _____ ☐
6. _____ ☐
7. _____ ☐
8. _____ ☐
9. _____ ☐
10. _____ ☐
11. _____ ☐
12. _____ ☐

I HAVE VISION

If an angel, a magical genie, or a multi-billionaire were to show up and instantly give you anything you could imagine in the next 15 minutes, what would you have 16 minutes from now? You have a good place to start because you've already developed your purpose, intentions and goals. But what does that *look* like? It's now time to create a master vision.

Exercise

Use one or more of the exercises below to turn your ideas into a detailed picture of your ideal life.

Remember, the angel, magical genie or multi-billionaire will give you anything you want, so don't limit your vision for any reason!

Vision Board: Gather pictures representing things you want from magazines, newspapers, brochures, printed from the internet, and books (used book stores are great for this project!). Cut out just the things you want from each page; usually this will mean cutting the pictures away from the logos and wording of advertisements. Then tape or glue the pictures to a large piece of poster board, cardboard or display board. You could also use a bulletin board or your refrigerator.

Vision Box: Collect pictures as described above and put them in a box. Paint and/or decorate the box any way that appeals to you.

Vision Book: Collect pictures as described above. Put the pictures in a photo album where the plastic cover of the pages peel back so you can arrange the things you want anywhere on the page. If you scrapbook, create a book with these pictures as if they were things you've already done.

Vision Photo Album: Collect pictures as described above. Take a close-up picture of each one with your cell phone. If possible, store these in a separate folder or album on your phone for easy access.

Vision Slide Show: Download pictures off the internet and create a slideshow of the things you want.

Vision Art: If you paint, sculpt or build models, create a piece or pieces that depict your vision.

Vision Track: Write a very detailed first-person story about living the life you envision. Write your story in the present tense and describe all of the wonderful things you're experiencing. Or, you may want to describe a single day in your perfect life that includes where you wake up, what you do, and who you're with. You could also talk about what you did yesterday, last week, last month in your ideal world, or what you'll be doing tomorrow, next week and next month. Elaborate on as many details as you possibly can, especially the senses. What do you hear; traffic, people, insects or animals? What do you feel; sunlight, the wind, cotton or silk against your skin, someone else's lips against yours? What do you smell; salty sea air, fresh baked bread, flowers? What do you taste; wine, warm cookies, coffee, your favorite meal? When you have completed your story, record yourself reading it. Save the recording on your laptop, tablet or cell phone.

> Quick Tip: Like your success project(s), keep in mind that some are more portable than others. Plan to spend about 15 minutes each day looking at or listening to your vision. If you travel often you may want to create a Vision Track and Vision Photo Album, which would be ideal to listen to on a road-trip or look at while you're waiting for your plane.

Mindful Living Worksheet

Check this item off of the Mindful Living Worksheet when you take 15 minutes or more daily to immerse yourself in your vision.

I will create a . . .

- ☐ Vision Board
- ☐ Vision Box
- ☐ Vision Book/Scrapbook
- ☐ Vision Photo Album (cell phone)
- ☐ Vision Slide Show
- ☐ Vision Art
- ☐ Vision Track
- ☐ Other: _____

I will review my vision project . . .

- ☐ When I wake up in the morning
- ☐ Before I go to sleep at night
- ☐ On my lunch break
- ☐ When I'm driving (Success Track)
- ☐ While I eat breakfast/lunch/dinner
- ☐ While I'm waiting for: _____

- ☐ Other: _____

There are only two ways to live your life.
One is as though nothing is a miracle.
The other is as though everything is a miracle.

—Albert Einstein

CHAPTER 5

Why do I deserve a wonderful life?

I AM GRATEFUL

What do you spend the most time thinking about?

What kinds of emotions do you generally feel?

Do you want more of what you're already getting, or do you need to focus on something different and better to have something different and feel better?

By taking time each day to think about the good things you are grateful for and want more of, you will see and attract more of these into your life.

Exercise

Begin the gratitude process by making a list on the opposite page of everything in your life that you are grateful for and want more of. This can include people you are happy to have in your life; material possessions such as a safe place to live, a car or a bed to sleep in; and experiences like taking vacations, participating in hobbies or spending time with your friends and family. Write down everything you love about your life.

Mindful Living Worksheet

Begin to look for things that you are thankful for on a daily basis. It's easier to be grateful for big things like getting a promotion or receiving a special gift. But are you also grateful for beautiful weather, someone giving you a sincere compliment or a delicious meal?

When you do come across something you appreciate, take a moment to really feel the emotion of gratitude. You may even want to say a prayer (silent or out loud) like, "Thank you for this _____." Or, "I am truly grateful for _____." Offer your appreciation as a gift to God, the Universe, Spirit, or however you perceive your higher power.

Complete the gratitude section of the Mindful Living Worksheet on a daily basis. When you write things you are thankful for in this section, they should be relevant to or something you experienced today. Check this item off each day that you are able to list ten things that you are grateful for.

> **Quick Tip: Completing the daily list of 10 things you are grateful for is *the most important section of the Mindful Living Worksheet*. Write this list, even if you do nothing else on your worksheet for the day.**

If you struggle with this exercise, it is probably an indication that you have been focusing on negative experiences. As you get in the habit of writing a daily gratitude list on the Mindful Living Worksheet, you will start to see more and more to be grateful for. Come back to the next page in your workbook after a few weeks and see if you have more to add to your overall list.

Mindful Living

I am grateful for . . .

My Relationships (family, friends, neighbors, co-workers): _____
_____
_____

My Personality Traits (compassionate, grounded, confident, loving): _____
_____
_____

My Skills (fixing things, typing, leadership abilities, sales): _____
_____
_____

My Physical Body (eyes, strong hands, hair, skin, smile): _____
_____
_____

My Experiences (education/knowledge, travel): _____
_____
_____

My Work (job, career, volunteering, source of income): _____
_____
_____

My Hobbies (cooking, scuba diving, singing, target shooting, kayaking, dancing): _____
_____
_____

My Environment (home, office, room): _____
_____
_____

My Material Possessions (clothes, car, tools, electronics): _____
_____
_____

I AM LOOKING FORWARD

If life has become a tribulation and you're just trying to get through the day, you need things to look forward to.

Finding things to look forward to is ultimately about taking responsibility for enjoying your life. It's your job to decide what you enjoy and how to include those experiences.

Exercise

On the opposite page write down what you're looking forward to today/tomorrow, this week, this month and in the next year. Use the following ideas to help you develop your list.

- Spending time with people who love and support you.
- Reaching a goal.
- Taking care of yourself (refer to your list on page 39).
- Wearing clothes, shoes, jewelry, make-up, or hair accessories that you feel great in.
- Having quiet time to yourself.
- Doing something FUN! (Refer to your list on page 23.)
- Getting to sleep in.
- A special meal or snack that you really enjoy.
- Going on vacation or just taking a day off from work.
- Doing something that makes you laugh (refer to your list on page 23).
- Surprising someone you care about with a gift.

Now that you have things to look forward to, get in the habit of mentally going through this list when you first wake up in the morning. Think about what you *want* to do during the day and what you're excited about.

Think about what you're looking forward to tomorrow or in the next few weeks. Is there anything you want to do today related to your future plans? For example, if you're looking forward to having a 'date night' with someone special, you could call and make a dinner reservation or choose what clothes you're going to wear. You might even look at the menu online.

Planning the small steps is beneficial in several ways. First, just thinking about the preliminary tasks gives you things to look forward to and builds excitement for many days. Second, taking action and completing these steps builds confidence in your ability to reach short-term goals. Finally, the experience is even more enjoyable because you've already taken care of the details. Using the previous example of gong to dinner, you wouldn't have to worry at the last minute about what to wear (and is it clean?) or waiting in line because you planned ahead.

Mindful Living Worksheet

When you complete the Mindful Living Worksheet for the day, be sure to jot down something you're looking forward to. If you're anticipating a lot of wonderful things, just list what you're looking forward to next or the most. But don't limit yourself to the worksheet alone! Thinking about things you're looking forward to is a great mental and emotional boost anytime.

Today and tomorrow I am looking forward to . . .

_____
_____
_____
_____
_____

This week I am looking forward to . . .

_____
_____
_____
_____
_____

This month I am looking forward to . . .

_____
_____
_____
_____
_____

This year I am looking forward to . . .

_____
_____
_____
_____
_____

In the future I am looking forward to . . .

_____
_____
_____
_____
_____

Life is an opportunity, benefit from it.
Life is beauty, admire it.
Life is a dream, realize it.
Life is a challenge, meet it.
Life is a duty, complete it.
Life is a game, play it.
Life is a promise, fulfill it.
Life is sorrow, overcome it.
Life is a song, sing it.
Life is a struggle, accept it.
Life is a tragedy, confront it.
Life is an adventure, dare it.
Life is luck, make it.
Life is too precious, do not destroy it.
Life is life, fight for it.

—Mother Teresa

Daily Journal

MINDFUL LIVING WORKSHEET

M Tu W Th F S S   Date:_____   Rate:_____

☐ I am content with: _____
☐ I am proud of: _____
☐ Success review
☐ I love myself because: _____ ☐
☐ Love, thanks, kindness and support for others:
    1. _____   2. _____
    3. _____   4. _____
☐ Love, thanks, kindness and support for me:
    1. _____   2. _____
    3. _____   4. _____
☐ Good Deed/Selfless Act/Random Kindness: _____
☐ I gave undivided attention to: _____
☐ I made things better by: _____
☐ I experienced joy, happiness, fun and/or laughter: _____
☐ I smiled _____ minutes
☐ Meditation/Prayer _____ minutes
☐ Inspiration (reading, video, music): _____
☐ I listened to my intuition: _____
☐ Physical activity _____ minutes
☐ I was 100% honest today
☐ I took care of myself by: _____
☐ Reviewed purpose 3 times
☐ Reviewed intentions 3 times
☐ Steps toward goals, intentions and purpose
    1. _____ 2. _____ 3. _____
☐ Reviewed vision
☐ I am grateful for:
    1. _____   6. _____
    2. _____   7. _____
    3. _____   8. _____
    4. _____   9. _____
    5. _____   10. _____

☐ I am looking forward to: _____

Notes: _____
_____
_____
_____

MINDFUL LIVING WORKSHEET

M Tu W Th F S S   Date:_____   Rate:_____

- ☐ I am content with: _____
- ☐ I am proud of: _____
- ☐ Success review
- ☐ I love myself because: _____ ☐
- ☐ Love, thanks, kindness and support for others:
  - 1. _____   2. _____
  - 3. _____   4. _____
- ☐ Love, thanks, kindness and support for me:
  - 1. _____   2. _____
  - 3. _____   4. _____
- ☐ Good Deed/Selfless Act/Random Kindness: _____
- ☐ I gave undivided attention to: _____
- ☐ I made things better by: _____
- ☐ I experienced joy, happiness, fun and/or laughter: _____
- ☐ I smiled _____ minutes
- ☐ Meditation/Prayer _____ minutes
- ☐ Inspiration (reading, video, music): _____
- ☐ I listened to my intuition: _____
- ☐ Physical activity _____ minutes
- ☐ I was 100% honest today
- ☐ I took care of myself by: _____
- ☐ Reviewed purpose 3 times
- ☐ Reviewed intentions 3 times
- ☐ Steps toward goals, intentions and purpose
  - 1. _____   2. _____   3. _____
- ☐ Reviewed vision
- ☐ I am grateful for:
  - 1. _____   6. _____
  - 2. _____   7. _____
  - 3. _____   8. _____
  - 4. _____   9. _____
  - 5. _____   10. _____

- ☐ I am looking forward to: _____

Notes: _____
_____
_____

MINDFUL LIVING WORKSHEET

M Tu W Th F S S   Date:_____   Rate:_____

- ☐ I am content with: _____
- ☐ I am proud of: _____
- ☐ Success review
- ☐ I love myself because: _____ ☐
- ☐ Love, thanks, kindness and support for others:
  - 1. _____   2. _____
  - 3. _____   4. _____
- ☐ Love, thanks, kindness and support for me:
  - 1. _____   2. _____
  - 3. _____   4. _____
- ☐ Good Deed/Selfless Act/Random Kindness: _____
- ☐ I gave undivided attention to: _____
- ☐ I made things better by: _____
- ☐ I experienced joy, happiness, fun and/or laughter: _____
- ☐ I smiled _____ minutes
- ☐ Meditation/Prayer _____ minutes
- ☐ Inspiration (reading, video, music): _____
- ☐ I listened to my intuition: _____
- ☐ Physical activity _____ minutes
- ☐ I was 100% honest today
- ☐ I took care of myself by: _____
- ☐ Reviewed purpose 3 times
- ☐ Reviewed intentions 3 times
- ☐ Steps toward goals, intentions and purpose
  - 1. _____   2. _____   3. _____
- ☐ Reviewed vision
- ☐ I am grateful for:
  - 1. _____   6. _____
  - 2. _____   7. _____
  - 3. _____   8. _____
  - 4. _____   9. _____
  - 5. _____   10. _____

- ☐ I am looking forward to: _____

Notes: _____
_____
_____
_____

Mindful Living Worksheet

M Tu W Th F S S   Date:_____   Rate:_____

- ☐ I am content with: _____
- ☐ I am proud of: _____
- ☐ Success review
- ☐ I love myself because: _____ ☐
- ☐ Love, thanks, kindness and support for others:
  - 1. _____   2. _____
  - 3. _____   4. _____
- ☐ Love, thanks, kindness and support for me:
  - 1. _____   2. _____
  - 3. _____   4. _____
- ☐ Good Deed/Selfless Act/Random Kindness: _____
- ☐ I gave undivided attention to: _____
- ☐ I made things better by: _____
- ☐ I experienced joy, happiness, fun and/or laughter: _____
- ☐ I smiled _____ minutes
- ☐ Meditation/Prayer _____ minutes
- ☐ Inspiration (reading, video, music): _____
- ☐ I listened to my intuition: _____
- ☐ Physical activity _____ minutes
- ☐ I was 100% honest today
- ☐ I took care of myself by: _____
- ☐ Reviewed purpose 3 times
- ☐ Reviewed intentions 3 times
- ☐ Steps toward goals, intentions and purpose
  - 1. _____   2. _____   3. _____
- ☐ Reviewed vision
- ☐ I am grateful for:
  - 1. _____   6. _____
  - 2. _____   7. _____
  - 3. _____   8. _____
  - 4. _____   9. _____
  - 5. _____   10. _____

- ☐ I am looking forward to: _____

Notes: _____
_____
_____
_____

MINDFUL LIVING WORKSHEET

M Tu W Th F S S   Date:_____   Rate:_____

- ☐ I am content with: _____
- ☐ I am proud of: _____
- ☐ Success review
- ☐ I love myself because: _____ ☐
- ☐ Love, thanks, kindness and support for others:
  - 1. _____   2. _____
  - 3. _____   4. _____
- ☐ Love, thanks, kindness and support for me:
  - 1. _____   2. _____
  - 3. _____   4. _____
- ☐ Good Deed/Selfless Act/Random Kindness: _____
- ☐ I gave undivided attention to: _____
- ☐ I made things better by: _____
- ☐ I experienced joy, happiness, fun and/or laughter: _____
- ☐ I smiled _____ minutes
- ☐ Meditation/Prayer _____ minutes
- ☐ Inspiration (reading, video, music): _____
- ☐ I listened to my intuition: _____
- ☐ Physical activity _____ minutes
- ☐ I was 100% honest today
- ☐ I took care of myself by: _____
- ☐ Reviewed purpose 3 times
- ☐ Reviewed intentions 3 times
- ☐ Steps toward goals, intentions and purpose
  - 1. _____   2. _____   3. _____
- ☐ Reviewed vision
- ☐ I am grateful for:
  - 1. _____   6. _____
  - 2. _____   7. _____
  - 3. _____   8. _____
  - 4. _____   9. _____
  - 5. _____   10. _____

- ☐ I am looking forward to: _____

Notes: _____
_____
_____
_____

MINDFUL LIVING WORKSHEET

M　Tu　W　Th　F　S　S　　　Date:_____　　　　　Rate:_____

- ☐ I am content with: _____
- ☐ I am proud of: _____
- ☐ Success review
- ☐ I love myself because: _____ ☐
- ☐ Love, thanks, kindness and support for others:
  - 1. _____ 2. _____
  - 3. _____ 4. _____
- ☐ Love, thanks, kindness and support for me:
  - 1. _____ 2. _____
  - 3. _____ 4. _____
- ☐ Good Deed/Selfless Act/Random Kindness: _____
- ☐ I gave undivided attention to: _____
- ☐ I made things better by: _____
- ☐ I experienced joy, happiness, fun and/or laughter: _____
- ☐ I smiled _____ minutes
- ☐ Meditation/Prayer _____ minutes
- ☐ Inspiration (reading, video, music): _____
- ☐ I listened to my intuition: _____
- ☐ Physical activity _____ minutes
- ☐ I was 100% honest today
- ☐ I took care of myself by: _____
- ☐ Reviewed purpose 3 times
- ☐ Reviewed intentions 3 times
- ☐ Steps toward goals, intentions and purpose
  - 1. _____ 2. _____ 3. _____
- ☐ Reviewed vision
- ☐ I am grateful for:
  - 1. _____ 6. _____
  - 2. _____ 7. _____
  - 3. _____ 8. _____
  - 4. _____ 9. _____
  - 5. _____ 10. _____

- ☐ I am looking forward to: _____

Notes: _____
_____
_____
_____

MINDFUL LIVING WORKSHEET

M Tu W Th F S S   Date:_____   Rate:_____

- ☐ I am content with: _____
- ☐ I am proud of: _____
- ☐ Success review
- ☐ I love myself because: _____ ☐
- ☐ Love, thanks, kindness and support for others:
    - 1. _____   2. _____
    - 3. _____   4. _____
- ☐ Love, thanks, kindness and support for me:
    - 1. _____   2. _____
    - 3. _____   4. _____
- ☐ Good Deed/Selfless Act/Random Kindness: _____
- ☐ I gave undivided attention to: _____
- ☐ I made things better by: _____
- ☐ I experienced joy, happiness, fun and/or laughter: _____
- ☐ I smiled _____ minutes
- ☐ Meditation/Prayer _____ minutes
- ☐ Inspiration (reading, video, music): _____
- ☐ I listened to my intuition: _____
- ☐ Physical activity _____ minutes
- ☐ I was 100% honest today
- ☐ I took care of myself by: _____
- ☐ Reviewed purpose 3 times
- ☐ Reviewed intentions 3 times
- ☐ Steps toward goals, intentions and purpose
    - 1. _____ 2. _____ 3. _____
- ☐ Reviewed vision
- ☐ I am grateful for:
    - 1. _____   6. _____
    - 2. _____   7. _____
    - 3. _____   8. _____
    - 4. _____   9. _____
    - 5. _____   10. _____

- ☐ I am looking forward to: _____

Notes: _____
_____
_____
_____

MINDFUL LIVING WORKSHEET

M Tu W Th F S S   Date:_____   Rate:_____

- ☐ I am content with: _____
- ☐ I am proud of: _____
- ☐ Success review
- ☐ I love myself because: _____ ☐
- ☐ Love, thanks, kindness and support for others:
  - 1. _____   2. _____
  - 3. _____   4. _____
- ☐ Love, thanks, kindness and support for me:
  - 1. _____   2. _____
  - 3. _____   4. _____
- ☐ Good Deed/Selfless Act/Random Kindness: _____
- ☐ I gave undivided attention to: _____
- ☐ I made things better by: _____
- ☐ I experienced joy, happiness, fun and/or laughter: _____
- ☐ I smiled _____ minutes
- ☐ Meditation/Prayer _____ minutes
- ☐ Inspiration (reading, video, music): _____
- ☐ I listened to my intuition: _____
- ☐ Physical activity _____ minutes
- ☐ I was 100% honest today
- ☐ I took care of myself by: _____
- ☐ Reviewed purpose 3 times
- ☐ Reviewed intentions 3 times
- ☐ Steps toward goals, intentions and purpose
  - 1. _____ 2. _____ 3. _____
- ☐ Reviewed vision
- ☐ I am grateful for:
  - 1. _____   6. _____
  - 2. _____   7. _____
  - 3. _____   8. _____
  - 4. _____   9. _____
  - 5. _____   10. _____

- ☐ I am looking forward to: _____

Notes: _____
_____
_____
_____

Mindful Living Worksheet

M Tu W Th F S S   Date:_____   Rate:_____

- ☐ I am content with: _____
- ☐ I am proud of: _____
- ☐ Success review
- ☐ I love myself because: _____ ☐
- ☐ Love, thanks, kindness and support for others:
  - 1. _____   2. _____
  - 3. _____   4. _____
- ☐ Love, thanks, kindness and support for me:
  - 1. _____   2. _____
  - 3. _____   4. _____
- ☐ Good Deed/Selfless Act/Random Kindness: _____
- ☐ I gave undivided attention to: _____
- ☐ I made things better by: _____
- ☐ I experienced joy, happiness, fun and/or laughter: _____
- ☐ I smiled _____ minutes
- ☐ Meditation/Prayer _____ minutes
- ☐ Inspiration (reading, video, music): _____
- ☐ I listened to my intuition: _____
- ☐ Physical activity _____ minutes
- ☐ I was 100% honest today
- ☐ I took care of myself by: _____
- ☐ Reviewed purpose 3 times
- ☐ Reviewed intentions 3 times
- ☐ Steps toward goals, intentions and purpose
  - 1. _____ 2. _____ 3. _____
- ☐ Reviewed vision
- ☐ I am grateful for:
  - 1. _____   6. _____
  - 2. _____   7. _____
  - 3. _____   8. _____
  - 4. _____   9. _____
  - 5. _____   10. _____

- ☐ I am looking forward to: _____

Notes: _____
_____
_____
_____

MINDFUL LIVING WORKSHEET

M Tu W Th F S S   Date:_____   Rate:_____

- ☐ I am content with: _____
- ☐ I am proud of: _____
- ☐ Success review
- ☐ I love myself because: _____ ☐
- ☐ Love, thanks, kindness and support for others:
  - 1. _____ 2. _____
  - 3. _____ 4. _____
- ☐ Love, thanks, kindness and support for me:
  - 1. _____ 2. _____
  - 3. _____ 4. _____
- ☐ Good Deed/Selfless Act/Random Kindness: _____
- ☐ I gave undivided attention to: _____
- ☐ I made things better by: _____
- ☐ I experienced joy, happiness, fun and/or laughter: _____
- ☐ I smiled _____ minutes
- ☐ Meditation/Prayer _____ minutes
- ☐ Inspiration (reading, video, music): _____
- ☐ I listened to my intuition: _____
- ☐ Physical activity _____ minutes
- ☐ I was 100% honest today
- ☐ I took care of myself by: _____
- ☐ Reviewed purpose 3 times
- ☐ Reviewed intentions 3 times
- ☐ Steps toward goals, intentions and purpose
  - 1. _____ 2. _____ 3. _____
- ☐ Reviewed vision
- ☐ I am grateful for:
  - 1. _____ 6. _____
  - 2. _____ 7. _____
  - 3. _____ 8. _____
  - 4. _____ 9. _____
  - 5. _____ 10. _____

- ☐ I am looking forward to: _____

Notes: _____
_____
_____
_____

MINDFUL LIVING WORKSHEET

M Tu W Th F S S   Date:_____   Rate:_____

- ☐ I am content with: _____
- ☐ I am proud of: _____
- ☐ Success review
- ☐ I love myself because: _____ ☐
- ☐ Love, thanks, kindness and support for others:
  - 1. _____   2. _____
  - 3. _____   4. _____
- ☐ Love, thanks, kindness and support for me:
  - 1. _____   2. _____
  - 3. _____   4. _____
- ☐ Good Deed/Selfless Act/Random Kindness: _____
- ☐ I gave undivided attention to: _____
- ☐ I made things better by: _____
- ☐ I experienced joy, happiness, fun and/or laughter: _____
- ☐ I smiled _____ minutes
- ☐ Meditation/Prayer _____ minutes
- ☐ Inspiration (reading, video, music): _____
- ☐ I listened to my intuition: _____
- ☐ Physical activity _____ minutes
- ☐ I was 100% honest today
- ☐ I took care of myself by: _____
- ☐ Reviewed purpose 3 times
- ☐ Reviewed intentions 3 times
- ☐ Steps toward goals, intentions and purpose
  - 1. _____   2. _____   3. _____
- ☐ Reviewed vision
- ☐ I am grateful for:
  - 1. _____   6. _____
  - 2. _____   7. _____
  - 3. _____   8. _____
  - 4. _____   9. _____
  - 5. _____   10. _____

- ☐ I am looking forward to: _____

Notes: _____
_____
_____
_____

MINDFUL LIVING WORKSHEET

M Tu W Th F S S   Date:_____   Rate:_____

- ☐ I am content with: _____
- ☐ I am proud of: _____
- ☐ Success review
- ☐ I love myself because: _____ ☐
- ☐ Love, thanks, kindness and support for others:
  - 1. _____   2. _____
  - 3. _____   4. _____
- ☐ Love, thanks, kindness and support for me:
  - 1. _____   2. _____
  - 3. _____   4. _____
- ☐ Good Deed/Selfless Act/Random Kindness: _____
- ☐ I gave undivided attention to: _____
- ☐ I made things better by: _____
- ☐ I experienced joy, happiness, fun and/or laughter: _____
- ☐ I smiled _____ minutes
- ☐ Meditation/Prayer _____ minutes
- ☐ Inspiration (reading, video, music): _____
- ☐ I listened to my intuition: _____
- ☐ Physical activity _____ minutes
- ☐ I was 100% honest today
- ☐ I took care of myself by: _____
- ☐ Reviewed purpose 3 times
- ☐ Reviewed intentions 3 times
- ☐ Steps toward goals, intentions and purpose
  - 1. _____ 2. _____ 3. _____
- ☐ Reviewed vision
- ☐ I am grateful for:
  - 1. _____   6. _____
  - 2. _____   7. _____
  - 3. _____   8. _____
  - 4. _____   9. _____
  - 5. _____   10. _____

- ☐ I am looking forward to: _____

Notes: _____
_____
_____
_____

MINDFUL LIVING WORKSHEET

M Tu W Th F S S   Date:_____   Rate:_____

- ☐ I am content with: _____
- ☐ I am proud of: _____
- ☐ Success review
- ☐ I love myself because: _____ ☐
- ☐ Love, thanks, kindness and support for others:
  - 1. _____   2. _____
  - 3. _____   4. _____
- ☐ Love, thanks, kindness and support for me:
  - 1. _____   2. _____
  - 3. _____   4. _____
- ☐ Good Deed/Selfless Act/Random Kindness: _____
- ☐ I gave undivided attention to: _____
- ☐ I made things better by: _____
- ☐ I experienced joy, happiness, fun and/or laughter: _____
- ☐ I smiled _____ minutes
- ☐ Meditation/Prayer _____ minutes
- ☐ Inspiration (reading, video, music): _____
- ☐ I listened to my intuition: _____
- ☐ Physical activity _____ minutes
- ☐ I was 100% honest today
- ☐ I took care of myself by: _____
- ☐ Reviewed purpose 3 times
- ☐ Reviewed intentions 3 times
- ☐ Steps toward goals, intentions and purpose
  - 1. _____   2. _____   3. _____
- ☐ Reviewed vision
- ☐ I am grateful for:
  - 1. _____   6. _____
  - 2. _____   7. _____
  - 3. _____   8. _____
  - 4. _____   9. _____
  - 5. _____   10. _____

- ☐ I am looking forward to: _____

Notes: _____
_____
_____
_____

MINDFUL LIVING WORKSHEET

M Tu W Th F S S   Date:_____   Rate:_____

- ☐ I am content with: _____
- ☐ I am proud of: _____
- ☐ Success review
- ☐ I love myself because: _____ ☐
- ☐ Love, thanks, kindness and support for others:
  - 1. _____ 2. _____
  - 3. _____ 4. _____
- ☐ Love, thanks, kindness and support for me:
  - 1. _____ 2. _____
  - 3. _____ 4. _____
- ☐ Good Deed/Selfless Act/Random Kindness: _____
- ☐ I gave undivided attention to: _____
- ☐ I made things better by: _____
- ☐ I experienced joy, happiness, fun and/or laughter: _____
- ☐ I smiled _____ minutes
- ☐ Meditation/Prayer _____ minutes
- ☐ Inspiration (reading, video, music): _____
- ☐ I listened to my intuition: _____
- ☐ Physical activity _____ minutes
- ☐ I was 100% honest today
- ☐ I took care of myself by: _____
- ☐ Reviewed purpose 3 times
- ☐ Reviewed intentions 3 times
- ☐ Steps toward goals, intentions and purpose
  - 1. _____ 2. _____ 3. _____
- ☐ Reviewed vision
- ☐ I am grateful for:
  - 1. _____ 6. _____
  - 2. _____ 7. _____
  - 3. _____ 8. _____
  - 4. _____ 9. _____
  - 5. _____ 10. _____

- ☐ I am looking forward to: _____

Notes: _____
_____
_____
_____

MINDFUL LIVING WORKSHEET

M Tu W Th F S S   Date:_____   Rate:_____

- ☐ I am content with: _____
- ☐ I am proud of: _____
- ☐ Success review
- ☐ I love myself because: _____ ☐
- ☐ Love, thanks, kindness and support for others:
    1. _____   2. _____
    3. _____   4. _____
- ☐ Love, thanks, kindness and support for me:
    1. _____   2. _____
    3. _____   4. _____
- ☐ Good Deed/Selfless Act/Random Kindness: _____
- ☐ I gave undivided attention to: _____
- ☐ I made things better by: _____
- ☐ I experienced joy, happiness, fun and/or laughter: _____
- ☐ I smiled _____ minutes
- ☐ Meditation/Prayer _____ minutes
- ☐ Inspiration (reading, video, music): _____
- ☐ I listened to my intuition: _____
- ☐ Physical activity _____ minutes
- ☐ I was 100% honest today
- ☐ I took care of myself by: _____
- ☐ Reviewed purpose 3 times
- ☐ Reviewed intentions 3 times
- ☐ Steps toward goals, intentions and purpose
    1. _____ 2. _____ 3. _____
- ☐ Reviewed vision
- ☐ I am grateful for:
    1. _____   6. _____
    2. _____   7. _____
    3. _____   8. _____
    4. _____   9. _____
    5. _____   10. _____

- ☐ I am looking forward to: _____

Notes: _____
_____
_____
_____

MINDFUL LIVING WORKSHEET

M   Tu   W   Th   F   S   S   Date:_____   Rate:_____

- ☐ I am content with: _____
- ☐ I am proud of: _____
- ☐ Success review
- ☐ I love myself because: _____ ☐
- ☐ Love, thanks, kindness and support for others:
    1. _____   2. _____
    3. _____   4. _____
- ☐ Love, thanks, kindness and support for me:
    1. _____   2. _____
    3. _____   4. _____
- ☐ Good Deed/Selfless Act/Random Kindness: _____
- ☐ I gave undivided attention to: _____
- ☐ I made things better by: _____
- ☐ I experienced joy, happiness, fun and/or laughter: _____
- ☐ I smiled _____ minutes
- ☐ Meditation/Prayer _____ minutes
- ☐ Inspiration (reading, video, music): _____
- ☐ I listened to my intuition: _____
- ☐ Physical activity _____ minutes
- ☐ I was 100% honest today
- ☐ I took care of myself by: _____
- ☐ Reviewed purpose 3 times
- ☐ Reviewed intentions 3 times
- ☐ Steps toward goals, intentions and purpose
    1. _____ 2. _____ 3. _____
- ☐ Reviewed vision
- ☐ I am grateful for:
    1. _____   6. _____
    2. _____   7. _____
    3. _____   8. _____
    4. _____   9. _____
    5. _____   10. _____

- ☐ I am looking forward to: _____

Notes: _____
_____
_____

MINDFUL LIVING WORKSHEET

M   Tu   W   Th   F   S   S   Date:_____   Rate:_____

- ☐ I am content with: _____
- ☐ I am proud of: _____
- ☐ Success review
- ☐ I love myself because: _____ ☐
- ☐ Love, thanks, kindness and support for others:
    1. _____   2. _____
    3. _____   4. _____
- ☐ Love, thanks, kindness and support for me:
    1. _____   2. _____
    3. _____   4. _____
- ☐ Good Deed/Selfless Act/Random Kindness: _____
- ☐ I gave undivided attention to: _____
- ☐ I made things better by: _____
- ☐ I experienced joy, happiness, fun and/or laughter: _____
- ☐ I smiled _____ minutes
- ☐ Meditation/Prayer _____ minutes
- ☐ Inspiration (reading, video, music): _____
- ☐ I listened to my intuition: _____
- ☐ Physical activity _____ minutes
- ☐ I was 100% honest today
- ☐ I took care of myself by: _____
- ☐ Reviewed purpose 3 times
- ☐ Reviewed intentions 3 times
- ☐ Steps toward goals, intentions and purpose
    1. _____   2. _____   3. _____
- ☐ Reviewed vision
- ☐ I am grateful for:
    1. _____   6. _____
    2. _____   7. _____
    3. _____   8. _____
    4. _____   9. _____
    5. _____   10. _____

- ☐ I am looking forward to: _____

Notes: _____
_____
_____
_____

MINDFUL LIVING WORKSHEET

M   Tu   W   Th   F   S   S   Date:_____   Rate:_____

- ☐ I am content with: _____
- ☐ I am proud of: _____
- ☐ Success review
- ☐ I love myself because: _____ ☐
- ☐ Love, thanks, kindness and support for others:
    - 1. _____   2. _____
    - 3. _____   4. _____
- ☐ Love, thanks, kindness and support for me:
    - 1. _____   2. _____
    - 3. _____   4. _____
- ☐ Good Deed/Selfless Act/Random Kindness: _____
- ☐ I gave undivided attention to: _____
- ☐ I made things better by: _____
- ☐ I experienced joy, happiness, fun and/or laughter: _____
- ☐ I smiled _____ minutes
- ☐ Meditation/Prayer _____ minutes
- ☐ Inspiration (reading, video, music): _____
- ☐ I listened to my intuition: _____
- ☐ Physical activity _____ minutes
- ☐ I was 100% honest today
- ☐ I took care of myself by: _____
- ☐ Reviewed purpose 3 times
- ☐ Reviewed intentions 3 times
- ☐ Steps toward goals, intentions and purpose
    - 1. _____   2. _____   3. _____
- ☐ Reviewed vision
- ☐ I am grateful for:
    - 1. _____   6. _____
    - 2. _____   7. _____
    - 3. _____   8. _____
    - 4. _____   9. _____
    - 5. _____   10. _____

- ☐ I am looking forward to: _____

Notes: _____
_____
_____

MINDFUL LIVING WORKSHEET

M   Tu   W   Th   F   S   S   Date:_____   Rate:_____

☐ I am content with: _____
☐ I am proud of: _____
☐ Success review
☐ I love myself because: _____ ☐
☐ Love, thanks, kindness and support for others:
     1. _____   2. _____
     3. _____   4. _____
☐ Love, thanks, kindness and support for me:
     1. _____   2. _____
     3. _____   4. _____
☐ Good Deed/Selfless Act/Random Kindness: _____
☐ I gave undivided attention to: _____
☐ I made things better by: _____
☐ I experienced joy, happiness, fun and/or laughter: _____
☐ I smiled _____ minutes
☐ Meditation/Prayer _____ minutes
☐ Inspiration (reading, video, music): _____
☐ I listened to my intuition: _____
☐ Physical activity _____ minutes
☐ I was 100% honest today
☐ I took care of myself by: _____
☐ Reviewed purpose 3 times
☐ Reviewed intentions 3 times
☐ Steps toward goals, intentions and purpose
     1. _____   2. _____   3. _____
☐ Reviewed vision
☐ I am grateful for:
     1. _____   6. _____
     2. _____   7. _____
     3. _____   8. _____
     4. _____   9. _____
     5. _____   10. _____

☐ I am looking forward to: _____

Notes: _____
_____
_____
_____

MINDFUL LIVING WORKSHEET

M Tu W Th F S S   Date:_____   Rate:_____

- ☐ I am content with: _____
- ☐ I am proud of: _____
- ☐ Success review
- ☐ I love myself because: _____ ☐
- ☐ Love, thanks, kindness and support for others:
  - 1. _____   2. _____
  - 3. _____   4. _____
- ☐ Love, thanks, kindness and support for me:
  - 1. _____   2. _____
  - 3. _____   4. _____
- ☐ Good Deed/Selfless Act/Random Kindness: _____
- ☐ I gave undivided attention to: _____
- ☐ I made things better by: _____
- ☐ I experienced joy, happiness, fun and/or laughter: _____
- ☐ I smiled _____ minutes
- ☐ Meditation/Prayer _____ minutes
- ☐ Inspiration (reading, video, music): _____
- ☐ I listened to my intuition: _____
- ☐ Physical activity _____ minutes
- ☐ I was 100% honest today
- ☐ I took care of myself by: _____
- ☐ Reviewed purpose 3 times
- ☐ Reviewed intentions 3 times
- ☐ Steps toward goals, intentions and purpose
  - 1. _____ 2. _____ 3. _____
- ☐ Reviewed vision
- ☐ I am grateful for:
  - 1. _____   6. _____
  - 2. _____   7. _____
  - 3. _____   8. _____
  - 4. _____   9. _____
  - 5. _____   10. _____

- ☐ I am looking forward to: _____

Notes: _____
_____
_____

MINDFUL LIVING WORKSHEET

M   Tu   W   Th   F   S   S   Date:_____   Rate:_____

- ☐ I am content with: _____
- ☐ I am proud of: _____
- ☐ Success review
- ☐ I love myself because: _____ ☐
- ☐ Love, thanks, kindness and support for others:
    1. _____   2. _____
    3. _____   4. _____
- ☐ Love, thanks, kindness and support for me:
    1. _____   2. _____
    3. _____   4. _____
- ☐ Good Deed/Selfless Act/Random Kindness: _____
- ☐ I gave undivided attention to: _____
- ☐ I made things better by: _____
- ☐ I experienced joy, happiness, fun and/or laughter: _____
- ☐ I smiled _____ minutes
- ☐ Meditation/Prayer _____ minutes
- ☐ Inspiration (reading, video, music): _____
- ☐ I listened to my intuition: _____
- ☐ Physical activity _____ minutes
- ☐ I was 100% honest today
- ☐ I took care of myself by: _____
- ☐ Reviewed purpose 3 times
- ☐ Reviewed intentions 3 times
- ☐ Steps toward goals, intentions and purpose
    1. _____   2. _____   3. _____
- ☐ Reviewed vision
- ☐ I am grateful for:
    1. _____   6. _____
    2. _____   7. _____
    3. _____   8. _____
    4. _____   9. _____
    5. _____   10. _____

- ☐ I am looking forward to: _____

Notes: _____
_____
_____
_____

MINDFUL LIVING WORKSHEET

M   Tu   W   Th   F   S   S   Date:_____   Rate:_____

- ☐ I am content with: _____
- ☐ I am proud of: _____
- ☐ Success review
- ☐ I love myself because: _____ ☐
- ☐ Love, thanks, kindness and support for others:
  - 1. _____   2. _____
  - 3. _____   4. _____
- ☐ Love, thanks, kindness and support for me:
  - 1. _____   2. _____
  - 3. _____   4. _____
- ☐ Good Deed/Selfless Act/Random Kindness: _____
- ☐ I gave undivided attention to: _____
- ☐ I made things better by: _____
- ☐ I experienced joy, happiness, fun and/or laughter: _____
- ☐ I smiled _____ minutes
- ☐ Meditation/Prayer _____ minutes
- ☐ Inspiration (reading, video, music): _____
- ☐ I listened to my intuition: _____
- ☐ Physical activity _____ minutes
- ☐ I was 100% honest today
- ☐ I took care of myself by: _____
- ☐ Reviewed purpose 3 times
- ☐ Reviewed intentions 3 times
- ☐ Steps toward goals, intentions and purpose
  - 1. _____   2. _____   3. _____
- ☐ Reviewed vision
- ☐ I am grateful for:
  - 1. _____   6. _____
  - 2. _____   7. _____
  - 3. _____   8. _____
  - 4. _____   9. _____
  - 5. _____   10. _____

- ☐ I am looking forward to: _____

Notes: _____
_____
_____

Mindful Living Worksheet

M Tu W Th F S S   Date:_____   Rate:_____

- ☐ I am content with: _____
- ☐ I am proud of: _____
- ☐ Success review
- ☐ I love myself because: _____ ☐
- ☐ Love, thanks, kindness and support for others:
    1. _____   2. _____
    3. _____   4. _____
- ☐ Love, thanks, kindness and support for me:
    1. _____   2. _____
    3. _____   4. _____
- ☐ Good Deed/Selfless Act/Random Kindness: _____
- ☐ I gave undivided attention to: _____
- ☐ I made things better by: _____
- ☐ I experienced joy, happiness, fun and/or laughter: _____
- ☐ I smiled _____ minutes
- ☐ Meditation/Prayer _____ minutes
- ☐ Inspiration (reading, video, music): _____
- ☐ I listened to my intuition: _____
- ☐ Physical activity _____ minutes
- ☐ I was 100% honest today
- ☐ I took care of myself by: _____
- ☐ Reviewed purpose 3 times
- ☐ Reviewed intentions 3 times
- ☐ Steps toward goals, intentions and purpose
    1. _____ 2. _____ 3. _____
- ☐ Reviewed vision
- ☐ I am grateful for:
    1. _____   6. _____
    2. _____   7. _____
    3. _____   8. _____
    4. _____   9. _____
    5. _____   10. _____

- ☐ I am looking forward to: _____

Notes: _____
_____
_____
_____

MINDFUL LIVING WORKSHEET

M Tu W Th F S S   Date:_____   Rate:_____

- ☐ I am content with: _____
- ☐ I am proud of: _____
- ☐ Success review
- ☐ I love myself because: _____ ☐
- ☐ Love, thanks, kindness and support for others:
    1. _____   2. _____
    3. _____   4. _____
- ☐ Love, thanks, kindness and support for me:
    1. _____   2. _____
    3. _____   4. _____
- ☐ Good Deed/Selfless Act/Random Kindness: _____
- ☐ I gave undivided attention to: _____
- ☐ I made things better by: _____
- ☐ I experienced joy, happiness, fun and/or laughter: _____
- ☐ I smiled _____ minutes
- ☐ Meditation/Prayer _____ minutes
- ☐ Inspiration (reading, video, music): _____
- ☐ I listened to my intuition: _____
- ☐ Physical activity _____ minutes
- ☐ I was 100% honest today
- ☐ I took care of myself by: _____
- ☐ Reviewed purpose 3 times
- ☐ Reviewed intentions 3 times
- ☐ Steps toward goals, intentions and purpose
    1. _____   2. _____   3. _____
- ☐ Reviewed vision
- ☐ I am grateful for:
    1. _____   6. _____
    2. _____   7. _____
    3. _____   8. _____
    4. _____   9. _____
    5. _____   10. _____

- ☐ I am looking forward to: _____

Notes: _____
_____
_____
_____

MINDFUL LIVING WORKSHEET

M   Tu   W   Th   F   S   S   Date:_____   Rate:_____

- ☐ I am content with: _____
- ☐ I am proud of: _____
- ☐ Success review
- ☐ I love myself because: _____ ☐
- ☐ Love, thanks, kindness and support for others:
  - 1. _____   2. _____
  - 3. _____   4. _____
- ☐ Love, thanks, kindness and support for me:
  - 1. _____   2. _____
  - 3. _____   4. _____
- ☐ Good Deed/Selfless Act/Random Kindness: _____
- ☐ I gave undivided attention to: _____
- ☐ I made things better by: _____
- ☐ I experienced joy, happiness, fun and/or laughter: _____
- ☐ I smiled _____ minutes
- ☐ Meditation/Prayer _____ minutes
- ☐ Inspiration (reading, video, music): _____
- ☐ I listened to my intuition: _____
- ☐ Physical activity _____ minutes
- ☐ I was 100% honest today
- ☐ I took care of myself by: _____
- ☐ Reviewed purpose 3 times
- ☐ Reviewed intentions 3 times
- ☐ Steps toward goals, intentions and purpose
  - 1. _____   2. _____   3. _____
- ☐ Reviewed vision
- ☐ I am grateful for:
  - 1. _____   6. _____
  - 2. _____   7. _____
  - 3. _____   8. _____
  - 4. _____   9. _____
  - 5. _____   10. _____

- ☐ I am looking forward to: _____

Notes: _____
_____
_____
_____

Mindful Living Worksheet

M Tu W Th F S S   Date:_____   Rate:_____

- ☐ I am content with: _____
- ☐ I am proud of: _____
- ☐ Success review
- ☐ I love myself because: _____ ☐
- ☐ Love, thanks, kindness and support for others:
   1. _____   2. _____
   3. _____   4. _____
- ☐ Love, thanks, kindness and support for me:
   1. _____   2. _____
   3. _____   4. _____
- ☐ Good Deed/Selfless Act/Random Kindness: _____
- ☐ I gave undivided attention to: _____
- ☐ I made things better by: _____
- ☐ I experienced joy, happiness, fun and/or laughter: _____
- ☐ I smiled _____ minutes
- ☐ Meditation/Prayer _____ minutes
- ☐ Inspiration (reading, video, music): _____
- ☐ I listened to my intuition: _____
- ☐ Physical activity _____ minutes
- ☐ I was 100% honest today
- ☐ I took care of myself by: _____
- ☐ Reviewed purpose 3 times
- ☐ Reviewed intentions 3 times
- ☐ Steps toward goals, intentions and purpose
   1. _____ 2. _____ 3. _____
- ☐ Reviewed vision
- ☐ I am grateful for:
   1. _____   6. _____
   2. _____   7. _____
   3. _____   8. _____
   4. _____   9. _____
   5. _____   10. _____

- ☐ I am looking forward to: _____

Notes: _____
_____
_____
_____

MINDFUL LIVING WORKSHEET

M Tu W Th F S S   Date:_____   Rate:_____

☐ I am content with: _____
☐ I am proud of: _____
☐ Success review
☐ I love myself because: _____ ☐
☐ Love, thanks, kindness and support for others:
    1. _____ 2. _____
    3. _____ 4. _____
☐ Love, thanks, kindness and support for me:
    1. _____ 2. _____
    3. _____ 4. _____
☐ Good Deed/Selfless Act/Random Kindness: _____
☐ I gave undivided attention to: _____
☐ I made things better by: _____
☐ I experienced joy, happiness, fun and/or laughter: _____
☐ I smiled _____ minutes
☐ Meditation/Prayer _____ minutes
☐ Inspiration (reading, video, music): _____
☐ I listened to my intuition: _____
☐ Physical activity _____ minutes
☐ I was 100% honest today
☐ I took care of myself by: _____
☐ Reviewed purpose 3 times
☐ Reviewed intentions 3 times
☐ Steps toward goals, intentions and purpose
    1. _____ 2. _____ 3. _____
☐ Reviewed vision
☐ I am grateful for:
    1. _____ 6. _____
    2. _____ 7. _____
    3. _____ 8. _____
    4. _____ 9. _____
    5. _____ 10. _____

☐ I am looking forward to: _____

Notes: _____
_____
_____
_____

MINDFUL LIVING WORKSHEET

M   Tu   W   Th   F   S   S   Date:_____   Rate:_____

- ☐ I am content with: _____
- ☐ I am proud of: _____
- ☐ Success review
- ☐ I love myself because: _____ ☐
- ☐ Love, thanks, kindness and support for others:
    - 1. _____   2. _____
    - 3. _____   4. _____
- ☐ Love, thanks, kindness and support for me:
    - 1. _____   2. _____
    - 3. _____   4. _____
- ☐ Good Deed/Selfless Act/Random Kindness: _____
- ☐ I gave undivided attention to: _____
- ☐ I made things better by: _____
- ☐ I experienced joy, happiness, fun and/or laughter: _____
- ☐ I smiled _____ minutes
- ☐ Meditation/Prayer _____ minutes
- ☐ Inspiration (reading, video, music): _____
- ☐ I listened to my intuition: _____
- ☐ Physical activity _____ minutes
- ☐ I was 100% honest today
- ☐ I took care of myself by: _____
- ☐ Reviewed purpose 3 times
- ☐ Reviewed intentions 3 times
- ☐ Steps toward goals, intentions and purpose
    - 1. _____   2. _____   3. _____
- ☐ Reviewed vision
- ☐ I am grateful for:
    - 1. _____   6. _____
    - 2. _____   7. _____
    - 3. _____   8. _____
    - 4. _____   9. _____
    - 5. _____   10. _____

- ☐ I am looking forward to: _____

Notes: _____
_____
_____
_____

MINDFUL LIVING WORKSHEET

M Tu W Th F S S   Date:_____   Rate:_____

- ☐ I am content with: _____
- ☐ I am proud of: _____
- ☐ Success review
- ☐ I love myself because: _____ ☐
- ☐ Love, thanks, kindness and support for others:
    1. _____   2. _____
    3. _____   4. _____
- ☐ Love, thanks, kindness and support for me:
    1. _____   2. _____
    3. _____   4. _____
- ☐ Good Deed/Selfless Act/Random Kindness: _____
- ☐ I gave undivided attention to: _____
- ☐ I made things better by: _____
- ☐ I experienced joy, happiness, fun and/or laughter: _____
- ☐ I smiled _____ minutes
- ☐ Meditation/Prayer _____ minutes
- ☐ Inspiration (reading, video, music): _____
- ☐ I listened to my intuition: _____
- ☐ Physical activity _____ minutes
- ☐ I was 100% honest today
- ☐ I took care of myself by: _____
- ☐ Reviewed purpose 3 times
- ☐ Reviewed intentions 3 times
- ☐ Steps toward goals, intentions and purpose
    1. _____ 2. _____ 3. _____
- ☐ Reviewed vision
- ☐ I am grateful for:
    1. _____   6. _____
    2. _____   7. _____
    3. _____   8. _____
    4. _____   9. _____
    5. _____   10. _____

- ☐ I am looking forward to: _____

Notes: _____
_____
_____
_____

MINDFUL LIVING WORKSHEET

M   Tu   W   Th   F   S   S   Date:_____   Rate:_____

- ☐ I am content with: _____
- ☐ I am proud of: _____
- ☐ Success review
- ☐ I love myself because: _____ ☐
- ☐ Love, thanks, kindness and support for others:
  - 1. _____   2. _____
  - 3. _____   4. _____
- ☐ Love, thanks, kindness and support for me:
  - 1. _____   2. _____
  - 3. _____   4. _____
- ☐ Good Deed/Selfless Act/Random Kindness: _____
- ☐ I gave undivided attention to: _____
- ☐ I made things better by: _____
- ☐ I experienced joy, happiness, fun and/or laughter: _____
- ☐ I smiled _____ minutes
- ☐ Meditation/Prayer _____ minutes
- ☐ Inspiration (reading, video, music): _____
- ☐ I listened to my intuition: _____
- ☐ Physical activity _____ minutes
- ☐ I was 100% honest today
- ☐ I took care of myself by: _____
- ☐ Reviewed purpose 3 times
- ☐ Reviewed intentions 3 times
- ☐ Steps toward goals, intentions and purpose
  - 1. _____   2. _____   3. _____
- ☐ Reviewed vision
- ☐ I am grateful for:
  - 1. _____   6. _____
  - 2. _____   7. _____
  - 3. _____   8. _____
  - 4. _____   9. _____
  - 5. _____   10. _____

- ☐ I am looking forward to: _____

Notes: _____
_____
_____
_____

Mindful Living Worksheet

M   Tu   W   Th   F   S   S   Date:_____   Rate:_____

- ☐ I am content with: _____
- ☐ I am proud of: _____
- ☐ Success review
- ☐ I love myself because: _____ ☐
- ☐ Love, thanks, kindness and support for others:
    1. _____   2. _____
    3. _____   4. _____
- ☐ Love, thanks, kindness and support for me:
    1. _____   2. _____
    3. _____   4. _____
- ☐ Good Deed/Selfless Act/Random Kindness: _____
- ☐ I gave undivided attention to: _____
- ☐ I made things better by: _____
- ☐ I experienced joy, happiness, fun and/or laughter: _____
- ☐ I smiled _____ minutes
- ☐ Meditation/Prayer _____ minutes
- ☐ Inspiration (reading, video, music): _____
- ☐ I listened to my intuition: _____
- ☐ Physical activity _____ minutes
- ☐ I was 100% honest today
- ☐ I took care of myself by: _____
- ☐ Reviewed purpose 3 times
- ☐ Reviewed intentions 3 times
- ☐ Steps toward goals, intentions and purpose
    1. _____   2. _____   3. _____
- ☐ Reviewed vision
- ☐ I am grateful for:
    1. _____   6. _____
    2. _____   7. _____
    3. _____   8. _____
    4. _____   9. _____
    5. _____   10. _____

- ☐ I am looking forward to: _____

Notes: _____
_____
_____
_____

MINDFUL LIVING WORKSHEET

M Tu W Th F S S   Date:_____   Rate:_____

- ☐ I am content with: _____
- ☐ I am proud of: _____
- ☐ Success review
- ☐ I love myself because: _____ ☐
- ☐ Love, thanks, kindness and support for others:
  - 1. _____   2. _____
  - 3. _____   4. _____
- ☐ Love, thanks, kindness and support for me:
  - 1. _____   2. _____
  - 3. _____   4. _____
- ☐ Good Deed/Selfless Act/Random Kindness: _____
- ☐ I gave undivided attention to: _____
- ☐ I made things better by: _____
- ☐ I experienced joy, happiness, fun and/or laughter: _____
- ☐ I smiled _____ minutes
- ☐ Meditation/Prayer _____ minutes
- ☐ Inspiration (reading, video, music): _____
- ☐ I listened to my intuition: _____
- ☐ Physical activity _____ minutes
- ☐ I was 100% honest today
- ☐ I took care of myself by: _____
- ☐ Reviewed purpose 3 times
- ☐ Reviewed intentions 3 times
- ☐ Steps toward goals, intentions and purpose
  - 1. _____   2. _____   3. _____
- ☐ Reviewed vision
- ☐ I am grateful for:
  - 1. _____   6. _____
  - 2. _____   7. _____
  - 3. _____   8. _____
  - 4. _____   9. _____
  - 5. _____   10. _____

- ☐ I am looking forward to: _____

Notes: _____
_____
_____

Mindful Living Worksheet

M Tu W Th F S S   Date:_____   Rate:_____

- ☐ I am content with: _____
- ☐ I am proud of: _____
- ☐ Success review
- ☐ I love myself because: _____ ☐
- ☐ Love, thanks, kindness and support for others:
  - 1. _____   2. _____
  - 3. _____   4. _____
- ☐ Love, thanks, kindness and support for me:
  - 1. _____   2. _____
  - 3. _____   4. _____
- ☐ Good Deed/Selfless Act/Random Kindness: _____
- ☐ I gave undivided attention to: _____
- ☐ I made things better by: _____
- ☐ I experienced joy, happiness, fun and/or laughter: _____
- ☐ I smiled _____ minutes
- ☐ Meditation/Prayer _____ minutes
- ☐ Inspiration (reading, video, music): _____
- ☐ I listened to my intuition: _____
- ☐ Physical activity _____ minutes
- ☐ I was 100% honest today
- ☐ I took care of myself by: _____
- ☐ Reviewed purpose 3 times
- ☐ Reviewed intentions 3 times
- ☐ Steps toward goals, intentions and purpose
  - 1. _____ 2. _____ 3. _____
- ☐ Reviewed vision
- ☐ I am grateful for:
  - 1. _____   6. _____
  - 2. _____   7. _____
  - 3. _____   8. _____
  - 4. _____   9. _____
  - 5. _____   10. _____
- ☐ I am looking forward to: _____

Notes: _____
_____
_____
_____

MINDFUL LIVING WORKSHEET

M   Tu   W   Th   F   S   S   Date:_____   Rate:_____

- ☐ I am content with: _____
- ☐ I am proud of: _____
- ☐ Success review
- ☐ I love myself because: _____ ☐
- ☐ Love, thanks, kindness and support for others:
  - 1. _____   2. _____
  - 3. _____   4. _____
- ☐ Love, thanks, kindness and support for me:
  - 1. _____   2. _____
  - 3. _____   4. _____
- ☐ Good Deed/Selfless Act/Random Kindness: _____
- ☐ I gave undivided attention to: _____
- ☐ I made things better by: _____
- ☐ I experienced joy, happiness, fun and/or laughter: _____
- ☐ I smiled _____ minutes
- ☐ Meditation/Prayer _____ minutes
- ☐ Inspiration (reading, video, music): _____
- ☐ I listened to my intuition: _____
- ☐ Physical activity _____ minutes
- ☐ I was 100% honest today
- ☐ I took care of myself by: _____
- ☐ Reviewed purpose 3 times
- ☐ Reviewed intentions 3 times
- ☐ Steps toward goals, intentions and purpose
  - 1. _____   2. _____   3. _____
- ☐ Reviewed vision
- ☐ I am grateful for:
  - 1. _____   6. _____
  - 2. _____   7. _____
  - 3. _____   8. _____
  - 4. _____   9. _____
  - 5. _____   10. _____

- ☐ I am looking forward to: _____

Notes: _____
_____
_____
_____

Mindful Living Worksheet

M Tu W Th F S S   Date:_____   Rate:_____

☐ I am content with: _____
☐ I am proud of: _____
☐ Success review
☐ I love myself because: _____ ☐
☐ Love, thanks, kindness and support for others:
    1. _____ 2. _____
    3. _____ 4. _____
☐ Love, thanks, kindness and support for me:
    1. _____ 2. _____
    3. _____ 4. _____
☐ Good Deed/Selfless Act/Random Kindness: _____
☐ I gave undivided attention to: _____
☐ I made things better by: _____
☐ I experienced joy, happiness, fun and/or laughter: _____
☐ I smiled _____ minutes
☐ Meditation/Prayer _____ minutes
☐ Inspiration (reading, video, music): _____
☐ I listened to my intuition: _____
☐ Physical activity _____ minutes
☐ I was 100% honest today
☐ I took care of myself by: _____
☐ Reviewed purpose 3 times
☐ Reviewed intentions 3 times
☐ Steps toward goals, intentions and purpose
    1. _____ 2. _____ 3. _____
☐ Reviewed vision
☐ I am grateful for:
    1. _____ 6. _____
    2. _____ 7. _____
    3. _____ 8. _____
    4. _____ 9. _____
    5. _____ 10. _____

☐ I am looking forward to: _____

Notes: _____
_____
_____
_____

MINDFUL LIVING WORKSHEET

M Tu W Th F S S   Date:_____   Rate:_____

- ☐ I am content with: _____
- ☐ I am proud of: _____
- ☐ Success review
- ☐ I love myself because: _____ ☐
- ☐ Love, thanks, kindness and support for others:
  - 1. _____   2. _____
  - 3. _____   4. _____
- ☐ Love, thanks, kindness and support for me:
  - 1. _____   2. _____
  - 3. _____   4. _____
- ☐ Good Deed/Selfless Act/Random Kindness: _____
- ☐ I gave undivided attention to: _____
- ☐ I made things better by: _____
- ☐ I experienced joy, happiness, fun and/or laughter: _____
- ☐ I smiled _____ minutes
- ☐ Meditation/Prayer _____ minutes
- ☐ Inspiration (reading, video, music): _____
- ☐ I listened to my intuition: _____
- ☐ Physical activity _____ minutes
- ☐ I was 100% honest today
- ☐ I took care of myself by: _____
- ☐ Reviewed purpose 3 times
- ☐ Reviewed intentions 3 times
- ☐ Steps toward goals, intentions and purpose
  - 1. _____   2. _____   3. _____
- ☐ Reviewed vision
- ☐ I am grateful for:
  - 1. _____   6. _____
  - 2. _____   7. _____
  - 3. _____   8. _____
  - 4. _____   9. _____
  - 5. _____   10. _____

- ☐ I am looking forward to: _____

Notes: _____
_____
_____
_____

MINDFUL LIVING WORKSHEET

M   Tu   W   Th   F   S   S   Date:_____   Rate:_____

- ☐ I am content with: _____
- ☐ I am proud of: _____
- ☐ Success review
- ☐ I love myself because: _____ ☐
- ☐ Love, thanks, kindness and support for others:
  - 1. _____   2. _____
  - 3. _____   4. _____
- ☐ Love, thanks, kindness and support for me:
  - 1. _____   2. _____
  - 3. _____   4. _____
- ☐ Good Deed/Selfless Act/Random Kindness: _____
- ☐ I gave undivided attention to: _____
- ☐ I made things better by: _____
- ☐ I experienced joy, happiness, fun and/or laughter: _____
- ☐ I smiled _____ minutes
- ☐ Meditation/Prayer _____ minutes
- ☐ Inspiration (reading, video, music): _____
- ☐ I listened to my intuition: _____
- ☐ Physical activity _____ minutes
- ☐ I was 100% honest today
- ☐ I took care of myself by: _____
- ☐ Reviewed purpose 3 times
- ☐ Reviewed intentions 3 times
- ☐ Steps toward goals, intentions and purpose
  - 1. _____   2. _____   3. _____
- ☐ Reviewed vision
- ☐ I am grateful for:
  - 1. _____   6. _____
  - 2. _____   7. _____
  - 3. _____   8. _____
  - 4. _____   9. _____
  - 5. _____   10. _____

- ☐ I am looking forward to: _____

Notes: _____
_____
_____
_____

MINDFUL LIVING WORKSHEET

M Tu W Th F S S   Date:_____   Rate:_____

- ☐ I am content with: _____
- ☐ I am proud of: _____
- ☐ Success review
- ☐ I love myself because: _____ ☐
- ☐ Love, thanks, kindness and support for others:
  - 1. _____   2. _____
  - 3. _____   4. _____
- ☐ Love, thanks, kindness and support for me:
  - 1. _____   2. _____
  - 3. _____   4. _____
- ☐ Good Deed/Selfless Act/Random Kindness: _____
- ☐ I gave undivided attention to: _____
- ☐ I made things better by: _____
- ☐ I experienced joy, happiness, fun and/or laughter: _____
- ☐ I smiled _____ minutes
- ☐ Meditation/Prayer _____ minutes
- ☐ Inspiration (reading, video, music): _____
- ☐ I listened to my intuition: _____
- ☐ Physical activity _____ minutes
- ☐ I was 100% honest today
- ☐ I took care of myself by: _____
- ☐ Reviewed purpose 3 times
- ☐ Reviewed intentions 3 times
- ☐ Steps toward goals, intentions and purpose
  - 1. _____   2. _____   3. _____
- ☐ Reviewed vision
- ☐ I am grateful for:
  - 1. _____   6. _____
  - 2. _____   7. _____
  - 3. _____   8. _____
  - 4. _____   9. _____
  - 5. _____   10. _____

- ☐ I am looking forward to: _____

Notes: _____
_____
_____
_____

MINDFUL LIVING WORKSHEET

M   Tu   W   Th   F   S   S   Date:_____   Rate:_____

- ☐ I am content with: _____
- ☐ I am proud of: _____
- ☐ Success review
- ☐ I love myself because: _____ ☐
- ☐ Love, thanks, kindness and support for others:
  - 1. _____   2. _____
  - 3. _____   4. _____
- ☐ Love, thanks, kindness and support for me:
  - 1. _____   2. _____
  - 3. _____   4. _____
- ☐ Good Deed/Selfless Act/Random Kindness: _____
- ☐ I gave undivided attention to: _____
- ☐ I made things better by: _____
- ☐ I experienced joy, happiness, fun and/or laughter: _____
- ☐ I smiled _____ minutes
- ☐ Meditation/Prayer _____ minutes
- ☐ Inspiration (reading, video, music): _____
- ☐ I listened to my intuition: _____
- ☐ Physical activity _____ minutes
- ☐ I was 100% honest today
- ☐ I took care of myself by: _____
- ☐ Reviewed purpose 3 times
- ☐ Reviewed intentions 3 times
- ☐ Steps toward goals, intentions and purpose
  - 1. _____ 2. _____ 3. _____
- ☐ Reviewed vision
- ☐ I am grateful for:
  - 1. _____   6. _____
  - 2. _____   7. _____
  - 3. _____   8. _____
  - 4. _____   9. _____
  - 5. _____   10. _____

- ☐ I am looking forward to: _____

Notes: _____
_____
_____

MINDFUL LIVING WORKSHEET

M Tu W Th F S S   Date:_____   Rate:_____

- ☐ I am content with: _____
- ☐ I am proud of: _____
- ☐ Success review
- ☐ I love myself because: _____ ☐
- ☐ Love, thanks, kindness and support for others:
  - 1. _____   2. _____
  - 3. _____   4. _____
- ☐ Love, thanks, kindness and support for me:
  - 1. _____   2. _____
  - 3. _____   4. _____
- ☐ Good Deed/Selfless Act/Random Kindness: _____
- ☐ I gave undivided attention to: _____
- ☐ I made things better by: _____
- ☐ I experienced joy, happiness, fun and/or laughter: _____
- ☐ I smiled _____ minutes
- ☐ Meditation/Prayer _____ minutes
- ☐ Inspiration (reading, video, music): _____
- ☐ I listened to my intuition: _____
- ☐ Physical activity _____ minutes
- ☐ I was 100% honest today
- ☐ I took care of myself by: _____
- ☐ Reviewed purpose 3 times
- ☐ Reviewed intentions 3 times
- ☐ Steps toward goals, intentions and purpose
  - 1. _____ 2. _____ 3. _____
- ☐ Reviewed vision
- ☐ I am grateful for:
  - 1. _____   6. _____
  - 2. _____   7. _____
  - 3. _____   8. _____
  - 4. _____   9. _____
  - 5. _____   10. _____

- ☐ I am looking forward to: _____

Notes: _____
_____
_____
_____

Mindful Living Worksheet

M Tu W Th F S S   Date:_____   Rate:_____

- ☐ I am content with: _____
- ☐ I am proud of: _____
- ☐ Success review
- ☐ I love myself because: _____ ☐
- ☐ Love, thanks, kindness and support for others:
  - 1. _____   2. _____
  - 3. _____   4. _____
- ☐ Love, thanks, kindness and support for me:
  - 1. _____   2. _____
  - 3. _____   4. _____
- ☐ Good Deed/Selfless Act/Random Kindness: _____
- ☐ I gave undivided attention to: _____
- ☐ I made things better by: _____
- ☐ I experienced joy, happiness, fun and/or laughter: _____
- ☐ I smiled _____ minutes
- ☐ Meditation/Prayer _____ minutes
- ☐ Inspiration (reading, video, music): _____
- ☐ I listened to my intuition: _____
- ☐ Physical activity _____ minutes
- ☐ I was 100% honest today
- ☐ I took care of myself by: _____
- ☐ Reviewed purpose 3 times
- ☐ Reviewed intentions 3 times
- ☐ Steps toward goals, intentions and purpose
  - 1. _____ 2. _____ 3. _____
- ☐ Reviewed vision
- ☐ I am grateful for:
  - 1. _____   6. _____
  - 2. _____   7. _____
  - 3. _____   8. _____
  - 4. _____   9. _____
  - 5. _____   10. _____

- ☐ I am looking forward to: _____

Notes: _____
_____
_____
_____

Mindful Living Worksheet

M   Tu   W   Th   F   S   S   Date:_____   Rate:_____

- ☐ I am content with: _____
- ☐ I am proud of: _____
- ☐ Success review
- ☐ I love myself because: _____ ☐
- ☐ Love, thanks, kindness and support for others:
  - 1. _____   2. _____
  - 3. _____   4. _____
- ☐ Love, thanks, kindness and support for me:
  - 1. _____   2. _____
  - 3. _____   4. _____
- ☐ Good Deed/Selfless Act/Random Kindness: _____
- ☐ I gave undivided attention to: _____
- ☐ I made things better by: _____
- ☐ I experienced joy, happiness, fun and/or laughter: _____
- ☐ I smiled _____ minutes
- ☐ Meditation/Prayer _____ minutes
- ☐ Inspiration (reading, video, music): _____
- ☐ I listened to my intuition: _____
- ☐ Physical activity _____ minutes
- ☐ I was 100% honest today
- ☐ I took care of myself by: _____
- ☐ Reviewed purpose 3 times
- ☐ Reviewed intentions 3 times
- ☐ Steps toward goals, intentions and purpose
  - 1. _____ 2. _____ 3. _____
- ☐ Reviewed vision
- ☐ I am grateful for:
  - 1. _____   6. _____
  - 2. _____   7. _____
  - 3. _____   8. _____
  - 4. _____   9. _____
  - 5. _____   10. _____

- ☐ I am looking forward to: _____

Notes: _____
_____
_____
_____

MINDFUL LIVING WORKSHEET

M Tu W Th F S S   Date:_____   Rate:_____

☐ I am content with: _____
☐ I am proud of: _____
☐ Success review
☐ I love myself because: _____ ☐
☐ Love, thanks, kindness and support for others:
    1. _____   2. _____
    3. _____   4. _____
☐ Love, thanks, kindness and support for me:
    1. _____   2. _____
    3. _____   4. _____
☐ Good Deed/Selfless Act/Random Kindness: _____
☐ I gave undivided attention to: _____
☐ I made things better by: _____
☐ I experienced joy, happiness, fun and/or laughter: _____
☐ I smiled _____ minutes
☐ Meditation/Prayer _____ minutes
☐ Inspiration (reading, video, music): _____
☐ I listened to my intuition: _____
☐ Physical activity _____ minutes
☐ I was 100% honest today
☐ I took care of myself by: _____
☐ Reviewed purpose 3 times
☐ Reviewed intentions 3 times
☐ Steps toward goals, intentions and purpose
    1. _____ 2. _____ 3. _____
☐ Reviewed vision
☐ I am grateful for:
    1. _____   6. _____
    2. _____   7. _____
    3. _____   8. _____
    4. _____   9. _____
    5. _____   10. _____

☐ I am looking forward to: _____

Notes: _____
_____
_____
_____

Mindful Living Worksheet

M Tu W Th F S S   Date:_____   Rate:_____

- ☐ I am content with: _____
- ☐ I am proud of: _____
- ☐ Success review
- ☐ I love myself because: _____ ☐
- ☐ Love, thanks, kindness and support for others:
    - 1. _____   2. _____
    - 3. _____   4. _____
- ☐ Love, thanks, kindness and support for me:
    - 1. _____   2. _____
    - 3. _____   4. _____
- ☐ Good Deed/Selfless Act/Random Kindness: _____
- ☐ I gave undivided attention to: _____
- ☐ I made things better by: _____
- ☐ I experienced joy, happiness, fun and/or laughter: _____
- ☐ I smiled _____ minutes
- ☐ Meditation/Prayer _____ minutes
- ☐ Inspiration (reading, video, music): _____
- ☐ I listened to my intuition: _____
- ☐ Physical activity _____ minutes
- ☐ I was 100% honest today
- ☐ I took care of myself by: _____
- ☐ Reviewed purpose 3 times
- ☐ Reviewed intentions 3 times
- ☐ Steps toward goals, intentions and purpose
    - 1. _____ 2. _____ 3. _____
- ☐ Reviewed vision
- ☐ I am grateful for:
    - 1. _____   6. _____
    - 2. _____   7. _____
    - 3. _____   8. _____
    - 4. _____   9. _____
    - 5. _____   10. _____

- ☐ I am looking forward to: _____

Notes: _____
_____
_____
_____

MINDFUL LIVING WORKSHEET

M Tu W Th F S S   Date:_____   Rate:_____

- ☐ I am content with: _____
- ☐ I am proud of: _____
- ☐ Success review
- ☐ I love myself because: _____ ☐
- ☐ Love, thanks, kindness and support for others:
     1. _____   2. _____
     3. _____   4. _____
- ☐ Love, thanks, kindness and support for me:
     1. _____   2. _____
     3. _____   4. _____
- ☐ Good Deed/Selfless Act/Random Kindness: _____
- ☐ I gave undivided attention to: _____
- ☐ I made things better by: _____
- ☐ I experienced joy, happiness, fun and/or laughter: _____
- ☐ I smiled _____ minutes
- ☐ Meditation/Prayer _____ minutes
- ☐ Inspiration (reading, video, music): _____
- ☐ I listened to my intuition: _____
- ☐ Physical activity _____ minutes
- ☐ I was 100% honest today
- ☐ I took care of myself by: _____
- ☐ Reviewed purpose 3 times
- ☐ Reviewed intentions 3 times
- ☐ Steps toward goals, intentions and purpose
     1. _____   2. _____   3. _____
- ☐ Reviewed vision
- ☐ I am grateful for:
     1. _____   6. _____
     2. _____   7. _____
     3. _____   8. _____
     4. _____   9. _____
     5. _____   10. _____

- ☐ I am looking forward to: _____

Notes: _____
_____
_____
_____

MINDFUL LIVING WORKSHEET

M   Tu   W   Th   F   S   S   Date:_____   Rate:_____

- ☐ I am content with: _____
- ☐ I am proud of: _____
- ☐ Success review
- ☐ I love myself because: _____ ☐
- ☐ Love, thanks, kindness and support for others:
    1. _____   2. _____
    3. _____   4. _____
- ☐ Love, thanks, kindness and support for me:
    1. _____   2. _____
    3. _____   4. _____
- ☐ Good Deed/Selfless Act/Random Kindness: _____
- ☐ I gave undivided attention to: _____
- ☐ I made things better by: _____
- ☐ I experienced joy, happiness, fun and/or laughter: _____
- ☐ I smiled _____ minutes
- ☐ Meditation/Prayer _____ minutes
- ☐ Inspiration (reading, video, music): _____
- ☐ I listened to my intuition: _____
- ☐ Physical activity _____ minutes
- ☐ I was 100% honest today
- ☐ I took care of myself by: _____
- ☐ Reviewed purpose 3 times
- ☐ Reviewed intentions 3 times
- ☐ Steps toward goals, intentions and purpose
    1. _____   2. _____   3. _____
- ☐ Reviewed vision
- ☐ I am grateful for:
    1. _____   6. _____
    2. _____   7. _____
    3. _____   8. _____
    4. _____   9. _____
    5. _____   10. _____

- ☐ I am looking forward to: _____

Notes: _____
_____
_____
_____

MINDFUL LIVING WORKSHEET

M   Tu   W   Th   F   S   S   Date:_____   Rate:_____

- ☐ I am content with: _____
- ☐ I am proud of: _____
- ☐ Success review
- ☐ I love myself because: _____ ☐
- ☐ Love, thanks, kindness and support for others:
   - 1. _____   2. _____
   - 3. _____   4. _____
- ☐ Love, thanks, kindness and support for me:
   - 1. _____   2. _____
   - 3. _____   4. _____
- ☐ Good Deed/Selfless Act/Random Kindness: _____
- ☐ I gave undivided attention to: _____
- ☐ I made things better by: _____
- ☐ I experienced joy, happiness, fun and/or laughter: _____
- ☐ I smiled _____ minutes
- ☐ Meditation/Prayer _____ minutes
- ☐ Inspiration (reading, video, music): _____
- ☐ I listened to my intuition: _____
- ☐ Physical activity _____ minutes
- ☐ I was 100% honest today
- ☐ I took care of myself by: _____
- ☐ Reviewed purpose 3 times
- ☐ Reviewed intentions 3 times
- ☐ Steps toward goals, intentions and purpose
   - 1. _____   2. _____   3. _____
- ☐ Reviewed vision
- ☐ I am grateful for:
   - 1. _____   6. _____
   - 2. _____   7. _____
   - 3. _____   8. _____
   - 4. _____   9. _____
   - 5. _____   10. _____

- ☐ I am looking forward to: _____

Notes: _____
_____
_____
_____

Mindful Living Worksheet

M Tu W Th F S S   Date:_____   Rate:_____

- ☐ I am content with: _____
- ☐ I am proud of: _____
- ☐ Success review
- ☐ I love myself because: _____ ☐
- ☐ Love, thanks, kindness and support for others:
  - 1. _____   2. _____
  - 3. _____   4. _____
- ☐ Love, thanks, kindness and support for me:
  - 1. _____   2. _____
  - 3. _____   4. _____
- ☐ Good Deed/Selfless Act/Random Kindness: _____
- ☐ I gave undivided attention to: _____
- ☐ I made things better by: _____
- ☐ I experienced joy, happiness, fun and/or laughter: _____
- ☐ I smiled _____ minutes
- ☐ Meditation/Prayer _____ minutes
- ☐ Inspiration (reading, video, music): _____
- ☐ I listened to my intuition: _____
- ☐ Physical activity _____ minutes
- ☐ I was 100% honest today
- ☐ I took care of myself by: _____
- ☐ Reviewed purpose 3 times
- ☐ Reviewed intentions 3 times
- ☐ Steps toward goals, intentions and purpose
  - 1. _____   2. _____   3. _____
- ☐ Reviewed vision
- ☐ I am grateful for:
  - 1. _____   6. _____
  - 2. _____   7. _____
  - 3. _____   8. _____
  - 4. _____   9. _____
  - 5. _____   10. _____

- ☐ I am looking forward to: _____

Notes: _____
_____
_____

Mindful Living Worksheet

M Tu W Th F S S   Date:_____   Rate:_____

- ☐ I am content with: _____
- ☐ I am proud of: _____
- ☐ Success review
- ☐ I love myself because: _____ ☐
- ☐ Love, thanks, kindness and support for others:
  - 1. _____   2. _____
  - 3. _____   4. _____
- ☐ Love, thanks, kindness and support for me:
  - 1. _____   2. _____
  - 3. _____   4. _____
- ☐ Good Deed/Selfless Act/Random Kindness: _____
- ☐ I gave undivided attention to: _____
- ☐ I made things better by: _____
- ☐ I experienced joy, happiness, fun and/or laughter: _____
- ☐ I smiled _____ minutes
- ☐ Meditation/Prayer _____ minutes
- ☐ Inspiration (reading, video, music): _____
- ☐ I listened to my intuition: _____
- ☐ Physical activity _____ minutes
- ☐ I was 100% honest today
- ☐ I took care of myself by: _____
- ☐ Reviewed purpose 3 times
- ☐ Reviewed intentions 3 times
- ☐ Steps toward goals, intentions and purpose
  - 1. _____ 2. _____ 3. _____
- ☐ Reviewed vision
- ☐ I am grateful for:
  - 1. _____   6. _____
  - 2. _____   7. _____
  - 3. _____   8. _____
  - 4. _____   9. _____
  - 5. _____   10. _____
- ☐ I am looking forward to: _____

Notes: _____
_____
_____
_____

MINDFUL LIVING WORKSHEET

M   Tu   W   Th   F   S   S   Date:_____   Rate:_____

- ☐ I am content with: _____
- ☐ I am proud of: _____
- ☐ Success review
- ☐ I love myself because: _____ ☐
- ☐ Love, thanks, kindness and support for others:
  - 1. _____   2. _____
  - 3. _____   4. _____
- ☐ Love, thanks, kindness and support for me:
  - 1. _____   2. _____
  - 3. _____   4. _____
- ☐ Good Deed/Selfless Act/Random Kindness: _____
- ☐ I gave undivided attention to: _____
- ☐ I made things better by: _____
- ☐ I experienced joy, happiness, fun and/or laughter: _____
- ☐ I smiled _____ minutes
- ☐ Meditation/Prayer _____ minutes
- ☐ Inspiration (reading, video, music): _____
- ☐ I listened to my intuition: _____
- ☐ Physical activity _____ minutes
- ☐ I was 100% honest today
- ☐ I took care of myself by: _____
- ☐ Reviewed purpose 3 times
- ☐ Reviewed intentions 3 times
- ☐ Steps toward goals, intentions and purpose
  - 1. _____   2. _____   3. _____
- ☐ Reviewed vision
- ☐ I am grateful for:
  - 1. _____   6. _____
  - 2. _____   7. _____
  - 3. _____   8. _____
  - 4. _____   9. _____
  - 5. _____   10. _____

- ☐ I am looking forward to: _____

Notes: _____
_____
_____

Mindful Living Worksheet

M Tu W Th F S S   Date:_____   Rate:_____

- ☐ I am content with: _____
- ☐ I am proud of: _____
- ☐ Success review
- ☐ I love myself because: _____ ☐
- ☐ Love, thanks, kindness and support for others:
    - 1. _____   2. _____
    - 3. _____   4. _____
- ☐ Love, thanks, kindness and support for me:
    - 1. _____   2. _____
    - 3. _____   4. _____
- ☐ Good Deed/Selfless Act/Random Kindness: _____
- ☐ I gave undivided attention to: _____
- ☐ I made things better by: _____
- ☐ I experienced joy, happiness, fun and/or laughter: _____
- ☐ I smiled _____ minutes
- ☐ Meditation/Prayer _____ minutes
- ☐ Inspiration (reading, video, music): _____
- ☐ I listened to my intuition: _____
- ☐ Physical activity _____ minutes
- ☐ I was 100% honest today
- ☐ I took care of myself by: _____
- ☐ Reviewed purpose 3 times
- ☐ Reviewed intentions 3 times
- ☐ Steps toward goals, intentions and purpose
    - 1. _____   2. _____   3. _____
- ☐ Reviewed vision
- ☐ I am grateful for:
    - 1. _____   6. _____
    - 2. _____   7. _____
    - 3. _____   8. _____
    - 4. _____   9. _____
    - 5. _____   10. _____

- ☐ I am looking forward to: _____

Notes: _____
_____
_____
_____

MINDFUL LIVING WORKSHEET

M Tu W Th F S S   Date:_____   Rate:_____

- ☐ I am content with: _____
- ☐ I am proud of: _____
- ☐ Success review
- ☐ I love myself because: _____ ☐
- ☐ Love, thanks, kindness and support for others:
  - 1. _____   2. _____
  - 3. _____   4. _____
- ☐ Love, thanks, kindness and support for me:
  - 1. _____   2. _____
  - 3. _____   4. _____
- ☐ Good Deed/Selfless Act/Random Kindness: _____
- ☐ I gave undivided attention to: _____
- ☐ I made things better by: _____
- ☐ I experienced joy, happiness, fun and/or laughter: _____
- ☐ I smiled _____ minutes
- ☐ Meditation/Prayer _____ minutes
- ☐ Inspiration (reading, video, music): _____
- ☐ I listened to my intuition: _____
- ☐ Physical activity _____ minutes
- ☐ I was 100% honest today
- ☐ I took care of myself by: _____
- ☐ Reviewed purpose 3 times
- ☐ Reviewed intentions 3 times
- ☐ Steps toward goals, intentions and purpose
  - 1. _____   2. _____   3. _____
- ☐ Reviewed vision
- ☐ I am grateful for:
  - 1. _____   6. _____
  - 2. _____   7. _____
  - 3. _____   8. _____
  - 4. _____   9. _____
  - 5. _____   10. _____

- ☐ I am looking forward to: _____

Notes: _____
_____
_____
_____

MINDFUL LIVING WORKSHEET

M Tu W Th F S S   Date:_____   Rate:_____

- ☐ I am content with: _____
- ☐ I am proud of: _____
- ☐ Success review
- ☐ I love myself because: _____ ☐
- ☐ Love, thanks, kindness and support for others:
  - 1. _____   2. _____
  - 3. _____   4. _____
- ☐ Love, thanks, kindness and support for me:
  - 1. _____   2. _____
  - 3. _____   4. _____
- ☐ Good Deed/Selfless Act/Random Kindness: _____
- ☐ I gave undivided attention to: _____
- ☐ I made things better by: _____
- ☐ I experienced joy, happiness, fun and/or laughter: _____
- ☐ I smiled _____ minutes
- ☐ Meditation/Prayer _____ minutes
- ☐ Inspiration (reading, video, music): _____
- ☐ I listened to my intuition: _____
- ☐ Physical activity _____ minutes
- ☐ I was 100% honest today
- ☐ I took care of myself by: _____
- ☐ Reviewed purpose 3 times
- ☐ Reviewed intentions 3 times
- ☐ Steps toward goals, intentions and purpose
  - 1. _____ 2. _____ 3. _____
- ☐ Reviewed vision
- ☐ I am grateful for:
  - 1. _____   6. _____
  - 2. _____   7. _____
  - 3. _____   8. _____
  - 4. _____   9. _____
  - 5. _____   10. _____

- ☐ I am looking forward to: _____

Notes: _____
_____
_____
_____

Mindful Living Worksheet

M Tu W Th F S S   Date:_____   Rate:_____

- ☐ I am content with: _____
- ☐ I am proud of: _____
- ☐ Success review
- ☐ I love myself because: _____ ☐
- ☐ Love, thanks, kindness and support for others:
    - 1. _____   2. _____
    - 3. _____   4. _____
- ☐ Love, thanks, kindness and support for me:
    - 1. _____   2. _____
    - 3. _____   4. _____
- ☐ Good Deed/Selfless Act/Random Kindness: _____
- ☐ I gave undivided attention to: _____
- ☐ I made things better by: _____
- ☐ I experienced joy, happiness, fun and/or laughter: _____
- ☐ I smiled _____ minutes
- ☐ Meditation/Prayer _____ minutes
- ☐ Inspiration (reading, video, music): _____
- ☐ I listened to my intuition: _____
- ☐ Physical activity _____ minutes
- ☐ I was 100% honest today
- ☐ I took care of myself by: _____
- ☐ Reviewed purpose 3 times
- ☐ Reviewed intentions 3 times
- ☐ Steps toward goals, intentions and purpose
    - 1. _____   2. _____   3. _____
- ☐ Reviewed vision
- ☐ I am grateful for:
    - 1. _____   6. _____
    - 2. _____   7. _____
    - 3. _____   8. _____
    - 4. _____   9. _____
    - 5. _____   10. _____

- ☐ I am looking forward to: _____

Notes: _____
_____
_____
_____

Mindful Living Worksheet

M Tu W Th F S S   Date:_____   Rate:_____

- ☐ I am content with: _____
- ☐ I am proud of: _____
- ☐ Success review
- ☐ I love myself because: _____ ☐
- ☐ Love, thanks, kindness and support for others:
    1. _____   2. _____
    3. _____   4. _____
- ☐ Love, thanks, kindness and support for me:
    1. _____   2. _____
    3. _____   4. _____
- ☐ Good Deed/Selfless Act/Random Kindness: _____
- ☐ I gave undivided attention to: _____
- ☐ I made things better by: _____
- ☐ I experienced joy, happiness, fun and/or laughter: _____
- ☐ I smiled _____ minutes
- ☐ Meditation/Prayer _____ minutes
- ☐ Inspiration (reading, video, music): _____
- ☐ I listened to my intuition: _____
- ☐ Physical activity _____ minutes
- ☐ I was 100% honest today
- ☐ I took care of myself by: _____
- ☐ Reviewed purpose 3 times
- ☐ Reviewed intentions 3 times
- ☐ Steps toward goals, intentions and purpose
    1. _____ 2. _____ 3. _____
- ☐ Reviewed vision
- ☐ I am grateful for:
    1. _____   6. _____
    2. _____   7. _____
    3. _____   8. _____
    4. _____   9. _____
    5. _____   10. _____

- ☐ I am looking forward to: _____

Notes: _____
_____
_____
_____

MINDFUL LIVING WORKSHEET

M Tu W Th F S S   Date:_____   Rate:_____

- ☐ I am content with: _____
- ☐ I am proud of: _____
- ☐ Success review
- ☐ I love myself because: _____ ☐
- ☐ Love, thanks, kindness and support for others:
  - 1. _____   2. _____
  - 3. _____   4. _____
- ☐ Love, thanks, kindness and support for me:
  - 1. _____   2. _____
  - 3. _____   4. _____
- ☐ Good Deed/Selfless Act/Random Kindness: _____
- ☐ I gave undivided attention to: _____
- ☐ I made things better by: _____
- ☐ I experienced joy, happiness, fun and/or laughter: _____
- ☐ I smiled _____ minutes
- ☐ Meditation/Prayer _____ minutes
- ☐ Inspiration (reading, video, music): _____
- ☐ I listened to my intuition: _____
- ☐ Physical activity _____ minutes
- ☐ I was 100% honest today
- ☐ I took care of myself by: _____
- ☐ Reviewed purpose 3 times
- ☐ Reviewed intentions 3 times
- ☐ Steps toward goals, intentions and purpose
  - 1. _____   2. _____   3. _____
- ☐ Reviewed vision
- ☐ I am grateful for:
  - 1. _____   6. _____
  - 2. _____   7. _____
  - 3. _____   8. _____
  - 4. _____   9. _____
  - 5. _____   10. _____

- ☐ I am looking forward to: _____

Notes: _____
_____
_____

MINDFUL LIVING WORKSHEET

M Tu W Th F S S   Date:_____   Rate:_____

- ☐ I am content with: _____
- ☐ I am proud of: _____
- ☐ Success review
- ☐ I love myself because: _____ ☐
- ☐ Love, thanks, kindness and support for others:
    - 1. _____   2. _____
    - 3. _____   4. _____
- ☐ Love, thanks, kindness and support for me:
    - 1. _____   2. _____
    - 3. _____   4. _____
- ☐ Good Deed/Selfless Act/Random Kindness: _____
- ☐ I gave undivided attention to: _____
- ☐ I made things better by: _____
- ☐ I experienced joy, happiness, fun and/or laughter: _____
- ☐ I smiled _____ minutes
- ☐ Meditation/Prayer _____ minutes
- ☐ Inspiration (reading, video, music): _____
- ☐ I listened to my intuition: _____
- ☐ Physical activity _____ minutes
- ☐ I was 100% honest today
- ☐ I took care of myself by: _____
- ☐ Reviewed purpose 3 times
- ☐ Reviewed intentions 3 times
- ☐ Steps toward goals, intentions and purpose
    - 1. _____   2. _____   3. _____
- ☐ Reviewed vision
- ☐ I am grateful for:
    - 1. _____   6. _____
    - 2. _____   7. _____
    - 3. _____   8. _____
    - 4. _____   9. _____
    - 5. _____   10. _____

- ☐ I am looking forward to: _____

Notes: _____
_____
_____
_____

MINDFUL LIVING WORKSHEET

M Tu W Th F S S   Date:_____   Rate:_____

- ☐ I am content with: _____
- ☐ I am proud of: _____
- ☐ Success review
- ☐ I love myself because: _____ ☐
- ☐ Love, thanks, kindness and support for others:
    - 1. _____   2. _____
    - 3. _____   4. _____
- ☐ Love, thanks, kindness and support for me:
    - 1. _____   2. _____
    - 3. _____   4. _____
- ☐ Good Deed/Selfless Act/Random Kindness: _____
- ☐ I gave undivided attention to: _____
- ☐ I made things better by: _____
- ☐ I experienced joy, happiness, fun and/or laughter: _____
- ☐ I smiled _____ minutes
- ☐ Meditation/Prayer _____ minutes
- ☐ Inspiration (reading, video, music): _____
- ☐ I listened to my intuition: _____
- ☐ Physical activity _____ minutes
- ☐ I was 100% honest today
- ☐ I took care of myself by: _____
- ☐ Reviewed purpose 3 times
- ☐ Reviewed intentions 3 times
- ☐ Steps toward goals, intentions and purpose
    - 1. _____   2. _____   3. _____
- ☐ Reviewed vision
- ☐ I am grateful for:
    - 1. _____   6. _____
    - 2. _____   7. _____
    - 3. _____   8. _____
    - 4. _____   9. _____
    - 5. _____   10. _____

- ☐ I am looking forward to: _____

Notes: _____
_____
_____
_____

MINDFUL LIVING WORKSHEET

M   Tu   W   Th   F   S   S   Date:_____   Rate:_____

- ☐ I am content with: _____
- ☐ I am proud of: _____
- ☐ Success review
- ☐ I love myself because: _____ ☐
- ☐ Love, thanks, kindness and support for others:
    1. _____   2. _____
    3. _____   4. _____
- ☐ Love, thanks, kindness and support for me:
    1. _____   2. _____
    3. _____   4. _____
- ☐ Good Deed/Selfless Act/Random Kindness: _____
- ☐ I gave undivided attention to: _____
- ☐ I made things better by: _____
- ☐ I experienced joy, happiness, fun and/or laughter: _____
- ☐ I smiled _____ minutes
- ☐ Meditation/Prayer _____ minutes
- ☐ Inspiration (reading, video, music): _____
- ☐ I listened to my intuition: _____
- ☐ Physical activity _____ minutes
- ☐ I was 100% honest today
- ☐ I took care of myself by: _____
- ☐ Reviewed purpose 3 times
- ☐ Reviewed intentions 3 times
- ☐ Steps toward goals, intentions and purpose
    1. _____   2. _____   3. _____
- ☐ Reviewed vision
- ☐ I am grateful for:
    1. _____   6. _____
    2. _____   7. _____
    3. _____   8. _____
    4. _____   9. _____
    5. _____   10. _____

- ☐ I am looking forward to: _____

Notes: _____
_____
_____
_____

MINDFUL LIVING WORKSHEET

M   Tu   W   Th   F   S   S   Date:_____   Rate:_____

- ☐ I am content with: _____
- ☐ I am proud of: _____
- ☐ Success review
- ☐ I love myself because: _____ ☐
- ☐ Love, thanks, kindness and support for others:
  - 1. _____   2. _____
  - 3. _____   4. _____
- ☐ Love, thanks, kindness and support for me:
  - 1. _____   2. _____
  - 3. _____   4. _____
- ☐ Good Deed/Selfless Act/Random Kindness: _____
- ☐ I gave undivided attention to: _____
- ☐ I made things better by: _____
- ☐ I experienced joy, happiness, fun and/or laughter: _____
- ☐ I smiled _____ minutes
- ☐ Meditation/Prayer _____ minutes
- ☐ Inspiration (reading, video, music): _____
- ☐ I listened to my intuition: _____
- ☐ Physical activity _____ minutes
- ☐ I was 100% honest today
- ☐ I took care of myself by: _____
- ☐ Reviewed purpose 3 times
- ☐ Reviewed intentions 3 times
- ☐ Steps toward goals, intentions and purpose
  - 1. _____   2. _____   3. _____
- ☐ Reviewed vision
- ☐ I am grateful for:
  - 1. _____   6. _____
  - 2. _____   7. _____
  - 3. _____   8. _____
  - 4. _____   9. _____
  - 5. _____   10. _____

- ☐ I am looking forward to: _____

Notes: _____
_____
_____

Mindful Living Worksheet

M Tu W Th F S S   Date:_____   Rate:_____

- ☐ I am content with: _____
- ☐ I am proud of: _____
- ☐ Success review
- ☐ I love myself because: _____ ☐
- ☐ Love, thanks, kindness and support for others:
    1. _____   2. _____
    3. _____   4. _____
- ☐ Love, thanks, kindness and support for me:
    1. _____   2. _____
    3. _____   4. _____
- ☐ Good Deed/Selfless Act/Random Kindness: _____
- ☐ I gave undivided attention to: _____
- ☐ I made things better by: _____
- ☐ I experienced joy, happiness, fun and/or laughter: _____
- ☐ I smiled _____ minutes
- ☐ Meditation/Prayer _____ minutes
- ☐ Inspiration (reading, video, music): _____
- ☐ I listened to my intuition: _____
- ☐ Physical activity _____ minutes
- ☐ I was 100% honest today
- ☐ I took care of myself by: _____
- ☐ Reviewed purpose 3 times
- ☐ Reviewed intentions 3 times
- ☐ Steps toward goals, intentions and purpose
    1. _____ 2. _____ 3. _____
- ☐ Reviewed vision
- ☐ I am grateful for:
    1. _____   6. _____
    2. _____   7. _____
    3. _____   8. _____
    4. _____   9. _____
    5. _____   10. _____

- ☐ I am looking forward to: _____

Notes: _____
_____
_____
_____

MINDFUL LIVING WORKSHEET

M Tu W Th F S S   Date:_____   Rate:_____

- ☐ I am content with: _____
- ☐ I am proud of: _____
- ☐ Success review
- ☐ I love myself because: _____ ☐
- ☐ Love, thanks, kindness and support for others:
    1. _____   2. _____
    3. _____   4. _____
- ☐ Love, thanks, kindness and support for me:
    1. _____   2. _____
    3. _____   4. _____
- ☐ Good Deed/Selfless Act/Random Kindness: _____
- ☐ I gave undivided attention to: _____
- ☐ I made things better by: _____
- ☐ I experienced joy, happiness, fun and/or laughter: _____
- ☐ I smiled _____ minutes
- ☐ Meditation/Prayer _____ minutes
- ☐ Inspiration (reading, video, music): _____
- ☐ I listened to my intuition: _____
- ☐ Physical activity _____ minutes
- ☐ I was 100% honest today
- ☐ I took care of myself by: _____
- ☐ Reviewed purpose 3 times
- ☐ Reviewed intentions 3 times
- ☐ Steps toward goals, intentions and purpose
    1. _____   2. _____   3. _____
- ☐ Reviewed vision
- ☐ I am grateful for:
    1. _____   6. _____
    2. _____   7. _____
    3. _____   8. _____
    4. _____   9. _____
    5. _____   10. _____

- ☐ I am looking forward to: _____

Notes: _____
_____
_____

Mindful Living Worksheet

M Tu W Th F S S   Date:_____   Rate:_____

- ☐ I am content with: _____
- ☐ I am proud of: _____
- ☐ Success review
- ☐ I love myself because: _____ ☐
- ☐ Love, thanks, kindness and support for others:
    - 1. _____ 2. _____
    - 3. _____ 4. _____
- ☐ Love, thanks, kindness and support for me:
    - 1. _____ 2. _____
    - 3. _____ 4. _____
- ☐ Good Deed/Selfless Act/Random Kindness: _____
- ☐ I gave undivided attention to: _____
- ☐ I made things better by: _____
- ☐ I experienced joy, happiness, fun and/or laughter: _____
- ☐ I smiled _____ minutes
- ☐ Meditation/Prayer _____ minutes
- ☐ Inspiration (reading, video, music): _____
- ☐ I listened to my intuition: _____
- ☐ Physical activity _____ minutes
- ☐ I was 100% honest today
- ☐ I took care of myself by: _____
- ☐ Reviewed purpose 3 times
- ☐ Reviewed intentions 3 times
- ☐ Steps toward goals, intentions and purpose
    - 1. _____ 2. _____ 3. _____
- ☐ Reviewed vision
- ☐ I am grateful for:
    - 1. _____ 6. _____
    - 2. _____ 7. _____
    - 3. _____ 8. _____
    - 4. _____ 9. _____
    - 5. _____ 10. _____

- ☐ I am looking forward to: _____

Notes: _____
_____
_____
_____

Mindful Living Worksheet

M Tu W Th F S S   Date:_____   Rate:_____

- ☐ I am content with: _____
- ☐ I am proud of: _____
- ☐ Success review
- ☐ I love myself because: _____ ☐
- ☐ Love, thanks, kindness and support for others:
  - 1. _____   2. _____
  - 3. _____   4. _____
- ☐ Love, thanks, kindness and support for me:
  - 1. _____   2. _____
  - 3. _____   4. _____
- ☐ Good Deed/Selfless Act/Random Kindness: _____
- ☐ I gave undivided attention to: _____
- ☐ I made things better by: _____
- ☐ I experienced joy, happiness, fun and/or laughter: _____
- ☐ I smiled _____ minutes
- ☐ Meditation/Prayer _____ minutes
- ☐ Inspiration (reading, video, music): _____
- ☐ I listened to my intuition: _____
- ☐ Physical activity _____ minutes
- ☐ I was 100% honest today
- ☐ I took care of myself by: _____
- ☐ Reviewed purpose 3 times
- ☐ Reviewed intentions 3 times
- ☐ Steps toward goals, intentions and purpose
  - 1. _____ 2. _____ 3. _____
- ☐ Reviewed vision
- ☐ I am grateful for:
  - 1. _____   6. _____
  - 2. _____   7. _____
  - 3. _____   8. _____
  - 4. _____   9. _____
  - 5. _____   10. _____

- ☐ I am looking forward to: _____

Notes: _____
_____
_____

MINDFUL LIVING WORKSHEET

M Tu W Th F S S   Date:_____   Rate:_____

- ☐ I am content with: _____
- ☐ I am proud of: _____
- ☐ Success review
- ☐ I love myself because: _____ ☐
- ☐ Love, thanks, kindness and support for others:
  - 1. _____   2. _____
  - 3. _____   4. _____
- ☐ Love, thanks, kindness and support for me:
  - 1. _____   2. _____
  - 3. _____   4. _____
- ☐ Good Deed/Selfless Act/Random Kindness: _____
- ☐ I gave undivided attention to: _____
- ☐ I made things better by: _____
- ☐ I experienced joy, happiness, fun and/or laughter: _____
- ☐ I smiled _____ minutes
- ☐ Meditation/Prayer _____ minutes
- ☐ Inspiration (reading, video, music): _____
- ☐ I listened to my intuition: _____
- ☐ Physical activity _____ minutes
- ☐ I was 100% honest today
- ☐ I took care of myself by: _____
- ☐ Reviewed purpose 3 times
- ☐ Reviewed intentions 3 times
- ☐ Steps toward goals, intentions and purpose
  - 1. _____ 2. _____ 3. _____
- ☐ Reviewed vision
- ☐ I am grateful for:
  - 1. _____   6. _____
  - 2. _____   7. _____
  - 3. _____   8. _____
  - 4. _____   9. _____
  - 5. _____   10. _____

- ☐ I am looking forward to: _____

Notes: _____
_____
_____
_____

MINDFUL LIVING WORKSHEET

M Tu W Th F S S   Date:_____   Rate:_____

- ☐ I am content with: _____
- ☐ I am proud of: _____
- ☐ Success review
- ☐ I love myself because: _____ ☐
- ☐ Love, thanks, kindness and support for others:
  - 1. _____   2. _____
  - 3. _____   4. _____
- ☐ Love, thanks, kindness and support for me:
  - 1. _____   2. _____
  - 3. _____   4. _____
- ☐ Good Deed/Selfless Act/Random Kindness: _____
- ☐ I gave undivided attention to: _____
- ☐ I made things better by: _____
- ☐ I experienced joy, happiness, fun and/or laughter: _____
- ☐ I smiled _____ minutes
- ☐ Meditation/Prayer _____ minutes
- ☐ Inspiration (reading, video, music): _____
- ☐ I listened to my intuition: _____
- ☐ Physical activity _____ minutes
- ☐ I was 100% honest today
- ☐ I took care of myself by: _____
- ☐ Reviewed purpose 3 times
- ☐ Reviewed intentions 3 times
- ☐ Steps toward goals, intentions and purpose
  - 1. _____ 2. _____ 3. _____
- ☐ Reviewed vision
- ☐ I am grateful for:
  - 1. _____   6. _____
  - 2. _____   7. _____
  - 3. _____   8. _____
  - 4. _____   9. _____
  - 5. _____   10. _____

- ☐ I am looking forward to: _____

Notes: _____
_____
_____
_____

MINDFUL LIVING WORKSHEET

M Tu W Th F S S   Date:_____   Rate:_____

- ☐ I am content with: _____
- ☐ I am proud of: _____
- ☐ Success review
- ☐ I love myself because: _____ ☐
- ☐ Love, thanks, kindness and support for others:
    1. _____   2. _____
    3. _____   4. _____
- ☐ Love, thanks, kindness and support for me:
    1. _____   2. _____
    3. _____   4. _____
- ☐ Good Deed/Selfless Act/Random Kindness: _____
- ☐ I gave undivided attention to: _____
- ☐ I made things better by: _____
- ☐ I experienced joy, happiness, fun and/or laughter: _____
- ☐ I smiled _____ minutes
- ☐ Meditation/Prayer _____ minutes
- ☐ Inspiration (reading, video, music): _____
- ☐ I listened to my intuition: _____
- ☐ Physical activity _____ minutes
- ☐ I was 100% honest today
- ☐ I took care of myself by: _____
- ☐ Reviewed purpose 3 times
- ☐ Reviewed intentions 3 times
- ☐ Steps toward goals, intentions and purpose
    1. _____ 2. _____ 3. _____
- ☐ Reviewed vision
- ☐ I am grateful for:
    1. _____   6. _____
    2. _____   7. _____
    3. _____   8. _____
    4. _____   9. _____
    5. _____   10. _____

- ☐ I am looking forward to: _____

Notes: _____
_____
_____
_____

MINDFUL LIVING WORKSHEET

M   Tu   W   Th   F   S   S   Date:_____   Rate:_____

☐ I am content with: _____
☐ I am proud of: _____
☐ Success review
☐ I love myself because: _____ ☐
☐ Love, thanks, kindness and support for others:
    1. _____   2. _____
    3. _____   4. _____
☐ Love, thanks, kindness and support for me:
    1. _____   2. _____
    3. _____   4. _____
☐ Good Deed/Selfless Act/Random Kindness: _____
☐ I gave undivided attention to: _____
☐ I made things better by: _____
☐ I experienced joy, happiness, fun and/or laughter: _____
☐ I smiled _____ minutes
☐ Meditation/Prayer _____ minutes
☐ Inspiration (reading, video, music): _____
☐ I listened to my intuition: _____
☐ Physical activity _____ minutes
☐ I was 100% honest today
☐ I took care of myself by: _____
☐ Reviewed purpose 3 times
☐ Reviewed intentions 3 times
☐ Steps toward goals, intentions and purpose
    1. _____   2. _____   3. _____
☐ Reviewed vision
☐ I am grateful for:
    1. _____   6. _____
    2. _____   7. _____
    3. _____   8. _____
    4. _____   9. _____
    5. _____   10. _____

☐ I am looking forward to: _____

Notes: _____
_____
_____

Mindful Living Worksheet

M Tu W Th F S S   Date:_____   Rate:_____

☐ I am content with: _____
☐ I am proud of: _____
☐ Success review
☐ I love myself because: _____ ☐
☐ Love, thanks, kindness and support for others:
    1. _____   2. _____
    3. _____   4. _____
☐ Love, thanks, kindness and support for me:
    1. _____   2. _____
    3. _____   4. _____
☐ Good Deed/Selfless Act/Random Kindness: _____
☐ I gave undivided attention to: _____
☐ I made things better by: _____
☐ I experienced joy, happiness, fun and/or laughter: _____
☐ I smiled _____ minutes
☐ Meditation/Prayer _____ minutes
☐ Inspiration (reading, video, music): _____
☐ I listened to my intuition: _____
☐ Physical activity _____ minutes
☐ I was 100% honest today
☐ I took care of myself by: _____
☐ Reviewed purpose 3 times
☐ Reviewed intentions 3 times
☐ Steps toward goals, intentions and purpose
    1. _____   2. _____   3. _____
☐ Reviewed vision
☐ I am grateful for:
    1. _____   6. _____
    2. _____   7. _____
    3. _____   8. _____
    4. _____   9. _____
    5. _____   10. _____

☐ I am looking forward to: _____

Notes: _____
_____
_____
_____

MINDFUL LIVING WORKSHEET

M   Tu   W   Th   F   S   S   Date:_____   Rate:_____

- ☐ I am content with: _____
- ☐ I am proud of: _____
- ☐ Success review
- ☐ I love myself because: _____ ☐
- ☐ Love, thanks, kindness and support for others:
  - 1. _____   2. _____
  - 3. _____   4. _____
- ☐ Love, thanks, kindness and support for me:
  - 1. _____   2. _____
  - 3. _____   4. _____
- ☐ Good Deed/Selfless Act/Random Kindness: _____
- ☐ I gave undivided attention to: _____
- ☐ I made things better by: _____
- ☐ I experienced joy, happiness, fun and/or laughter: _____
- ☐ I smiled _____ minutes
- ☐ Meditation/Prayer _____ minutes
- ☐ Inspiration (reading, video, music): _____
- ☐ I listened to my intuition: _____
- ☐ Physical activity _____ minutes
- ☐ I was 100% honest today
- ☐ I took care of myself by: _____
- ☐ Reviewed purpose 3 times
- ☐ Reviewed intentions 3 times
- ☐ Steps toward goals, intentions and purpose
  - 1. _____   2. _____   3. _____
- ☐ Reviewed vision
- ☐ I am grateful for:
  - 1. _____   6. _____
  - 2. _____   7. _____
  - 3. _____   8. _____
  - 4. _____   9. _____
  - 5. _____   10. _____

- ☐ I am looking forward to: _____

Notes: _____
_____
_____
_____

Mindful Living Worksheet

M Tu W Th F S S   Date:_____   Rate:_____

- ☐ I am content with: _____
- ☐ I am proud of: _____
- ☐ Success review
- ☐ I love myself because: _____ ☐
- ☐ Love, thanks, kindness and support for others:
  - 1. _____   2. _____
  - 3. _____   4. _____
- ☐ Love, thanks, kindness and support for me:
  - 1. _____   2. _____
  - 3. _____   4. _____
- ☐ Good Deed/Selfless Act/Random Kindness: _____
- ☐ I gave undivided attention to: _____
- ☐ I made things better by: _____
- ☐ I experienced joy, happiness, fun and/or laughter: _____
- ☐ I smiled _____ minutes
- ☐ Meditation/Prayer _____ minutes
- ☐ Inspiration (reading, video, music): _____
- ☐ I listened to my intuition: _____
- ☐ Physical activity _____ minutes
- ☐ I was 100% honest today
- ☐ I took care of myself by: _____
- ☐ Reviewed purpose 3 times
- ☐ Reviewed intentions 3 times
- ☐ Steps toward goals, intentions and purpose
  - 1. _____ 2. _____ 3. _____
- ☐ Reviewed vision
- ☐ I am grateful for:
  - 1. _____   6. _____
  - 2. _____   7. _____
  - 3. _____   8. _____
  - 4. _____   9. _____
  - 5. _____   10. _____

- ☐ I am looking forward to: _____

Notes: _____
_____
_____

Mindful Living Worksheet

M Tu W Th F S S   Date:_____   Rate:_____

- ☐ I am content with: _____
- ☐ I am proud of: _____
- ☐ Success review
- ☐ I love myself because: _____ ☐
- ☐ Love, thanks, kindness and support for others:
  - 1. _____   2. _____
  - 3. _____   4. _____
- ☐ Love, thanks, kindness and support for me:
  - 1. _____   2. _____
  - 3. _____   4. _____
- ☐ Good Deed/Selfless Act/Random Kindness: _____
- ☐ I gave undivided attention to: _____
- ☐ I made things better by: _____
- ☐ I experienced joy, happiness, fun and/or laughter: _____
- ☐ I smiled _____ minutes
- ☐ Meditation/Prayer _____ minutes
- ☐ Inspiration (reading, video, music): _____
- ☐ I listened to my intuition: _____
- ☐ Physical activity _____ minutes
- ☐ I was 100% honest today
- ☐ I took care of myself by: _____
- ☐ Reviewed purpose 3 times
- ☐ Reviewed intentions 3 times
- ☐ Steps toward goals, intentions and purpose
  - 1. _____   2. _____   3. _____
- ☐ Reviewed vision
- ☐ I am grateful for:
  - 1. _____   6. _____
  - 2. _____   7. _____
  - 3. _____   8. _____
  - 4. _____   9. _____
  - 5. _____   10. _____

- ☐ I am looking forward to: _____

Notes: _____
_____
_____

MINDFUL LIVING WORKSHEET

M Tu W Th F S S   Date:_____   Rate:_____

- ☐ I am content with: _____
- ☐ I am proud of: _____
- ☐ Success review
- ☐ I love myself because: _____ ☐
- ☐ Love, thanks, kindness and support for others:
    1. _____   2. _____
    3. _____   4. _____
- ☐ Love, thanks, kindness and support for me:
    1. _____   2. _____
    3. _____   4. _____
- ☐ Good Deed/Selfless Act/Random Kindness: _____
- ☐ I gave undivided attention to: _____
- ☐ I made things better by: _____
- ☐ I experienced joy, happiness, fun and/or laughter: _____
- ☐ I smiled _____ minutes
- ☐ Meditation/Prayer _____ minutes
- ☐ Inspiration (reading, video, music): _____
- ☐ I listened to my intuition: _____
- ☐ Physical activity _____ minutes
- ☐ I was 100% honest today
- ☐ I took care of myself by: _____
- ☐ Reviewed purpose 3 times
- ☐ Reviewed intentions 3 times
- ☐ Steps toward goals, intentions and purpose
    1. _____ 2. _____ 3. _____
- ☐ Reviewed vision
- ☐ I am grateful for:
    1. _____   6. _____
    2. _____   7. _____
    3. _____   8. _____
    4. _____   9. _____
    5. _____   10. _____

- ☐ I am looking forward to: _____

Notes: _____
_____
_____
_____

MINDFUL LIVING WORKSHEET

M Tu W Th F S S   Date:_____   Rate:_____

- ☐ I am content with: _____
- ☐ I am proud of: _____
- ☐ Success review
- ☐ I love myself because: _____ ☐
- ☐ Love, thanks, kindness and support for others:
    1. _____   2. _____
    3. _____   4. _____
- ☐ Love, thanks, kindness and support for me:
    1. _____   2. _____
    3. _____   4. _____
- ☐ Good Deed/Selfless Act/Random Kindness: _____
- ☐ I gave undivided attention to: _____
- ☐ I made things better by: _____
- ☐ I experienced joy, happiness, fun and/or laughter: _____
- ☐ I smiled _____ minutes
- ☐ Meditation/Prayer _____ minutes
- ☐ Inspiration (reading, video, music): _____
- ☐ I listened to my intuition: _____
- ☐ Physical activity _____ minutes
- ☐ I was 100% honest today
- ☐ I took care of myself by: _____
- ☐ Reviewed purpose 3 times
- ☐ Reviewed intentions 3 times
- ☐ Steps toward goals, intentions and purpose
    1. _____ 2. _____ 3. _____
- ☐ Reviewed vision
- ☐ I am grateful for:
    1. _____   6. _____
    2. _____   7. _____
    3. _____   8. _____
    4. _____   9. _____
    5. _____   10. _____

- ☐ I am looking forward to: _____

Notes: _____
_____
_____
_____

MINDFUL LIVING WORKSHEET

M Tu W Th F S S   Date:_____   Rate:_____

- ☐ I am content with: _____
- ☐ I am proud of: _____
- ☐ Success review
- ☐ I love myself because: _____ ☐
- ☐ Love, thanks, kindness and support for others:
  - 1. _____   2. _____
  - 3. _____   4. _____
- ☐ Love, thanks, kindness and support for me:
  - 1. _____   2. _____
  - 3. _____   4. _____
- ☐ Good Deed/Selfless Act/Random Kindness: _____
- ☐ I gave undivided attention to: _____
- ☐ I made things better by: _____
- ☐ I experienced joy, happiness, fun and/or laughter: _____
- ☐ I smiled _____ minutes
- ☐ Meditation/Prayer _____ minutes
- ☐ Inspiration (reading, video, music): _____
- ☐ I listened to my intuition: _____
- ☐ Physical activity _____ minutes
- ☐ I was 100% honest today
- ☐ I took care of myself by: _____
- ☐ Reviewed purpose 3 times
- ☐ Reviewed intentions 3 times
- ☐ Steps toward goals, intentions and purpose
  - 1. _____ 2. _____ 3. _____
- ☐ Reviewed vision
- ☐ I am grateful for:
  - 1. _____   6. _____
  - 2. _____   7. _____
  - 3. _____   8. _____
  - 4. _____   9. _____
  - 5. _____   10. _____
- ☐ I am looking forward to: _____

Notes: _____
_____
_____
_____

MINDFUL LIVING WORKSHEET

M   Tu   W   Th   F   S   S   Date:_____   Rate:_____

- ☐ I am content with: _____
- ☐ I am proud of: _____
- ☐ Success review
- ☐ I love myself because: _____ ☐
- ☐ Love, thanks, kindness and support for others:
  - 1. _____   2. _____
  - 3. _____   4. _____
- ☐ Love, thanks, kindness and support for me:
  - 1. _____   2. _____
  - 3. _____   4. _____
- ☐ Good Deed/Selfless Act/Random Kindness: _____
- ☐ I gave undivided attention to: _____
- ☐ I made things better by: _____
- ☐ I experienced joy, happiness, fun and/or laughter: _____
- ☐ I smiled _____ minutes
- ☐ Meditation/Prayer _____ minutes
- ☐ Inspiration (reading, video, music): _____
- ☐ I listened to my intuition: _____
- ☐ Physical activity _____ minutes
- ☐ I was 100% honest today
- ☐ I took care of myself by: _____
- ☐ Reviewed purpose 3 times
- ☐ Reviewed intentions 3 times
- ☐ Steps toward goals, intentions and purpose
  - 1. _____   2. _____   3. _____
- ☐ Reviewed vision
- ☐ I am grateful for:
  - 1. _____   6. _____
  - 2. _____   7. _____
  - 3. _____   8. _____
  - 4. _____   9. _____
  - 5. _____   10. _____
- ☐ I am looking forward to: _____

Notes: _____
_____
_____

Mindful Living Worksheet

M   Tu   W   Th   F   S   S   Date:_____   Rate:_____

- ☐ I am content with: _____
- ☐ I am proud of: _____
- ☐ Success review
- ☐ I love myself because: _____ ☐
- ☐ Love, thanks, kindness and support for others:
    1. _____   2. _____
    3. _____   4. _____
- ☐ Love, thanks, kindness and support for me:
    1. _____   2. _____
    3. _____   4. _____
- ☐ Good Deed/Selfless Act/Random Kindness: _____
- ☐ I gave undivided attention to: _____
- ☐ I made things better by: _____
- ☐ I experienced joy, happiness, fun and/or laughter: _____
- ☐ I smiled _____ minutes
- ☐ Meditation/Prayer _____ minutes
- ☐ Inspiration (reading, video, music): _____
- ☐ I listened to my intuition: _____
- ☐ Physical activity _____ minutes
- ☐ I was 100% honest today
- ☐ I took care of myself by: _____
- ☐ Reviewed purpose 3 times
- ☐ Reviewed intentions 3 times
- ☐ Steps toward goals, intentions and purpose
    1. _____ 2. _____ 3. _____
- ☐ Reviewed vision
- ☐ I am grateful for:
    1. _____   6. _____
    2. _____   7. _____
    3. _____   8. _____
    4. _____   9. _____
    5. _____   10. _____

- ☐ I am looking forward to: _____

Notes: _____
_____
_____
_____

Mindful Living Worksheet

M Tu W Th F S S   Date:_____   Rate:_____

- ☐ I am content with: _____
- ☐ I am proud of: _____
- ☐ Success review
- ☐ I love myself because: _____ ☐
- ☐ Love, thanks, kindness and support for others:
  - 1. _____   2. _____
  - 3. _____   4. _____
- ☐ Love, thanks, kindness and support for me:
  - 1. _____   2. _____
  - 3. _____   4. _____
- ☐ Good Deed/Selfless Act/Random Kindness: _____
- ☐ I gave undivided attention to: _____
- ☐ I made things better by: _____
- ☐ I experienced joy, happiness, fun and/or laughter: _____
- ☐ I smiled _____ minutes
- ☐ Meditation/Prayer _____ minutes
- ☐ Inspiration (reading, video, music): _____
- ☐ I listened to my intuition: _____
- ☐ Physical activity _____ minutes
- ☐ I was 100% honest today
- ☐ I took care of myself by: _____
- ☐ Reviewed purpose 3 times
- ☐ Reviewed intentions 3 times
- ☐ Steps toward goals, intentions and purpose
  - 1. _____   2. _____   3. _____
- ☐ Reviewed vision
- ☐ I am grateful for:
  - 1. _____   6. _____
  - 2. _____   7. _____
  - 3. _____   8. _____
  - 4. _____   9. _____
  - 5. _____   10. _____

- ☐ I am looking forward to: _____

Notes: _____
_____
_____
_____

MINDFUL LIVING WORKSHEET

M Tu W Th F S S   Date:_____   Rate:_____

☐ I am content with: _____
☐ I am proud of: _____
☐ Success review
☐ I love myself because: _____ ☐
☐ Love, thanks, kindness and support for others:
    1. _____ 2. _____
    3. _____ 4. _____
☐ Love, thanks, kindness and support for me:
    1. _____ 2. _____
    3. _____ 4. _____
☐ Good Deed/Selfless Act/Random Kindness: _____
☐ I gave undivided attention to: _____
☐ I made things better by: _____
☐ I experienced joy, happiness, fun and/or laughter: _____
☐ I smiled _____ minutes
☐ Meditation/Prayer _____ minutes
☐ Inspiration (reading, video, music): _____
☐ I listened to my intuition: _____
☐ Physical activity _____ minutes
☐ I was 100% honest today
☐ I took care of myself by: _____
☐ Reviewed purpose 3 times
☐ Reviewed intentions 3 times
☐ Steps toward goals, intentions and purpose
    1. _____ 2. _____ 3. _____
☐ Reviewed vision
☐ I am grateful for:
    1. _____ 6. _____
    2. _____ 7. _____
    3. _____ 8. _____
    4. _____ 9. _____
    5. _____ 10. _____

☐ I am looking forward to: _____

Notes: _____
_____
_____
_____

MINDFUL LIVING WORKSHEET

M Tu W Th F S S   Date:_____   Rate:_____

- ☐ I am content with: _____
- ☐ I am proud of: _____
- ☐ Success review
- ☐ I love myself because: _____ ☐
- ☐ Love, thanks, kindness and support for others:
    1. _____   2. _____
    3. _____   4. _____
- ☐ Love, thanks, kindness and support for me:
    1. _____   2. _____
    3. _____   4. _____
- ☐ Good Deed/Selfless Act/Random Kindness: _____
- ☐ I gave undivided attention to: _____
- ☐ I made things better by: _____
- ☐ I experienced joy, happiness, fun and/or laughter: _____
- ☐ I smiled _____ minutes
- ☐ Meditation/Prayer _____ minutes
- ☐ Inspiration (reading, video, music): _____
- ☐ I listened to my intuition: _____
- ☐ Physical activity _____ minutes
- ☐ I was 100% honest today
- ☐ I took care of myself by: _____
- ☐ Reviewed purpose 3 times
- ☐ Reviewed intentions 3 times
- ☐ Steps toward goals, intentions and purpose
    1. _____ 2. _____ 3. _____
- ☐ Reviewed vision
- ☐ I am grateful for:
    1. _____   6. _____
    2. _____   7. _____
    3. _____   8. _____
    4. _____   9. _____
    5. _____   10. _____

- ☐ I am looking forward to: _____

Notes: _____
_____
_____
_____

Mindful Living Worksheet

M Tu W Th F S S   Date:_____   Rate:_____

- ☐ I am content with: _____
- ☐ I am proud of: _____
- ☐ Success review
- ☐ I love myself because: _____ ☐
- ☐ Love, thanks, kindness and support for others:
    1. _____   2. _____
    3. _____   4. _____
- ☐ Love, thanks, kindness and support for me:
    1. _____   2. _____
    3. _____   4. _____
- ☐ Good Deed/Selfless Act/Random Kindness: _____
- ☐ I gave undivided attention to: _____
- ☐ I made things better by: _____
- ☐ I experienced joy, happiness, fun and/or laughter: _____
- ☐ I smiled _____ minutes
- ☐ Meditation/Prayer _____ minutes
- ☐ Inspiration (reading, video, music): _____
- ☐ I listened to my intuition: _____
- ☐ Physical activity _____ minutes
- ☐ I was 100% honest today
- ☐ I took care of myself by: _____
- ☐ Reviewed purpose 3 times
- ☐ Reviewed intentions 3 times
- ☐ Steps toward goals, intentions and purpose
    1. _____ 2. _____ 3. _____
- ☐ Reviewed vision
- ☐ I am grateful for:
    1. _____   6. _____
    2. _____   7. _____
    3. _____   8. _____
    4. _____   9. _____
    5. _____   10. _____

- ☐ I am looking forward to: _____

Notes: _____
_____
_____
_____

MINDFUL LIVING WORKSHEET

M   Tu   W   Th   F   S   S   Date:_____   Rate:_____

- ☐ I am content with: _____
- ☐ I am proud of: _____
- ☐ Success review
- ☐ I love myself because: _____ ☐
- ☐ Love, thanks, kindness and support for others:
    - 1. _____   2. _____
    - 3. _____   4. _____
- ☐ Love, thanks, kindness and support for me:
    - 1. _____   2. _____
    - 3. _____   4. _____
- ☐ Good Deed/Selfless Act/Random Kindness: _____
- ☐ I gave undivided attention to: _____
- ☐ I made things better by: _____
- ☐ I experienced joy, happiness, fun and/or laughter: _____
- ☐ I smiled _____ minutes
- ☐ Meditation/Prayer _____ minutes
- ☐ Inspiration (reading, video, music): _____
- ☐ I listened to my intuition: _____
- ☐ Physical activity _____ minutes
- ☐ I was 100% honest today
- ☐ I took care of myself by: _____
- ☐ Reviewed purpose 3 times
- ☐ Reviewed intentions 3 times
- ☐ Steps toward goals, intentions and purpose
    - 1. _____ 2. _____ 3. _____
- ☐ Reviewed vision
- ☐ I am grateful for:
    - 1. _____   6. _____
    - 2. _____   7. _____
    - 3. _____   8. _____
    - 4. _____   9. _____
    - 5. _____   10. _____

- ☐ I am looking forward to: _____

Notes: _____
_____
_____
_____

MINDFUL LIVING WORKSHEET

M Tu W Th F S S   Date:_____   Rate:_____

- ☐ I am content with: _____
- ☐ I am proud of: _____
- ☐ Success review
- ☐ I love myself because: _____ ☐
- ☐ Love, thanks, kindness and support for others:
  - 1. _____   2. _____
  - 3. _____   4. _____
- ☐ Love, thanks, kindness and support for me:
  - 1. _____   2. _____
  - 3. _____   4. _____
- ☐ Good Deed/Selfless Act/Random Kindness: _____
- ☐ I gave undivided attention to: _____
- ☐ I made things better by: _____
- ☐ I experienced joy, happiness, fun and/or laughter: _____
- ☐ I smiled _____ minutes
- ☐ Meditation/Prayer _____ minutes
- ☐ Inspiration (reading, video, music): _____
- ☐ I listened to my intuition: _____
- ☐ Physical activity _____ minutes
- ☐ I was 100% honest today
- ☐ I took care of myself by: _____
- ☐ Reviewed purpose 3 times
- ☐ Reviewed intentions 3 times
- ☐ Steps toward goals, intentions and purpose
  - 1. _____ 2. _____ 3. _____
- ☐ Reviewed vision
- ☐ I am grateful for:
  - 1. _____   6. _____
  - 2. _____   7. _____
  - 3. _____   8. _____
  - 4. _____   9. _____
  - 5. _____   10. _____

- ☐ I am looking forward to: _____

Notes: _____
_____
_____

MINDFUL LIVING WORKSHEET

M   Tu   W   Th   F   S   S   Date:_____   Rate:_____

☐ I am content with: _____
☐ I am proud of: _____
☐ Success review
☐ I love myself because: _____ ☐
☐ Love, thanks, kindness and support for others:
    1. _____ 2. _____
    3. _____ 4. _____
☐ Love, thanks, kindness and support for me:
    1. _____ 2. _____
    3. _____ 4. _____
☐ Good Deed/Selfless Act/Random Kindness: _____
☐ I gave undivided attention to: _____
☐ I made things better by: _____
☐ I experienced joy, happiness, fun and/or laughter: _____
☐ I smiled _____ minutes
☐ Meditation/Prayer _____ minutes
☐ Inspiration (reading, video, music): _____
☐ I listened to my intuition: _____
☐ Physical activity _____ minutes
☐ I was 100% honest today
☐ I took care of myself by: _____
☐ Reviewed purpose 3 times
☐ Reviewed intentions 3 times
☐ Steps toward goals, intentions and purpose
    1. _____ 2. _____ 3. _____
☐ Reviewed vision
☐ I am grateful for:
    1. _____ 6. _____
    2. _____ 7. _____
    3. _____ 8. _____
    4. _____ 9. _____
    5. _____ 10. _____

☐ I am looking forward to: _____

Notes: _____
_____
_____

MINDFUL LIVING WORKSHEET

M   Tu   W   Th   F   S   S   Date:_____   Rate:_____

- ☐ I am content with: _____
- ☐ I am proud of: _____
- ☐ Success review
- ☐ I love myself because: _____ ☐
- ☐ Love, thanks, kindness and support for others:
  - 1. _____   2. _____
  - 3. _____   4. _____
- ☐ Love, thanks, kindness and support for me:
  - 1. _____   2. _____
  - 3. _____   4. _____
- ☐ Good Deed/Selfless Act/Random Kindness: _____
- ☐ I gave undivided attention to: _____
- ☐ I made things better by: _____
- ☐ I experienced joy, happiness, fun and/or laughter: _____
- ☐ I smiled _____ minutes
- ☐ Meditation/Prayer _____ minutes
- ☐ Inspiration (reading, video, music): _____
- ☐ I listened to my intuition: _____
- ☐ Physical activity _____ minutes
- ☐ I was 100% honest today
- ☐ I took care of myself by: _____
- ☐ Reviewed purpose 3 times
- ☐ Reviewed intentions 3 times
- ☐ Steps toward goals, intentions and purpose
  - 1. _____ 2. _____ 3. _____
- ☐ Reviewed vision
- ☐ I am grateful for:
  - 1. _____   6. _____
  - 2. _____   7. _____
  - 3. _____   8. _____
  - 4. _____   9. _____
  - 5. _____   10. _____

- ☐ I am looking forward to: _____

Notes: _____
_____
_____
_____

MINDFUL LIVING WORKSHEET

M Tu W Th F S S   Date:_____   Rate:_____

- ☐ I am content with: _____
- ☐ I am proud of: _____
- ☐ Success review
- ☐ I love myself because: _____ ☐
- ☐ Love, thanks, kindness and support for others:
  - 1. _____   2. _____
  - 3. _____   4. _____
- ☐ Love, thanks, kindness and support for me:
  - 1. _____   2. _____
  - 3. _____   4. _____
- ☐ Good Deed/Selfless Act/Random Kindness: _____
- ☐ I gave undivided attention to: _____
- ☐ I made things better by: _____
- ☐ I experienced joy, happiness, fun and/or laughter: _____
- ☐ I smiled _____ minutes
- ☐ Meditation/Prayer _____ minutes
- ☐ Inspiration (reading, video, music): _____
- ☐ I listened to my intuition: _____
- ☐ Physical activity _____ minutes
- ☐ I was 100% honest today
- ☐ I took care of myself by: _____
- ☐ Reviewed purpose 3 times
- ☐ Reviewed intentions 3 times
- ☐ Steps toward goals, intentions and purpose
  - 1. _____ 2. _____ 3. _____
- ☐ Reviewed vision
- ☐ I am grateful for:
  - 1. _____   6. _____
  - 2. _____   7. _____
  - 3. _____   8. _____
  - 4. _____   9. _____
  - 5. _____   10. _____

- ☐ I am looking forward to: _____

Notes: _____
_____
_____
_____

Mindful Living Worksheet

M Tu W Th F S S   Date:_____   Rate:_____

- ☐ I am content with: _____
- ☐ I am proud of: _____
- ☐ Success review
- ☐ I love myself because: _____ ☐
- ☐ Love, thanks, kindness and support for others:
    1. _____   2. _____
    3. _____   4. _____
- ☐ Love, thanks, kindness and support for me:
    1. _____   2. _____
    3. _____   4. _____
- ☐ Good Deed/Selfless Act/Random Kindness: _____
- ☐ I gave undivided attention to: _____
- ☐ I made things better by: _____
- ☐ I experienced joy, happiness, fun and/or laughter: _____
- ☐ I smiled _____ minutes
- ☐ Meditation/Prayer _____ minutes
- ☐ Inspiration (reading, video, music): _____
- ☐ I listened to my intuition: _____
- ☐ Physical activity _____ minutes
- ☐ I was 100% honest today
- ☐ I took care of myself by: _____
- ☐ Reviewed purpose 3 times
- ☐ Reviewed intentions 3 times
- ☐ Steps toward goals, intentions and purpose
    1. _____   2. _____   3. _____
- ☐ Reviewed vision
- ☐ I am grateful for:
    1. _____   6. _____
    2. _____   7. _____
    3. _____   8. _____
    4. _____   9. _____
    5. _____   10. _____

- ☐ I am looking forward to: _____

Notes: _____
_____
_____
_____

MINDFUL LIVING WORKSHEET

M Tu W Th F S S   Date:_____   Rate:_____

- ☐ I am content with: _____
- ☐ I am proud of: _____
- ☐ Success review
- ☐ I love myself because: _____ ☐
- ☐ Love, thanks, kindness and support for others:
  - 1. _____   2. _____
  - 3. _____   4. _____
- ☐ Love, thanks, kindness and support for me:
  - 1. _____   2. _____
  - 3. _____   4. _____
- ☐ Good Deed/Selfless Act/Random Kindness: _____
- ☐ I gave undivided attention to: _____
- ☐ I made things better by: _____
- ☐ I experienced joy, happiness, fun and/or laughter: _____
- ☐ I smiled _____ minutes
- ☐ Meditation/Prayer _____ minutes
- ☐ Inspiration (reading, video, music): _____
- ☐ I listened to my intuition: _____
- ☐ Physical activity _____ minutes
- ☐ I was 100% honest today
- ☐ I took care of myself by: _____
- ☐ Reviewed purpose 3 times
- ☐ Reviewed intentions 3 times
- ☐ Steps toward goals, intentions and purpose
  - 1. _____ 2. _____ 3. _____
- ☐ Reviewed vision
- ☐ I am grateful for:
  - 1. _____   6. _____
  - 2. _____   7. _____
  - 3. _____   8. _____
  - 4. _____   9. _____
  - 5. _____   10. _____

- ☐ I am looking forward to: _____

Notes: _____
_____
_____

MINDFUL LIVING WORKSHEET

M   Tu   W   Th   F   S   S   Date:_____   Rate:_____

☐ I am content with: _____
☐ I am proud of: _____
☐ Success review
☐ I love myself because: _____ ☐
☐ Love, thanks, kindness and support for others:
    1. _____   2. _____
    3. _____   4. _____
☐ Love, thanks, kindness and support for me:
    1. _____   2. _____
    3. _____   4. _____
☐ Good Deed/Selfless Act/Random Kindness: _____
☐ I gave undivided attention to: _____
☐ I made things better by: _____
☐ I experienced joy, happiness, fun and/or laughter: _____
☐ I smiled _____ minutes
☐ Meditation/Prayer _____ minutes
☐ Inspiration (reading, video, music): _____
☐ I listened to my intuition: _____
☐ Physical activity _____ minutes
☐ I was 100% honest today
☐ I took care of myself by: _____
☐ Reviewed purpose 3 times
☐ Reviewed intentions 3 times
☐ Steps toward goals, intentions and purpose
    1. _____   2. _____   3. _____
☐ Reviewed vision
☐ I am grateful for:
    1. _____   6. _____
    2. _____   7. _____
    3. _____   8. _____
    4. _____   9. _____
    5. _____   10. _____

☐ I am looking forward to: _____

Notes: _____
_____
_____
_____

MINDFUL LIVING WORKSHEET

M Tu W Th F S S   Date:_____   Rate:_____

☐ I am content with: _____
☐ I am proud of: _____
☐ Success review
☐ I love myself because: _____ ☐
☐ Love, thanks, kindness and support for others:
    1. _____   2. _____
    3. _____   4. _____
☐ Love, thanks, kindness and support for me:
    1. _____   2. _____
    3. _____   4. _____
☐ Good Deed/Selfless Act/Random Kindness: _____
☐ I gave undivided attention to: _____
☐ I made things better by: _____
☐ I experienced joy, happiness, fun and/or laughter: _____
☐ I smiled _____ minutes
☐ Meditation/Prayer _____ minutes
☐ Inspiration (reading, video, music): _____
☐ I listened to my intuition: _____
☐ Physical activity _____ minutes
☐ I was 100% honest today
☐ I took care of myself by: _____
☐ Reviewed purpose 3 times
☐ Reviewed intentions 3 times
☐ Steps toward goals, intentions and purpose
    1. _____   2. _____   3. _____
☐ Reviewed vision
☐ I am grateful for:
    1. _____   6. _____
    2. _____   7. _____
    3. _____   8. _____
    4. _____   9. _____
    5. _____   10. _____

☐ I am looking forward to: _____

Notes: _____
_____
_____
_____

MINDFUL LIVING WORKSHEET

M Tu W Th F S S   Date:_____   Rate:_____

- ☐ I am content with: _____
- ☐ I am proud of: _____
- ☐ Success review
- ☐ I love myself because: _____ ☐
- ☐ Love, thanks, kindness and support for others:
  - 1. _____   2. _____
  - 3. _____   4. _____
- ☐ Love, thanks, kindness and support for me:
  - 1. _____   2. _____
  - 3. _____   4. _____
- ☐ Good Deed/Selfless Act/Random Kindness: _____
- ☐ I gave undivided attention to: _____
- ☐ I made things better by: _____
- ☐ I experienced joy, happiness, fun and/or laughter: _____
- ☐ I smiled _____ minutes
- ☐ Meditation/Prayer _____ minutes
- ☐ Inspiration (reading, video, music): _____
- ☐ I listened to my intuition: _____
- ☐ Physical activity _____ minutes
- ☐ I was 100% honest today
- ☐ I took care of myself by: _____
- ☐ Reviewed purpose 3 times
- ☐ Reviewed intentions 3 times
- ☐ Steps toward goals, intentions and purpose
  - 1. _____ 2. _____ 3. _____
- ☐ Reviewed vision
- ☐ I am grateful for:
  - 1. _____   6. _____
  - 2. _____   7. _____
  - 3. _____   8. _____
  - 4. _____   9. _____
  - 5. _____   10. _____
- ☐ I am looking forward to: _____

Notes: _____
_____
_____
_____

MINDFUL LIVING WORKSHEET

M   Tu   W   Th   F   S   S   Date:_____   Rate:_____

- ☐ I am content with: _____
- ☐ I am proud of: _____
- ☐ Success review
- ☐ I love myself because: _____ ☐
- ☐ Love, thanks, kindness and support for others:
  - 1. _____ 2. _____
  - 3. _____ 4. _____
- ☐ Love, thanks, kindness and support for me:
  - 1. _____ 2. _____
  - 3. _____ 4. _____
- ☐ Good Deed/Selfless Act/Random Kindness: _____
- ☐ I gave undivided attention to: _____
- ☐ I made things better by: _____
- ☐ I experienced joy, happiness, fun and/or laughter: _____
- ☐ I smiled _____ minutes
- ☐ Meditation/Prayer _____ minutes
- ☐ Inspiration (reading, video, music): _____
- ☐ I listened to my intuition: _____
- ☐ Physical activity _____ minutes
- ☐ I was 100% honest today
- ☐ I took care of myself by: _____
- ☐ Reviewed purpose 3 times
- ☐ Reviewed intentions 3 times
- ☐ Steps toward goals, intentions and purpose
  - 1. _____ 2. _____ 3. _____
- ☐ Reviewed vision
- ☐ I am grateful for:
  - 1. _____ 6. _____
  - 2. _____ 7. _____
  - 3. _____ 8. _____
  - 4. _____ 9. _____
  - 5. _____ 10. _____

- ☐ I am looking forward to: _____

Notes: _____
_____
_____
_____

Mindful Living Worksheet

M Tu W Th F S S   Date:_____   Rate:_____

- ☐ I am content with: _____
- ☐ I am proud of: _____
- ☐ Success review
- ☐ I love myself because: _____ ☐
- ☐ Love, thanks, kindness and support for others:
  - 1. _____   2. _____
  - 3. _____   4. _____
- ☐ Love, thanks, kindness and support for me:
  - 1. _____   2. _____
  - 3. _____   4. _____
- ☐ Good Deed/Selfless Act/Random Kindness: _____
- ☐ I gave undivided attention to: _____
- ☐ I made things better by: _____
- ☐ I experienced joy, happiness, fun and/or laughter: _____
- ☐ I smiled _____ minutes
- ☐ Meditation/Prayer _____ minutes
- ☐ Inspiration (reading, video, music): _____
- ☐ I listened to my intuition: _____
- ☐ Physical activity _____ minutes
- ☐ I was 100% honest today
- ☐ I took care of myself by: _____
- ☐ Reviewed purpose 3 times
- ☐ Reviewed intentions 3 times
- ☐ Steps toward goals, intentions and purpose
  - 1. _____   2. _____   3. _____
- ☐ Reviewed vision
- ☐ I am grateful for:
  - 1. _____   6. _____
  - 2. _____   7. _____
  - 3. _____   8. _____
  - 4. _____   9. _____
  - 5. _____   10. _____

- ☐ I am looking forward to: _____

Notes: _____
_____
_____
_____

MINDFUL LIVING WORKSHEET

M Tu W Th F S S   Date:_____   Rate:_____

- ☐ I am content with: _____
- ☐ I am proud of: _____
- ☐ Success review
- ☐ I love myself because: _____ ☐
- ☐ Love, thanks, kindness and support for others:
  - 1. _____   2. _____
  - 3. _____   4. _____
- ☐ Love, thanks, kindness and support for me:
  - 1. _____   2. _____
  - 3. _____   4. _____
- ☐ Good Deed/Selfless Act/Random Kindness: _____
- ☐ I gave undivided attention to: _____
- ☐ I made things better by: _____
- ☐ I experienced joy, happiness, fun and/or laughter: _____
- ☐ I smiled _____ minutes
- ☐ Meditation/Prayer _____ minutes
- ☐ Inspiration (reading, video, music): _____
- ☐ I listened to my intuition: _____
- ☐ Physical activity _____ minutes
- ☐ I was 100% honest today
- ☐ I took care of myself by: _____
- ☐ Reviewed purpose 3 times
- ☐ Reviewed intentions 3 times
- ☐ Steps toward goals, intentions and purpose
  - 1. _____ 2. _____ 3. _____
- ☐ Reviewed vision
- ☐ I am grateful for:
  - 1. _____   6. _____
  - 2. _____   7. _____
  - 3. _____   8. _____
  - 4. _____   9. _____
  - 5. _____   10. _____

- ☐ I am looking forward to: _____

Notes: _____
_____
_____

Mindful Living Worksheet

M Tu W Th F S S   Date:_____   Rate:_____

- ☐ I am content with: _____
- ☐ I am proud of: _____
- ☐ Success review
- ☐ I love myself because: _____ ☐
- ☐ Love, thanks, kindness and support for others:
    1. _____   2. _____
    3. _____   4. _____
- ☐ Love, thanks, kindness and support for me:
    1. _____   2. _____
    3. _____   4. _____
- ☐ Good Deed/Selfless Act/Random Kindness: _____
- ☐ I gave undivided attention to: _____
- ☐ I made things better by: _____
- ☐ I experienced joy, happiness, fun and/or laughter: _____
- ☐ I smiled _____ minutes
- ☐ Meditation/Prayer _____ minutes
- ☐ Inspiration (reading, video, music): _____
- ☐ I listened to my intuition: _____
- ☐ Physical activity _____ minutes
- ☐ I was 100% honest today
- ☐ I took care of myself by: _____
- ☐ Reviewed purpose 3 times
- ☐ Reviewed intentions 3 times
- ☐ Steps toward goals, intentions and purpose
    1. _____   2. _____   3. _____
- ☐ Reviewed vision
- ☐ I am grateful for:
    1. _____   6. _____
    2. _____   7. _____
    3. _____   8. _____
    4. _____   9. _____
    5. _____   10. _____

- ☐ I am looking forward to: _____

Notes: _____
_____
_____
_____

Mindful Living Worksheet

M Tu W Th F S S   Date: _____   Rate: _____

- ☐ I am content with: _____
- ☐ I am proud of: _____
- ☐ Success review
- ☐ I love myself because: _____ ☐
- ☐ Love, thanks, kindness and support for others:
    1. _____   2. _____
    3. _____   4. _____
- ☐ Love, thanks, kindness and support for me:
    1. _____   2. _____
    3. _____   4. _____
- ☐ Good Deed/Selfless Act/Random Kindness: _____
- ☐ I gave undivided attention to: _____
- ☐ I made things better by: _____
- ☐ I experienced joy, happiness, fun and/or laughter: _____
- ☐ I smiled _____ minutes
- ☐ Meditation/Prayer _____ minutes
- ☐ Inspiration (reading, video, music): _____
- ☐ I listened to my intuition: _____
- ☐ Physical activity _____ minutes
- ☐ I was 100% honest today
- ☐ I took care of myself by: _____
- ☐ Reviewed purpose 3 times
- ☐ Reviewed intentions 3 times
- ☐ Steps toward goals, intentions and purpose
    1. _____ 2. _____ 3. _____
- ☐ Reviewed vision
- ☐ I am grateful for:
    1. _____   6. _____
    2. _____   7. _____
    3. _____   8. _____
    4. _____   9. _____
    5. _____   10. _____

- ☐ I am looking forward to: _____

Notes: _____
_____
_____
_____

MINDFUL LIVING WORKSHEET

M Tu W Th F S S   Date:_____   Rate:_____

☐ I am content with: _____
☐ I am proud of: _____
☐ Success review
☐ I love myself because: _____ ☐
☐ Love, thanks, kindness and support for others:
    1. _____   2. _____
    3. _____   4. _____
☐ Love, thanks, kindness and support for me:
    1. _____   2. _____
    3. _____   4. _____
☐ Good Deed/Selfless Act/Random Kindness: _____
☐ I gave undivided attention to: _____
☐ I made things better by: _____
☐ I experienced joy, happiness, fun and/or laughter: _____
☐ I smiled _____ minutes
☐ Meditation/Prayer _____ minutes
☐ Inspiration (reading, video, music): _____
☐ I listened to my intuition: _____
☐ Physical activity _____ minutes
☐ I was 100% honest today
☐ I took care of myself by: _____
☐ Reviewed purpose 3 times
☐ Reviewed intentions 3 times
☐ Steps toward goals, intentions and purpose
    1. _____   2. _____   3. _____
☐ Reviewed vision
☐ I am grateful for:
    1. _____   6. _____
    2. _____   7. _____
    3. _____   8. _____
    4. _____   9. _____
    5. _____   10. _____

☐ I am looking forward to: _____

Notes: _____
_____
_____
_____

MINDFUL LIVING WORKSHEET

M Tu W Th F S S   Date:_____   Rate:_____

- ☐ I am content with: _____
- ☐ I am proud of: _____
- ☐ Success review
- ☐ I love myself because: _____ ☐
- ☐ Love, thanks, kindness and support for others:
  - 1. _____   2. _____
  - 3. _____   4. _____
- ☐ Love, thanks, kindness and support for me:
  - 1. _____   2. _____
  - 3. _____   4. _____
- ☐ Good Deed/Selfless Act/Random Kindness: _____
- ☐ I gave undivided attention to: _____
- ☐ I made things better by: _____
- ☐ I experienced joy, happiness, fun and/or laughter: _____
- ☐ I smiled _____ minutes
- ☐ Meditation/Prayer _____ minutes
- ☐ Inspiration (reading, video, music): _____
- ☐ I listened to my intuition: _____
- ☐ Physical activity _____ minutes
- ☐ I was 100% honest today
- ☐ I took care of myself by: _____
- ☐ Reviewed purpose 3 times
- ☐ Reviewed intentions 3 times
- ☐ Steps toward goals, intentions and purpose
  - 1. _____ 2. _____ 3. _____
- ☐ Reviewed vision
- ☐ I am grateful for:
  - 1. _____   6. _____
  - 2. _____   7. _____
  - 3. _____   8. _____
  - 4. _____   9. _____
  - 5. _____   10. _____

- ☐ I am looking forward to: _____

Notes: _____
_____
_____

MINDFUL LIVING WORKSHEET

M Tu W Th F S S   Date:_____   Rate:_____

- ☐ I am content with: _____
- ☐ I am proud of: _____
- ☐ Success review
- ☐ I love myself because: _____ ☐
- ☐ Love, thanks, kindness and support for others:
    1. _____   2. _____
    3. _____   4. _____
- ☐ Love, thanks, kindness and support for me:
    1. _____   2. _____
    3. _____   4. _____
- ☐ Good Deed/Selfless Act/Random Kindness: _____
- ☐ I gave undivided attention to: _____
- ☐ I made things better by: _____
- ☐ I experienced joy, happiness, fun and/or laughter: _____
- ☐ I smiled _____ minutes
- ☐ Meditation/Prayer _____ minutes
- ☐ Inspiration (reading, video, music): _____
- ☐ I listened to my intuition: _____
- ☐ Physical activity _____ minutes
- ☐ I was 100% honest today
- ☐ I took care of myself by: _____
- ☐ Reviewed purpose 3 times
- ☐ Reviewed intentions 3 times
- ☐ Steps toward goals, intentions and purpose
    1. _____   2. _____   3. _____
- ☐ Reviewed vision
- ☐ I am grateful for:
    1. _____   6. _____
    2. _____   7. _____
    3. _____   8. _____
    4. _____   9. _____
    5. _____   10. _____

- ☐ I am looking forward to: _____

Notes: _____
_____
_____
_____

Mindful Living Worksheet

M Tu W Th F S S   Date:_____   Rate:_____

- ☐ I am content with: _____
- ☐ I am proud of: _____
- ☐ Success review
- ☐ I love myself because: _____ ☐
- ☐ Love, thanks, kindness and support for others:
    - 1. _____   2. _____
    - 3. _____   4. _____
- ☐ Love, thanks, kindness and support for me:
    - 1. _____   2. _____
    - 3. _____   4. _____
- ☐ Good Deed/Selfless Act/Random Kindness: _____
- ☐ I gave undivided attention to: _____
- ☐ I made things better by: _____
- ☐ I experienced joy, happiness, fun and/or laughter: _____
- ☐ I smiled _____ minutes
- ☐ Meditation/Prayer _____ minutes
- ☐ Inspiration (reading, video, music): _____
- ☐ I listened to my intuition: _____
- ☐ Physical activity _____ minutes
- ☐ I was 100% honest today
- ☐ I took care of myself by: _____
- ☐ Reviewed purpose 3 times
- ☐ Reviewed intentions 3 times
- ☐ Steps toward goals, intentions and purpose
    - 1. _____   2. _____   3. _____
- ☐ Reviewed vision
- ☐ I am grateful for:
    - 1. _____   6. _____
    - 2. _____   7. _____
    - 3. _____   8. _____
    - 4. _____   9. _____
    - 5. _____   10. _____

- ☐ I am looking forward to: _____

Notes: _____
_____
_____

MINDFUL LIVING WORKSHEET

M Tu W Th F S S   Date:_____   Rate:_____

- ☐ I am content with: _____
- ☐ I am proud of: _____
- ☐ Success review
- ☐ I love myself because: _____ ☐
- ☐ Love, thanks, kindness and support for others:
    1. _____   2. _____
    3. _____   4. _____
- ☐ Love, thanks, kindness and support for me:
    1. _____   2. _____
    3. _____   4. _____
- ☐ Good Deed/Selfless Act/Random Kindness: _____
- ☐ I gave undivided attention to: _____
- ☐ I made things better by: _____
- ☐ I experienced joy, happiness, fun and/or laughter: _____
- ☐ I smiled _____ minutes
- ☐ Meditation/Prayer _____ minutes
- ☐ Inspiration (reading, video, music): _____
- ☐ I listened to my intuition: _____
- ☐ Physical activity _____ minutes
- ☐ I was 100% honest today
- ☐ I took care of myself by: _____
- ☐ Reviewed purpose 3 times
- ☐ Reviewed intentions 3 times
- ☐ Steps toward goals, intentions and purpose
    1. _____   2. _____   3. _____
- ☐ Reviewed vision
- ☐ I am grateful for:
    1. _____   6. _____
    2. _____   7. _____
    3. _____   8. _____
    4. _____   9. _____
    5. _____   10. _____

- ☐ I am looking forward to: _____

Notes: _____
_____
_____
_____

MINDFUL LIVING WORKSHEET

M   Tu   W   Th   F   S   S   Date:_____   Rate:_____

☐ I am content with: _____
☐ I am proud of: _____
☐ Success review
☐ I love myself because: _____ ☐
☐ Love, thanks, kindness and support for others:
    1. _____   2. _____
    3. _____   4. _____
☐ Love, thanks, kindness and support for me:
    1. _____   2. _____
    3. _____   4. _____
☐ Good Deed/Selfless Act/Random Kindness: _____
☐ I gave undivided attention to: _____
☐ I made things better by: _____
☐ I experienced joy, happiness, fun and/or laughter: _____
☐ I smiled _____ minutes
☐ Meditation/Prayer _____ minutes
☐ Inspiration (reading, video, music): _____
☐ I listened to my intuition: _____
☐ Physical activity _____ minutes
☐ I was 100% honest today
☐ I took care of myself by: _____
☐ Reviewed purpose 3 times
☐ Reviewed intentions 3 times
☐ Steps toward goals, intentions and purpose
    1. _____   2. _____   3. _____
☐ Reviewed vision
☐ I am grateful for:
    1. _____   6. _____
    2. _____   7. _____
    3. _____   8. _____
    4. _____   9. _____
    5. _____   10. _____

☐ I am looking forward to: _____

Notes: _____
_____
_____

MINDFUL LIVING WORKSHEET

M Tu W Th F S S   Date:_____   Rate:_____

- ☐ I am content with: _____
- ☐ I am proud of: _____
- ☐ Success review
- ☐ I love myself because: _____ ☐
- ☐ Love, thanks, kindness and support for others:
  - 1. _____ 2. _____
  - 3. _____ 4. _____
- ☐ Love, thanks, kindness and support for me:
  - 1. _____ 2. _____
  - 3. _____ 4. _____
- ☐ Good Deed/Selfless Act/Random Kindness: _____
- ☐ I gave undivided attention to: _____
- ☐ I made things better by: _____
- ☐ I experienced joy, happiness, fun and/or laughter: _____
- ☐ I smiled _____ minutes
- ☐ Meditation/Prayer _____ minutes
- ☐ Inspiration (reading, video, music): _____
- ☐ I listened to my intuition: _____
- ☐ Physical activity _____ minutes
- ☐ I was 100% honest today
- ☐ I took care of myself by: _____
- ☐ Reviewed purpose 3 times
- ☐ Reviewed intentions 3 times
- ☐ Steps toward goals, intentions and purpose
  - 1. _____ 2. _____ 3. _____
- ☐ Reviewed vision
- ☐ I am grateful for:
  - 1. _____ 6. _____
  - 2. _____ 7. _____
  - 3. _____ 8. _____
  - 4. _____ 9. _____
  - 5. _____ 10. _____

- ☐ I am looking forward to: _____

Notes: _____
_____
_____
_____

Mindful Living Worksheet

M Tu W Th F S S   Date:_____   Rate:_____

- ☐ I am content with: _____
- ☐ I am proud of: _____
- ☐ Success review
- ☐ I love myself because: _____ ☐
- ☐ Love, thanks, kindness and support for others:
  - 1. _____   2. _____
  - 3. _____   4. _____
- ☐ Love, thanks, kindness and support for me:
  - 1. _____   2. _____
  - 3. _____   4. _____
- ☐ Good Deed/Selfless Act/Random Kindness: _____
- ☐ I gave undivided attention to: _____
- ☐ I made things better by: _____
- ☐ I experienced joy, happiness, fun and/or laughter: _____
- ☐ I smiled _____ minutes
- ☐ Meditation/Prayer _____ minutes
- ☐ Inspiration (reading, video, music): _____
- ☐ I listened to my intuition: _____
- ☐ Physical activity _____ minutes
- ☐ I was 100% honest today
- ☐ I took care of myself by: _____
- ☐ Reviewed purpose 3 times
- ☐ Reviewed intentions 3 times
- ☐ Steps toward goals, intentions and purpose
  - 1. _____   2. _____   3. _____
- ☐ Reviewed vision
- ☐ I am grateful for:
  - 1. _____   6. _____
  - 2. _____   7. _____
  - 3. _____   8. _____
  - 4. _____   9. _____
  - 5. _____   10. _____

- ☐ I am looking forward to: _____

Notes: _____
_____
_____

MINDFUL LIVING WORKSHEET

M Tu W Th F S S   Date:_____   Rate:_____

- ☐ I am content with: _____
- ☐ I am proud of: _____
- ☐ Success review
- ☐ I love myself because: _____ ☐
- ☐ Love, thanks, kindness and support for others:
    1. _____   2. _____
    3. _____   4. _____
- ☐ Love, thanks, kindness and support for me:
    1. _____   2. _____
    3. _____   4. _____
- ☐ Good Deed/Selfless Act/Random Kindness: _____
- ☐ I gave undivided attention to: _____
- ☐ I made things better by: _____
- ☐ I experienced joy, happiness, fun and/or laughter: _____
- ☐ I smiled _____ minutes
- ☐ Meditation/Prayer _____ minutes
- ☐ Inspiration (reading, video, music): _____
- ☐ I listened to my intuition: _____
- ☐ Physical activity _____ minutes
- ☐ I was 100% honest today
- ☐ I took care of myself by: _____
- ☐ Reviewed purpose 3 times
- ☐ Reviewed intentions 3 times
- ☐ Steps toward goals, intentions and purpose
    1. _____   2. _____   3. _____
- ☐ Reviewed vision
- ☐ I am grateful for:
    1. _____   6. _____
    2. _____   7. _____
    3. _____   8. _____
    4. _____   9. _____
    5. _____   10. _____

- ☐ I am looking forward to: _____

Notes: _____
_____
_____
_____

Mindful Living Worksheet

M   Tu   W   Th   F   S   S   Date:_____   Rate:_____

- ☐ I am content with: _____
- ☐ I am proud of: _____
- ☐ Success review
- ☐ I love myself because: _____ ☐
- ☐ Love, thanks, kindness and support for others:
  - 1. _____   2. _____
  - 3. _____   4. _____
- ☐ Love, thanks, kindness and support for me:
  - 1. _____   2. _____
  - 3. _____   4. _____
- ☐ Good Deed/Selfless Act/Random Kindness: _____
- ☐ I gave undivided attention to: _____
- ☐ I made things better by: _____
- ☐ I experienced joy, happiness, fun and/or laughter: _____
- ☐ I smiled _____ minutes
- ☐ Meditation/Prayer _____ minutes
- ☐ Inspiration (reading, video, music): _____
- ☐ I listened to my intuition: _____
- ☐ Physical activity _____ minutes
- ☐ I was 100% honest today
- ☐ I took care of myself by: _____
- ☐ Reviewed purpose 3 times
- ☐ Reviewed intentions 3 times
- ☐ Steps toward goals, intentions and purpose
  - 1. _____   2. _____   3. _____
- ☐ Reviewed vision
- ☐ I am grateful for:
  - 1. _____   6. _____
  - 2. _____   7. _____
  - 3. _____   8. _____
  - 4. _____   9. _____
  - 5. _____   10. _____

- ☐ I am looking forward to: _____

Notes: _____
_____
_____

MINDFUL LIVING WORKSHEET

M Tu W Th F S S   Date:_____   Rate:_____

- ☐ I am content with: _____
- ☐ I am proud of: _____
- ☐ Success review
- ☐ I love myself because: _____ ☐
- ☐ Love, thanks, kindness and support for others:
  - 1. _____   2. _____
  - 3. _____   4. _____
- ☐ Love, thanks, kindness and support for me:
  - 1. _____   2. _____
  - 3. _____   4. _____
- ☐ Good Deed/Selfless Act/Random Kindness: _____
- ☐ I gave undivided attention to: _____
- ☐ I made things better by: _____
- ☐ I experienced joy, happiness, fun and/or laughter: _____
- ☐ I smiled _____ minutes
- ☐ Meditation/Prayer _____ minutes
- ☐ Inspiration (reading, video, music): _____
- ☐ I listened to my intuition: _____
- ☐ Physical activity _____ minutes
- ☐ I was 100% honest today
- ☐ I took care of myself by: _____
- ☐ Reviewed purpose 3 times
- ☐ Reviewed intentions 3 times
- ☐ Steps toward goals, intentions and purpose
  - 1. _____   2. _____   3. _____
- ☐ Reviewed vision
- ☐ I am grateful for:
  - 1. _____   6. _____
  - 2. _____   7. _____
  - 3. _____   8. _____
  - 4. _____   9. _____
  - 5. _____   10. _____

- ☐ I am looking forward to: _____

Notes: _____
_____
_____

MINDFUL LIVING WORKSHEET

M Tu W Th F S S   Date:_____   Rate:_____

- ☐ I am content with: _____
- ☐ I am proud of: _____
- ☐ Success review
- ☐ I love myself because: _____ ☐
- ☐ Love, thanks, kindness and support for others:
    - 1. _____ 2. _____
    - 3. _____ 4. _____
- ☐ Love, thanks, kindness and support for me:
    - 1. _____ 2. _____
    - 3. _____ 4. _____
- ☐ Good Deed/Selfless Act/Random Kindness: _____
- ☐ I gave undivided attention to: _____
- ☐ I made things better by: _____
- ☐ I experienced joy, happiness, fun and/or laughter: _____
- ☐ I smiled _____ minutes
- ☐ Meditation/Prayer _____ minutes
- ☐ Inspiration (reading, video, music): _____
- ☐ I listened to my intuition: _____
- ☐ Physical activity _____ minutes
- ☐ I was 100% honest today
- ☐ I took care of myself by: _____
- ☐ Reviewed purpose 3 times
- ☐ Reviewed intentions 3 times
- ☐ Steps toward goals, intentions and purpose
    - 1. _____ 2. _____ 3. _____
- ☐ Reviewed vision
- ☐ I am grateful for:
    - 1. _____   6. _____
    - 2. _____   7. _____
    - 3. _____   8. _____
    - 4. _____   9. _____
    - 5. _____   10. _____

- ☐ I am looking forward to: _____

Notes: _____
_____
_____

MINDFUL LIVING WORKSHEET

M   Tu   W   Th   F   S   S   Date:_____   Rate:_____

- ☐ I am content with: _____
- ☐ I am proud of: _____
- ☐ Success review
- ☐ I love myself because: _____ ☐
- ☐ Love, thanks, kindness and support for others:
    1. _____   2. _____
    3. _____   4. _____
- ☐ Love, thanks, kindness and support for me:
    1. _____   2. _____
    3. _____   4. _____
- ☐ Good Deed/Selfless Act/Random Kindness: _____
- ☐ I gave undivided attention to: _____
- ☐ I made things better by: _____
- ☐ I experienced joy, happiness, fun and/or laughter: _____
- ☐ I smiled _____ minutes
- ☐ Meditation/Prayer _____ minutes
- ☐ Inspiration (reading, video, music): _____
- ☐ I listened to my intuition: _____
- ☐ Physical activity _____ minutes
- ☐ I was 100% honest today
- ☐ I took care of myself by: _____
- ☐ Reviewed purpose 3 times
- ☐ Reviewed intentions 3 times
- ☐ Steps toward goals, intentions and purpose
    1. _____ 2. _____ 3. _____
- ☐ Reviewed vision
- ☐ I am grateful for:
    1. _____   6. _____
    2. _____   7. _____
    3. _____   8. _____
    4. _____   9. _____
    5. _____   10. _____

- ☐ I am looking forward to: _____

Notes: _____
_____
_____

MINDFUL LIVING WORKSHEET

M   Tu   W   Th   F   S   S   Date:_____   Rate:_____

- ☐ I am content with: _____
- ☐ I am proud of: _____
- ☐ Success review
- ☐ I love myself because: _____ ☐
- ☐ Love, thanks, kindness and support for others:
    1. _____   2. _____
    3. _____   4. _____
- ☐ Love, thanks, kindness and support for me:
    1. _____   2. _____
    3. _____   4. _____
- ☐ Good Deed/Selfless Act/Random Kindness: _____
- ☐ I gave undivided attention to: _____
- ☐ I made things better by: _____
- ☐ I experienced joy, happiness, fun and/or laughter: _____
- ☐ I smiled _____ minutes
- ☐ Meditation/Prayer _____ minutes
- ☐ Inspiration (reading, video, music): _____
- ☐ I listened to my intuition: _____
- ☐ Physical activity _____ minutes
- ☐ I was 100% honest today
- ☐ I took care of myself by: _____
- ☐ Reviewed purpose 3 times
- ☐ Reviewed intentions 3 times
- ☐ Steps toward goals, intentions and purpose
    1. _____ 2. _____ 3. _____
- ☐ Reviewed vision
- ☐ I am grateful for:
    1. _____   6. _____
    2. _____   7. _____
    3. _____   8. _____
    4. _____   9. _____
    5. _____   10. _____

- ☐ I am looking forward to: _____

Notes: _____
_____
_____
_____

MINDFUL LIVING WORKSHEET

M   Tu   W   Th   F   S   S   Date:_____   Rate:_____

- ☐ I am content with: _____
- ☐ I am proud of: _____
- ☐ Success review
- ☐ I love myself because: _____ ☐
- ☐ Love, thanks, kindness and support for others:
  - 1. _____ 2. _____
  - 3. _____ 4. _____
- ☐ Love, thanks, kindness and support for me:
  - 1. _____ 2. _____
  - 3. _____ 4. _____
- ☐ Good Deed/Selfless Act/Random Kindness: _____
- ☐ I gave undivided attention to: _____
- ☐ I made things better by: _____
- ☐ I experienced joy, happiness, fun and/or laughter: _____
- ☐ I smiled _____ minutes
- ☐ Meditation/Prayer _____ minutes
- ☐ Inspiration (reading, video, music): _____
- ☐ I listened to my intuition: _____
- ☐ Physical activity _____ minutes
- ☐ I was 100% honest today
- ☐ I took care of myself by: _____
- ☐ Reviewed purpose 3 times
- ☐ Reviewed intentions 3 times
- ☐ Steps toward goals, intentions and purpose
  - 1. _____ 2. _____ 3. _____
- ☐ Reviewed vision
- ☐ I am grateful for:
  - 1. _____ 6. _____
  - 2. _____ 7. _____
  - 3. _____ 8. _____
  - 4. _____ 9. _____
  - 5. _____ 10. _____
- ☐ I am looking forward to: _____

Notes: _____
_____
_____
_____

Mindful Living Worksheet

M Tu W Th F S S   Date:_____   Rate:_____

- ☐ I am content with: _____
- ☐ I am proud of: _____
- ☐ Success review
- ☐ I love myself because: _____ ☐
- ☐ Love, thanks, kindness and support for others:
    1. _____   2. _____
    3. _____   4. _____
- ☐ Love, thanks, kindness and support for me:
    1. _____   2. _____
    3. _____   4. _____
- ☐ Good Deed/Selfless Act/Random Kindness: _____
- ☐ I gave undivided attention to: _____
- ☐ I made things better by: _____
- ☐ I experienced joy, happiness, fun and/or laughter: _____
- ☐ I smiled _____ minutes
- ☐ Meditation/Prayer _____ minutes
- ☐ Inspiration (reading, video, music): _____
- ☐ I listened to my intuition: _____
- ☐ Physical activity _____ minutes
- ☐ I was 100% honest today
- ☐ I took care of myself by: _____
- ☐ Reviewed purpose 3 times
- ☐ Reviewed intentions 3 times
- ☐ Steps toward goals, intentions and purpose
    1. _____   2. _____   3. _____
- ☐ Reviewed vision
- ☐ I am grateful for:
    1. _____   6. _____
    2. _____   7. _____
    3. _____   8. _____
    4. _____   9. _____
    5. _____   10. _____

- ☐ I am looking forward to: _____

Notes: _____
_____
_____
_____

MINDFUL LIVING WORKSHEET

M Tu W Th F S S   Date:_____   Rate:_____

- ☐ I am content with: _____
- ☐ I am proud of: _____
- ☐ Success review
- ☐ I love myself because: _____ ☐
- ☐ Love, thanks, kindness and support for others:
    1. _____   2. _____
    3. _____   4. _____
- ☐ Love, thanks, kindness and support for me:
    1. _____   2. _____
    3. _____   4. _____
- ☐ Good Deed/Selfless Act/Random Kindness: _____
- ☐ I gave undivided attention to: _____
- ☐ I made things better by: _____
- ☐ I experienced joy, happiness, fun and/or laughter: _____
- ☐ I smiled _____ minutes
- ☐ Meditation/Prayer _____ minutes
- ☐ Inspiration (reading, video, music): _____
- ☐ I listened to my intuition: _____
- ☐ Physical activity _____ minutes
- ☐ I was 100% honest today
- ☐ I took care of myself by: _____
- ☐ Reviewed purpose 3 times
- ☐ Reviewed intentions 3 times
- ☐ Steps toward goals, intentions and purpose
    1. _____ 2. _____ 3. _____
- ☐ Reviewed vision
- ☐ I am grateful for:
    1. _____   6. _____
    2. _____   7. _____
    3. _____   8. _____
    4. _____   9. _____
    5. _____   10. _____

- ☐ I am looking forward to: _____

Notes: _____
_____
_____
_____

MINDFUL LIVING WORKSHEET

M Tu W Th F S S   Date:_____   Rate:_____

- ☐ I am content with: _____
- ☐ I am proud of: _____
- ☐ Success review
- ☐ I love myself because: _____ ☐
- ☐ Love, thanks, kindness and support for others:
  - 1. _____   2. _____
  - 3. _____   4. _____
- ☐ Love, thanks, kindness and support for me:
  - 1. _____   2. _____
  - 3. _____   4. _____
- ☐ Good Deed/Selfless Act/Random Kindness: _____
- ☐ I gave undivided attention to: _____
- ☐ I made things better by: _____
- ☐ I experienced joy, happiness, fun and/or laughter: _____
- ☐ I smiled _____ minutes
- ☐ Meditation/Prayer _____ minutes
- ☐ Inspiration (reading, video, music): _____
- ☐ I listened to my intuition: _____
- ☐ Physical activity _____ minutes
- ☐ I was 100% honest today
- ☐ I took care of myself by: _____
- ☐ Reviewed purpose 3 times
- ☐ Reviewed intentions 3 times
- ☐ Steps toward goals, intentions and purpose
  - 1. _____ 2. _____ 3. _____
- ☐ Reviewed vision
- ☐ I am grateful for:
  - 1. _____   6. _____
  - 2. _____   7. _____
  - 3. _____   8. _____
  - 4. _____   9. _____
  - 5. _____   10. _____

- ☐ I am looking forward to: _____

Notes: _____
_____
_____
_____

MINDFUL LIVING WORKSHEET

M Tu W Th F S S   Date:_____   Rate:_____

- ☐ I am content with: _____
- ☐ I am proud of: _____
- ☐ Success review
- ☐ I love myself because: _____ ☐
- ☐ Love, thanks, kindness and support for others:
  - 1. _____   2. _____
  - 3. _____   4. _____
- ☐ Love, thanks, kindness and support for me:
  - 1. _____   2. _____
  - 3. _____   4. _____
- ☐ Good Deed/Selfless Act/Random Kindness: _____
- ☐ I gave undivided attention to: _____
- ☐ I made things better by: _____
- ☐ I experienced joy, happiness, fun and/or laughter: _____
- ☐ I smiled _____ minutes
- ☐ Meditation/Prayer _____ minutes
- ☐ Inspiration (reading, video, music): _____
- ☐ I listened to my intuition: _____
- ☐ Physical activity _____ minutes
- ☐ I was 100% honest today
- ☐ I took care of myself by: _____
- ☐ Reviewed purpose 3 times
- ☐ Reviewed intentions 3 times
- ☐ Steps toward goals, intentions and purpose
  - 1. _____   2. _____   3. _____
- ☐ Reviewed vision
- ☐ I am grateful for:
  - 1. _____   6. _____
  - 2. _____   7. _____
  - 3. _____   8. _____
  - 4. _____   9. _____
  - 5. _____   10. _____
- ☐ I am looking forward to: _____

Notes: _____
_____
_____

MINDFUL LIVING WORKSHEET

M Tu W Th F S S   Date:_____   Rate:_____

- ☐ I am content with: _____
- ☐ I am proud of: _____
- ☐ Success review
- ☐ I love myself because: _____ ☐
- ☐ Love, thanks, kindness and support for others:
    1. _____   2. _____
    3. _____   4. _____
- ☐ Love, thanks, kindness and support for me:
    1. _____   2. _____
    3. _____   4. _____
- ☐ Good Deed/Selfless Act/Random Kindness: _____
- ☐ I gave undivided attention to: _____
- ☐ I made things better by: _____
- ☐ I experienced joy, happiness, fun and/or laughter: _____
- ☐ I smiled _____ minutes
- ☐ Meditation/Prayer _____ minutes
- ☐ Inspiration (reading, video, music): _____
- ☐ I listened to my intuition: _____
- ☐ Physical activity _____ minutes
- ☐ I was 100% honest today
- ☐ I took care of myself by: _____
- ☐ Reviewed purpose 3 times
- ☐ Reviewed intentions 3 times
- ☐ Steps toward goals, intentions and purpose
    1. _____ 2. _____ 3. _____
- ☐ Reviewed vision
- ☐ I am grateful for:
    1. _____   6. _____
    2. _____   7. _____
    3. _____   8. _____
    4. _____   9. _____
    5. _____   10. _____

- ☐ I am looking forward to: _____

Notes: _____
_____
_____
_____

Mindful Living Worksheet

M Tu W Th F S S   Date:_____   Rate:_____

- ☐ I am content with: _____
- ☐ I am proud of: _____
- ☐ Success review
- ☐ I love myself because: _____ ☐
- ☐ Love, thanks, kindness and support for others:
    1. _____   2. _____
    3. _____   4. _____
- ☐ Love, thanks, kindness and support for me:
    1. _____   2. _____
    3. _____   4. _____
- ☐ Good Deed/Selfless Act/Random Kindness: _____
- ☐ I gave undivided attention to: _____
- ☐ I made things better by: _____
- ☐ I experienced joy, happiness, fun and/or laughter: _____
- ☐ I smiled _____ minutes
- ☐ Meditation/Prayer _____ minutes
- ☐ Inspiration (reading, video, music): _____
- ☐ I listened to my intuition: _____
- ☐ Physical activity _____ minutes
- ☐ I was 100% honest today
- ☐ I took care of myself by: _____
- ☐ Reviewed purpose 3 times
- ☐ Reviewed intentions 3 times
- ☐ Steps toward goals, intentions and purpose
    1. _____ 2. _____ 3. _____
- ☐ Reviewed vision
- ☐ I am grateful for:
    1. _____   6. _____
    2. _____   7. _____
    3. _____   8. _____
    4. _____   9. _____
    5. _____   10. _____

- ☐ I am looking forward to: _____

Notes: _____
_____
_____

MINDFUL LIVING WORKSHEET

M Tu W Th F S S   Date: _____   Rate: _____

- ☐ I am content with: _____
- ☐ I am proud of: _____
- ☐ Success review
- ☐ I love myself because: _____ ☐
- ☐ Love, thanks, kindness and support for others:
  - 1. _____   2. _____
  - 3. _____   4. _____
- ☐ Love, thanks, kindness and support for me:
  - 1. _____   2. _____
  - 3. _____   4. _____
- ☐ Good Deed/Selfless Act/Random Kindness: _____
- ☐ I gave undivided attention to: _____
- ☐ I made things better by: _____
- ☐ I experienced joy, happiness, fun and/or laughter: _____
- ☐ I smiled _____ minutes
- ☐ Meditation/Prayer _____ minutes
- ☐ Inspiration (reading, video, music): _____
- ☐ I listened to my intuition: _____
- ☐ Physical activity _____ minutes
- ☐ I was 100% honest today
- ☐ I took care of myself by: _____
- ☐ Reviewed purpose 3 times
- ☐ Reviewed intentions 3 times
- ☐ Steps toward goals, intentions and purpose
  - 1. _____   2. _____   3. _____
- ☐ Reviewed vision
- ☐ I am grateful for:
  - 1. _____   6. _____
  - 2. _____   7. _____
  - 3. _____   8. _____
  - 4. _____   9. _____
  - 5. _____   10. _____

- ☐ I am looking forward to: _____

Notes: _____
_____
_____

MINDFUL LIVING WORKSHEET

M Tu W Th F S S   Date:_____   Rate:_____

☐ I am content with: _____
☐ I am proud of: _____
☐ Success review
☐ I love myself because: _____ ☐
☐ Love, thanks, kindness and support for others:
    1. _____ 2. _____
    3. _____ 4. _____
☐ Love, thanks, kindness and support for me:
    1. _____ 2. _____
    3. _____ 4. _____
☐ Good Deed/Selfless Act/Random Kindness: _____
☐ I gave undivided attention to: _____
☐ I made things better by: _____
☐ I experienced joy, happiness, fun and/or laughter: _____
☐ I smiled _____ minutes
☐ Meditation/Prayer _____ minutes
☐ Inspiration (reading, video, music): _____
☐ I listened to my intuition: _____
☐ Physical activity _____ minutes
☐ I was 100% honest today
☐ I took care of myself by: _____
☐ Reviewed purpose 3 times
☐ Reviewed intentions 3 times
☐ Steps toward goals, intentions and purpose
    1. _____ 2. _____ 3. _____
☐ Reviewed vision
☐ I am grateful for:
    1. _____ 6. _____
    2. _____ 7. _____
    3. _____ 8. _____
    4. _____ 9. _____
    5. _____ 10. _____

☐ I am looking forward to: _____

Notes: _____
_____
_____
_____

MINDFUL LIVING WORKSHEET

M   Tu   W   Th   F   S   S   Date:_____   Rate:_____

- ☐ I am content with: _____
- ☐ I am proud of: _____
- ☐ Success review
- ☐ I love myself because: _____ ☐
- ☐ Love, thanks, kindness and support for others:
    - 1. _____   2. _____
    - 3. _____   4. _____
- ☐ Love, thanks, kindness and support for me:
    - 1. _____   2. _____
    - 3. _____   4. _____
- ☐ Good Deed/Selfless Act/Random Kindness: _____
- ☐ I gave undivided attention to: _____
- ☐ I made things better by: _____
- ☐ I experienced joy, happiness, fun and/or laughter: _____
- ☐ I smiled _____ minutes
- ☐ Meditation/Prayer _____ minutes
- ☐ Inspiration (reading, video, music): _____
- ☐ I listened to my intuition: _____
- ☐ Physical activity _____ minutes
- ☐ I was 100% honest today
- ☐ I took care of myself by: _____
- ☐ Reviewed purpose 3 times
- ☐ Reviewed intentions 3 times
- ☐ Steps toward goals, intentions and purpose
    - 1. _____   2. _____   3. _____
- ☐ Reviewed vision
- ☐ I am grateful for:
    - 1. _____   6. _____
    - 2. _____   7. _____
    - 3. _____   8. _____
    - 4. _____   9. _____
    - 5. _____   10. _____

- ☐ I am looking forward to: _____

Notes: _____
_____
_____
_____

MINDFUL LIVING WORKSHEET

M Tu W Th F S S   Date:_____   Rate:_____

- ☐ I am content with: _____
- ☐ I am proud of: _____
- ☐ Success review
- ☐ I love myself because: _____ ☐
- ☐ Love, thanks, kindness and support for others:
  - 1. _____   2. _____
  - 3. _____   4. _____
- ☐ Love, thanks, kindness and support for me:
  - 1. _____   2. _____
  - 3. _____   4. _____
- ☐ Good Deed/Selfless Act/Random Kindness: _____
- ☐ I gave undivided attention to: _____
- ☐ I made things better by: _____
- ☐ I experienced joy, happiness, fun and/or laughter: _____
- ☐ I smiled _____ minutes
- ☐ Meditation/Prayer _____ minutes
- ☐ Inspiration (reading, video, music): _____
- ☐ I listened to my intuition: _____
- ☐ Physical activity _____ minutes
- ☐ I was 100% honest today
- ☐ I took care of myself by: _____
- ☐ Reviewed purpose 3 times
- ☐ Reviewed intentions 3 times
- ☐ Steps toward goals, intentions and purpose
  - 1. _____ 2. _____ 3. _____
- ☐ Reviewed vision
- ☐ I am grateful for:
  - 1. _____   6. _____
  - 2. _____   7. _____
  - 3. _____   8. _____
  - 4. _____   9. _____
  - 5. _____   10. _____

- ☐ I am looking forward to: _____

Notes: _____
_____
_____
_____

MINDFUL LIVING WORKSHEET

M　Tu　W　Th　F　S　S　　　Date: _____　　　　Rate: _____

- ☐ I am content with: _____
- ☐ I am proud of: _____
- ☐ Success review
- ☐ I love myself because: _____ ☐
- ☐ Love, thanks, kindness and support for others:
    - 1. _____ 2. _____
    - 3. _____ 4. _____
- ☐ Love, thanks, kindness and support for me:
    - 1. _____ 2. _____
    - 3. _____ 4. _____
- ☐ Good Deed/Selfless Act/Random Kindness: _____
- ☐ I gave undivided attention to: _____
- ☐ I made things better by: _____
- ☐ I experienced joy, happiness, fun and/or laughter: _____
- ☐ I smiled _____ minutes
- ☐ Meditation/Prayer _____ minutes
- ☐ Inspiration (reading, video, music): _____
- ☐ I listened to my intuition: _____
- ☐ Physical activity _____ minutes
- ☐ I was 100% honest today
- ☐ I took care of myself by: _____
- ☐ Reviewed purpose 3 times
- ☐ Reviewed intentions 3 times
- ☐ Steps toward goals, intentions and purpose
    - 1. _____ 2. _____ 3. _____
- ☐ Reviewed vision
- ☐ I am grateful for:
    - 1. _____ 6. _____
    - 2. _____ 7. _____
    - 3. _____ 8. _____
    - 4. _____ 9. _____
    - 5. _____ 10. _____

- ☐ I am looking forward to: _____

Notes: _____
_____
_____
_____

MINDFUL LIVING WORKSHEET

M   Tu   W   Th   F   S   S   Date:_____   Rate:_____

- ☐ I am content with: _____
- ☐ I am proud of: _____
- ☐ Success review
- ☐ I love myself because: _____ ☐
- ☐ Love, thanks, kindness and support for others:
    1. _____   2. _____
    3. _____   4. _____
- ☐ Love, thanks, kindness and support for me:
    1. _____   2. _____
    3. _____   4. _____
- ☐ Good Deed/Selfless Act/Random Kindness: _____
- ☐ I gave undivided attention to: _____
- ☐ I made things better by: _____
- ☐ I experienced joy, happiness, fun and/or laughter: _____
- ☐ I smiled _____ minutes
- ☐ Meditation/Prayer _____ minutes
- ☐ Inspiration (reading, video, music): _____
- ☐ I listened to my intuition: _____
- ☐ Physical activity _____ minutes
- ☐ I was 100% honest today
- ☐ I took care of myself by: _____
- ☐ Reviewed purpose 3 times
- ☐ Reviewed intentions 3 times
- ☐ Steps toward goals, intentions and purpose
    1. _____   2. _____   3. _____
- ☐ Reviewed vision
- ☐ I am grateful for:
    1. _____   6. _____
    2. _____   7. _____
    3. _____   8. _____
    4. _____   9. _____
    5. _____   10. _____

- ☐ I am looking forward to: _____

Notes: _____
_____
_____
_____

Mindful Living Worksheet

M   Tu   W   Th   F   S   S   Date:_____   Rate:_____

- ☐ I am content with: _____
- ☐ I am proud of: _____
- ☐ Success review
- ☐ I love myself because: _____ ☐
- ☐ Love, thanks, kindness and support for others:
  - 1. _____   2. _____
  - 3. _____   4. _____
- ☐ Love, thanks, kindness and support for me:
  - 1. _____   2. _____
  - 3. _____   4. _____
- ☐ Good Deed/Selfless Act/Random Kindness: _____
- ☐ I gave undivided attention to: _____
- ☐ I made things better by: _____
- ☐ I experienced joy, happiness, fun and/or laughter: _____
- ☐ I smiled _____ minutes
- ☐ Meditation/Prayer _____ minutes
- ☐ Inspiration (reading, video, music): _____
- ☐ I listened to my intuition: _____
- ☐ Physical activity _____ minutes
- ☐ I was 100% honest today
- ☐ I took care of myself by: _____
- ☐ Reviewed purpose 3 times
- ☐ Reviewed intentions 3 times
- ☐ Steps toward goals, intentions and purpose
  - 1. _____   2. _____   3. _____
- ☐ Reviewed vision
- ☐ I am grateful for:
  - 1. _____   6. _____
  - 2. _____   7. _____
  - 3. _____   8. _____
  - 4. _____   9. _____
  - 5. _____   10. _____

- ☐ I am looking forward to: _____

Notes: _____
_____
_____
_____

Mindful Living Worksheet

M Tu W Th F S S   Date:_____   Rate:_____

- ☐ I am content with: _____
- ☐ I am proud of: _____
- ☐ Success review
- ☐ I love myself because: _____ ☐
- ☐ Love, thanks, kindness and support for others:
  - 1. _____   2. _____
  - 3. _____   4. _____
- ☐ Love, thanks, kindness and support for me:
  - 1. _____   2. _____
  - 3. _____   4. _____
- ☐ Good Deed/Selfless Act/Random Kindness: _____
- ☐ I gave undivided attention to: _____
- ☐ I made things better by: _____
- ☐ I experienced joy, happiness, fun and/or laughter: _____
- ☐ I smiled _____ minutes
- ☐ Meditation/Prayer _____ minutes
- ☐ Inspiration (reading, video, music): _____
- ☐ I listened to my intuition: _____
- ☐ Physical activity _____ minutes
- ☐ I was 100% honest today
- ☐ I took care of myself by: _____
- ☐ Reviewed purpose 3 times
- ☐ Reviewed intentions 3 times
- ☐ Steps toward goals, intentions and purpose
  - 1. _____   2. _____   3. _____
- ☐ Reviewed vision
- ☐ I am grateful for:
  - 1. _____   6. _____
  - 2. _____   7. _____
  - 3. _____   8. _____
  - 4. _____   9. _____
  - 5. _____   10. _____
- ☐ I am looking forward to: _____

Notes: _____
_____
_____
_____

MINDFUL LIVING WORKSHEET

M Tu W Th F S S   Date: _____   Rate: _____

- ☐ I am content with: _____
- ☐ I am proud of: _____
- ☐ Success review
- ☐ I love myself because: _____ ☐
- ☐ Love, thanks, kindness and support for others:
    - 1. _____   2. _____
    - 3. _____   4. _____
- ☐ Love, thanks, kindness and support for me:
    - 1. _____   2. _____
    - 3. _____   4. _____
- ☐ Good Deed/Selfless Act/Random Kindness: _____
- ☐ I gave undivided attention to: _____
- ☐ I made things better by: _____
- ☐ I experienced joy, happiness, fun and/or laughter: _____
- ☐ I smiled _____ minutes
- ☐ Meditation/Prayer _____ minutes
- ☐ Inspiration (reading, video, music): _____
- ☐ I listened to my intuition: _____
- ☐ Physical activity _____ minutes
- ☐ I was 100% honest today
- ☐ I took care of myself by: _____
- ☐ Reviewed purpose 3 times
- ☐ Reviewed intentions 3 times
- ☐ Steps toward goals, intentions and purpose
    - 1. _____   2. _____   3. _____
- ☐ Reviewed vision
- ☐ I am grateful for:
    - 1. _____   6. _____
    - 2. _____   7. _____
    - 3. _____   8. _____
    - 4. _____   9. _____
    - 5. _____   10. _____

- ☐ I am looking forward to: _____

Notes: _____
_____
_____
_____

MINDFUL LIVING WORKSHEET

M   Tu   W   Th   F   S   S   Date:_____   Rate:_____

- ☐ I am content with: _____
- ☐ I am proud of: _____
- ☐ Success review
- ☐ I love myself because: _____ ☐
- ☐ Love, thanks, kindness and support for others:
  - 1. _____   2. _____
  - 3. _____   4. _____
- ☐ Love, thanks, kindness and support for me:
  - 1. _____   2. _____
  - 3. _____   4. _____
- ☐ Good Deed/Selfless Act/Random Kindness: _____
- ☐ I gave undivided attention to: _____
- ☐ I made things better by: _____
- ☐ I experienced joy, happiness, fun and/or laughter: _____
- ☐ I smiled _____ minutes
- ☐ Meditation/Prayer _____ minutes
- ☐ Inspiration (reading, video, music): _____
- ☐ I listened to my intuition: _____
- ☐ Physical activity _____ minutes
- ☐ I was 100% honest today
- ☐ I took care of myself by: _____
- ☐ Reviewed purpose 3 times
- ☐ Reviewed intentions 3 times
- ☐ Steps toward goals, intentions and purpose
  - 1. _____   2. _____   3. _____
- ☐ Reviewed vision
- ☐ I am grateful for:
  - 1. _____   6. _____
  - 2. _____   7. _____
  - 3. _____   8. _____
  - 4. _____   9. _____
  - 5. _____   10. _____

- ☐ I am looking forward to: _____

Notes: _____
_____
_____
_____

MINDFUL LIVING WORKSHEET

M Tu W Th F S S   Date:_____   Rate:_____

☐ I am content with: _____
☐ I am proud of: _____
☐ Success review
☐ I love myself because: _____ ☐
☐ Love, thanks, kindness and support for others:
    1. _____ 2. _____
    3. _____ 4. _____
☐ Love, thanks, kindness and support for me:
    1. _____ 2. _____
    3. _____ 4. _____
☐ Good Deed/Selfless Act/Random Kindness: _____
☐ I gave undivided attention to: _____
☐ I made things better by: _____
☐ I experienced joy, happiness, fun and/or laughter: _____
☐ I smiled _____ minutes
☐ Meditation/Prayer _____ minutes
☐ Inspiration (reading, video, music): _____
☐ I listened to my intuition: _____
☐ Physical activity _____ minutes
☐ I was 100% honest today
☐ I took care of myself by: _____
☐ Reviewed purpose 3 times
☐ Reviewed intentions 3 times
☐ Steps toward goals, intentions and purpose
    1. _____ 2. _____ 3. _____
☐ Reviewed vision
☐ I am grateful for:
    1. _____ 6. _____
    2. _____ 7. _____
    3. _____ 8. _____
    4. _____ 9. _____
    5. _____ 10. _____

☐ I am looking forward to: _____

Notes: _____
_____
_____
_____

MINDFUL LIVING WORKSHEET

M Tu W Th F S S   Date:_____   Rate:_____

- ☐ I am content with: _____
- ☐ I am proud of: _____
- ☐ Success review
- ☐ I love myself because: _____ ☐
- ☐ Love, thanks, kindness and support for others:
  - 1. _____   2. _____
  - 3. _____   4. _____
- ☐ Love, thanks, kindness and support for me:
  - 1. _____   2. _____
  - 3. _____   4. _____
- ☐ Good Deed/Selfless Act/Random Kindness: _____
- ☐ I gave undivided attention to: _____
- ☐ I made things better by: _____
- ☐ I experienced joy, happiness, fun and/or laughter: _____
- ☐ I smiled _____ minutes
- ☐ Meditation/Prayer _____ minutes
- ☐ Inspiration (reading, video, music): _____
- ☐ I listened to my intuition: _____
- ☐ Physical activity _____ minutes
- ☐ I was 100% honest today
- ☐ I took care of myself by: _____
- ☐ Reviewed purpose 3 times
- ☐ Reviewed intentions 3 times
- ☐ Steps toward goals, intentions and purpose
  - 1. _____   2. _____   3. _____
- ☐ Reviewed vision
- ☐ I am grateful for:
  - 1. _____   6. _____
  - 2. _____   7. _____
  - 3. _____   8. _____
  - 4. _____   9. _____
  - 5. _____   10. _____

- ☐ I am looking forward to: _____

Notes: _____
_____
_____

MINDFUL LIVING WORKSHEET

M Tu W Th F S S   Date:_____   Rate:_____

- ☐ I am content with: _____
- ☐ I am proud of: _____
- ☐ Success review
- ☐ I love myself because: _____ ☐
- ☐ Love, thanks, kindness and support for others:
    - 1. _____   2. _____
    - 3. _____   4. _____
- ☐ Love, thanks, kindness and support for me:
    - 1. _____   2. _____
    - 3. _____   4. _____
- ☐ Good Deed/Selfless Act/Random Kindness: _____
- ☐ I gave undivided attention to: _____
- ☐ I made things better by: _____
- ☐ I experienced joy, happiness, fun and/or laughter: _____
- ☐ I smiled _____ minutes
- ☐ Meditation/Prayer _____ minutes
- ☐ Inspiration (reading, video, music): _____
- ☐ I listened to my intuition: _____
- ☐ Physical activity _____ minutes
- ☐ I was 100% honest today
- ☐ I took care of myself by: _____
- ☐ Reviewed purpose 3 times
- ☐ Reviewed intentions 3 times
- ☐ Steps toward goals, intentions and purpose
    - 1. _____   2. _____   3. _____
- ☐ Reviewed vision
- ☐ I am grateful for:
    - 1. _____   6. _____
    - 2. _____   7. _____
    - 3. _____   8. _____
    - 4. _____   9. _____
    - 5. _____   10. _____

- ☐ I am looking forward to: _____

Notes: _____
_____
_____

MINDFUL LIVING WORKSHEET

M   Tu   W   Th   F   S   S   Date:_____   Rate:_____

- ☐ I am content with: _____
- ☐ I am proud of: _____
- ☐ Success review
- ☐ I love myself because: _____ ☐
- ☐ Love, thanks, kindness and support for others:
    - 1. _____   2. _____
    - 3. _____   4. _____
- ☐ Love, thanks, kindness and support for me:
    - 1. _____   2. _____
    - 3. _____   4. _____
- ☐ Good Deed/Selfless Act/Random Kindness: _____
- ☐ I gave undivided attention to: _____
- ☐ I made things better by: _____
- ☐ I experienced joy, happiness, fun and/or laughter: _____
- ☐ I smiled _____ minutes
- ☐ Meditation/Prayer _____ minutes
- ☐ Inspiration (reading, video, music): _____
- ☐ I listened to my intuition: _____
- ☐ Physical activity _____ minutes
- ☐ I was 100% honest today
- ☐ I took care of myself by: _____
- ☐ Reviewed purpose 3 times
- ☐ Reviewed intentions 3 times
- ☐ Steps toward goals, intentions and purpose
    - 1. _____   2. _____   3. _____
- ☐ Reviewed vision
- ☐ I am grateful for:
    - 1. _____   6. _____
    - 2. _____   7. _____
    - 3. _____   8. _____
    - 4. _____   9. _____
    - 5. _____   10. _____

- ☐ I am looking forward to: _____

Notes: _____
_____
_____
_____

MINDFUL LIVING WORKSHEET

M   Tu   W   Th   F   S   S   Date: _____   Rate: _____

- ☐ I am content with: _____
- ☐ I am proud of: _____
- ☐ Success review
- ☐ I love myself because: _____ ☐
- ☐ Love, thanks, kindness and support for others:
    - 1. _____   2. _____
    - 3. _____   4. _____
- ☐ Love, thanks, kindness and support for me:
    - 1. _____   2. _____
    - 3. _____   4. _____
- ☐ Good Deed/Selfless Act/Random Kindness: _____
- ☐ I gave undivided attention to: _____
- ☐ I made things better by: _____
- ☐ I experienced joy, happiness, fun and/or laughter: _____
- ☐ I smiled _____ minutes
- ☐ Meditation/Prayer _____ minutes
- ☐ Inspiration (reading, video, music): _____
- ☐ I listened to my intuition: _____
- ☐ Physical activity _____ minutes
- ☐ I was 100% honest today
- ☐ I took care of myself by: _____
- ☐ Reviewed purpose 3 times
- ☐ Reviewed intentions 3 times
- ☐ Steps toward goals, intentions and purpose
    - 1. _____   2. _____   3. _____
- ☐ Reviewed vision
- ☐ I am grateful for:
    - 1. _____   6. _____
    - 2. _____   7. _____
    - 3. _____   8. _____
    - 4. _____   9. _____
    - 5. _____   10. _____

- ☐ I am looking forward to: _____

Notes: _____
_____
_____

MINDFUL LIVING WORKSHEET

M Tu W Th F S S   Date:_____   Rate:_____

- ☐ I am content with: _____
- ☐ I am proud of: _____
- ☐ Success review
- ☐ I love myself because: _____ ☐
- ☐ Love, thanks, kindness and support for others:
    1. _____   2. _____
    3. _____   4. _____
- ☐ Love, thanks, kindness and support for me:
    1. _____   2. _____
    3. _____   4. _____
- ☐ Good Deed/Selfless Act/Random Kindness: _____
- ☐ I gave undivided attention to: _____
- ☐ I made things better by: _____
- ☐ I experienced joy, happiness, fun and/or laughter: _____
- ☐ I smiled _____ minutes
- ☐ Meditation/Prayer _____ minutes
- ☐ Inspiration (reading, video, music): _____
- ☐ I listened to my intuition: _____
- ☐ Physical activity _____ minutes
- ☐ I was 100% honest today
- ☐ I took care of myself by: _____
- ☐ Reviewed purpose 3 times
- ☐ Reviewed intentions 3 times
- ☐ Steps toward goals, intentions and purpose
    1. _____ 2. _____ 3. _____
- ☐ Reviewed vision
- ☐ I am grateful for:
    1. _____   6. _____
    2. _____   7. _____
    3. _____   8. _____
    4. _____   9. _____
    5. _____   10. _____

- ☐ I am looking forward to: _____

Notes: _____
_____
_____
_____

MINDFUL LIVING WORKSHEET

M Tu W Th F S S   Date:_____   Rate:_____

☐ I am content with: _____
☐ I am proud of: _____
☐ Success review
☐ I love myself because: _____ ☐
☐ Love, thanks, kindness and support for others:
    1. _____   2. _____
    3. _____   4. _____
☐ Love, thanks, kindness and support for me:
    1. _____   2. _____
    3. _____   4. _____
☐ Good Deed/Selfless Act/Random Kindness: _____
☐ I gave undivided attention to: _____
☐ I made things better by: _____
☐ I experienced joy, happiness, fun and/or laughter: _____
☐ I smiled _____ minutes
☐ Meditation/Prayer _____ minutes
☐ Inspiration (reading, video, music): _____
☐ I listened to my intuition: _____
☐ Physical activity _____ minutes
☐ I was 100% honest today
☐ I took care of myself by: _____
☐ Reviewed purpose 3 times
☐ Reviewed intentions 3 times
☐ Steps toward goals, intentions and purpose
    1. _____ 2. _____ 3. _____
☐ Reviewed vision
☐ I am grateful for:
    1. _____   6. _____
    2. _____   7. _____
    3. _____   8. _____
    4. _____   9. _____
    5. _____   10. _____

☐ I am looking forward to: _____

Notes: _____
_____
_____
_____

MINDFUL LIVING WORKSHEET

M   Tu   W   Th   F   S   S   Date:_____   Rate:_____

- ☐ I am content with: _____
- ☐ I am proud of: _____
- ☐ Success review
- ☐ I love myself because: _____ ☐
- ☐ Love, thanks, kindness and support for others:
    - 1. _____   2. _____
    - 3. _____   4. _____
- ☐ Love, thanks, kindness and support for me:
    - 1. _____   2. _____
    - 3. _____   4. _____
- ☐ Good Deed/Selfless Act/Random Kindness: _____
- ☐ I gave undivided attention to: _____
- ☐ I made things better by: _____
- ☐ I experienced joy, happiness, fun and/or laughter: _____
- ☐ I smiled _____ minutes
- ☐ Meditation/Prayer _____ minutes
- ☐ Inspiration (reading, video, music): _____
- ☐ I listened to my intuition: _____
- ☐ Physical activity _____ minutes
- ☐ I was 100% honest today
- ☐ I took care of myself by: _____
- ☐ Reviewed purpose 3 times
- ☐ Reviewed intentions 3 times
- ☐ Steps toward goals, intentions and purpose
    - 1. _____   2. _____   3. _____
- ☐ Reviewed vision
- ☐ I am grateful for:
    - 1. _____   6. _____
    - 2. _____   7. _____
    - 3. _____   8. _____
    - 4. _____   9. _____
    - 5. _____   10. _____
- ☐ I am looking forward to: _____

Notes: _____
_____
_____
_____

MINDFUL LIVING WORKSHEET

M   Tu   W   Th   F   S   S   Date:_____   Rate:_____

- ☐ I am content with: _____
- ☐ I am proud of: _____
- ☐ Success review
- ☐ I love myself because: _____ ☐
- ☐ Love, thanks, kindness and support for others:
    1. _____   2. _____
    3. _____   4. _____
- ☐ Love, thanks, kindness and support for me:
    1. _____   2. _____
    3. _____   4. _____
- ☐ Good Deed/Selfless Act/Random Kindness: _____
- ☐ I gave undivided attention to: _____
- ☐ I made things better by: _____
- ☐ I experienced joy, happiness, fun and/or laughter: _____
- ☐ I smiled _____ minutes
- ☐ Meditation/Prayer _____ minutes
- ☐ Inspiration (reading, video, music): _____
- ☐ I listened to my intuition: _____
- ☐ Physical activity _____ minutes
- ☐ I was 100% honest today
- ☐ I took care of myself by: _____
- ☐ Reviewed purpose 3 times
- ☐ Reviewed intentions 3 times
- ☐ Steps toward goals, intentions and purpose
    1. _____   2. _____   3. _____
- ☐ Reviewed vision
- ☐ I am grateful for:
    1. _____   6. _____
    2. _____   7. _____
    3. _____   8. _____
    4. _____   9. _____
    5. _____   10. _____

- ☐ I am looking forward to: _____

Notes: _____
_____
_____
_____

MINDFUL LIVING WORKSHEET

M Tu W Th F S S   Date:_____   Rate:_____

- ☐ I am content with: _____
- ☐ I am proud of: _____
- ☐ Success review
- ☐ I love myself because: _____ ☐
- ☐ Love, thanks, kindness and support for others:
  - 1. _____ 2. _____
  - 3. _____ 4. _____
- ☐ Love, thanks, kindness and support for me:
  - 1. _____ 2. _____
  - 3. _____ 4. _____
- ☐ Good Deed/Selfless Act/Random Kindness: _____
- ☐ I gave undivided attention to: _____
- ☐ I made things better by: _____
- ☐ I experienced joy, happiness, fun and/or laughter: _____
- ☐ I smiled _____ minutes
- ☐ Meditation/Prayer _____ minutes
- ☐ Inspiration (reading, video, music): _____
- ☐ I listened to my intuition: _____
- ☐ Physical activity _____ minutes
- ☐ I was 100% honest today
- ☐ I took care of myself by: _____
- ☐ Reviewed purpose 3 times
- ☐ Reviewed intentions 3 times
- ☐ Steps toward goals, intentions and purpose
  - 1. _____ 2. _____ 3. _____
- ☐ Reviewed vision
- ☐ I am grateful for:
  - 1. _____ 6. _____
  - 2. _____ 7. _____
  - 3. _____ 8. _____
  - 4. _____ 9. _____
  - 5. _____ 10. _____

- ☐ I am looking forward to: _____

Notes: _____
_____
_____
_____

MINDFUL LIVING WORKSHEET

M   Tu   W   Th   F   S   S   Date:_____   Rate:_____

- ☐ I am content with: _____
- ☐ I am proud of: _____
- ☐ Success review
- ☐ I love myself because: _____ ☐
- ☐ Love, thanks, kindness and support for others:
    1. _____   2. _____
    3. _____   4. _____
- ☐ Love, thanks, kindness and support for me:
    1. _____   2. _____
    3. _____   4. _____
- ☐ Good Deed/Selfless Act/Random Kindness: _____
- ☐ I gave undivided attention to: _____
- ☐ I made things better by: _____
- ☐ I experienced joy, happiness, fun and/or laughter: _____
- ☐ I smiled _____ minutes
- ☐ Meditation/Prayer _____ minutes
- ☐ Inspiration (reading, video, music): _____
- ☐ I listened to my intuition: _____
- ☐ Physical activity _____ minutes
- ☐ I was 100% honest today
- ☐ I took care of myself by: _____
- ☐ Reviewed purpose 3 times
- ☐ Reviewed intentions 3 times
- ☐ Steps toward goals, intentions and purpose
    1. _____ 2. _____ 3. _____
- ☐ Reviewed vision
- ☐ I am grateful for:
    1. _____   6. _____
    2. _____   7. _____
    3. _____   8. _____
    4. _____   9. _____
    5. _____   10. _____

- ☐ I am looking forward to: _____

Notes: _____
_____
_____

Mindful Living Worksheet

M Tu W Th F S S   Date:_____   Rate:_____

- ☐ I am content with: _____
- ☐ I am proud of: _____
- ☐ Success review
- ☐ I love myself because: _____ ☐
- ☐ Love, thanks, kindness and support for others:
  - 1. _____ 2. _____
  - 3. _____ 4. _____
- ☐ Love, thanks, kindness and support for me:
  - 1. _____ 2. _____
  - 3. _____ 4. _____
- ☐ Good Deed/Selfless Act/Random Kindness: _____
- ☐ I gave undivided attention to: _____
- ☐ I made things better by: _____
- ☐ I experienced joy, happiness, fun and/or laughter: _____
- ☐ I smiled _____ minutes
- ☐ Meditation/Prayer _____ minutes
- ☐ Inspiration (reading, video, music): _____
- ☐ I listened to my intuition: _____
- ☐ Physical activity _____ minutes
- ☐ I was 100% honest today
- ☐ I took care of myself by: _____
- ☐ Reviewed purpose 3 times
- ☐ Reviewed intentions 3 times
- ☐ Steps toward goals, intentions and purpose
  - 1. _____ 2. _____ 3. _____
- ☐ Reviewed vision
- ☐ I am grateful for:
  - 1. _____ 6. _____
  - 2. _____ 7. _____
  - 3. _____ 8. _____
  - 4. _____ 9. _____
  - 5. _____ 10. _____

- ☐ I am looking forward to: _____

Notes: _____
_____
_____
_____

MINDFUL LIVING WORKSHEET

M Tu W Th F S S   Date:_____   Rate:_____

- ☐ I am content with: _____
- ☐ I am proud of: _____
- ☐ Success review
- ☐ I love myself because: _____ ☐
- ☐ Love, thanks, kindness and support for others:
    1. _____   2. _____
    3. _____   4. _____
- ☐ Love, thanks, kindness and support for me:
    1. _____   2. _____
    3. _____   4. _____
- ☐ Good Deed/Selfless Act/Random Kindness: _____
- ☐ I gave undivided attention to: _____
- ☐ I made things better by: _____
- ☐ I experienced joy, happiness, fun and/or laughter: _____
- ☐ I smiled _____ minutes
- ☐ Meditation/Prayer _____ minutes
- ☐ Inspiration (reading, video, music): _____
- ☐ I listened to my intuition: _____
- ☐ Physical activity _____ minutes
- ☐ I was 100% honest today
- ☐ I took care of myself by: _____
- ☐ Reviewed purpose 3 times
- ☐ Reviewed intentions 3 times
- ☐ Steps toward goals, intentions and purpose
    1. _____ 2. _____ 3. _____
- ☐ Reviewed vision
- ☐ I am grateful for:
    1. _____   6. _____
    2. _____   7. _____
    3. _____   8. _____
    4. _____   9. _____
    5. _____   10. _____

- ☐ I am looking forward to: _____

Notes: _____
_____
_____

MINDFUL LIVING WORKSHEET

M Tu W Th F S S   Date:_____   Rate:_____

- ☐ I am content with: _____
- ☐ I am proud of: _____
- ☐ Success review
- ☐ I love myself because: _____ ☐
- ☐ Love, thanks, kindness and support for others:
    1. _____   2. _____
    3. _____   4. _____
- ☐ Love, thanks, kindness and support for me:
    1. _____   2. _____
    3. _____   4. _____
- ☐ Good Deed/Selfless Act/Random Kindness: _____
- ☐ I gave undivided attention to: _____
- ☐ I made things better by: _____
- ☐ I experienced joy, happiness, fun and/or laughter: _____
- ☐ I smiled _____ minutes
- ☐ Meditation/Prayer _____ minutes
- ☐ Inspiration (reading, video, music): _____
- ☐ I listened to my intuition: _____
- ☐ Physical activity _____ minutes
- ☐ I was 100% honest today
- ☐ I took care of myself by: _____
- ☐ Reviewed purpose 3 times
- ☐ Reviewed intentions 3 times
- ☐ Steps toward goals, intentions and purpose
    1. _____ 2. _____ 3. _____
- ☐ Reviewed vision
- ☐ I am grateful for:
    1. _____   6. _____
    2. _____   7. _____
    3. _____   8. _____
    4. _____   9. _____
    5. _____   10. _____

- ☐ I am looking forward to: _____

Notes: _____
_____
_____
_____

MINDFUL LIVING WORKSHEET

M Tu W Th F S S   Date: _____   Rate: _____

- ☐ I am content with: _____
- ☐ I am proud of: _____
- ☐ Success review
- ☐ I love myself because: _____ ☐
- ☐ Love, thanks, kindness and support for others:
  - 1. _____   2. _____
  - 3. _____   4. _____
- ☐ Love, thanks, kindness and support for me:
  - 1. _____   2. _____
  - 3. _____   4. _____
- ☐ Good Deed/Selfless Act/Random Kindness: _____
- ☐ I gave undivided attention to: _____
- ☐ I made things better by: _____
- ☐ I experienced joy, happiness, fun and/or laughter: _____
- ☐ I smiled _____ minutes
- ☐ Meditation/Prayer _____ minutes
- ☐ Inspiration (reading, video, music): _____
- ☐ I listened to my intuition: _____
- ☐ Physical activity _____ minutes
- ☐ I was 100% honest today
- ☐ I took care of myself by: _____
- ☐ Reviewed purpose 3 times
- ☐ Reviewed intentions 3 times
- ☐ Steps toward goals, intentions and purpose
  - 1. _____   2. _____   3. _____
- ☐ Reviewed vision
- ☐ I am grateful for:
  - 1. _____   6. _____
  - 2. _____   7. _____
  - 3. _____   8. _____
  - 4. _____   9. _____
  - 5. _____   10. _____

- ☐ I am looking forward to: _____

Notes: _____
_____
_____

MINDFUL LIVING WORKSHEET

M Tu W Th F S S   Date: _____   Rate: _____

- ☐ I am content with: _____
- ☐ I am proud of: _____
- ☐ Success review
- ☐ I love myself because: _____ ☐
- ☐ Love, thanks, kindness and support for others:
    1. _____   2. _____
    3. _____   4. _____
- ☐ Love, thanks, kindness and support for me:
    1. _____   2. _____
    3. _____   4. _____
- ☐ Good Deed/Selfless Act/Random Kindness: _____
- ☐ I gave undivided attention to: _____
- ☐ I made things better by: _____
- ☐ I experienced joy, happiness, fun and/or laughter: _____
- ☐ I smiled _____ minutes
- ☐ Meditation/Prayer _____ minutes
- ☐ Inspiration (reading, video, music): _____
- ☐ I listened to my intuition: _____
- ☐ Physical activity _____ minutes
- ☐ I was 100% honest today
- ☐ I took care of myself by: _____
- ☐ Reviewed purpose 3 times
- ☐ Reviewed intentions 3 times
- ☐ Steps toward goals, intentions and purpose
    1. _____ 2. _____ 3. _____
- ☐ Reviewed vision
- ☐ I am grateful for:
    1. _____   6. _____
    2. _____   7. _____
    3. _____   8. _____
    4. _____   9. _____
    5. _____   10. _____

- ☐ I am looking forward to: _____

Notes: _____
_____
_____
_____

MINDFUL LIVING WORKSHEET

M Tu W Th F S S   Date:_____   Rate:_____

- ☐ I am content with: _____
- ☐ I am proud of: _____
- ☐ Success review
- ☐ I love myself because: _____ ☐
- ☐ Love, thanks, kindness and support for others:
    1. _____   2. _____
    3. _____   4. _____
- ☐ Love, thanks, kindness and support for me:
    1. _____   2. _____
    3. _____   4. _____
- ☐ Good Deed/Selfless Act/Random Kindness: _____
- ☐ I gave undivided attention to: _____
- ☐ I made things better by: _____
- ☐ I experienced joy, happiness, fun and/or laughter: _____
- ☐ I smiled _____ minutes
- ☐ Meditation/Prayer _____ minutes
- ☐ Inspiration (reading, video, music): _____
- ☐ I listened to my intuition: _____
- ☐ Physical activity _____ minutes
- ☐ I was 100% honest today
- ☐ I took care of myself by: _____
- ☐ Reviewed purpose 3 times
- ☐ Reviewed intentions 3 times
- ☐ Steps toward goals, intentions and purpose
    1. _____ 2. _____ 3. _____
- ☐ Reviewed vision
- ☐ I am grateful for:
    1. _____   6. _____
    2. _____   7. _____
    3. _____   8. _____
    4. _____   9. _____
    5. _____   10. _____

- ☐ I am looking forward to: _____

Notes: _____
_____
_____

Mindful Living Worksheet

M Tu W Th F S S   Date:_____   Rate:_____

- ☐ I am content with: _____
- ☐ I am proud of: _____
- ☐ Success review
- ☐ I love myself because: _____ ☐
- ☐ Love, thanks, kindness and support for others:
  - 1. _____   2. _____
  - 3. _____   4. _____
- ☐ Love, thanks, kindness and support for me:
  - 1. _____   2. _____
  - 3. _____   4. _____
- ☐ Good Deed/Selfless Act/Random Kindness: _____
- ☐ I gave undivided attention to: _____
- ☐ I made things better by: _____
- ☐ I experienced joy, happiness, fun and/or laughter: _____
- ☐ I smiled _____ minutes
- ☐ Meditation/Prayer _____ minutes
- ☐ Inspiration (reading, video, music): _____
- ☐ I listened to my intuition: _____
- ☐ Physical activity _____ minutes
- ☐ I was 100% honest today
- ☐ I took care of myself by: _____
- ☐ Reviewed purpose 3 times
- ☐ Reviewed intentions 3 times
- ☐ Steps toward goals, intentions and purpose
  - 1. _____   2. _____   3. _____
- ☐ Reviewed vision
- ☐ I am grateful for:
  - 1. _____   6. _____
  - 2. _____   7. _____
  - 3. _____   8. _____
  - 4. _____   9. _____
  - 5. _____   10. _____
- ☐ I am looking forward to: _____

Notes: _____
_____
_____

Mindful Living Worksheet

M Tu W Th F S S   Date:_____   Rate:_____

- ☐ I am content with: _____
- ☐ I am proud of: _____
- ☐ Success review
- ☐ I love myself because: _____ ☐
- ☐ Love, thanks, kindness and support for others:
  - 1. _____   2. _____
  - 3. _____   4. _____
- ☐ Love, thanks, kindness and support for me:
  - 1. _____   2. _____
  - 3. _____   4. _____
- ☐ Good Deed/Selfless Act/Random Kindness: _____
- ☐ I gave undivided attention to: _____
- ☐ I made things better by: _____
- ☐ I experienced joy, happiness, fun and/or laughter: _____
- ☐ I smiled _____ minutes
- ☐ Meditation/Prayer _____ minutes
- ☐ Inspiration (reading, video, music): _____
- ☐ I listened to my intuition: _____
- ☐ Physical activity _____ minutes
- ☐ I was 100% honest today
- ☐ I took care of myself by: _____
- ☐ Reviewed purpose 3 times
- ☐ Reviewed intentions 3 times
- ☐ Steps toward goals, intentions and purpose
  - 1. _____   2. _____   3. _____
- ☐ Reviewed vision
- ☐ I am grateful for:
  - 1. _____   6. _____
  - 2. _____   7. _____
  - 3. _____   8. _____
  - 4. _____   9. _____
  - 5. _____   10. _____

- ☐ I am looking forward to: _____

Notes: _____
_____
_____
_____

Mindful Living Worksheet

M Tu W Th F S S   Date:_____   Rate:_____

- ☐ I am content with: _____
- ☐ I am proud of: _____
- ☐ Success review
- ☐ I love myself because: _____ ☐
- ☐ Love, thanks, kindness and support for others:
  - 1. _____ 2. _____
  - 3. _____ 4. _____
- ☐ Love, thanks, kindness and support for me:
  - 1. _____ 2. _____
  - 3. _____ 4. _____
- ☐ Good Deed/Selfless Act/Random Kindness: _____
- ☐ I gave undivided attention to: _____
- ☐ I made things better by: _____
- ☐ I experienced joy, happiness, fun and/or laughter: _____
- ☐ I smiled _____ minutes
- ☐ Meditation/Prayer _____ minutes
- ☐ Inspiration (reading, video, music): _____
- ☐ I listened to my intuition: _____
- ☐ Physical activity _____ minutes
- ☐ I was 100% honest today
- ☐ I took care of myself by: _____
- ☐ Reviewed purpose 3 times
- ☐ Reviewed intentions 3 times
- ☐ Steps toward goals, intentions and purpose
  - 1. _____ 2. _____ 3. _____
- ☐ Reviewed vision
- ☐ I am grateful for:
  - 1. _____ 6. _____
  - 2. _____ 7. _____
  - 3. _____ 8. _____
  - 4. _____ 9. _____
  - 5. _____ 10. _____

- ☐ I am looking forward to: _____

Notes: _____
_____
_____
_____

MINDFUL LIVING WORKSHEET

M   Tu   W   Th   F   S   S   Date:_____   Rate:_____

- ☐ I am content with: _____
- ☐ I am proud of: _____
- ☐ Success review
- ☐ I love myself because: _____ ☐
- ☐ Love, thanks, kindness and support for others:
    1. _____   2. _____
    3. _____   4. _____
- ☐ Love, thanks, kindness and support for me:
    1. _____   2. _____
    3. _____   4. _____
- ☐ Good Deed/Selfless Act/Random Kindness: _____
- ☐ I gave undivided attention to: _____
- ☐ I made things better by: _____
- ☐ I experienced joy, happiness, fun and/or laughter: _____
- ☐ I smiled _____ minutes
- ☐ Meditation/Prayer _____ minutes
- ☐ Inspiration (reading, video, music): _____
- ☐ I listened to my intuition: _____
- ☐ Physical activity _____ minutes
- ☐ I was 100% honest today
- ☐ I took care of myself by: _____
- ☐ Reviewed purpose 3 times
- ☐ Reviewed intentions 3 times
- ☐ Steps toward goals, intentions and purpose
    1. _____   2. _____   3. _____
- ☐ Reviewed vision
- ☐ I am grateful for:
    1. _____   6. _____
    2. _____   7. _____
    3. _____   8. _____
    4. _____   9. _____
    5. _____   10. _____

- ☐ I am looking forward to: _____

Notes: _____
_____
_____

MINDFUL LIVING WORKSHEET

M Tu W Th F S S   Date:_____   Rate:_____

- ☐ I am content with: _____
- ☐ I am proud of: _____
- ☐ Success review
- ☐ I love myself because: _____ ☐
- ☐ Love, thanks, kindness and support for others:
    - 1. _____   2. _____
    - 3. _____   4. _____
- ☐ Love, thanks, kindness and support for me:
    - 1. _____   2. _____
    - 3. _____   4. _____
- ☐ Good Deed/Selfless Act/Random Kindness: _____
- ☐ I gave undivided attention to: _____
- ☐ I made things better by: _____
- ☐ I experienced joy, happiness, fun and/or laughter: _____
- ☐ I smiled _____ minutes
- ☐ Meditation/Prayer _____ minutes
- ☐ Inspiration (reading, video, music): _____
- ☐ I listened to my intuition: _____
- ☐ Physical activity _____ minutes
- ☐ I was 100% honest today
- ☐ I took care of myself by: _____
- ☐ Reviewed purpose 3 times
- ☐ Reviewed intentions 3 times
- ☐ Steps toward goals, intentions and purpose
    - 1. _____   2. _____   3. _____
- ☐ Reviewed vision
- ☐ I am grateful for:
    - 1. _____   6. _____
    - 2. _____   7. _____
    - 3. _____   8. _____
    - 4. _____   9. _____
    - 5. _____   10. _____

- ☐ I am looking forward to: _____

Notes: _____
_____
_____

MINDFUL LIVING WORKSHEET

M Tu W Th F S S   Date:_____   Rate:_____

- ☐ I am content with: _____
- ☐ I am proud of: _____
- ☐ Success review
- ☐ I love myself because: _____ ☐
- ☐ Love, thanks, kindness and support for others:
    - 1. _____   2. _____
    - 3. _____   4. _____
- ☐ Love, thanks, kindness and support for me:
    - 1. _____   2. _____
    - 3. _____   4. _____
- ☐ Good Deed/Selfless Act/Random Kindness: _____
- ☐ I gave undivided attention to: _____
- ☐ I made things better by: _____
- ☐ I experienced joy, happiness, fun and/or laughter: _____
- ☐ I smiled _____ minutes
- ☐ Meditation/Prayer _____ minutes
- ☐ Inspiration (reading, video, music): _____
- ☐ I listened to my intuition: _____
- ☐ Physical activity _____ minutes
- ☐ I was 100% honest today
- ☐ I took care of myself by: _____
- ☐ Reviewed purpose 3 times
- ☐ Reviewed intentions 3 times
- ☐ Steps toward goals, intentions and purpose
    - 1. _____   2. _____   3. _____
- ☐ Reviewed vision
- ☐ I am grateful for:
    - 1. _____   6. _____
    - 2. _____   7. _____
    - 3. _____   8. _____
    - 4. _____   9. _____
    - 5. _____   10. _____

- ☐ I am looking forward to: _____

Notes: _____
_____
_____
_____

Mindful Living Worksheet

M Tu W Th F S S   Date:_____   Rate:_____

- ☐ I am content with: _____
- ☐ I am proud of: _____
- ☐ Success review
- ☐ I love myself because: _____ ☐
- ☐ Love, thanks, kindness and support for others:
    - 1. _____   2. _____
    - 3. _____   4. _____
- ☐ Love, thanks, kindness and support for me:
    - 1. _____   2. _____
    - 3. _____   4. _____
- ☐ Good Deed/Selfless Act/Random Kindness: _____
- ☐ I gave undivided attention to: _____
- ☐ I made things better by: _____
- ☐ I experienced joy, happiness, fun and/or laughter: _____
- ☐ I smiled _____ minutes
- ☐ Meditation/Prayer _____ minutes
- ☐ Inspiration (reading, video, music): _____
- ☐ I listened to my intuition: _____
- ☐ Physical activity _____ minutes
- ☐ I was 100% honest today
- ☐ I took care of myself by: _____
- ☐ Reviewed purpose 3 times
- ☐ Reviewed intentions 3 times
- ☐ Steps toward goals, intentions and purpose
    - 1. _____ 2. _____ 3. _____
- ☐ Reviewed vision
- ☐ I am grateful for:
    - 1. _____   6. _____
    - 2. _____   7. _____
    - 3. _____   8. _____
    - 4. _____   9. _____
    - 5. _____   10. _____

- ☐ I am looking forward to: _____

Notes: _____
_____
_____

MINDFUL LIVING WORKSHEET

M   Tu   W   Th   F   S   S   Date:_____   Rate:_____

- ☐ I am content with: _____
- ☐ I am proud of: _____
- ☐ Success review
- ☐ I love myself because: _____ ☐
- ☐ Love, thanks, kindness and support for others:
  - 1. _____   2. _____
  - 3. _____   4. _____
- ☐ Love, thanks, kindness and support for me:
  - 1. _____   2. _____
  - 3. _____   4. _____
- ☐ Good Deed/Selfless Act/Random Kindness: _____
- ☐ I gave undivided attention to: _____
- ☐ I made things better by: _____
- ☐ I experienced joy, happiness, fun and/or laughter: _____
- ☐ I smiled _____ minutes
- ☐ Meditation/Prayer _____ minutes
- ☐ Inspiration (reading, video, music): _____
- ☐ I listened to my intuition: _____
- ☐ Physical activity _____ minutes
- ☐ I was 100% honest today
- ☐ I took care of myself by: _____
- ☐ Reviewed purpose 3 times
- ☐ Reviewed intentions 3 times
- ☐ Steps toward goals, intentions and purpose
  - 1. _____   2. _____   3. _____
- ☐ Reviewed vision
- ☐ I am grateful for:
  - 1. _____   6. _____
  - 2. _____   7. _____
  - 3. _____   8. _____
  - 4. _____   9. _____
  - 5. _____   10. _____

- ☐ I am looking forward to: _____

Notes: _____
_____
_____

MINDFUL LIVING WORKSHEET

M Tu W Th F S S   Date:_____   Rate:_____

- ☐ I am content with: _____
- ☐ I am proud of: _____
- ☐ Success review
- ☐ I love myself because: _____ ☐
- ☐ Love, thanks, kindness and support for others:
  - 1. _____   2. _____
  - 3. _____   4. _____
- ☐ Love, thanks, kindness and support for me:
  - 1. _____   2. _____
  - 3. _____   4. _____
- ☐ Good Deed/Selfless Act/Random Kindness: _____
- ☐ I gave undivided attention to: _____
- ☐ I made things better by: _____
- ☐ I experienced joy, happiness, fun and/or laughter: _____
- ☐ I smiled _____ minutes
- ☐ Meditation/Prayer _____ minutes
- ☐ Inspiration (reading, video, music): _____
- ☐ I listened to my intuition: _____
- ☐ Physical activity _____ minutes
- ☐ I was 100% honest today
- ☐ I took care of myself by: _____
- ☐ Reviewed purpose 3 times
- ☐ Reviewed intentions 3 times
- ☐ Steps toward goals, intentions and purpose
  - 1. _____ 2. _____ 3. _____
- ☐ Reviewed vision
- ☐ I am grateful for:
  - 1. _____   6. _____
  - 2. _____   7. _____
  - 3. _____   8. _____
  - 4. _____   9. _____
  - 5. _____   10. _____

- ☐ I am looking forward to: _____

Notes: _____
_____
_____
_____

Mindful Living Worksheet

M Tu W Th F S S   Date:_____   Rate:_____

- ☐ I am content with: _____
- ☐ I am proud of: _____
- ☐ Success review
- ☐ I love myself because: _____ ☐
- ☐ Love, thanks, kindness and support for others:
  - 1. _____   2. _____
  - 3. _____   4. _____
- ☐ Love, thanks, kindness and support for me:
  - 1. _____   2. _____
  - 3. _____   4. _____
- ☐ Good Deed/Selfless Act/Random Kindness: _____
- ☐ I gave undivided attention to: _____
- ☐ I made things better by: _____
- ☐ I experienced joy, happiness, fun and/or laughter: _____
- ☐ I smiled _____ minutes
- ☐ Meditation/Prayer _____ minutes
- ☐ Inspiration (reading, video, music): _____
- ☐ I listened to my intuition: _____
- ☐ Physical activity _____ minutes
- ☐ I was 100% honest today
- ☐ I took care of myself by: _____
- ☐ Reviewed purpose 3 times
- ☐ Reviewed intentions 3 times
- ☐ Steps toward goals, intentions and purpose
  - 1. _____   2. _____   3. _____
- ☐ Reviewed vision
- ☐ I am grateful for:
  - 1. _____   6. _____
  - 2. _____   7. _____
  - 3. _____   8. _____
  - 4. _____   9. _____
  - 5. _____   10. _____
- ☐ I am looking forward to: _____

Notes: _____
_____
_____
_____

MINDFUL LIVING WORKSHEET

M Tu W Th F S S   Date:_____   Rate:_____

- ☐ I am content with: _____
- ☐ I am proud of: _____
- ☐ Success review
- ☐ I love myself because: _____ ☐
- ☐ Love, thanks, kindness and support for others:
    1. _____   2. _____
    3. _____   4. _____
- ☐ Love, thanks, kindness and support for me:
    1. _____   2. _____
    3. _____   4. _____
- ☐ Good Deed/Selfless Act/Random Kindness: _____
- ☐ I gave undivided attention to: _____
- ☐ I made things better by: _____
- ☐ I experienced joy, happiness, fun and/or laughter: _____
- ☐ I smiled _____ minutes
- ☐ Meditation/Prayer _____ minutes
- ☐ Inspiration (reading, video, music): _____
- ☐ I listened to my intuition: _____
- ☐ Physical activity _____ minutes
- ☐ I was 100% honest today
- ☐ I took care of myself by: _____
- ☐ Reviewed purpose 3 times
- ☐ Reviewed intentions 3 times
- ☐ Steps toward goals, intentions and purpose
    1. _____ 2. _____ 3. _____
- ☐ Reviewed vision
- ☐ I am grateful for:
    1. _____   6. _____
    2. _____   7. _____
    3. _____   8. _____
    4. _____   9. _____
    5. _____   10. _____

- ☐ I am looking forward to: _____

Notes: _____
_____
_____

Mindful Living Worksheet

M Tu W Th F S S   Date:_____   Rate:_____

- ☐ I am content with: _____
- ☐ I am proud of: _____
- ☐ Success review
- ☐ I love myself because: _____ ☐
- ☐ Love, thanks, kindness and support for others:
  - 1. _____   2. _____
  - 3. _____   4. _____
- ☐ Love, thanks, kindness and support for me:
  - 1. _____   2. _____
  - 3. _____   4. _____
- ☐ Good Deed/Selfless Act/Random Kindness: _____
- ☐ I gave undivided attention to: _____
- ☐ I made things better by: _____
- ☐ I experienced joy, happiness, fun and/or laughter: _____
- ☐ I smiled _____ minutes
- ☐ Meditation/Prayer _____ minutes
- ☐ Inspiration (reading, video, music): _____
- ☐ I listened to my intuition: _____
- ☐ Physical activity _____ minutes
- ☐ I was 100% honest today
- ☐ I took care of myself by: _____
- ☐ Reviewed purpose 3 times
- ☐ Reviewed intentions 3 times
- ☐ Steps toward goals, intentions and purpose
  - 1. _____   2. _____   3. _____
- ☐ Reviewed vision
- ☐ I am grateful for:
  - 1. _____   6. _____
  - 2. _____   7. _____
  - 3. _____   8. _____
  - 4. _____   9. _____
  - 5. _____   10. _____

- ☐ I am looking forward to: _____

Notes: _____
_____
_____

MINDFUL LIVING WORKSHEET

M Tu W Th F S S   Date:_____   Rate:_____

- ☐ I am content with: _____
- ☐ I am proud of: _____
- ☐ Success review
- ☐ I love myself because: _____ ☐
- ☐ Love, thanks, kindness and support for others:
  - 1. _____   2. _____
  - 3. _____   4. _____
- ☐ Love, thanks, kindness and support for me:
  - 1. _____   2. _____
  - 3. _____   4. _____
- ☐ Good Deed/Selfless Act/Random Kindness: _____
- ☐ I gave undivided attention to: _____
- ☐ I made things better by: _____
- ☐ I experienced joy, happiness, fun and/or laughter: _____
- ☐ I smiled _____ minutes
- ☐ Meditation/Prayer _____ minutes
- ☐ Inspiration (reading, video, music): _____
- ☐ I listened to my intuition: _____
- ☐ Physical activity _____ minutes
- ☐ I was 100% honest today
- ☐ I took care of myself by: _____
- ☐ Reviewed purpose 3 times
- ☐ Reviewed intentions 3 times
- ☐ Steps toward goals, intentions and purpose
  - 1. _____ 2. _____ 3. _____
- ☐ Reviewed vision
- ☐ I am grateful for:
  - 1. _____   6. _____
  - 2. _____   7. _____
  - 3. _____   8. _____
  - 4. _____   9. _____
  - 5. _____   10. _____

- ☐ I am looking forward to: _____

Notes: _____
_____
_____
_____

MINDFUL LIVING WORKSHEET

M Tu W Th F S S   Date:_____   Rate:_____

- ☐ I am content with: _____
- ☐ I am proud of: _____
- ☐ Success review
- ☐ I love myself because: _____ ☐
- ☐ Love, thanks, kindness and support for others:
    1. _____   2. _____
    3. _____   4. _____
- ☐ Love, thanks, kindness and support for me:
    1. _____   2. _____
    3. _____   4. _____
- ☐ Good Deed/Selfless Act/Random Kindness: _____
- ☐ I gave undivided attention to: _____
- ☐ I made things better by: _____
- ☐ I experienced joy, happiness, fun and/or laughter: _____
- ☐ I smiled _____ minutes
- ☐ Meditation/Prayer _____ minutes
- ☐ Inspiration (reading, video, music): _____
- ☐ I listened to my intuition: _____
- ☐ Physical activity _____ minutes
- ☐ I was 100% honest today
- ☐ I took care of myself by: _____
- ☐ Reviewed purpose 3 times
- ☐ Reviewed intentions 3 times
- ☐ Steps toward goals, intentions and purpose
    1. _____   2. _____   3. _____
- ☐ Reviewed vision
- ☐ I am grateful for:
    1. _____   6. _____
    2. _____   7. _____
    3. _____   8. _____
    4. _____   9. _____
    5. _____   10. _____

- ☐ I am looking forward to: _____

Notes: _____
_____
_____

MINDFUL LIVING WORKSHEET

M Tu W Th F S S   Date:_____   Rate:_____

- ☐ I am content with: _____
- ☐ I am proud of: _____
- ☐ Success review
- ☐ I love myself because: _____ ☐
- ☐ Love, thanks, kindness and support for others:
     1. _____   2. _____
     3. _____   4. _____
- ☐ Love, thanks, kindness and support for me:
     1. _____   2. _____
     3. _____   4. _____
- ☐ Good Deed/Selfless Act/Random Kindness: _____
- ☐ I gave undivided attention to: _____
- ☐ I made things better by: _____
- ☐ I experienced joy, happiness, fun and/or laughter: _____
- ☐ I smiled _____ minutes
- ☐ Meditation/Prayer _____ minutes
- ☐ Inspiration (reading, video, music): _____
- ☐ I listened to my intuition: _____
- ☐ Physical activity _____ minutes
- ☐ I was 100% honest today
- ☐ I took care of myself by: _____
- ☐ Reviewed purpose 3 times
- ☐ Reviewed intentions 3 times
- ☐ Steps toward goals, intentions and purpose
     1. _____   2. _____   3. _____
- ☐ Reviewed vision
- ☐ I am grateful for:
     1. _____   6. _____
     2. _____   7. _____
     3. _____   8. _____
     4. _____   9. _____
     5. _____   10. _____

- ☐ I am looking forward to: _____

Notes: _____
_____
_____
_____

Mindful Living Worksheet

M Tu W Th F S S   Date:_____   Rate:_____

- ☐ I am content with: _____
- ☐ I am proud of: _____
- ☐ Success review
- ☐ I love myself because: _____ ☐
- ☐ Love, thanks, kindness and support for others:
  - 1. _____   2. _____
  - 3. _____   4. _____
- ☐ Love, thanks, kindness and support for me:
  - 1. _____   2. _____
  - 3. _____   4. _____
- ☐ Good Deed/Selfless Act/Random Kindness: _____
- ☐ I gave undivided attention to: _____
- ☐ I made things better by: _____
- ☐ I experienced joy, happiness, fun and/or laughter: _____
- ☐ I smiled _____ minutes
- ☐ Meditation/Prayer _____ minutes
- ☐ Inspiration (reading, video, music): _____
- ☐ I listened to my intuition: _____
- ☐ Physical activity _____ minutes
- ☐ I was 100% honest today
- ☐ I took care of myself by: _____
- ☐ Reviewed purpose 3 times
- ☐ Reviewed intentions 3 times
- ☐ Steps toward goals, intentions and purpose
  - 1. _____   2. _____   3. _____
- ☐ Reviewed vision
- ☐ I am grateful for:
  - 1. _____   6. _____
  - 2. _____   7. _____
  - 3. _____   8. _____
  - 4. _____   9. _____
  - 5. _____   10. _____

- ☐ I am looking forward to: _____

Notes: _____
_____
_____

Mindful Living Worksheet

M Tu W Th F S S   Date:_____   Rate:_____

- ☐ I am content with: _____
- ☐ I am proud of: _____
- ☐ Success review
- ☐ I love myself because: _____ ☐
- ☐ Love, thanks, kindness and support for others:
    1. _____   2. _____
    3. _____   4. _____
- ☐ Love, thanks, kindness and support for me:
    1. _____   2. _____
    3. _____   4. _____
- ☐ Good Deed/Selfless Act/Random Kindness: _____
- ☐ I gave undivided attention to: _____
- ☐ I made things better by: _____
- ☐ I experienced joy, happiness, fun and/or laughter: _____
- ☐ I smiled _____ minutes
- ☐ Meditation/Prayer _____ minutes
- ☐ Inspiration (reading, video, music): _____
- ☐ I listened to my intuition: _____
- ☐ Physical activity _____ minutes
- ☐ I was 100% honest today
- ☐ I took care of myself by: _____
- ☐ Reviewed purpose 3 times
- ☐ Reviewed intentions 3 times
- ☐ Steps toward goals, intentions and purpose
    1. _____ 2. _____ 3. _____
- ☐ Reviewed vision
- ☐ I am grateful for:
    1. _____   6. _____
    2. _____   7. _____
    3. _____   8. _____
    4. _____   9. _____
    5. _____   10. _____

- ☐ I am looking forward to: _____

Notes: _____
_____
_____
_____

MINDFUL LIVING WORKSHEET

M   Tu   W   Th   F   S   S   Date:_____   Rate:_____

- ☐ I am content with: _____
- ☐ I am proud of: _____
- ☐ Success review
- ☐ I love myself because: _____ ☐
- ☐ Love, thanks, kindness and support for others:
    1. _____   2. _____
    3. _____   4. _____
- ☐ Love, thanks, kindness and support for me:
    1. _____   2. _____
    3. _____   4. _____
- ☐ Good Deed/Selfless Act/Random Kindness: _____
- ☐ I gave undivided attention to: _____
- ☐ I made things better by: _____
- ☐ I experienced joy, happiness, fun and/or laughter: _____
- ☐ I smiled _____ minutes
- ☐ Meditation/Prayer _____ minutes
- ☐ Inspiration (reading, video, music): _____
- ☐ I listened to my intuition: _____
- ☐ Physical activity _____ minutes
- ☐ I was 100% honest today
- ☐ I took care of myself by: _____
- ☐ Reviewed purpose 3 times
- ☐ Reviewed intentions 3 times
- ☐ Steps toward goals, intentions and purpose
    1. _____   2. _____   3. _____
- ☐ Reviewed vision
- ☐ I am grateful for:
    1. _____   6. _____
    2. _____   7. _____
    3. _____   8. _____
    4. _____   9. _____
    5. _____   10. _____

- ☐ I am looking forward to: _____

Notes: _____
_____
_____
_____

Mindful Living Worksheet

M Tu W Th F S S   Date:_____   Rate:_____

- ☐ I am content with: _____
- ☐ I am proud of: _____
- ☐ Success review
- ☐ I love myself because: _____ ☐
- ☐ Love, thanks, kindness and support for others:
    1. _____   2. _____
    3. _____   4. _____
- ☐ Love, thanks, kindness and support for me:
    1. _____   2. _____
    3. _____   4. _____
- ☐ Good Deed/Selfless Act/Random Kindness: _____
- ☐ I gave undivided attention to: _____
- ☐ I made things better by: _____
- ☐ I experienced joy, happiness, fun and/or laughter: _____
- ☐ I smiled _____ minutes
- ☐ Meditation/Prayer _____ minutes
- ☐ Inspiration (reading, video, music): _____
- ☐ I listened to my intuition: _____
- ☐ Physical activity _____ minutes
- ☐ I was 100% honest today
- ☐ I took care of myself by: _____
- ☐ Reviewed purpose 3 times
- ☐ Reviewed intentions 3 times
- ☐ Steps toward goals, intentions and purpose
    1. _____ 2. _____ 3. _____
- ☐ Reviewed vision
- ☐ I am grateful for:
    1. _____   6. _____
    2. _____   7. _____
    3. _____   8. _____
    4. _____   9. _____
    5. _____   10. _____

- ☐ I am looking forward to: _____

Notes: _____
_____
_____

MINDFUL LIVING WORKSHEET

M Tu W Th F S S   Date:_____   Rate:_____

- ☐ I am content with: _____
- ☐ I am proud of: _____
- ☐ Success review
- ☐ I love myself because: _____ ☐
- ☐ Love, thanks, kindness and support for others:
  - 1. _____   2. _____
  - 3. _____   4. _____
- ☐ Love, thanks, kindness and support for me:
  - 1. _____   2. _____
  - 3. _____   4. _____
- ☐ Good Deed/Selfless Act/Random Kindness: _____
- ☐ I gave undivided attention to: _____
- ☐ I made things better by: _____
- ☐ I experienced joy, happiness, fun and/or laughter: _____
- ☐ I smiled _____ minutes
- ☐ Meditation/Prayer _____ minutes
- ☐ Inspiration (reading, video, music): _____
- ☐ I listened to my intuition: _____
- ☐ Physical activity _____ minutes
- ☐ I was 100% honest today
- ☐ I took care of myself by: _____
- ☐ Reviewed purpose 3 times
- ☐ Reviewed intentions 3 times
- ☐ Steps toward goals, intentions and purpose
  - 1. _____ 2. _____ 3. _____
- ☐ Reviewed vision
- ☐ I am grateful for:
  - 1. _____   6. _____
  - 2. _____   7. _____
  - 3. _____   8. _____
  - 4. _____   9. _____
  - 5. _____   10. _____

- ☐ I am looking forward to: _____

Notes: _____
_____
_____
_____

MINDFUL LIVING WORKSHEET

M   Tu   W   Th   F   S   S   Date:_____   Rate:_____

- ☐ I am content with: _____
- ☐ I am proud of: _____
- ☐ Success review
- ☐ I love myself because: _____ ☐
- ☐ Love, thanks, kindness and support for others:
    - 1. _____   2. _____
    - 3. _____   4. _____
- ☐ Love, thanks, kindness and support for me:
    - 1. _____   2. _____
    - 3. _____   4. _____
- ☐ Good Deed/Selfless Act/Random Kindness: _____
- ☐ I gave undivided attention to: _____
- ☐ I made things better by: _____
- ☐ I experienced joy, happiness, fun and/or laughter: _____
- ☐ I smiled _____ minutes
- ☐ Meditation/Prayer _____ minutes
- ☐ Inspiration (reading, video, music): _____
- ☐ I listened to my intuition: _____
- ☐ Physical activity _____ minutes
- ☐ I was 100% honest today
- ☐ I took care of myself by: _____
- ☐ Reviewed purpose 3 times
- ☐ Reviewed intentions 3 times
- ☐ Steps toward goals, intentions and purpose
    - 1. _____   2. _____   3. _____
- ☐ Reviewed vision
- ☐ I am grateful for:
    - 1. _____   6. _____
    - 2. _____   7. _____
    - 3. _____   8. _____
    - 4. _____   9. _____
    - 5. _____   10. _____

- ☐ I am looking forward to: _____

Notes: _____
_____
_____
_____

MINDFUL LIVING WORKSHEET

M Tu W Th F S S   Date: _____   Rate: _____

- ☐ I am content with: _____
- ☐ I am proud of: _____
- ☐ Success review
- ☐ I love myself because: _____ ☐
- ☐ Love, thanks, kindness and support for others:
  - 1. _____   2. _____
  - 3. _____   4. _____
- ☐ Love, thanks, kindness and support for me:
  - 1. _____   2. _____
  - 3. _____   4. _____
- ☐ Good Deed/Selfless Act/Random Kindness: _____
- ☐ I gave undivided attention to: _____
- ☐ I made things better by: _____
- ☐ I experienced joy, happiness, fun and/or laughter: _____
- ☐ I smiled _____ minutes
- ☐ Meditation/Prayer _____ minutes
- ☐ Inspiration (reading, video, music): _____
- ☐ I listened to my intuition: _____
- ☐ Physical activity _____ minutes
- ☐ I was 100% honest today
- ☐ I took care of myself by: _____
- ☐ Reviewed purpose 3 times
- ☐ Reviewed intentions 3 times
- ☐ Steps toward goals, intentions and purpose
  - 1. _____   2. _____   3. _____
- ☐ Reviewed vision
- ☐ I am grateful for:
  - 1. _____   6. _____
  - 2. _____   7. _____
  - 3. _____   8. _____
  - 4. _____   9. _____
  - 5. _____   10. _____

- ☐ I am looking forward to: _____

Notes: _____
_____
_____

MINDFUL LIVING WORKSHEET

M Tu W Th F S S   Date:_____   Rate:_____

- ☐ I am content with: _____
- ☐ I am proud of: _____
- ☐ Success review
- ☐ I love myself because: _____ ☐
- ☐ Love, thanks, kindness and support for others:
    1. _____   2. _____
    3. _____   4. _____
- ☐ Love, thanks, kindness and support for me:
    1. _____   2. _____
    3. _____   4. _____
- ☐ Good Deed/Selfless Act/Random Kindness: _____
- ☐ I gave undivided attention to: _____
- ☐ I made things better by: _____
- ☐ I experienced joy, happiness, fun and/or laughter: _____
- ☐ I smiled _____ minutes
- ☐ Meditation/Prayer _____ minutes
- ☐ Inspiration (reading, video, music): _____
- ☐ I listened to my intuition: _____
- ☐ Physical activity _____ minutes
- ☐ I was 100% honest today
- ☐ I took care of myself by: _____
- ☐ Reviewed purpose 3 times
- ☐ Reviewed intentions 3 times
- ☐ Steps toward goals, intentions and purpose
    1. _____ 2. _____ 3. _____
- ☐ Reviewed vision
- ☐ I am grateful for:
    1. _____   6. _____
    2. _____   7. _____
    3. _____   8. _____
    4. _____   9. _____
    5. _____   10. _____

- ☐ I am looking forward to: _____

Notes: _____
_____
_____

Mindful Living Worksheet

M Tu W Th F S S   Date:_____   Rate:_____

- ☐ I am content with: _____
- ☐ I am proud of: _____
- ☐ Success review
- ☐ I love myself because: _____ ☐
- ☐ Love, thanks, kindness and support for others:
  - 1. _____   2. _____
  - 3. _____   4. _____
- ☐ Love, thanks, kindness and support for me:
  - 1. _____   2. _____
  - 3. _____   4. _____
- ☐ Good Deed/Selfless Act/Random Kindness: _____
- ☐ I gave undivided attention to: _____
- ☐ I made things better by: _____
- ☐ I experienced joy, happiness, fun and/or laughter: _____
- ☐ I smiled _____ minutes
- ☐ Meditation/Prayer _____ minutes
- ☐ Inspiration (reading, video, music): _____
- ☐ I listened to my intuition: _____
- ☐ Physical activity _____ minutes
- ☐ I was 100% honest today
- ☐ I took care of myself by: _____
- ☐ Reviewed purpose 3 times
- ☐ Reviewed intentions 3 times
- ☐ Steps toward goals, intentions and purpose
  - 1. _____   2. _____   3. _____
- ☐ Reviewed vision
- ☐ I am grateful for:
  - 1. _____   6. _____
  - 2. _____   7. _____
  - 3. _____   8. _____
  - 4. _____   9. _____
  - 5. _____   10. _____

- ☐ I am looking forward to: _____

Notes: _____
_____
_____
_____

MINDFUL LIVING WORKSHEET

M   Tu   W   Th   F   S   S   Date:_____   Rate:_____

☐ I am content with: _____
☐ I am proud of: _____
☐ Success review
☐ I love myself because: _____ ☐
☐ Love, thanks, kindness and support for others:
    1. _____   2. _____
    3. _____   4. _____
☐ Love, thanks, kindness and support for me:
    1. _____   2. _____
    3. _____   4. _____
☐ Good Deed/Selfless Act/Random Kindness: _____
☐ I gave undivided attention to: _____
☐ I made things better by: _____
☐ I experienced joy, happiness, fun and/or laughter: _____
☐ I smiled _____ minutes
☐ Meditation/Prayer _____ minutes
☐ Inspiration (reading, video, music): _____
☐ I listened to my intuition: _____
☐ Physical activity _____ minutes
☐ I was 100% honest today
☐ I took care of myself by: _____
☐ Reviewed purpose 3 times
☐ Reviewed intentions 3 times
☐ Steps toward goals, intentions and purpose
    1. _____ 2. _____ 3. _____
☐ Reviewed vision
☐ I am grateful for:
    1. _____   6. _____
    2. _____   7. _____
    3. _____   8. _____
    4. _____   9. _____
    5. _____   10. _____

☐ I am looking forward to: _____

Notes: _____
_____
_____
_____

Mindful Living Worksheet

M Tu W Th F S S   Date:_____   Rate:_____

- ☐ I am content with: _____
- ☐ I am proud of: _____
- ☐ Success review
- ☐ I love myself because: _____ ☐
- ☐ Love, thanks, kindness and support for others:
  - 1. _____   2. _____
  - 3. _____   4. _____
- ☐ Love, thanks, kindness and support for me:
  - 1. _____   2. _____
  - 3. _____   4. _____
- ☐ Good Deed/Selfless Act/Random Kindness: _____
- ☐ I gave undivided attention to: _____
- ☐ I made things better by: _____
- ☐ I experienced joy, happiness, fun and/or laughter: _____
- ☐ I smiled _____ minutes
- ☐ Meditation/Prayer _____ minutes
- ☐ Inspiration (reading, video, music): _____
- ☐ I listened to my intuition: _____
- ☐ Physical activity _____ minutes
- ☐ I was 100% honest today
- ☐ I took care of myself by: _____
- ☐ Reviewed purpose 3 times
- ☐ Reviewed intentions 3 times
- ☐ Steps toward goals, intentions and purpose
  - 1. _____   2. _____   3. _____
- ☐ Reviewed vision
- ☐ I am grateful for:
  - 1. _____   6. _____
  - 2. _____   7. _____
  - 3. _____   8. _____
  - 4. _____   9. _____
  - 5. _____   10. _____

- ☐ I am looking forward to: _____

Notes: _____
_____
_____

MINDFUL LIVING WORKSHEET

M Tu W Th F S S   Date:_____   Rate:_____

- ☐ I am content with: _____
- ☐ I am proud of: _____
- ☐ Success review
- ☐ I love myself because: _____ ☐
- ☐ Love, thanks, kindness and support for others:
  - 1. _____   2. _____
  - 3. _____   4. _____
- ☐ Love, thanks, kindness and support for me:
  - 1. _____   2. _____
  - 3. _____   4. _____
- ☐ Good Deed/Selfless Act/Random Kindness: _____
- ☐ I gave undivided attention to: _____
- ☐ I made things better by: _____
- ☐ I experienced joy, happiness, fun and/or laughter: _____
- ☐ I smiled _____ minutes
- ☐ Meditation/Prayer _____ minutes
- ☐ Inspiration (reading, video, music): _____
- ☐ I listened to my intuition: _____
- ☐ Physical activity _____ minutes
- ☐ I was 100% honest today
- ☐ I took care of myself by: _____
- ☐ Reviewed purpose 3 times
- ☐ Reviewed intentions 3 times
- ☐ Steps toward goals, intentions and purpose
  - 1. _____   2. _____   3. _____
- ☐ Reviewed vision
- ☐ I am grateful for:
  - 1. _____   6. _____
  - 2. _____   7. _____
  - 3. _____   8. _____
  - 4. _____   9. _____
  - 5. _____   10. _____

- ☐ I am looking forward to: _____

Notes: _____
_____
_____
_____

MINDFUL LIVING WORKSHEET

M   Tu   W   Th   F   S   S   Date:_____   Rate:_____

- ☐ I am content with: _____
- ☐ I am proud of: _____
- ☐ Success review
- ☐ I love myself because: _____ ☐
- ☐ Love, thanks, kindness and support for others:
  - 1. _____   2. _____
  - 3. _____   4. _____
- ☐ Love, thanks, kindness and support for me:
  - 1. _____   2. _____
  - 3. _____   4. _____
- ☐ Good Deed/Selfless Act/Random Kindness: _____
- ☐ I gave undivided attention to: _____
- ☐ I made things better by: _____
- ☐ I experienced joy, happiness, fun and/or laughter: _____
- ☐ I smiled _____ minutes
- ☐ Meditation/Prayer _____ minutes
- ☐ Inspiration (reading, video, music): _____
- ☐ I listened to my intuition: _____
- ☐ Physical activity _____ minutes
- ☐ I was 100% honest today
- ☐ I took care of myself by: _____
- ☐ Reviewed purpose 3 times
- ☐ Reviewed intentions 3 times
- ☐ Steps toward goals, intentions and purpose
  - 1. _____ 2. _____ 3. _____
- ☐ Reviewed vision
- ☐ I am grateful for:
  - 1. _____   6. _____
  - 2. _____   7. _____
  - 3. _____   8. _____
  - 4. _____   9. _____
  - 5. _____   10. _____

- ☐ I am looking forward to: _____

Notes: _____
_____
_____
_____

MINDFUL LIVING WORKSHEET

M Tu W Th F S S   Date:_____   Rate:_____

☐ I am content with: _____
☐ I am proud of: _____
☐ Success review
☐ I love myself because: _____ ☐
☐ Love, thanks, kindness and support for others:
    1. _____   2. _____
    3. _____   4. _____
☐ Love, thanks, kindness and support for me:
    1. _____   2. _____
    3. _____   4. _____
☐ Good Deed/Selfless Act/Random Kindness: _____
☐ I gave undivided attention to: _____
☐ I made things better by: _____
☐ I experienced joy, happiness, fun and/or laughter: _____
☐ I smiled _____ minutes
☐ Meditation/Prayer _____ minutes
☐ Inspiration (reading, video, music): _____
☐ I listened to my intuition: _____
☐ Physical activity _____ minutes
☐ I was 100% honest today
☐ I took care of myself by: _____
☐ Reviewed purpose 3 times
☐ Reviewed intentions 3 times
☐ Steps toward goals, intentions and purpose
    1. _____ 2. _____ 3. _____
☐ Reviewed vision
☐ I am grateful for:
    1. _____   6. _____
    2. _____   7. _____
    3. _____   8. _____
    4. _____   9. _____
    5. _____   10. _____

☐ I am looking forward to: _____

Notes: _____
_____
_____
_____

MINDFUL LIVING WORKSHEET

M Tu W Th F S S   Date:_____   Rate:_____

- ☐ I am content with: _____
- ☐ I am proud of: _____
- ☐ Success review
- ☐ I love myself because: _____ ☐
- ☐ Love, thanks, kindness and support for others:
    1. _____   2. _____
    3. _____   4. _____
- ☐ Love, thanks, kindness and support for me:
    1. _____   2. _____
    3. _____   4. _____
- ☐ Good Deed/Selfless Act/Random Kindness: _____
- ☐ I gave undivided attention to: _____
- ☐ I made things better by: _____
- ☐ I experienced joy, happiness, fun and/or laughter: _____
- ☐ I smiled _____ minutes
- ☐ Meditation/Prayer _____ minutes
- ☐ Inspiration (reading, video, music): _____
- ☐ I listened to my intuition: _____
- ☐ Physical activity _____ minutes
- ☐ I was 100% honest today
- ☐ I took care of myself by: _____
- ☐ Reviewed purpose 3 times
- ☐ Reviewed intentions 3 times
- ☐ Steps toward goals, intentions and purpose
    1. _____   2. _____   3. _____
- ☐ Reviewed vision
- ☐ I am grateful for:
    1. _____   6. _____
    2. _____   7. _____
    3. _____   8. _____
    4. _____   9. _____
    5. _____   10. _____

- ☐ I am looking forward to: _____

Notes: _____
_____
_____
_____

MINDFUL LIVING WORKSHEET

M Tu W Th F S S   Date:_____   Rate:_____

- ☐ I am content with: _____
- ☐ I am proud of: _____
- ☐ Success review
- ☐ I love myself because: _____ ☐
- ☐ Love, thanks, kindness and support for others:
    1. _____   2. _____
    3. _____   4. _____
- ☐ Love, thanks, kindness and support for me:
    1. _____   2. _____
    3. _____   4. _____
- ☐ Good Deed/Selfless Act/Random Kindness: _____
- ☐ I gave undivided attention to: _____
- ☐ I made things better by: _____
- ☐ I experienced joy, happiness, fun and/or laughter: _____
- ☐ I smiled _____ minutes
- ☐ Meditation/Prayer _____ minutes
- ☐ Inspiration (reading, video, music): _____
- ☐ I listened to my intuition: _____
- ☐ Physical activity _____ minutes
- ☐ I was 100% honest today
- ☐ I took care of myself by: _____
- ☐ Reviewed purpose 3 times
- ☐ Reviewed intentions 3 times
- ☐ Steps toward goals, intentions and purpose
    1. _____   2. _____   3. _____
- ☐ Reviewed vision
- ☐ I am grateful for:
    1. _____   6. _____
    2. _____   7. _____
    3. _____   8. _____
    4. _____   9. _____
    5. _____   10. _____

- ☐ I am looking forward to: _____

Notes: _____
_____
_____

Mindful Living Worksheet

M Tu W Th F S S   Date:_____   Rate:_____

- ☐ I am content with: _____
- ☐ I am proud of: _____
- ☐ Success review
- ☐ I love myself because: _____ ☐
- ☐ Love, thanks, kindness and support for others:
  - 1. _____   2. _____
  - 3. _____   4. _____
- ☐ Love, thanks, kindness and support for me:
  - 1. _____   2. _____
  - 3. _____   4. _____
- ☐ Good Deed/Selfless Act/Random Kindness: _____
- ☐ I gave undivided attention to: _____
- ☐ I made things better by: _____
- ☐ I experienced joy, happiness, fun and/or laughter: _____
- ☐ I smiled _____ minutes
- ☐ Meditation/Prayer _____ minutes
- ☐ Inspiration (reading, video, music): _____
- ☐ I listened to my intuition: _____
- ☐ Physical activity _____ minutes
- ☐ I was 100% honest today
- ☐ I took care of myself by: _____
- ☐ Reviewed purpose 3 times
- ☐ Reviewed intentions 3 times
- ☐ Steps toward goals, intentions and purpose
  - 1. _____ 2. _____ 3. _____
- ☐ Reviewed vision
- ☐ I am grateful for:
  - 1. _____   6. _____
  - 2. _____   7. _____
  - 3. _____   8. _____
  - 4. _____   9. _____
  - 5. _____   10. _____

- ☐ I am looking forward to: _____

Notes: _____
_____
_____

MINDFUL LIVING WORKSHEET

M   Tu   W   Th   F   S   S   Date:_____   Rate:_____

- ☐ I am content with: _____
- ☐ I am proud of: _____
- ☐ Success review
- ☐ I love myself because: _____ ☐
- ☐ Love, thanks, kindness and support for others:
    1. _____   2. _____
    3. _____   4. _____
- ☐ Love, thanks, kindness and support for me:
    1. _____   2. _____
    3. _____   4. _____
- ☐ Good Deed/Selfless Act/Random Kindness: _____
- ☐ I gave undivided attention to: _____
- ☐ I made things better by: _____
- ☐ I experienced joy, happiness, fun and/or laughter: _____
- ☐ I smiled _____ minutes
- ☐ Meditation/Prayer _____ minutes
- ☐ Inspiration (reading, video, music): _____
- ☐ I listened to my intuition: _____
- ☐ Physical activity _____ minutes
- ☐ I was 100% honest today
- ☐ I took care of myself by: _____
- ☐ Reviewed purpose 3 times
- ☐ Reviewed intentions 3 times
- ☐ Steps toward goals, intentions and purpose
    1. _____   2. _____   3. _____
- ☐ Reviewed vision
- ☐ I am grateful for:
    1. _____   6. _____
    2. _____   7. _____
    3. _____   8. _____
    4. _____   9. _____
    5. _____   10. _____

- ☐ I am looking forward to: _____

Notes: _____
_____
_____
_____

MINDFUL LIVING WORKSHEET

M Tu W Th F S S   Date:_____   Rate:_____

☐ I am content with: _____
☐ I am proud of: _____
☐ Success review
☐ I love myself because: _____ ☐
☐ Love, thanks, kindness and support for others:
    1. _____   2. _____
    3. _____   4. _____
☐ Love, thanks, kindness and support for me:
    1. _____   2. _____
    3. _____   4. _____
☐ Good Deed/Selfless Act/Random Kindness: _____
☐ I gave undivided attention to: _____
☐ I made things better by: _____
☐ I experienced joy, happiness, fun and/or laughter: _____
☐ I smiled _____ minutes
☐ Meditation/Prayer _____ minutes
☐ Inspiration (reading, video, music): _____
☐ I listened to my intuition: _____
☐ Physical activity _____ minutes
☐ I was 100% honest today
☐ I took care of myself by: _____
☐ Reviewed purpose 3 times
☐ Reviewed intentions 3 times
☐ Steps toward goals, intentions and purpose
    1. _____ 2. _____ 3. _____
☐ Reviewed vision
☐ I am grateful for:
    1. _____   6. _____
    2. _____   7. _____
    3. _____   8. _____
    4. _____   9. _____
    5. _____   10. _____

☐ I am looking forward to: _____

Notes: _____
_____
_____
_____

Mindful Living Worksheet

M Tu W Th F S S   Date:_____   Rate:_____

- ☐ I am content with: _____
- ☐ I am proud of: _____
- ☐ Success review
- ☐ I love myself because: _____ ☐
- ☐ Love, thanks, kindness and support for others:
    1. _____   2. _____
    3. _____   4. _____
- ☐ Love, thanks, kindness and support for me:
    1. _____   2. _____
    3. _____   4. _____
- ☐ Good Deed/Selfless Act/Random Kindness: _____
- ☐ I gave undivided attention to: _____
- ☐ I made things better by: _____
- ☐ I experienced joy, happiness, fun and/or laughter: _____
- ☐ I smiled _____ minutes
- ☐ Meditation/Prayer _____ minutes
- ☐ Inspiration (reading, video, music): _____
- ☐ I listened to my intuition: _____
- ☐ Physical activity _____ minutes
- ☐ I was 100% honest today
- ☐ I took care of myself by: _____
- ☐ Reviewed purpose 3 times
- ☐ Reviewed intentions 3 times
- ☐ Steps toward goals, intentions and purpose
    1. _____   2. _____   3. _____
- ☐ Reviewed vision
- ☐ I am grateful for:
    1. _____   6. _____
    2. _____   7. _____
    3. _____   8. _____
    4. _____   9. _____
    5. _____   10. _____

- ☐ I am looking forward to: _____

Notes: _____
_____
_____

MINDFUL LIVING WORKSHEET

M   Tu   W   Th   F   S   S   Date:_____   Rate:_____

- ☐ I am content with: _____
- ☐ I am proud of: _____
- ☐ Success review
- ☐ I love myself because: _____ ☐
- ☐ Love, thanks, kindness and support for others:
    1. _____   2. _____
    3. _____   4. _____
- ☐ Love, thanks, kindness and support for me:
    1. _____   2. _____
    3. _____   4. _____
- ☐ Good Deed/Selfless Act/Random Kindness: _____
- ☐ I gave undivided attention to: _____
- ☐ I made things better by: _____
- ☐ I experienced joy, happiness, fun and/or laughter: _____
- ☐ I smiled _____ minutes
- ☐ Meditation/Prayer _____ minutes
- ☐ Inspiration (reading, video, music): _____
- ☐ I listened to my intuition: _____
- ☐ Physical activity _____ minutes
- ☐ I was 100% honest today
- ☐ I took care of myself by: _____
- ☐ Reviewed purpose 3 times
- ☐ Reviewed intentions 3 times
- ☐ Steps toward goals, intentions and purpose
    1. _____   2. _____   3. _____
- ☐ Reviewed vision
- ☐ I am grateful for:
    1. _____   6. _____
    2. _____   7. _____
    3. _____   8. _____
    4. _____   9. _____
    5. _____   10. _____

- ☐ I am looking forward to: _____

Notes: _____
_____
_____

Mindful Living Worksheet

M Tu W Th F S S   Date:_____   Rate:_____

- ☐ I am content with: _____
- ☐ I am proud of: _____
- ☐ Success review
- ☐ I love myself because: _____ ☐
- ☐ Love, thanks, kindness and support for others:
    1. _____   2. _____
    3. _____   4. _____
- ☐ Love, thanks, kindness and support for me:
    1. _____   2. _____
    3. _____   4. _____
- ☐ Good Deed/Selfless Act/Random Kindness: _____
- ☐ I gave undivided attention to: _____
- ☐ I made things better by: _____
- ☐ I experienced joy, happiness, fun and/or laughter: _____
- ☐ I smiled _____ minutes
- ☐ Meditation/Prayer _____ minutes
- ☐ Inspiration (reading, video, music): _____
- ☐ I listened to my intuition: _____
- ☐ Physical activity _____ minutes
- ☐ I was 100% honest today
- ☐ I took care of myself by: _____
- ☐ Reviewed purpose 3 times
- ☐ Reviewed intentions 3 times
- ☐ Steps toward goals, intentions and purpose
    1. _____   2. _____   3. _____
- ☐ Reviewed vision
- ☐ I am grateful for:
    1. _____   6. _____
    2. _____   7. _____
    3. _____   8. _____
    4. _____   9. _____
    5. _____   10. _____

- ☐ I am looking forward to: _____

Notes: _____
_____
_____

Mindful Living Worksheet

M   Tu   W   Th   F   S   S   Date:_____   Rate:_____

- ☐ I am content with: _____
- ☐ I am proud of: _____
- ☐ Success review
- ☐ I love myself because: _____ ☐
- ☐ Love, thanks, kindness and support for others:
    1. _____   2. _____
    3. _____   4. _____
- ☐ Love, thanks, kindness and support for me:
    1. _____   2. _____
    3. _____   4. _____
- ☐ Good Deed/Selfless Act/Random Kindness: _____
- ☐ I gave undivided attention to: _____
- ☐ I made things better by: _____
- ☐ I experienced joy, happiness, fun and/or laughter: _____
- ☐ I smiled _____ minutes
- ☐ Meditation/Prayer _____ minutes
- ☐ Inspiration (reading, video, music): _____
- ☐ I listened to my intuition: _____
- ☐ Physical activity _____ minutes
- ☐ I was 100% honest today
- ☐ I took care of myself by: _____
- ☐ Reviewed purpose 3 times
- ☐ Reviewed intentions 3 times
- ☐ Steps toward goals, intentions and purpose
    1. _____   2. _____   3. _____
- ☐ Reviewed vision
- ☐ I am grateful for:
    1. _____   6. _____
    2. _____   7. _____
    3. _____   8. _____
    4. _____   9. _____
    5. _____   10. _____

- ☐ I am looking forward to: _____

Notes: _____
_____
_____
_____

MINDFUL LIVING WORKSHEET

M Tu W Th F S S   Date: _____   Rate: _____

- ☐ I am content with: _____
- ☐ I am proud of: _____
- ☐ Success review
- ☐ I love myself because: _____ ☐
- ☐ Love, thanks, kindness and support for others:
  - 1. _____   2. _____
  - 3. _____   4. _____
- ☐ Love, thanks, kindness and support for me:
  - 1. _____   2. _____
  - 3. _____   4. _____
- ☐ Good Deed/Selfless Act/Random Kindness: _____
- ☐ I gave undivided attention to: _____
- ☐ I made things better by: _____
- ☐ I experienced joy, happiness, fun and/or laughter: _____
- ☐ I smiled _____ minutes
- ☐ Meditation/Prayer _____ minutes
- ☐ Inspiration (reading, video, music): _____
- ☐ I listened to my intuition: _____
- ☐ Physical activity _____ minutes
- ☐ I was 100% honest today
- ☐ I took care of myself by: _____
- ☐ Reviewed purpose 3 times
- ☐ Reviewed intentions 3 times
- ☐ Steps toward goals, intentions and purpose
  - 1. _____ 2. _____ 3. _____
- ☐ Reviewed vision
- ☐ I am grateful for:
  - 1. _____   6. _____
  - 2. _____   7. _____
  - 3. _____   8. _____
  - 4. _____   9. _____
  - 5. _____   10. _____

- ☐ I am looking forward to: _____

Notes: _____
_____
_____
_____

Mindful Living Worksheet

M Tu W Th F S S   Date: _____   Rate: _____

- ☐ I am content with: _____
- ☐ I am proud of: _____
- ☐ Success review
- ☐ I love myself because: _____ ☐
- ☐ Love, thanks, kindness and support for others:
    1. _____   2. _____
    3. _____   4. _____
- ☐ Love, thanks, kindness and support for me:
    1. _____   2. _____
    3. _____   4. _____
- ☐ Good Deed/Selfless Act/Random Kindness: _____
- ☐ I gave undivided attention to: _____
- ☐ I made things better by: _____
- ☐ I experienced joy, happiness, fun and/or laughter: _____
- ☐ I smiled _____ minutes
- ☐ Meditation/Prayer _____ minutes
- ☐ Inspiration (reading, video, music): _____
- ☐ I listened to my intuition: _____
- ☐ Physical activity _____ minutes
- ☐ I was 100% honest today
- ☐ I took care of myself by: _____
- ☐ Reviewed purpose 3 times
- ☐ Reviewed intentions 3 times
- ☐ Steps toward goals, intentions and purpose
    1. _____ 2. _____ 3. _____
- ☐ Reviewed vision
- ☐ I am grateful for:
    1. _____   6. _____
    2. _____   7. _____
    3. _____   8. _____
    4. _____   9. _____
    5. _____   10. _____

- ☐ I am looking forward to: _____

Notes: _____
_____
_____
_____

MINDFUL LIVING WORKSHEET

M Tu W Th F S S   Date:_____   Rate:_____

- ☐ I am content with: _____
- ☐ I am proud of: _____
- ☐ Success review
- ☐ I love myself because: _____ ☐
- ☐ Love, thanks, kindness and support for others:
  - 1. _____   2. _____
  - 3. _____   4. _____
- ☐ Love, thanks, kindness and support for me:
  - 1. _____   2. _____
  - 3. _____   4. _____
- ☐ Good Deed/Selfless Act/Random Kindness: _____
- ☐ I gave undivided attention to: _____
- ☐ I made things better by: _____
- ☐ I experienced joy, happiness, fun and/or laughter: _____
- ☐ I smiled _____ minutes
- ☐ Meditation/Prayer _____ minutes
- ☐ Inspiration (reading, video, music): _____
- ☐ I listened to my intuition: _____
- ☐ Physical activity _____ minutes
- ☐ I was 100% honest today
- ☐ I took care of myself by: _____
- ☐ Reviewed purpose 3 times
- ☐ Reviewed intentions 3 times
- ☐ Steps toward goals, intentions and purpose
  - 1. _____ 2. _____ 3. _____
- ☐ Reviewed vision
- ☐ I am grateful for:
  - 1. _____   6. _____
  - 2. _____   7. _____
  - 3. _____   8. _____
  - 4. _____   9. _____
  - 5. _____   10. _____

- ☐ I am looking forward to: _____

Notes: _____
_____
_____
_____

MINDFUL LIVING WORKSHEET

M Tu W Th F S S   Date:_____   Rate:_____

- ☐ I am content with: _____
- ☐ I am proud of: _____
- ☐ Success review
- ☐ I love myself because: _____ ☐
- ☐ Love, thanks, kindness and support for others:
  - 1. _____   2. _____
  - 3. _____   4. _____
- ☐ Love, thanks, kindness and support for me:
  - 1. _____   2. _____
  - 3. _____   4. _____
- ☐ Good Deed/Selfless Act/Random Kindness: _____
- ☐ I gave undivided attention to: _____
- ☐ I made things better by: _____
- ☐ I experienced joy, happiness, fun and/or laughter: _____
- ☐ I smiled _____ minutes
- ☐ Meditation/Prayer _____ minutes
- ☐ Inspiration (reading, video, music): _____
- ☐ I listened to my intuition: _____
- ☐ Physical activity _____ minutes
- ☐ I was 100% honest today
- ☐ I took care of myself by: _____
- ☐ Reviewed purpose 3 times
- ☐ Reviewed intentions 3 times
- ☐ Steps toward goals, intentions and purpose
  - 1. _____ 2. _____ 3. _____
- ☐ Reviewed vision
- ☐ I am grateful for:
  - 1. _____   6. _____
  - 2. _____   7. _____
  - 3. _____   8. _____
  - 4. _____   9. _____
  - 5. _____   10. _____

- ☐ I am looking forward to: _____

Notes: _____
_____
_____
_____

MINDFUL LIVING WORKSHEET

M Tu W Th F S S   Date:_____   Rate:_____

- ☐ I am content with: _____
- ☐ I am proud of: _____
- ☐ Success review
- ☐ I love myself because: _____ ☐
- ☐ Love, thanks, kindness and support for others:
    - 1. _____   2. _____
    - 3. _____   4. _____
- ☐ Love, thanks, kindness and support for me:
    - 1. _____   2. _____
    - 3. _____   4. _____
- ☐ Good Deed/Selfless Act/Random Kindness: _____
- ☐ I gave undivided attention to: _____
- ☐ I made things better by: _____
- ☐ I experienced joy, happiness, fun and/or laughter: _____
- ☐ I smiled _____ minutes
- ☐ Meditation/Prayer _____ minutes
- ☐ Inspiration (reading, video, music): _____
- ☐ I listened to my intuition: _____
- ☐ Physical activity _____ minutes
- ☐ I was 100% honest today
- ☐ I took care of myself by: _____
- ☐ Reviewed purpose 3 times
- ☐ Reviewed intentions 3 times
- ☐ Steps toward goals, intentions and purpose
    - 1. _____ 2. _____ 3. _____
- ☐ Reviewed vision
- ☐ I am grateful for:
    - 1. _____   6. _____
    - 2. _____   7. _____
    - 3. _____   8. _____
    - 4. _____   9. _____
    - 5. _____   10. _____

- ☐ I am looking forward to: _____

Notes: _____
_____
_____
_____

Mindful Living Worksheet

M Tu W Th F S S   Date:_____   Rate:_____

- ☐ I am content with: _____
- ☐ I am proud of: _____
- ☐ Success review
- ☐ I love myself because: _____ ☐
- ☐ Love, thanks, kindness and support for others:
  - 1. _____   2. _____
  - 3. _____   4. _____
- ☐ Love, thanks, kindness and support for me:
  - 1. _____   2. _____
  - 3. _____   4. _____
- ☐ Good Deed/Selfless Act/Random Kindness: _____
- ☐ I gave undivided attention to: _____
- ☐ I made things better by: _____
- ☐ I experienced joy, happiness, fun and/or laughter: _____
- ☐ I smiled _____ minutes
- ☐ Meditation/Prayer _____ minutes
- ☐ Inspiration (reading, video, music): _____
- ☐ I listened to my intuition: _____
- ☐ Physical activity _____ minutes
- ☐ I was 100% honest today
- ☐ I took care of myself by: _____
- ☐ Reviewed purpose 3 times
- ☐ Reviewed intentions 3 times
- ☐ Steps toward goals, intentions and purpose
  - 1. _____ 2. _____ 3. _____
- ☐ Reviewed vision
- ☐ I am grateful for:
  - 1. _____   6. _____
  - 2. _____   7. _____
  - 3. _____   8. _____
  - 4. _____   9. _____
  - 5. _____   10. _____

- ☐ I am looking forward to: _____

Notes: _____
_____
_____

MINDFUL LIVING WORKSHEET

M   Tu   W   Th   F   S   S   Date:_____   Rate:_____

- ☐ I am content with: _____
- ☐ I am proud of: _____
- ☐ Success review
- ☐ I love myself because: _____ ☐
- ☐ Love, thanks, kindness and support for others:
    1. _____   2. _____
    3. _____   4. _____
- ☐ Love, thanks, kindness and support for me:
    1. _____   2. _____
    3. _____   4. _____
- ☐ Good Deed/Selfless Act/Random Kindness: _____
- ☐ I gave undivided attention to: _____
- ☐ I made things better by: _____
- ☐ I experienced joy, happiness, fun and/or laughter: _____
- ☐ I smiled _____ minutes
- ☐ Meditation/Prayer _____ minutes
- ☐ Inspiration (reading, video, music): _____
- ☐ I listened to my intuition: _____
- ☐ Physical activity _____ minutes
- ☐ I was 100% honest today
- ☐ I took care of myself by: _____
- ☐ Reviewed purpose 3 times
- ☐ Reviewed intentions 3 times
- ☐ Steps toward goals, intentions and purpose
    1. _____   2. _____   3. _____
- ☐ Reviewed vision
- ☐ I am grateful for:
    1. _____   6. _____
    2. _____   7. _____
    3. _____   8. _____
    4. _____   9. _____
    5. _____   10. _____

- ☐ I am looking forward to: _____

Notes: _____
_____
_____
_____

MINDFUL LIVING WORKSHEET

M   Tu   W   Th   F   S   S   Date:_____   Rate:_____

- ☐ I am content with: _____
- ☐ I am proud of: _____
- ☐ Success review
- ☐ I love myself because: _____ ☐
- ☐ Love, thanks, kindness and support for others:
    - 1. _____   2. _____
    - 3. _____   4. _____
- ☐ Love, thanks, kindness and support for me:
    - 1. _____   2. _____
    - 3. _____   4. _____
- ☐ Good Deed/Selfless Act/Random Kindness: _____
- ☐ I gave undivided attention to: _____
- ☐ I made things better by: _____
- ☐ I experienced joy, happiness, fun and/or laughter: _____
- ☐ I smiled _____ minutes
- ☐ Meditation/Prayer _____ minutes
- ☐ Inspiration (reading, video, music): _____
- ☐ I listened to my intuition: _____
- ☐ Physical activity _____ minutes
- ☐ I was 100% honest today
- ☐ I took care of myself by: _____
- ☐ Reviewed purpose 3 times
- ☐ Reviewed intentions 3 times
- ☐ Steps toward goals, intentions and purpose
    - 1. _____   2. _____   3. _____
- ☐ Reviewed vision
- ☐ I am grateful for:
    - 1. _____   6. _____
    - 2. _____   7. _____
    - 3. _____   8. _____
    - 4. _____   9. _____
    - 5. _____   10. _____
- ☐ I am looking forward to: _____

Notes: _____
_____
_____

MINDFUL LIVING WORKSHEET

M   Tu   W   Th   F   S   S   Date:_____   Rate:_____

- ☐ I am content with: _____
- ☐ I am proud of: _____
- ☐ Success review
- ☐ I love myself because: _____ ☐
- ☐ Love, thanks, kindness and support for others:
    1. _____   2. _____
    3. _____   4. _____
- ☐ Love, thanks, kindness and support for me:
    1. _____   2. _____
    3. _____   4. _____
- ☐ Good Deed/Selfless Act/Random Kindness: _____
- ☐ I gave undivided attention to: _____
- ☐ I made things better by: _____
- ☐ I experienced joy, happiness, fun and/or laughter: _____
- ☐ I smiled _____ minutes
- ☐ Meditation/Prayer _____ minutes
- ☐ Inspiration (reading, video, music): _____
- ☐ I listened to my intuition: _____
- ☐ Physical activity _____ minutes
- ☐ I was 100% honest today
- ☐ I took care of myself by: _____
- ☐ Reviewed purpose 3 times
- ☐ Reviewed intentions 3 times
- ☐ Steps toward goals, intentions and purpose
    1. _____ 2. _____ 3. _____
- ☐ Reviewed vision
- ☐ I am grateful for:
    1. _____   6. _____
    2. _____   7. _____
    3. _____   8. _____
    4. _____   9. _____
    5. _____   10. _____

- ☐ I am looking forward to: _____

Notes: _____
_____
_____
_____

MINDFUL LIVING WORKSHEET

M Tu W Th F S S   Date:_____   Rate:_____

- ☐ I am content with: _____
- ☐ I am proud of: _____
- ☐ Success review
- ☐ I love myself because: _____ ☐
- ☐ Love, thanks, kindness and support for others:
  - 1. _____   2. _____
  - 3. _____   4. _____
- ☐ Love, thanks, kindness and support for me:
  - 1. _____   2. _____
  - 3. _____   4. _____
- ☐ Good Deed/Selfless Act/Random Kindness: _____
- ☐ I gave undivided attention to: _____
- ☐ I made things better by: _____
- ☐ I experienced joy, happiness, fun and/or laughter: _____
- ☐ I smiled _____ minutes
- ☐ Meditation/Prayer _____ minutes
- ☐ Inspiration (reading, video, music): _____
- ☐ I listened to my intuition: _____
- ☐ Physical activity _____ minutes
- ☐ I was 100% honest today
- ☐ I took care of myself by: _____
- ☐ Reviewed purpose 3 times
- ☐ Reviewed intentions 3 times
- ☐ Steps toward goals, intentions and purpose
  - 1. _____ 2. _____ 3. _____
- ☐ Reviewed vision
- ☐ I am grateful for:
  - 1. _____   6. _____
  - 2. _____   7. _____
  - 3. _____   8. _____
  - 4. _____   9. _____
  - 5. _____   10. _____

- ☐ I am looking forward to: _____

Notes: _____
_____
_____
_____

MINDFUL LIVING WORKSHEET

M Tu W Th F S S   Date:_____   Rate:_____

- ☐ I am content with: _____
- ☐ I am proud of: _____
- ☐ Success review
- ☐ I love myself because: _____ ☐
- ☐ Love, thanks, kindness and support for others:
    1. _____   2. _____
    3. _____   4. _____
- ☐ Love, thanks, kindness and support for me:
    1. _____   2. _____
    3. _____   4. _____
- ☐ Good Deed/Selfless Act/Random Kindness: _____
- ☐ I gave undivided attention to: _____
- ☐ I made things better by: _____
- ☐ I experienced joy, happiness, fun and/or laughter: _____
- ☐ I smiled _____ minutes
- ☐ Meditation/Prayer _____ minutes
- ☐ Inspiration (reading, video, music): _____
- ☐ I listened to my intuition: _____
- ☐ Physical activity _____ minutes
- ☐ I was 100% honest today
- ☐ I took care of myself by: _____
- ☐ Reviewed purpose 3 times
- ☐ Reviewed intentions 3 times
- ☐ Steps toward goals, intentions and purpose
    1. _____ 2. _____ 3. _____
- ☐ Reviewed vision
- ☐ I am grateful for:
    1. _____   6. _____
    2. _____   7. _____
    3. _____   8. _____
    4. _____   9. _____
    5. _____   10. _____

- ☐ I am looking forward to: _____

Notes: _____
_____
_____
_____

MINDFUL LIVING WORKSHEET

M Tu W Th F S S   Date:_____   Rate:_____

- ☐ I am content with: _____
- ☐ I am proud of: _____
- ☐ Success review
- ☐ I love myself because: _____ ☐
- ☐ Love, thanks, kindness and support for others:
    1. _____   2. _____
    3. _____   4. _____
- ☐ Love, thanks, kindness and support for me:
    1. _____   2. _____
    3. _____   4. _____
- ☐ Good Deed/Selfless Act/Random Kindness: _____
- ☐ I gave undivided attention to: _____
- ☐ I made things better by: _____
- ☐ I experienced joy, happiness, fun and/or laughter: _____
- ☐ I smiled _____ minutes
- ☐ Meditation/Prayer _____ minutes
- ☐ Inspiration (reading, video, music): _____
- ☐ I listened to my intuition: _____
- ☐ Physical activity _____ minutes
- ☐ I was 100% honest today
- ☐ I took care of myself by: _____
- ☐ Reviewed purpose 3 times
- ☐ Reviewed intentions 3 times
- ☐ Steps toward goals, intentions and purpose
    1. _____   2. _____   3. _____
- ☐ Reviewed vision
- ☐ I am grateful for:
    1. _____   6. _____
    2. _____   7. _____
    3. _____   8. _____
    4. _____   9. _____
    5. _____   10. _____

- ☐ I am looking forward to: _____

Notes: _____
_____
_____
_____

MINDFUL LIVING WORKSHEET

M Tu W Th F S S   Date:_____   Rate:_____

- ☐ I am content with: _____
- ☐ I am proud of: _____
- ☐ Success review
- ☐ I love myself because: _____ ☐
- ☐ Love, thanks, kindness and support for others:
    - 1. _____ 2. _____
    - 3. _____ 4. _____
- ☐ Love, thanks, kindness and support for me:
    - 1. _____ 2. _____
    - 3. _____ 4. _____
- ☐ Good Deed/Selfless Act/Random Kindness: _____
- ☐ I gave undivided attention to: _____
- ☐ I made things better by: _____
- ☐ I experienced joy, happiness, fun and/or laughter: _____
- ☐ I smiled _____ minutes
- ☐ Meditation/Prayer _____ minutes
- ☐ Inspiration (reading, video, music): _____
- ☐ I listened to my intuition: _____
- ☐ Physical activity _____ minutes
- ☐ I was 100% honest today
- ☐ I took care of myself by: _____
- ☐ Reviewed purpose 3 times
- ☐ Reviewed intentions 3 times
- ☐ Steps toward goals, intentions and purpose
    - 1. _____ 2. _____ 3. _____
- ☐ Reviewed vision
- ☐ I am grateful for:
    - 1. _____ 6. _____
    - 2. _____ 7. _____
    - 3. _____ 8. _____
    - 4. _____ 9. _____
    - 5. _____ 10. _____

- ☐ I am looking forward to: _____

Notes: _____
_____
_____
_____

MINDFUL LIVING WORKSHEET

M Tu W Th F S S   Date:_____   Rate:_____

- ☐ I am content with: _____
- ☐ I am proud of: _____
- ☐ Success review
- ☐ I love myself because: _____ ☐
- ☐ Love, thanks, kindness and support for others:
  - 1. _____   2. _____
  - 3. _____   4. _____
- ☐ Love, thanks, kindness and support for me:
  - 1. _____   2. _____
  - 3. _____   4. _____
- ☐ Good Deed/Selfless Act/Random Kindness: _____
- ☐ I gave undivided attention to: _____
- ☐ I made things better by: _____
- ☐ I experienced joy, happiness, fun and/or laughter: _____
- ☐ I smiled _____ minutes
- ☐ Meditation/Prayer _____ minutes
- ☐ Inspiration (reading, video, music): _____
- ☐ I listened to my intuition: _____
- ☐ Physical activity _____ minutes
- ☐ I was 100% honest today
- ☐ I took care of myself by: _____
- ☐ Reviewed purpose 3 times
- ☐ Reviewed intentions 3 times
- ☐ Steps toward goals, intentions and purpose
  - 1. _____ 2. _____ 3. _____
- ☐ Reviewed vision
- ☐ I am grateful for:
  - 1. _____   6. _____
  - 2. _____   7. _____
  - 3. _____   8. _____
  - 4. _____   9. _____
  - 5. _____   10. _____

- ☐ I am looking forward to: _____

Notes: _____
_____
_____

MINDFUL LIVING WORKSHEET

M Tu W Th F S S   Date:_____   Rate:_____

- ☐ I am content with: _____
- ☐ I am proud of: _____
- ☐ Success review
- ☐ I love myself because: _____ ☐
- ☐ Love, thanks, kindness and support for others:
    1. _____   2. _____
    3. _____   4. _____
- ☐ Love, thanks, kindness and support for me:
    1. _____   2. _____
    3. _____   4. _____
- ☐ Good Deed/Selfless Act/Random Kindness: _____
- ☐ I gave undivided attention to: _____
- ☐ I made things better by: _____
- ☐ I experienced joy, happiness, fun and/or laughter: _____
- ☐ I smiled _____ minutes
- ☐ Meditation/Prayer _____ minutes
- ☐ Inspiration (reading, video, music): _____
- ☐ I listened to my intuition: _____
- ☐ Physical activity _____ minutes
- ☐ I was 100% honest today
- ☐ I took care of myself by: _____
- ☐ Reviewed purpose 3 times
- ☐ Reviewed intentions 3 times
- ☐ Steps toward goals, intentions and purpose
    1. _____ 2. _____ 3. _____
- ☐ Reviewed vision
- ☐ I am grateful for:
    1. _____   6. _____
    2. _____   7. _____
    3. _____   8. _____
    4. _____   9. _____
    5. _____   10. _____

- ☐ I am looking forward to: _____

Notes: _____
_____
_____
_____

Mindful Living Worksheet

M Tu W Th F S S   Date:_____   Rate:_____

- ☐ I am content with: _____
- ☐ I am proud of: _____
- ☐ Success review
- ☐ I love myself because: _____ ☐
- ☐ Love, thanks, kindness and support for others:
    1. _____   2. _____
    3. _____   4. _____
- ☐ Love, thanks, kindness and support for me:
    1. _____   2. _____
    3. _____   4. _____
- ☐ Good Deed/Selfless Act/Random Kindness: _____
- ☐ I gave undivided attention to: _____
- ☐ I made things better by: _____
- ☐ I experienced joy, happiness, fun and/or laughter: _____
- ☐ I smiled _____ minutes
- ☐ Meditation/Prayer _____ minutes
- ☐ Inspiration (reading, video, music): _____
- ☐ I listened to my intuition: _____
- ☐ Physical activity _____ minutes
- ☐ I was 100% honest today
- ☐ I took care of myself by: _____
- ☐ Reviewed purpose 3 times
- ☐ Reviewed intentions 3 times
- ☐ Steps toward goals, intentions and purpose
    1. _____   2. _____   3. _____
- ☐ Reviewed vision
- ☐ I am grateful for:
    1. _____   6. _____
    2. _____   7. _____
    3. _____   8. _____
    4. _____   9. _____
    5. _____   10. _____

- ☐ I am looking forward to: _____

Notes: _____
_____
_____
_____

MINDFUL LIVING WORKSHEET

M Tu W Th F S S   Date:_____   Rate:_____

- ☐ I am content with: _____
- ☐ I am proud of: _____
- ☐ Success review
- ☐ I love myself because: _____ ☐
- ☐ Love, thanks, kindness and support for others:
  - 1. _____   2. _____
  - 3. _____   4. _____
- ☐ Love, thanks, kindness and support for me:
  - 1. _____   2. _____
  - 3. _____   4. _____
- ☐ Good Deed/Selfless Act/Random Kindness: _____
- ☐ I gave undivided attention to: _____
- ☐ I made things better by: _____
- ☐ I experienced joy, happiness, fun and/or laughter: _____
- ☐ I smiled _____ minutes
- ☐ Meditation/Prayer _____ minutes
- ☐ Inspiration (reading, video, music): _____
- ☐ I listened to my intuition: _____
- ☐ Physical activity _____ minutes
- ☐ I was 100% honest today
- ☐ I took care of myself by: _____
- ☐ Reviewed purpose 3 times
- ☐ Reviewed intentions 3 times
- ☐ Steps toward goals, intentions and purpose
  - 1. _____   2. _____   3. _____
- ☐ Reviewed vision
- ☐ I am grateful for:
  - 1. _____   6. _____
  - 2. _____   7. _____
  - 3. _____   8. _____
  - 4. _____   9. _____
  - 5. _____   10. _____

- ☐ I am looking forward to: _____

Notes: _____
_____
_____
_____

Mindful Living Worksheet

M   Tu   W   Th   F   S   S   Date:_____   Rate:_____

- ☐ I am content with: _____
- ☐ I am proud of: _____
- ☐ Success review
- ☐ I love myself because: _____   ☐
- ☐ Love, thanks, kindness and support for others:
    - 1. _____   2. _____
    - 3. _____   4. _____
- ☐ Love, thanks, kindness and support for me:
    - 1. _____   2. _____
    - 3. _____   4. _____
- ☐ Good Deed/Selfless Act/Random Kindness: _____
- ☐ I gave undivided attention to: _____
- ☐ I made things better by: _____
- ☐ I experienced joy, happiness, fun and/or laughter: _____
- ☐ I smiled _____ minutes
- ☐ Meditation/Prayer _____ minutes
- ☐ Inspiration (reading, video, music): _____
- ☐ I listened to my intuition: _____
- ☐ Physical activity _____ minutes
- ☐ I was 100% honest today
- ☐ I took care of myself by: _____
- ☐ Reviewed purpose 3 times
- ☐ Reviewed intentions 3 times
- ☐ Steps toward goals, intentions and purpose
    - 1. _____   2. _____   3. _____
- ☐ Reviewed vision
- ☐ I am grateful for:
    - 1. _____   6. _____
    - 2. _____   7. _____
    - 3. _____   8. _____
    - 4. _____   9. _____
    - 5. _____   10. _____

- ☐ I am looking forward to: _____

Notes: _____
_____
_____
_____

MINDFUL LIVING WORKSHEET

M Tu W Th F S S   Date:_____   Rate:_____

- ☐ I am content with: _____
- ☐ I am proud of: _____
- ☐ Success review
- ☐ I love myself because: _____ ☐
- ☐ Love, thanks, kindness and support for others:
  - 1. _____   2. _____
  - 3. _____   4. _____
- ☐ Love, thanks, kindness and support for me:
  - 1. _____   2. _____
  - 3. _____   4. _____
- ☐ Good Deed/Selfless Act/Random Kindness: _____
- ☐ I gave undivided attention to: _____
- ☐ I made things better by: _____
- ☐ I experienced joy, happiness, fun and/or laughter: _____
- ☐ I smiled _____ minutes
- ☐ Meditation/Prayer _____ minutes
- ☐ Inspiration (reading, video, music): _____
- ☐ I listened to my intuition: _____
- ☐ Physical activity _____ minutes
- ☐ I was 100% honest today
- ☐ I took care of myself by: _____
- ☐ Reviewed purpose 3 times
- ☐ Reviewed intentions 3 times
- ☐ Steps toward goals, intentions and purpose
  - 1. _____ 2. _____ 3. _____
- ☐ Reviewed vision
- ☐ I am grateful for:
  - 1. _____   6. _____
  - 2. _____   7. _____
  - 3. _____   8. _____
  - 4. _____   9. _____
  - 5. _____   10. _____

- ☐ I am looking forward to: _____

Notes: _____
_____
_____

MINDFUL LIVING WORKSHEET

M Tu W Th F S S   Date:_____   Rate:_____

- ☐ I am content with: _____
- ☐ I am proud of: _____
- ☐ Success review
- ☐ I love myself because: _____ ☐
- ☐ Love, thanks, kindness and support for others:
  - 1. _____   2. _____
  - 3. _____   4. _____
- ☐ Love, thanks, kindness and support for me:
  - 1. _____   2. _____
  - 3. _____   4. _____
- ☐ Good Deed/Selfless Act/Random Kindness: _____
- ☐ I gave undivided attention to: _____
- ☐ I made things better by: _____
- ☐ I experienced joy, happiness, fun and/or laughter: _____
- ☐ I smiled _____ minutes
- ☐ Meditation/Prayer _____ minutes
- ☐ Inspiration (reading, video, music): _____
- ☐ I listened to my intuition: _____
- ☐ Physical activity _____ minutes
- ☐ I was 100% honest today
- ☐ I took care of myself by: _____
- ☐ Reviewed purpose 3 times
- ☐ Reviewed intentions 3 times
- ☐ Steps toward goals, intentions and purpose
  - 1. _____ 2. _____ 3. _____
- ☐ Reviewed vision
- ☐ I am grateful for:
  - 1. _____   6. _____
  - 2. _____   7. _____
  - 3. _____   8. _____
  - 4. _____   9. _____
  - 5. _____   10. _____

- ☐ I am looking forward to: _____

Notes: _____
_____
_____

Mindful Living Worksheet

M Tu W Th F S S   Date:_____   Rate:_____

- ☐ I am content with: _____
- ☐ I am proud of: _____
- ☐ Success review
- ☐ I love myself because: _____ ☐
- ☐ Love, thanks, kindness and support for others:
  - 1. _____   2. _____
  - 3. _____   4. _____
- ☐ Love, thanks, kindness and support for me:
  - 1. _____   2. _____
  - 3. _____   4. _____
- ☐ Good Deed/Selfless Act/Random Kindness: _____
- ☐ I gave undivided attention to: _____
- ☐ I made things better by: _____
- ☐ I experienced joy, happiness, fun and/or laughter: _____
- ☐ I smiled _____ minutes
- ☐ Meditation/Prayer _____ minutes
- ☐ Inspiration (reading, video, music): _____
- ☐ I listened to my intuition: _____
- ☐ Physical activity _____ minutes
- ☐ I was 100% honest today
- ☐ I took care of myself by: _____
- ☐ Reviewed purpose 3 times
- ☐ Reviewed intentions 3 times
- ☐ Steps toward goals, intentions and purpose
  - 1. _____ 2. _____ 3. _____
- ☐ Reviewed vision
- ☐ I am grateful for:
  - 1. _____   6. _____
  - 2. _____   7. _____
  - 3. _____   8. _____
  - 4. _____   9. _____
  - 5. _____   10. _____

- ☐ I am looking forward to: _____

Notes: _____
_____
_____

Mindful Living Worksheet

M Tu W Th F S S   Date:_____   Rate:_____

- ☐ I am content with: _____
- ☐ I am proud of: _____
- ☐ Success review
- ☐ I love myself because: _____ ☐
- ☐ Love, thanks, kindness and support for others:
  - 1. _____   2. _____
  - 3. _____   4. _____
- ☐ Love, thanks, kindness and support for me:
  - 1. _____   2. _____
  - 3. _____   4. _____
- ☐ Good Deed/Selfless Act/Random Kindness: _____
- ☐ I gave undivided attention to: _____
- ☐ I made things better by: _____
- ☐ I experienced joy, happiness, fun and/or laughter: _____
- ☐ I smiled _____ minutes
- ☐ Meditation/Prayer _____ minutes
- ☐ Inspiration (reading, video, music): _____
- ☐ I listened to my intuition: _____
- ☐ Physical activity _____ minutes
- ☐ I was 100% honest today
- ☐ I took care of myself by: _____
- ☐ Reviewed purpose 3 times
- ☐ Reviewed intentions 3 times
- ☐ Steps toward goals, intentions and purpose
  - 1. _____   2. _____   3. _____
- ☐ Reviewed vision
- ☐ I am grateful for:
  - 1. _____   6. _____
  - 2. _____   7. _____
  - 3. _____   8. _____
  - 4. _____   9. _____
  - 5. _____   10. _____

- ☐ I am looking forward to: _____

Notes: _____
_____
_____

Mindful Living Worksheet

M Tu W Th F S S   Date:_____   Rate:_____

- ☐ I am content with: _____
- ☐ I am proud of: _____
- ☐ Success review
- ☐ I love myself because: _____ ☐
- ☐ Love, thanks, kindness and support for others:
    1. _____   2. _____
    3. _____   4. _____
- ☐ Love, thanks, kindness and support for me:
    1. _____   2. _____
    3. _____   4. _____
- ☐ Good Deed/Selfless Act/Random Kindness: _____
- ☐ I gave undivided attention to: _____
- ☐ I made things better by: _____
- ☐ I experienced joy, happiness, fun and/or laughter: _____
- ☐ I smiled _____ minutes
- ☐ Meditation/Prayer _____ minutes
- ☐ Inspiration (reading, video, music): _____
- ☐ I listened to my intuition: _____
- ☐ Physical activity _____ minutes
- ☐ I was 100% honest today
- ☐ I took care of myself by: _____
- ☐ Reviewed purpose 3 times
- ☐ Reviewed intentions 3 times
- ☐ Steps toward goals, intentions and purpose
    1. _____   2. _____   3. _____
- ☐ Reviewed vision
- ☐ I am grateful for:
    1. _____   6. _____
    2. _____   7. _____
    3. _____   8. _____
    4. _____   9. _____
    5. _____   10. _____

- ☐ I am looking forward to: _____

Notes: _____
_____
_____
_____

Mindful Living Worksheet

M Tu W Th F S S   Date:_____   Rate:_____

- ☐ I am content with: _____
- ☐ I am proud of: _____
- ☐ Success review
- ☐ I love myself because: _____ ☐
- ☐ Love, thanks, kindness and support for others:
  - 1. _____ 2. _____
  - 3. _____ 4. _____
- ☐ Love, thanks, kindness and support for me:
  - 1. _____ 2. _____
  - 3. _____ 4. _____
- ☐ Good Deed/Selfless Act/Random Kindness: _____
- ☐ I gave undivided attention to: _____
- ☐ I made things better by: _____
- ☐ I experienced joy, happiness, fun and/or laughter: _____
- ☐ I smiled _____ minutes
- ☐ Meditation/Prayer _____ minutes
- ☐ Inspiration (reading, video, music): _____
- ☐ I listened to my intuition: _____
- ☐ Physical activity _____ minutes
- ☐ I was 100% honest today
- ☐ I took care of myself by: _____
- ☐ Reviewed purpose 3 times
- ☐ Reviewed intentions 3 times
- ☐ Steps toward goals, intentions and purpose
  - 1. _____ 2. _____ 3. _____
- ☐ Reviewed vision
- ☐ I am grateful for:
  - 1. _____ 6. _____
  - 2. _____ 7. _____
  - 3. _____ 8. _____
  - 4. _____ 9. _____
  - 5. _____ 10. _____

- ☐ I am looking forward to: _____

Notes: _____
_____
_____
_____

MINDFUL LIVING WORKSHEET

M Tu W Th F S S   Date:_____   Rate:_____

- ☐ I am content with: _____
- ☐ I am proud of: _____
- ☐ Success review
- ☐ I love myself because: _____ ☐
- ☐ Love, thanks, kindness and support for others:
    1. _____ 2. _____
    3. _____ 4. _____
- ☐ Love, thanks, kindness and support for me:
    1. _____ 2. _____
    3. _____ 4. _____
- ☐ Good Deed/Selfless Act/Random Kindness: _____
- ☐ I gave undivided attention to: _____
- ☐ I made things better by: _____
- ☐ I experienced joy, happiness, fun and/or laughter: _____
- ☐ I smiled _____ minutes
- ☐ Meditation/Prayer _____ minutes
- ☐ Inspiration (reading, video, music): _____
- ☐ I listened to my intuition: _____
- ☐ Physical activity _____ minutes
- ☐ I was 100% honest today
- ☐ I took care of myself by: _____
- ☐ Reviewed purpose 3 times
- ☐ Reviewed intentions 3 times
- ☐ Steps toward goals, intentions and purpose
    1. _____ 2. _____ 3. _____
- ☐ Reviewed vision
- ☐ I am grateful for:
    1. _____ 6. _____
    2. _____ 7. _____
    3. _____ 8. _____
    4. _____ 9. _____
    5. _____ 10. _____

- ☐ I am looking forward to: _____

Notes: _____
_____
_____
_____

MINDFUL LIVING WORKSHEET

M Tu W Th F S S   Date:_____   Rate:_____

- ☐ I am content with: _____
- ☐ I am proud of: _____
- ☐ Success review
- ☐ I love myself because: _____ ☐
- ☐ Love, thanks, kindness and support for others:
  - 1. _____   2. _____
  - 3. _____   4. _____
- ☐ Love, thanks, kindness and support for me:
  - 1. _____   2. _____
  - 3. _____   4. _____
- ☐ Good Deed/Selfless Act/Random Kindness: _____
- ☐ I gave undivided attention to: _____
- ☐ I made things better by: _____
- ☐ I experienced joy, happiness, fun and/or laughter: _____
- ☐ I smiled _____ minutes
- ☐ Meditation/Prayer _____ minutes
- ☐ Inspiration (reading, video, music): _____
- ☐ I listened to my intuition: _____
- ☐ Physical activity _____ minutes
- ☐ I was 100% honest today
- ☐ I took care of myself by: _____
- ☐ Reviewed purpose 3 times
- ☐ Reviewed intentions 3 times
- ☐ Steps toward goals, intentions and purpose
  - 1. _____ 2. _____ 3. _____
- ☐ Reviewed vision
- ☐ I am grateful for:
  - 1. _____   6. _____
  - 2. _____   7. _____
  - 3. _____   8. _____
  - 4. _____   9. _____
  - 5. _____   10. _____

- ☐ I am looking forward to: _____

Notes: _____
_____
_____

MINDFUL LIVING WORKSHEET

M   Tu   W   Th   F   S   S   Date:_____   Rate:_____

- ☐ I am content with: _____
- ☐ I am proud of: _____
- ☐ Success review
- ☐ I love myself because: _____ ☐
- ☐ Love, thanks, kindness and support for others:
    - 1. _____   2. _____
    - 3. _____   4. _____
- ☐ Love, thanks, kindness and support for me:
    - 1. _____   2. _____
    - 3. _____   4. _____
- ☐ Good Deed/Selfless Act/Random Kindness: _____
- ☐ I gave undivided attention to: _____
- ☐ I made things better by: _____
- ☐ I experienced joy, happiness, fun and/or laughter: _____
- ☐ I smiled _____ minutes
- ☐ Meditation/Prayer _____ minutes
- ☐ Inspiration (reading, video, music): _____
- ☐ I listened to my intuition: _____
- ☐ Physical activity _____ minutes
- ☐ I was 100% honest today
- ☐ I took care of myself by: _____
- ☐ Reviewed purpose 3 times
- ☐ Reviewed intentions 3 times
- ☐ Steps toward goals, intentions and purpose
    - 1. _____   2. _____   3. _____
- ☐ Reviewed vision
- ☐ I am grateful for:
    - 1. _____   6. _____
    - 2. _____   7. _____
    - 3. _____   8. _____
    - 4. _____   9. _____
    - 5. _____   10. _____

- ☐ I am looking forward to: _____

Notes: _____
_____
_____
_____

MINDFUL LIVING WORKSHEET

M   Tu   W   Th   F   S   S   Date:_____   Rate:_____

- ☐ I am content with: _____
- ☐ I am proud of: _____
- ☐ Success review
- ☐ I love myself because: _____ ☐
- ☐ Love, thanks, kindness and support for others:
  - 1. _____   2. _____
  - 3. _____   4. _____
- ☐ Love, thanks, kindness and support for me:
  - 1. _____   2. _____
  - 3. _____   4. _____
- ☐ Good Deed/Selfless Act/Random Kindness: _____
- ☐ I gave undivided attention to: _____
- ☐ I made things better by: _____
- ☐ I experienced joy, happiness, fun and/or laughter: _____
- ☐ I smiled _____ minutes
- ☐ Meditation/Prayer _____ minutes
- ☐ Inspiration (reading, video, music): _____
- ☐ I listened to my intuition: _____
- ☐ Physical activity _____ minutes
- ☐ I was 100% honest today
- ☐ I took care of myself by: _____
- ☐ Reviewed purpose 3 times
- ☐ Reviewed intentions 3 times
- ☐ Steps toward goals, intentions and purpose
  - 1. _____   2. _____   3. _____
- ☐ Reviewed vision
- ☐ I am grateful for:
  - 1. _____   6. _____
  - 2. _____   7. _____
  - 3. _____   8. _____
  - 4. _____   9. _____
  - 5. _____   10. _____

- ☐ I am looking forward to: _____

Notes: _____
_____
_____

MINDFUL LIVING WORKSHEET

M Tu W Th F S S   Date:_____   Rate:_____

- ☐ I am content with: _____
- ☐ I am proud of: _____
- ☐ Success review
- ☐ I love myself because: _____ ☐
- ☐ Love, thanks, kindness and support for others:
    1. _____   2. _____
    3. _____   4. _____
- ☐ Love, thanks, kindness and support for me:
    1. _____   2. _____
    3. _____   4. _____
- ☐ Good Deed/Selfless Act/Random Kindness: _____
- ☐ I gave undivided attention to: _____
- ☐ I made things better by: _____
- ☐ I experienced joy, happiness, fun and/or laughter: _____
- ☐ I smiled _____ minutes
- ☐ Meditation/Prayer _____ minutes
- ☐ Inspiration (reading, video, music): _____
- ☐ I listened to my intuition: _____
- ☐ Physical activity _____ minutes
- ☐ I was 100% honest today
- ☐ I took care of myself by: _____
- ☐ Reviewed purpose 3 times
- ☐ Reviewed intentions 3 times
- ☐ Steps toward goals, intentions and purpose
    1. _____   2. _____   3. _____
- ☐ Reviewed vision
- ☐ I am grateful for:
    1. _____   6. _____
    2. _____   7. _____
    3. _____   8. _____
    4. _____   9. _____
    5. _____   10. _____

- ☐ I am looking forward to: _____

Notes: _____
_____
_____
_____

Mindful Living Worksheet

M Tu W Th F S S   Date:_____   Rate:_____

- ☐ I am content with: _____
- ☐ I am proud of: _____
- ☐ Success review
- ☐ I love myself because: _____ ☐
- ☐ Love, thanks, kindness and support for others:
  - 1. _____ 2. _____
  - 3. _____ 4. _____
- ☐ Love, thanks, kindness and support for me:
  - 1. _____ 2. _____
  - 3. _____ 4. _____
- ☐ Good Deed/Selfless Act/Random Kindness: _____
- ☐ I gave undivided attention to: _____
- ☐ I made things better by: _____
- ☐ I experienced joy, happiness, fun and/or laughter: _____
- ☐ I smiled _____ minutes
- ☐ Meditation/Prayer _____ minutes
- ☐ Inspiration (reading, video, music): _____
- ☐ I listened to my intuition: _____
- ☐ Physical activity _____ minutes
- ☐ I was 100% honest today
- ☐ I took care of myself by: _____
- ☐ Reviewed purpose 3 times
- ☐ Reviewed intentions 3 times
- ☐ Steps toward goals, intentions and purpose
  - 1. _____ 2. _____ 3. _____
- ☐ Reviewed vision
- ☐ I am grateful for:
  - 1. _____ 6. _____
  - 2. _____ 7. _____
  - 3. _____ 8. _____
  - 4. _____ 9. _____
  - 5. _____ 10. _____

- ☐ I am looking forward to: _____

Notes: _____
_____
_____

Mindful Living Worksheet

M Tu W Th F S S   Date:_____   Rate:_____

- ☐ I am content with: _____
- ☐ I am proud of: _____
- ☐ Success review
- ☐ I love myself because: _____ ☐
- ☐ Love, thanks, kindness and support for others:
    1. _____   2. _____
    3. _____   4. _____
- ☐ Love, thanks, kindness and support for me:
    1. _____   2. _____
    3. _____   4. _____
- ☐ Good Deed/Selfless Act/Random Kindness: _____
- ☐ I gave undivided attention to: _____
- ☐ I made things better by: _____
- ☐ I experienced joy, happiness, fun and/or laughter: _____
- ☐ I smiled _____ minutes
- ☐ Meditation/Prayer _____ minutes
- ☐ Inspiration (reading, video, music): _____
- ☐ I listened to my intuition: _____
- ☐ Physical activity _____ minutes
- ☐ I was 100% honest today
- ☐ I took care of myself by: _____
- ☐ Reviewed purpose 3 times
- ☐ Reviewed intentions 3 times
- ☐ Steps toward goals, intentions and purpose
    1. _____ 2. _____ 3. _____
- ☐ Reviewed vision
- ☐ I am grateful for:
    1. _____   6. _____
    2. _____   7. _____
    3. _____   8. _____
    4. _____   9. _____
    5. _____   10. _____

- ☐ I am looking forward to: _____

Notes: _____
_____
_____

Mindful Living Worksheet

M Tu W Th F S S   Date:_____   Rate:_____

☐ I am content with: _____
☐ I am proud of: _____
☐ Success review
☐ I love myself because: _____ ☐
☐ Love, thanks, kindness and support for others:
    1. _____ 2. _____
    3. _____ 4. _____
☐ Love, thanks, kindness and support for me:
    1. _____ 2. _____
    3. _____ 4. _____
☐ Good Deed/Selfless Act/Random Kindness: _____
☐ I gave undivided attention to: _____
☐ I made things better by: _____
☐ I experienced joy, happiness, fun and/or laughter: _____
☐ I smiled _____ minutes
☐ Meditation/Prayer _____ minutes
☐ Inspiration (reading, video, music): _____
☐ I listened to my intuition: _____
☐ Physical activity _____ minutes
☐ I was 100% honest today
☐ I took care of myself by: _____
☐ Reviewed purpose 3 times
☐ Reviewed intentions 3 times
☐ Steps toward goals, intentions and purpose
    1. _____ 2. _____ 3. _____
☐ Reviewed vision
☐ I am grateful for:
    1. _____ 6. _____
    2. _____ 7. _____
    3. _____ 8. _____
    4. _____ 9. _____
    5. _____ 10. _____

☐ I am looking forward to: _____

Notes: _____
_____
_____
_____

MINDFUL LIVING WORKSHEET

M   Tu   W   Th   F   S   S   Date:_____   Rate:_____

- ☐ I am content with: _____
- ☐ I am proud of: _____
- ☐ Success review
- ☐ I love myself because: _____ ☐
- ☐ Love, thanks, kindness and support for others:
    - 1. _____   2. _____
    - 3. _____   4. _____
- ☐ Love, thanks, kindness and support for me:
    - 1. _____   2. _____
    - 3. _____   4. _____
- ☐ Good Deed/Selfless Act/Random Kindness: _____
- ☐ I gave undivided attention to: _____
- ☐ I made things better by: _____
- ☐ I experienced joy, happiness, fun and/or laughter: _____
- ☐ I smiled _____ minutes
- ☐ Meditation/Prayer _____ minutes
- ☐ Inspiration (reading, video, music): _____
- ☐ I listened to my intuition: _____
- ☐ Physical activity _____ minutes
- ☐ I was 100% honest today
- ☐ I took care of myself by: _____
- ☐ Reviewed purpose 3 times
- ☐ Reviewed intentions 3 times
- ☐ Steps toward goals, intentions and purpose
    - 1. _____   2. _____   3. _____
- ☐ Reviewed vision
- ☐ I am grateful for:
    - 1. _____   6. _____
    - 2. _____   7. _____
    - 3. _____   8. _____
    - 4. _____   9. _____
    - 5. _____   10. _____

- ☐ I am looking forward to: _____

Notes: _____
_____
_____

Mindful Living Worksheet

M Tu W Th F S S   Date:_____   Rate:_____

- [ ] I am content with: _____
- [ ] I am proud of: _____
- [ ] Success review
- [ ] I love myself because: _____ [ ]
- [ ] Love, thanks, kindness and support for others:
    1. _____   2. _____
    3. _____   4. _____
- [ ] Love, thanks, kindness and support for me:
    1. _____   2. _____
    3. _____   4. _____
- [ ] Good Deed/Selfless Act/Random Kindness: _____
- [ ] I gave undivided attention to: _____
- [ ] I made things better by: _____
- [ ] I experienced joy, happiness, fun and/or laughter: _____
- [ ] I smiled _____ minutes
- [ ] Meditation/Prayer _____ minutes
- [ ] Inspiration (reading, video, music): _____
- [ ] I listened to my intuition: _____
- [ ] Physical activity _____ minutes
- [ ] I was 100% honest today
- [ ] I took care of myself by: _____
- [ ] Reviewed purpose 3 times
- [ ] Reviewed intentions 3 times
- [ ] Steps toward goals, intentions and purpose
    1. _____ 2. _____ 3. _____
- [ ] Reviewed vision
- [ ] I am grateful for:
    1. _____   6. _____
    2. _____   7. _____
    3. _____   8. _____
    4. _____   9. _____
    5. _____   10. _____

- [ ] I am looking forward to: _____

Notes: _____
_____
_____
_____

MINDFUL LIVING WORKSHEET

M Tu W Th F S S   Date:_____   Rate:_____

- ☐ I am content with: _____
- ☐ I am proud of: _____
- ☐ Success review
- ☐ I love myself because: _____ ☐
- ☐ Love, thanks, kindness and support for others:
    - 1. _____   2. _____
    - 3. _____   4. _____
- ☐ Love, thanks, kindness and support for me:
    - 1. _____   2. _____
    - 3. _____   4. _____
- ☐ Good Deed/Selfless Act/Random Kindness: _____
- ☐ I gave undivided attention to: _____
- ☐ I made things better by: _____
- ☐ I experienced joy, happiness, fun and/or laughter: _____
- ☐ I smiled _____ minutes
- ☐ Meditation/Prayer _____ minutes
- ☐ Inspiration (reading, video, music): _____
- ☐ I listened to my intuition: _____
- ☐ Physical activity _____ minutes
- ☐ I was 100% honest today
- ☐ I took care of myself by: _____
- ☐ Reviewed purpose 3 times
- ☐ Reviewed intentions 3 times
- ☐ Steps toward goals, intentions and purpose
    - 1. _____ 2. _____ 3. _____
- ☐ Reviewed vision
- ☐ I am grateful for:
    - 1. _____   6. _____
    - 2. _____   7. _____
    - 3. _____   8. _____
    - 4. _____   9. _____
    - 5. _____   10. _____

- ☐ I am looking forward to: _____

Notes: _____
_____
_____
_____

Mindful Living Worksheet

M Tu W Th F S S   Date:_____   Rate:_____

- ☐ I am content with: _____
- ☐ I am proud of: _____
- ☐ Success review
- ☐ I love myself because: _____ ☐
- ☐ Love, thanks, kindness and support for others:
  - 1. _____   2. _____
  - 3. _____   4. _____
- ☐ Love, thanks, kindness and support for me:
  - 1. _____   2. _____
  - 3. _____   4. _____
- ☐ Good Deed/Selfless Act/Random Kindness: _____
- ☐ I gave undivided attention to: _____
- ☐ I made things better by: _____
- ☐ I experienced joy, happiness, fun and/or laughter: _____
- ☐ I smiled _____ minutes
- ☐ Meditation/Prayer _____ minutes
- ☐ Inspiration (reading, video, music): _____
- ☐ I listened to my intuition: _____
- ☐ Physical activity _____ minutes
- ☐ I was 100% honest today
- ☐ I took care of myself by: _____
- ☐ Reviewed purpose 3 times
- ☐ Reviewed intentions 3 times
- ☐ Steps toward goals, intentions and purpose
  - 1. _____ 2. _____ 3. _____
- ☐ Reviewed vision
- ☐ I am grateful for:
  - 1. _____   6. _____
  - 2. _____   7. _____
  - 3. _____   8. _____
  - 4. _____   9. _____
  - 5. _____   10. _____

- ☐ I am looking forward to: _____

Notes: _____
_____
_____
_____

MINDFUL LIVING WORKSHEET

M   Tu   W   Th   F   S   S   Date:_____   Rate:_____

- ☐ I am content with: _____
- ☐ I am proud of: _____
- ☐ Success review
- ☐ I love myself because: _____ ☐
- ☐ Love, thanks, kindness and support for others:
  - 1. _____   2. _____
  - 3. _____   4. _____
- ☐ Love, thanks, kindness and support for me:
  - 1. _____   2. _____
  - 3. _____   4. _____
- ☐ Good Deed/Selfless Act/Random Kindness: _____
- ☐ I gave undivided attention to: _____
- ☐ I made things better by: _____
- ☐ I experienced joy, happiness, fun and/or laughter: _____
- ☐ I smiled _____ minutes
- ☐ Meditation/Prayer _____ minutes
- ☐ Inspiration (reading, video, music): _____
- ☐ I listened to my intuition: _____
- ☐ Physical activity _____ minutes
- ☐ I was 100% honest today
- ☐ I took care of myself by: _____
- ☐ Reviewed purpose 3 times
- ☐ Reviewed intentions 3 times
- ☐ Steps toward goals, intentions and purpose
  - 1. _____   2. _____   3. _____
- ☐ Reviewed vision
- ☐ I am grateful for:
  - 1. _____   6. _____
  - 2. _____   7. _____
  - 3. _____   8. _____
  - 4. _____   9. _____
  - 5. _____   10. _____
- ☐ I am looking forward to: _____

Notes: _____
_____
_____

Mindful Living Worksheet

M Tu W Th F S S   Date:_____   Rate:_____

- ☐ I am content with: _____
- ☐ I am proud of: _____
- ☐ Success review
- ☐ I love myself because: _____ ☐
- ☐ Love, thanks, kindness and support for others:
  - 1. _____   2. _____
  - 3. _____   4. _____
- ☐ Love, thanks, kindness and support for me:
  - 1. _____   2. _____
  - 3. _____   4. _____
- ☐ Good Deed/Selfless Act/Random Kindness: _____
- ☐ I gave undivided attention to: _____
- ☐ I made things better by: _____
- ☐ I experienced joy, happiness, fun and/or laughter: _____
- ☐ I smiled _____ minutes
- ☐ Meditation/Prayer _____ minutes
- ☐ Inspiration (reading, video, music): _____
- ☐ I listened to my intuition: _____
- ☐ Physical activity _____ minutes
- ☐ I was 100% honest today
- ☐ I took care of myself by: _____
- ☐ Reviewed purpose 3 times
- ☐ Reviewed intentions 3 times
- ☐ Steps toward goals, intentions and purpose
  - 1. _____ 2. _____ 3. _____
- ☐ Reviewed vision
- ☐ I am grateful for:
  - 1. _____   6. _____
  - 2. _____   7. _____
  - 3. _____   8. _____
  - 4. _____   9. _____
  - 5. _____   10. _____
- ☐ I am looking forward to: _____

Notes: _____
_____
_____
_____

Mindful Living Worksheet

M   Tu   W   Th   F   S   S   Date:_____   Rate:_____

- ☐ I am content with: _____
- ☐ I am proud of: _____
- ☐ Success review
- ☐ I love myself because: _____ ☐
- ☐ Love, thanks, kindness and support for others:
  - 1. _____   2. _____
  - 3. _____   4. _____
- ☐ Love, thanks, kindness and support for me:
  - 1. _____   2. _____
  - 3. _____   4. _____
- ☐ Good Deed/Selfless Act/Random Kindness: _____
- ☐ I gave undivided attention to: _____
- ☐ I made things better by: _____
- ☐ I experienced joy, happiness, fun and/or laughter: _____
- ☐ I smiled _____ minutes
- ☐ Meditation/Prayer _____ minutes
- ☐ Inspiration (reading, video, music): _____
- ☐ I listened to my intuition: _____
- ☐ Physical activity _____ minutes
- ☐ I was 100% honest today
- ☐ I took care of myself by: _____
- ☐ Reviewed purpose 3 times
- ☐ Reviewed intentions 3 times
- ☐ Steps toward goals, intentions and purpose
  - 1. _____   2. _____   3. _____
- ☐ Reviewed vision
- ☐ I am grateful for:
  - 1. _____   6. _____
  - 2. _____   7. _____
  - 3. _____   8. _____
  - 4. _____   9. _____
  - 5. _____   10. _____

- ☐ I am looking forward to: _____

Notes: _____
_____
_____

MINDFUL LIVING WORKSHEET

M Tu W Th F S S   Date:_____   Rate:_____

- ☐ I am content with: _____
- ☐ I am proud of: _____
- ☐ Success review
- ☐ I love myself because: _____ ☐
- ☐ Love, thanks, kindness and support for others:
  - 1. _____ 2. _____
  - 3. _____ 4. _____
- ☐ Love, thanks, kindness and support for me:
  - 1. _____ 2. _____
  - 3. _____ 4. _____
- ☐ Good Deed/Selfless Act/Random Kindness: _____
- ☐ I gave undivided attention to: _____
- ☐ I made things better by: _____
- ☐ I experienced joy, happiness, fun and/or laughter: _____
- ☐ I smiled _____ minutes
- ☐ Meditation/Prayer _____ minutes
- ☐ Inspiration (reading, video, music): _____
- ☐ I listened to my intuition: _____
- ☐ Physical activity _____ minutes
- ☐ I was 100% honest today
- ☐ I took care of myself by: _____
- ☐ Reviewed purpose 3 times
- ☐ Reviewed intentions 3 times
- ☐ Steps toward goals, intentions and purpose
  - 1. _____ 2. _____ 3. _____
- ☐ Reviewed vision
- ☐ I am grateful for:
  - 1. _____ 6. _____
  - 2. _____ 7. _____
  - 3. _____ 8. _____
  - 4. _____ 9. _____
  - 5. _____ 10. _____

- ☐ I am looking forward to: _____

Notes: _____
_____
_____

MINDFUL LIVING WORKSHEET

M Tu W Th F S S   Date:_____   Rate:_____

- ☐ I am content with: _____
- ☐ I am proud of: _____
- ☐ Success review
- ☐ I love myself because: _____ ☐
- ☐ Love, thanks, kindness and support for others:
    1. _____   2. _____
    3. _____   4. _____
- ☐ Love, thanks, kindness and support for me:
    1. _____   2. _____
    3. _____   4. _____
- ☐ Good Deed/Selfless Act/Random Kindness: _____
- ☐ I gave undivided attention to: _____
- ☐ I made things better by: _____
- ☐ I experienced joy, happiness, fun and/or laughter: _____
- ☐ I smiled _____ minutes
- ☐ Meditation/Prayer _____ minutes
- ☐ Inspiration (reading, video, music): _____
- ☐ I listened to my intuition: _____
- ☐ Physical activity _____ minutes
- ☐ I was 100% honest today
- ☐ I took care of myself by: _____
- ☐ Reviewed purpose 3 times
- ☐ Reviewed intentions 3 times
- ☐ Steps toward goals, intentions and purpose
    1. _____ 2. _____ 3. _____
- ☐ Reviewed vision
- ☐ I am grateful for:
    1. _____   6. _____
    2. _____   7. _____
    3. _____   8. _____
    4. _____   9. _____
    5. _____   10. _____

- ☐ I am looking forward to: _____

Notes: _____
_____
_____

MINDFUL LIVING WORKSHEET

M   Tu   W   Th   F   S   S   Date:_____   Rate:_____

- ☐ I am content with: _____
- ☐ I am proud of: _____
- ☐ Success review
- ☐ I love myself because: _____ ☐
- ☐ Love, thanks, kindness and support for others:
  - 1. _____   2. _____
  - 3. _____   4. _____
- ☐ Love, thanks, kindness and support for me:
  - 1. _____   2. _____
  - 3. _____   4. _____
- ☐ Good Deed/Selfless Act/Random Kindness: _____
- ☐ I gave undivided attention to: _____
- ☐ I made things better by: _____
- ☐ I experienced joy, happiness, fun and/or laughter: _____
- ☐ I smiled _____ minutes
- ☐ Meditation/Prayer _____ minutes
- ☐ Inspiration (reading, video, music): _____
- ☐ I listened to my intuition: _____
- ☐ Physical activity _____ minutes
- ☐ I was 100% honest today
- ☐ I took care of myself by: _____
- ☐ Reviewed purpose 3 times
- ☐ Reviewed intentions 3 times
- ☐ Steps toward goals, intentions and purpose
  - 1. _____   2. _____   3. _____
- ☐ Reviewed vision
- ☐ I am grateful for:
  - 1. _____   6. _____
  - 2. _____   7. _____
  - 3. _____   8. _____
  - 4. _____   9. _____
  - 5. _____   10. _____

- ☐ I am looking forward to: _____

Notes: _____
_____
_____
_____

MINDFUL LIVING WORKSHEET

M   Tu   W   Th   F   S   S   Date:_____   Rate:_____

- ☐ I am content with: _____
- ☐ I am proud of: _____
- ☐ Success review
- ☐ I love myself because: _____ ☐
- ☐ Love, thanks, kindness and support for others:
  - 1. _____   2. _____
  - 3. _____   4. _____
- ☐ Love, thanks, kindness and support for me:
  - 1. _____   2. _____
  - 3. _____   4. _____
- ☐ Good Deed/Selfless Act/Random Kindness: _____
- ☐ I gave undivided attention to: _____
- ☐ I made things better by: _____
- ☐ I experienced joy, happiness, fun and/or laughter: _____
- ☐ I smiled _____ minutes
- ☐ Meditation/Prayer _____ minutes
- ☐ Inspiration (reading, video, music): _____
- ☐ I listened to my intuition: _____
- ☐ Physical activity _____ minutes
- ☐ I was 100% honest today
- ☐ I took care of myself by: _____
- ☐ Reviewed purpose 3 times
- ☐ Reviewed intentions 3 times
- ☐ Steps toward goals, intentions and purpose
  - 1. _____   2. _____   3. _____
- ☐ Reviewed vision
- ☐ I am grateful for:
  - 1. _____   6. _____
  - 2. _____   7. _____
  - 3. _____   8. _____
  - 4. _____   9. _____
  - 5. _____   10. _____

- ☐ I am looking forward to: _____

Notes: _____
_____
_____

Mindful Living Worksheet

M   Tu   W   Th   F   S   S   Date:_____   Rate:_____

- ☐ I am content with: _____
- ☐ I am proud of: _____
- ☐ Success review
- ☐ I love myself because: _____ ☐
- ☐ Love, thanks, kindness and support for others:
    1. _____   2. _____
    3. _____   4. _____
- ☐ Love, thanks, kindness and support for me:
    1. _____   2. _____
    3. _____   4. _____
- ☐ Good Deed/Selfless Act/Random Kindness: _____
- ☐ I gave undivided attention to: _____
- ☐ I made things better by: _____
- ☐ I experienced joy, happiness, fun and/or laughter: _____
- ☐ I smiled _____ minutes
- ☐ Meditation/Prayer _____ minutes
- ☐ Inspiration (reading, video, music): _____
- ☐ I listened to my intuition: _____
- ☐ Physical activity _____ minutes
- ☐ I was 100% honest today
- ☐ I took care of myself by: _____
- ☐ Reviewed purpose 3 times
- ☐ Reviewed intentions 3 times
- ☐ Steps toward goals, intentions and purpose
    1. _____   2. _____   3. _____
- ☐ Reviewed vision
- ☐ I am grateful for:
    1. _____   6. _____
    2. _____   7. _____
    3. _____   8. _____
    4. _____   9. _____
    5. _____   10. _____

- ☐ I am looking forward to: _____

Notes: _____
_____
_____
_____

MINDFUL LIVING WORKSHEET

M Tu W Th F S S   Date:_____   Rate:_____

- ☐ I am content with: _____
- ☐ I am proud of: _____
- ☐ Success review
- ☐ I love myself because: _____ ☐
- ☐ Love, thanks, kindness and support for others:
  - 1. _____   2. _____
  - 3. _____   4. _____
- ☐ Love, thanks, kindness and support for me:
  - 1. _____   2. _____
  - 3. _____   4. _____
- ☐ Good Deed/Selfless Act/Random Kindness: _____
- ☐ I gave undivided attention to: _____
- ☐ I made things better by: _____
- ☐ I experienced joy, happiness, fun and/or laughter: _____
- ☐ I smiled _____ minutes
- ☐ Meditation/Prayer _____ minutes
- ☐ Inspiration (reading, video, music): _____
- ☐ I listened to my intuition: _____
- ☐ Physical activity _____ minutes
- ☐ I was 100% honest today
- ☐ I took care of myself by: _____
- ☐ Reviewed purpose 3 times
- ☐ Reviewed intentions 3 times
- ☐ Steps toward goals, intentions and purpose
  - 1. _____ 2. _____ 3. _____
- ☐ Reviewed vision
- ☐ I am grateful for:
  - 1. _____   6. _____
  - 2. _____   7. _____
  - 3. _____   8. _____
  - 4. _____   9. _____
  - 5. _____   10. _____

- ☐ I am looking forward to: _____

Notes: _____
_____
_____

Mindful Living Worksheet

M Tu W Th F S S   Date:_____   Rate:_____

- ☐ I am content with: _____
- ☐ I am proud of: _____
- ☐ Success review
- ☐ I love myself because: _____ ☐
- ☐ Love, thanks, kindness and support for others:
  - 1. _____   2. _____
  - 3. _____   4. _____
- ☐ Love, thanks, kindness and support for me:
  - 1. _____   2. _____
  - 3. _____   4. _____
- ☐ Good Deed/Selfless Act/Random Kindness: _____
- ☐ I gave undivided attention to: _____
- ☐ I made things better by: _____
- ☐ I experienced joy, happiness, fun and/or laughter: _____
- ☐ I smiled _____ minutes
- ☐ Meditation/Prayer _____ minutes
- ☐ Inspiration (reading, video, music): _____
- ☐ I listened to my intuition: _____
- ☐ Physical activity _____ minutes
- ☐ I was 100% honest today
- ☐ I took care of myself by: _____
- ☐ Reviewed purpose 3 times
- ☐ Reviewed intentions 3 times
- ☐ Steps toward goals, intentions and purpose
  - 1. _____   2. _____   3. _____
- ☐ Reviewed vision
- ☐ I am grateful for:
  - 1. _____   6. _____
  - 2. _____   7. _____
  - 3. _____   8. _____
  - 4. _____   9. _____
  - 5. _____   10. _____

- ☐ I am looking forward to: _____

Notes: _____
_____
_____
_____

MINDFUL LIVING WORKSHEET

M Tu W Th F S S   Date:_____   Rate:_____

- ☐ I am content with: _____
- ☐ I am proud of: _____
- ☐ Success review
- ☐ I love myself because: _____ ☐
- ☐ Love, thanks, kindness and support for others:
    1. _____   2. _____
    3. _____   4. _____
- ☐ Love, thanks, kindness and support for me:
    1. _____   2. _____
    3. _____   4. _____
- ☐ Good Deed/Selfless Act/Random Kindness: _____
- ☐ I gave undivided attention to: _____
- ☐ I made things better by: _____
- ☐ I experienced joy, happiness, fun and/or laughter: _____
- ☐ I smiled _____ minutes
- ☐ Meditation/Prayer _____ minutes
- ☐ Inspiration (reading, video, music): _____
- ☐ I listened to my intuition: _____
- ☐ Physical activity _____ minutes
- ☐ I was 100% honest today
- ☐ I took care of myself by: _____
- ☐ Reviewed purpose 3 times
- ☐ Reviewed intentions 3 times
- ☐ Steps toward goals, intentions and purpose
    1. _____ 2. _____ 3. _____
- ☐ Reviewed vision
- ☐ I am grateful for:
    1. _____   6. _____
    2. _____   7. _____
    3. _____   8. _____
    4. _____   9. _____
    5. _____   10. _____

- ☐ I am looking forward to: _____

Notes: _____
_____
_____
_____

Mindful Living Worksheet

M   Tu   W   Th   F   S   S   Date:_____   Rate:_____

- ☐ I am content with: _____
- ☐ I am proud of: _____
- ☐ Success review
- ☐ I love myself because: _____ ☐
- ☐ Love, thanks, kindness and support for others:
  - 1. _____   2. _____
  - 3. _____   4. _____
- ☐ Love, thanks, kindness and support for me:
  - 1. _____   2. _____
  - 3. _____   4. _____
- ☐ Good Deed/Selfless Act/Random Kindness: _____
- ☐ I gave undivided attention to: _____
- ☐ I made things better by: _____
- ☐ I experienced joy, happiness, fun and/or laughter: _____
- ☐ I smiled _____ minutes
- ☐ Meditation/Prayer _____ minutes
- ☐ Inspiration (reading, video, music): _____
- ☐ I listened to my intuition: _____
- ☐ Physical activity _____ minutes
- ☐ I was 100% honest today
- ☐ I took care of myself by: _____
- ☐ Reviewed purpose 3 times
- ☐ Reviewed intentions 3 times
- ☐ Steps toward goals, intentions and purpose
  - 1. _____ 2. _____ 3. _____
- ☐ Reviewed vision
- ☐ I am grateful for:
  - 1. _____   6. _____
  - 2. _____   7. _____
  - 3. _____   8. _____
  - 4. _____   9. _____
  - 5. _____   10. _____
- ☐ I am looking forward to: _____

Notes: _____
_____
_____
_____

Mindful Living Worksheet

M   Tu   W   Th   F   S   S   Date: _____   Rate: _____

- ☐ I am content with: _____
- ☐ I am proud of: _____
- ☐ Success review
- ☐ I love myself because: _____ ☐
- ☐ Love, thanks, kindness and support for others:
    1. _____   2. _____
    3. _____   4. _____
- ☐ Love, thanks, kindness and support for me:
    1. _____   2. _____
    3. _____   4. _____
- ☐ Good Deed/Selfless Act/Random Kindness: _____
- ☐ I gave undivided attention to: _____
- ☐ I made things better by: _____
- ☐ I experienced joy, happiness, fun and/or laughter: _____
- ☐ I smiled _____ minutes
- ☐ Meditation/Prayer _____ minutes
- ☐ Inspiration (reading, video, music): _____
- ☐ I listened to my intuition: _____
- ☐ Physical activity _____ minutes
- ☐ I was 100% honest today
- ☐ I took care of myself by: _____
- ☐ Reviewed purpose 3 times
- ☐ Reviewed intentions 3 times
- ☐ Steps toward goals, intentions and purpose
    1. _____ 2. _____ 3. _____
- ☐ Reviewed vision
- ☐ I am grateful for:
    1. _____   6. _____
    2. _____   7. _____
    3. _____   8. _____
    4. _____   9. _____
    5. _____   10. _____

- ☐ I am looking forward to: _____

Notes: _____
_____
_____

Mindful Living Worksheet

M   Tu   W   Th   F   S   S   Date:_____   Rate:_____

☐ I am content with: _____
☐ I am proud of: _____
☐ Success review
☐ I love myself because: _____ ☐
☐ Love, thanks, kindness and support for others:
    1. _____   2. _____
    3. _____   4. _____
☐ Love, thanks, kindness and support for me:
    1. _____   2. _____
    3. _____   4. _____
☐ Good Deed/Selfless Act/Random Kindness: _____
☐ I gave undivided attention to: _____
☐ I made things better by: _____
☐ I experienced joy, happiness, fun and/or laughter: _____
☐ I smiled _____ minutes
☐ Meditation/Prayer _____ minutes
☐ Inspiration (reading, video, music): _____
☐ I listened to my intuition: _____
☐ Physical activity _____ minutes
☐ I was 100% honest today
☐ I took care of myself by: _____
☐ Reviewed purpose 3 times
☐ Reviewed intentions 3 times
☐ Steps toward goals, intentions and purpose
    1. _____   2. _____   3. _____
☐ Reviewed vision
☐ I am grateful for:
    1. _____   6. _____
    2. _____   7. _____
    3. _____   8. _____
    4. _____   9. _____
    5. _____   10. _____

☐ I am looking forward to: _____

Notes: _____
_____
_____
_____

MINDFUL LIVING WORKSHEET

M Tu W Th F S S   Date:_____   Rate:_____

- ☐ I am content with: _____
- ☐ I am proud of: _____
- ☐ Success review
- ☐ I love myself because: _____ ☐
- ☐ Love, thanks, kindness and support for others:
  - 1. _____   2. _____
  - 3. _____   4. _____
- ☐ Love, thanks, kindness and support for me:
  - 1. _____   2. _____
  - 3. _____   4. _____
- ☐ Good Deed/Selfless Act/Random Kindness: _____
- ☐ I gave undivided attention to: _____
- ☐ I made things better by: _____
- ☐ I experienced joy, happiness, fun and/or laughter: _____
- ☐ I smiled _____ minutes
- ☐ Meditation/Prayer _____ minutes
- ☐ Inspiration (reading, video, music): _____
- ☐ I listened to my intuition: _____
- ☐ Physical activity _____ minutes
- ☐ I was 100% honest today
- ☐ I took care of myself by: _____
- ☐ Reviewed purpose 3 times
- ☐ Reviewed intentions 3 times
- ☐ Steps toward goals, intentions and purpose
  - 1. _____ 2. _____ 3. _____
- ☐ Reviewed vision
- ☐ I am grateful for:
  - 1. _____   6. _____
  - 2. _____   7. _____
  - 3. _____   8. _____
  - 4. _____   9. _____
  - 5. _____   10. _____

- ☐ I am looking forward to: _____

Notes: _____
_____
_____
_____

Mindful Living Worksheet

M   Tu   W   Th   F   S   S   Date:_____   Rate:_____

- ☐ I am content with: _____
- ☐ I am proud of: _____
- ☐ Success review
- ☐ I love myself because: _____ ☐
- ☐ Love, thanks, kindness and support for others:
  - 1. _____   2. _____
  - 3. _____   4. _____
- ☐ Love, thanks, kindness and support for me:
  - 1. _____   2. _____
  - 3. _____   4. _____
- ☐ Good Deed/Selfless Act/Random Kindness: _____
- ☐ I gave undivided attention to: _____
- ☐ I made things better by: _____
- ☐ I experienced joy, happiness, fun and/or laughter: _____
- ☐ I smiled _____ minutes
- ☐ Meditation/Prayer _____ minutes
- ☐ Inspiration (reading, video, music): _____
- ☐ I listened to my intuition: _____
- ☐ Physical activity _____ minutes
- ☐ I was 100% honest today
- ☐ I took care of myself by: _____
- ☐ Reviewed purpose 3 times
- ☐ Reviewed intentions 3 times
- ☐ Steps toward goals, intentions and purpose
  - 1. _____ 2. _____ 3. _____
- ☐ Reviewed vision
- ☐ I am grateful for:
  - 1. _____   6. _____
  - 2. _____   7. _____
  - 3. _____   8. _____
  - 4. _____   9. _____
  - 5. _____   10. _____

- ☐ I am looking forward to: _____

Notes: _____
_____
_____
_____

MINDFUL LIVING WORKSHEET

M Tu W Th F S S   Date:_____   Rate:_____

- ☐ I am content with: _____
- ☐ I am proud of: _____
- ☐ Success review
- ☐ I love myself because: _____ ☐
- ☐ Love, thanks, kindness and support for others:
    1. _____   2. _____
    3. _____   4. _____
- ☐ Love, thanks, kindness and support for me:
    1. _____   2. _____
    3. _____   4. _____
- ☐ Good Deed/Selfless Act/Random Kindness: _____
- ☐ I gave undivided attention to: _____
- ☐ I made things better by: _____
- ☐ I experienced joy, happiness, fun and/or laughter: _____
- ☐ I smiled _____ minutes
- ☐ Meditation/Prayer _____ minutes
- ☐ Inspiration (reading, video, music): _____
- ☐ I listened to my intuition: _____
- ☐ Physical activity _____ minutes
- ☐ I was 100% honest today
- ☐ I took care of myself by: _____
- ☐ Reviewed purpose 3 times
- ☐ Reviewed intentions 3 times
- ☐ Steps toward goals, intentions and purpose
    1. _____ 2. _____ 3. _____
- ☐ Reviewed vision
- ☐ I am grateful for:
    1. _____   6. _____
    2. _____   7. _____
    3. _____   8. _____
    4. _____   9. _____
    5. _____   10. _____

- ☐ I am looking forward to: _____

Notes: _____
_____
_____

MINDFUL LIVING WORKSHEET

M   Tu   W   Th   F   S   S   Date:_____   Rate:_____

- ☐ I am content with: _____
- ☐ I am proud of: _____
- ☐ Success review
- ☐ I love myself because: _____ ☐
- ☐ Love, thanks, kindness and support for others:
  - 1. _____   2. _____
  - 3. _____   4. _____
- ☐ Love, thanks, kindness and support for me:
  - 1. _____   2. _____
  - 3. _____   4. _____
- ☐ Good Deed/Selfless Act/Random Kindness: _____
- ☐ I gave undivided attention to: _____
- ☐ I made things better by: _____
- ☐ I experienced joy, happiness, fun and/or laughter: _____
- ☐ I smiled _____ minutes
- ☐ Meditation/Prayer _____ minutes
- ☐ Inspiration (reading, video, music): _____
- ☐ I listened to my intuition: _____
- ☐ Physical activity _____ minutes
- ☐ I was 100% honest today
- ☐ I took care of myself by: _____
- ☐ Reviewed purpose 3 times
- ☐ Reviewed intentions 3 times
- ☐ Steps toward goals, intentions and purpose
  - 1. _____   2. _____   3. _____
- ☐ Reviewed vision
- ☐ I am grateful for:
  - 1. _____   6. _____
  - 2. _____   7. _____
  - 3. _____   8. _____
  - 4. _____   9. _____
  - 5. _____   10. _____

- ☐ I am looking forward to: _____

Notes: _____
_____
_____

MINDFUL LIVING WORKSHEET

M Tu W Th F S S   Date:_____   Rate:_____

- ☐ I am content with: _____
- ☐ I am proud of: _____
- ☐ Success review
- ☐ I love myself because: _____ ☐
- ☐ Love, thanks, kindness and support for others:
    1. _____   2. _____
    3. _____   4. _____
- ☐ Love, thanks, kindness and support for me:
    1. _____   2. _____
    3. _____   4. _____
- ☐ Good Deed/Selfless Act/Random Kindness: _____
- ☐ I gave undivided attention to: _____
- ☐ I made things better by: _____
- ☐ I experienced joy, happiness, fun and/or laughter: _____
- ☐ I smiled _____ minutes
- ☐ Meditation/Prayer _____ minutes
- ☐ Inspiration (reading, video, music): _____
- ☐ I listened to my intuition: _____
- ☐ Physical activity _____ minutes
- ☐ I was 100% honest today
- ☐ I took care of myself by: _____
- ☐ Reviewed purpose 3 times
- ☐ Reviewed intentions 3 times
- ☐ Steps toward goals, intentions and purpose
    1. _____ 2. _____ 3. _____
- ☐ Reviewed vision
- ☐ I am grateful for:
    1. _____   6. _____
    2. _____   7. _____
    3. _____   8. _____
    4. _____   9. _____
    5. _____   10. _____

- ☐ I am looking forward to: _____

Notes: _____
_____
_____
_____

Mindful Living Worksheet

M Tu W Th F S S   Date:_____   Rate:_____

- ☐ I am content with: _____
- ☐ I am proud of: _____
- ☐ Success review
- ☐ I love myself because: _____ ☐
- ☐ Love, thanks, kindness and support for others:
    1. _____   2. _____
    3. _____   4. _____
- ☐ Love, thanks, kindness and support for me:
    1. _____   2. _____
    3. _____   4. _____
- ☐ Good Deed/Selfless Act/Random Kindness: _____
- ☐ I gave undivided attention to: _____
- ☐ I made things better by: _____
- ☐ I experienced joy, happiness, fun and/or laughter: _____
- ☐ I smiled _____ minutes
- ☐ Meditation/Prayer _____ minutes
- ☐ Inspiration (reading, video, music): _____
- ☐ I listened to my intuition: _____
- ☐ Physical activity _____ minutes
- ☐ I was 100% honest today
- ☐ I took care of myself by: _____
- ☐ Reviewed purpose 3 times
- ☐ Reviewed intentions 3 times
- ☐ Steps toward goals, intentions and purpose
    1. _____   2. _____   3. _____
- ☐ Reviewed vision
- ☐ I am grateful for:
    1. _____   6. _____
    2. _____   7. _____
    3. _____   8. _____
    4. _____   9. _____
    5. _____   10. _____

- ☐ I am looking forward to: _____

Notes: _____
_____
_____

Mindful Living Worksheet

M   Tu   W   Th   F   S   S   Date:_____   Rate:_____

- ☐ I am content with: _____
- ☐ I am proud of: _____
- ☐ Success review
- ☐ I love myself because: _____ ☐
- ☐ Love, thanks, kindness and support for others:
    1. _____   2. _____
    3. _____   4. _____
- ☐ Love, thanks, kindness and support for me:
    1. _____   2. _____
    3. _____   4. _____
- ☐ Good Deed/Selfless Act/Random Kindness: _____
- ☐ I gave undivided attention to: _____
- ☐ I made things better by: _____
- ☐ I experienced joy, happiness, fun and/or laughter: _____
- ☐ I smiled _____ minutes
- ☐ Meditation/Prayer _____ minutes
- ☐ Inspiration (reading, video, music): _____
- ☐ I listened to my intuition: _____
- ☐ Physical activity _____ minutes
- ☐ I was 100% honest today
- ☐ I took care of myself by: _____
- ☐ Reviewed purpose 3 times
- ☐ Reviewed intentions 3 times
- ☐ Steps toward goals, intentions and purpose
    1. _____   2. _____   3. _____
- ☐ Reviewed vision
- ☐ I am grateful for:
    1. _____   6. _____
    2. _____   7. _____
    3. _____   8. _____
    4. _____   9. _____
    5. _____   10. _____

- ☐ I am looking forward to: _____

Notes: _____
_____
_____

MINDFUL LIVING WORKSHEET

M Tu W Th F S S   Date:_____   Rate:_____

☐ I am content with: _____
☐ I am proud of: _____
☐ Success review
☐ I love myself because: _____ ☐
☐ Love, thanks, kindness and support for others:
    1. _____   2. _____
    3. _____   4. _____
☐ Love, thanks, kindness and support for me:
    1. _____   2. _____
    3. _____   4. _____
☐ Good Deed/Selfless Act/Random Kindness: _____
☐ I gave undivided attention to: _____
☐ I made things better by: _____
☐ I experienced joy, happiness, fun and/or laughter: _____
☐ I smiled _____ minutes
☐ Meditation/Prayer _____ minutes
☐ Inspiration (reading, video, music): _____
☐ I listened to my intuition: _____
☐ Physical activity _____ minutes
☐ I was 100% honest today
☐ I took care of myself by: _____
☐ Reviewed purpose 3 times
☐ Reviewed intentions 3 times
☐ Steps toward goals, intentions and purpose
    1. _____ 2. _____ 3. _____
☐ Reviewed vision
☐ I am grateful for:
    1. _____   6. _____
    2. _____   7. _____
    3. _____   8. _____
    4. _____   9. _____
    5. _____   10. _____

☐ I am looking forward to: _____

Notes: _____
_____
_____
_____

MINDFUL LIVING WORKSHEET

M Tu W Th F S S 　　Date:_____　　　　　Rate:_____

- ☐ I am content with: _____
- ☐ I am proud of: _____
- ☐ Success review
- ☐ I love myself because: _____ ☐
- ☐ Love, thanks, kindness and support for others:
    - 1. _____ 2. _____
    - 3. _____ 4. _____
- ☐ Love, thanks, kindness and support for me:
    - 1. _____ 2. _____
    - 3. _____ 4. _____
- ☐ Good Deed/Selfless Act/Random Kindness: _____
- ☐ I gave undivided attention to: _____
- ☐ I made things better by: _____
- ☐ I experienced joy, happiness, fun and/or laughter: _____
- ☐ I smiled _____ minutes
- ☐ Meditation/Prayer _____ minutes
- ☐ Inspiration (reading, video, music): _____
- ☐ I listened to my intuition: _____
- ☐ Physical activity _____ minutes
- ☐ I was 100% honest today
- ☐ I took care of myself by: _____
- ☐ Reviewed purpose 3 times
- ☐ Reviewed intentions 3 times
- ☐ Steps toward goals, intentions and purpose
    - 1. _____ 2. _____ 3. _____
- ☐ Reviewed vision
- ☐ I am grateful for:
    - 1. _____ 6. _____
    - 2. _____ 7. _____
    - 3. _____ 8. _____
    - 4. _____ 9. _____
    - 5. _____ 10. _____

- ☐ I am looking forward to: _____

Notes: _____
_____
_____

Mindful Living Worksheet

M Tu W Th F S S   Date:_____   Rate:_____

- ☐ I am content with: _____
- ☐ I am proud of: _____
- ☐ Success review
- ☐ I love myself because: _____ ☐
- ☐ Love, thanks, kindness and support for others:
  - 1. _____   2. _____
  - 3. _____   4. _____
- ☐ Love, thanks, kindness and support for me:
  - 1. _____   2. _____
  - 3. _____   4. _____
- ☐ Good Deed/Selfless Act/Random Kindness: _____
- ☐ I gave undivided attention to: _____
- ☐ I made things better by: _____
- ☐ I experienced joy, happiness, fun and/or laughter: _____
- ☐ I smiled _____ minutes
- ☐ Meditation/Prayer _____ minutes
- ☐ Inspiration (reading, video, music): _____
- ☐ I listened to my intuition: _____
- ☐ Physical activity _____ minutes
- ☐ I was 100% honest today
- ☐ I took care of myself by: _____
- ☐ Reviewed purpose 3 times
- ☐ Reviewed intentions 3 times
- ☐ Steps toward goals, intentions and purpose
  - 1. _____   2. _____   3. _____
- ☐ Reviewed vision
- ☐ I am grateful for:
  - 1. _____   6. _____
  - 2. _____   7. _____
  - 3. _____   8. _____
  - 4. _____   9. _____
  - 5. _____   10. _____

- ☐ I am looking forward to: _____

Notes: _____
_____
_____

Mindful Living Worksheet

M Tu W Th F S S   Date:_____   Rate:_____

- ☐ I am content with: _____
- ☐ I am proud of: _____
- ☐ Success review
- ☐ I love myself because: _____ ☐
- ☐ Love, thanks, kindness and support for others:
    1. _____ 2. _____
    3. _____ 4. _____
- ☐ Love, thanks, kindness and support for me:
    1. _____ 2. _____
    3. _____ 4. _____
- ☐ Good Deed/Selfless Act/Random Kindness: _____
- ☐ I gave undivided attention to: _____
- ☐ I made things better by: _____
- ☐ I experienced joy, happiness, fun and/or laughter: _____
- ☐ I smiled _____ minutes
- ☐ Meditation/Prayer _____ minutes
- ☐ Inspiration (reading, video, music): _____
- ☐ I listened to my intuition: _____
- ☐ Physical activity _____ minutes
- ☐ I was 100% honest today
- ☐ I took care of myself by: _____
- ☐ Reviewed purpose 3 times
- ☐ Reviewed intentions 3 times
- ☐ Steps toward goals, intentions and purpose
    1. _____ 2. _____ 3. _____
- ☐ Reviewed vision
- ☐ I am grateful for:
    1. _____ 6. _____
    2. _____ 7. _____
    3. _____ 8. _____
    4. _____ 9. _____
    5. _____ 10. _____

- ☐ I am looking forward to: _____

Notes: _____
_____
_____

MINDFUL LIVING WORKSHEET

M Tu W Th F S S   Date:_____   Rate:_____

- ☐ I am content with: _____
- ☐ I am proud of: _____
- ☐ Success review
- ☐ I love myself because: _____ ☐
- ☐ Love, thanks, kindness and support for others:
  - 1. _____ 2. _____
  - 3. _____ 4. _____
- ☐ Love, thanks, kindness and support for me:
  - 1. _____ 2. _____
  - 3. _____ 4. _____
- ☐ Good Deed/Selfless Act/Random Kindness: _____
- ☐ I gave undivided attention to: _____
- ☐ I made things better by: _____
- ☐ I experienced joy, happiness, fun and/or laughter: _____
- ☐ I smiled _____ minutes
- ☐ Meditation/Prayer _____ minutes
- ☐ Inspiration (reading, video, music): _____
- ☐ I listened to my intuition: _____
- ☐ Physical activity _____ minutes
- ☐ I was 100% honest today
- ☐ I took care of myself by: _____
- ☐ Reviewed purpose 3 times
- ☐ Reviewed intentions 3 times
- ☐ Steps toward goals, intentions and purpose
  - 1. _____ 2. _____ 3. _____
- ☐ Reviewed vision
- ☐ I am grateful for:
  - 1. _____ 6. _____
  - 2. _____ 7. _____
  - 3. _____ 8. _____
  - 4. _____ 9. _____
  - 5. _____ 10. _____
- ☐ I am looking forward to: _____

Notes: _____
_____
_____

MINDFUL LIVING WORKSHEET

M   Tu   W   Th   F   S   S   Date:_____   Rate:_____

- ☐ I am content with: _____
- ☐ I am proud of: _____
- ☐ Success review
- ☐ I love myself because: _____ ☐
- ☐ Love, thanks, kindness and support for others:
    1. _____   2. _____
    3. _____   4. _____
- ☐ Love, thanks, kindness and support for me:
    1. _____   2. _____
    3. _____   4. _____
- ☐ Good Deed/Selfless Act/Random Kindness: _____
- ☐ I gave undivided attention to: _____
- ☐ I made things better by: _____
- ☐ I experienced joy, happiness, fun and/or laughter: _____
- ☐ I smiled _____ minutes
- ☐ Meditation/Prayer _____ minutes
- ☐ Inspiration (reading, video, music): _____
- ☐ I listened to my intuition: _____
- ☐ Physical activity _____ minutes
- ☐ I was 100% honest today
- ☐ I took care of myself by: _____
- ☐ Reviewed purpose 3 times
- ☐ Reviewed intentions 3 times
- ☐ Steps toward goals, intentions and purpose
    1. _____   2. _____   3. _____
- ☐ Reviewed vision
- ☐ I am grateful for:
    1. _____   6. _____
    2. _____   7. _____
    3. _____   8. _____
    4. _____   9. _____
    5. _____   10. _____

- ☐ I am looking forward to: _____

Notes: _____
_____
_____

MINDFUL LIVING WORKSHEET

M Tu W Th F S S   Date:_____   Rate:_____

- ☐ I am content with: _____
- ☐ I am proud of: _____
- ☐ Success review
- ☐ I love myself because: _____ ☐
- ☐ Love, thanks, kindness and support for others:
    - 1. _____   2. _____
    - 3. _____   4. _____
- ☐ Love, thanks, kindness and support for me:
    - 1. _____   2. _____
    - 3. _____   4. _____
- ☐ Good Deed/Selfless Act/Random Kindness: _____
- ☐ I gave undivided attention to: _____
- ☐ I made things better by: _____
- ☐ I experienced joy, happiness, fun and/or laughter: _____
- ☐ I smiled _____ minutes
- ☐ Meditation/Prayer _____ minutes
- ☐ Inspiration (reading, video, music): _____
- ☐ I listened to my intuition: _____
- ☐ Physical activity _____ minutes
- ☐ I was 100% honest today
- ☐ I took care of myself by: _____
- ☐ Reviewed purpose 3 times
- ☐ Reviewed intentions 3 times
- ☐ Steps toward goals, intentions and purpose
    - 1. _____   2. _____   3. _____
- ☐ Reviewed vision
- ☐ I am grateful for:
    - 1. _____   6. _____
    - 2. _____   7. _____
    - 3. _____   8. _____
    - 4. _____   9. _____
    - 5. _____   10. _____

- ☐ I am looking forward to: _____

Notes: _____
_____
_____
_____

Mindful Living Worksheet

M   Tu   W   Th   F   S   S   Date:_____   Rate:_____

- ☐ I am content with: _____
- ☐ I am proud of: _____
- ☐ Success review
- ☐ I love myself because: _____ ☐
- ☐ Love, thanks, kindness and support for others:
  - 1. _____   2. _____
  - 3. _____   4. _____
- ☐ Love, thanks, kindness and support for me:
  - 1. _____   2. _____
  - 3. _____   4. _____
- ☐ Good Deed/Selfless Act/Random Kindness: _____
- ☐ I gave undivided attention to: _____
- ☐ I made things better by: _____
- ☐ I experienced joy, happiness, fun and/or laughter: _____
- ☐ I smiled _____ minutes
- ☐ Meditation/Prayer _____ minutes
- ☐ Inspiration (reading, video, music): _____
- ☐ I listened to my intuition: _____
- ☐ Physical activity _____ minutes
- ☐ I was 100% honest today
- ☐ I took care of myself by: _____
- ☐ Reviewed purpose 3 times
- ☐ Reviewed intentions 3 times
- ☐ Steps toward goals, intentions and purpose
  - 1. _____   2. _____   3. _____
- ☐ Reviewed vision
- ☐ I am grateful for:
  - 1. _____   6. _____
  - 2. _____   7. _____
  - 3. _____   8. _____
  - 4. _____   9. _____
  - 5. _____   10. _____
- ☐ I am looking forward to: _____

Notes: _____
_____
_____

MINDFUL LIVING WORKSHEET

M Tu W Th F S S   Date:_____   Rate:_____

☐ I am content with: _____
☐ I am proud of: _____
☐ Success review
☐ I love myself because: _____ ☐
☐ Love, thanks, kindness and support for others:
    1. _____   2. _____
    3. _____   4. _____
☐ Love, thanks, kindness and support for me:
    1. _____   2. _____
    3. _____   4. _____
☐ Good Deed/Selfless Act/Random Kindness: _____
☐ I gave undivided attention to: _____
☐ I made things better by: _____
☐ I experienced joy, happiness, fun and/or laughter: _____
☐ I smiled _____ minutes
☐ Meditation/Prayer _____ minutes
☐ Inspiration (reading, video, music): _____
☐ I listened to my intuition: _____
☐ Physical activity _____ minutes
☐ I was 100% honest today
☐ I took care of myself by: _____
☐ Reviewed purpose 3 times
☐ Reviewed intentions 3 times
☐ Steps toward goals, intentions and purpose
    1. _____   2. _____   3. _____
☐ Reviewed vision
☐ I am grateful for:
    1. _____   6. _____
    2. _____   7. _____
    3. _____   8. _____
    4. _____   9. _____
    5. _____   10. _____

☐ I am looking forward to: _____

Notes: _____
_____
_____

MINDFUL LIVING WORKSHEET

M   Tu   W   Th   F   S   S   Date:_____   Rate:_____

- ☐ I am content with: _____
- ☐ I am proud of: _____
- ☐ Success review
- ☐ I love myself because: _____ ☐
- ☐ Love, thanks, kindness and support for others:
  - 1. _____   2. _____
  - 3. _____   4. _____
- ☐ Love, thanks, kindness and support for me:
  - 1. _____   2. _____
  - 3. _____   4. _____
- ☐ Good Deed/Selfless Act/Random Kindness: _____
- ☐ I gave undivided attention to: _____
- ☐ I made things better by: _____
- ☐ I experienced joy, happiness, fun and/or laughter: _____
- ☐ I smiled _____ minutes
- ☐ Meditation/Prayer _____ minutes
- ☐ Inspiration (reading, video, music): _____
- ☐ I listened to my intuition: _____
- ☐ Physical activity _____ minutes
- ☐ I was 100% honest today
- ☐ I took care of myself by: _____
- ☐ Reviewed purpose 3 times
- ☐ Reviewed intentions 3 times
- ☐ Steps toward goals, intentions and purpose
  - 1. _____ 2. _____ 3. _____
- ☐ Reviewed vision
- ☐ I am grateful for:
  - 1. _____   6. _____
  - 2. _____   7. _____
  - 3. _____   8. _____
  - 4. _____   9. _____
  - 5. _____   10. _____

- ☐ I am looking forward to: _____

Notes: _____
_____
_____

MINDFUL LIVING WORKSHEET

M   Tu   W   Th   F   S   S   Date:_____   Rate:_____

- ☐ I am content with: _____
- ☐ I am proud of: _____
- ☐ Success review
- ☐ I love myself because: _____ ☐
- ☐ Love, thanks, kindness and support for others:
  - 1. _____   2. _____
  - 3. _____   4. _____
- ☐ Love, thanks, kindness and support for me:
  - 1. _____   2. _____
  - 3. _____   4. _____
- ☐ Good Deed/Selfless Act/Random Kindness: _____
- ☐ I gave undivided attention to: _____
- ☐ I made things better by: _____
- ☐ I experienced joy, happiness, fun and/or laughter: _____
- ☐ I smiled _____ minutes
- ☐ Meditation/Prayer _____ minutes
- ☐ Inspiration (reading, video, music): _____
- ☐ I listened to my intuition: _____
- ☐ Physical activity _____ minutes
- ☐ I was 100% honest today
- ☐ I took care of myself by: _____
- ☐ Reviewed purpose 3 times
- ☐ Reviewed intentions 3 times
- ☐ Steps toward goals, intentions and purpose
  - 1. _____   2. _____   3. _____
- ☐ Reviewed vision
- ☐ I am grateful for:
  - 1. _____   6. _____
  - 2. _____   7. _____
  - 3. _____   8. _____
  - 4. _____   9. _____
  - 5. _____   10. _____

- ☐ I am looking forward to: _____

Notes: _____
_____
_____

Mindful Living Worksheet

M Tu W Th F S S   Date:_____   Rate:_____

- ☐ I am content with: _____
- ☐ I am proud of: _____
- ☐ Success review
- ☐ I love myself because: _____ ☐
- ☐ Love, thanks, kindness and support for others:
    1. _____   2. _____
    3. _____   4. _____
- ☐ Love, thanks, kindness and support for me:
    1. _____   2. _____
    3. _____   4. _____
- ☐ Good Deed/Selfless Act/Random Kindness: _____
- ☐ I gave undivided attention to: _____
- ☐ I made things better by: _____
- ☐ I experienced joy, happiness, fun and/or laughter: _____
- ☐ I smiled _____ minutes
- ☐ Meditation/Prayer _____ minutes
- ☐ Inspiration (reading, video, music): _____
- ☐ I listened to my intuition: _____
- ☐ Physical activity _____ minutes
- ☐ I was 100% honest today
- ☐ I took care of myself by: _____
- ☐ Reviewed purpose 3 times
- ☐ Reviewed intentions 3 times
- ☐ Steps toward goals, intentions and purpose
    1. _____ 2. _____ 3. _____
- ☐ Reviewed vision
- ☐ I am grateful for:
    1. _____   6. _____
    2. _____   7. _____
    3. _____   8. _____
    4. _____   9. _____
    5. _____   10. _____

- ☐ I am looking forward to: _____

Notes: _____
_____
_____

Mindful Living Worksheet

M Tu W Th F S S   Date:_____   Rate:_____

- ☐ I am content with: _____
- ☐ I am proud of: _____
- ☐ Success review
- ☐ I love myself because: _____ ☐
- ☐ Love, thanks, kindness and support for others:
    - 1. _____   2. _____
    - 3. _____   4. _____
- ☐ Love, thanks, kindness and support for me:
    - 1. _____   2. _____
    - 3. _____   4. _____
- ☐ Good Deed/Selfless Act/Random Kindness: _____
- ☐ I gave undivided attention to: _____
- ☐ I made things better by: _____
- ☐ I experienced joy, happiness, fun and/or laughter: _____
- ☐ I smiled _____ minutes
- ☐ Meditation/Prayer _____ minutes
- ☐ Inspiration (reading, video, music): _____
- ☐ I listened to my intuition: _____
- ☐ Physical activity _____ minutes
- ☐ I was 100% honest today
- ☐ I took care of myself by: _____
- ☐ Reviewed purpose 3 times
- ☐ Reviewed intentions 3 times
- ☐ Steps toward goals, intentions and purpose
    - 1. _____ 2. _____ 3. _____
- ☐ Reviewed vision
- ☐ I am grateful for:
    - 1. _____   6. _____
    - 2. _____   7. _____
    - 3. _____   8. _____
    - 4. _____   9. _____
    - 5. _____   10. _____

- ☐ I am looking forward to: _____

Notes: _____
_____
_____

MINDFUL LIVING WORKSHEET

M Tu W Th F S S   Date:_____   Rate:_____

- ☐ I am content with: _____
- ☐ I am proud of: _____
- ☐ Success review
- ☐ I love myself because: _____ ☐
- ☐ Love, thanks, kindness and support for others:
  - 1. _____   2. _____
  - 3. _____   4. _____
- ☐ Love, thanks, kindness and support for me:
  - 1. _____   2. _____
  - 3. _____   4. _____
- ☐ Good Deed/Selfless Act/Random Kindness: _____
- ☐ I gave undivided attention to: _____
- ☐ I made things better by: _____
- ☐ I experienced joy, happiness, fun and/or laughter: _____
- ☐ I smiled _____ minutes
- ☐ Meditation/Prayer _____ minutes
- ☐ Inspiration (reading, video, music): _____
- ☐ I listened to my intuition: _____
- ☐ Physical activity _____ minutes
- ☐ I was 100% honest today
- ☐ I took care of myself by: _____
- ☐ Reviewed purpose 3 times
- ☐ Reviewed intentions 3 times
- ☐ Steps toward goals, intentions and purpose
  - 1. _____ 2. _____ 3. _____
- ☐ Reviewed vision
- ☐ I am grateful for:
  - 1. _____   6. _____
  - 2. _____   7. _____
  - 3. _____   8. _____
  - 4. _____   9. _____
  - 5. _____   10. _____

- ☐ I am looking forward to: _____

Notes: _____
_____
_____

MINDFUL LIVING WORKSHEET

M Tu W Th F S S   Date:_____   Rate:_____

- ☐ I am content with: _____
- ☐ I am proud of: _____
- ☐ Success review
- ☐ I love myself because: _____ ☐
- ☐ Love, thanks, kindness and support for others:
  - 1. _____   2. _____
  - 3. _____   4. _____
- ☐ Love, thanks, kindness and support for me:
  - 1. _____   2. _____
  - 3. _____   4. _____
- ☐ Good Deed/Selfless Act/Random Kindness: _____
- ☐ I gave undivided attention to: _____
- ☐ I made things better by: _____
- ☐ I experienced joy, happiness, fun and/or laughter: _____
- ☐ I smiled _____ minutes
- ☐ Meditation/Prayer _____ minutes
- ☐ Inspiration (reading, video, music): _____
- ☐ I listened to my intuition: _____
- ☐ Physical activity _____ minutes
- ☐ I was 100% honest today
- ☐ I took care of myself by: _____
- ☐ Reviewed purpose 3 times
- ☐ Reviewed intentions 3 times
- ☐ Steps toward goals, intentions and purpose
  - 1. _____ 2. _____ 3. _____
- ☐ Reviewed vision
- ☐ I am grateful for:
  - 1. _____   6. _____
  - 2. _____   7. _____
  - 3. _____   8. _____
  - 4. _____   9. _____
  - 5. _____   10. _____
- ☐ I am looking forward to: _____

Notes: _____
_____
_____

MINDFUL LIVING WORKSHEET

M Tu W Th F S S   Date:_____   Rate:_____

- ☐ I am content with: _____
- ☐ I am proud of: _____
- ☐ Success review
- ☐ I love myself because: _____ ☐
- ☐ Love, thanks, kindness and support for others:
  - 1. _____   2. _____
  - 3. _____   4. _____
- ☐ Love, thanks, kindness and support for me:
  - 1. _____   2. _____
  - 3. _____   4. _____
- ☐ Good Deed/Selfless Act/Random Kindness: _____
- ☐ I gave undivided attention to: _____
- ☐ I made things better by: _____
- ☐ I experienced joy, happiness, fun and/or laughter: _____
- ☐ I smiled _____ minutes
- ☐ Meditation/Prayer _____ minutes
- ☐ Inspiration (reading, video, music): _____
- ☐ I listened to my intuition: _____
- ☐ Physical activity _____ minutes
- ☐ I was 100% honest today
- ☐ I took care of myself by: _____
- ☐ Reviewed purpose 3 times
- ☐ Reviewed intentions 3 times
- ☐ Steps toward goals, intentions and purpose
  - 1. _____   2. _____   3. _____
- ☐ Reviewed vision
- ☐ I am grateful for:
  - 1. _____   6. _____
  - 2. _____   7. _____
  - 3. _____   8. _____
  - 4. _____   9. _____
  - 5. _____   10. _____

- ☐ I am looking forward to: _____

Notes: _____
_____
_____
_____

Mindful Living Worksheet

M Tu W Th F S S   Date:_____   Rate:_____

- ☐ I am content with: _____
- ☐ I am proud of: _____
- ☐ Success review
- ☐ I love myself because: _____ ☐
- ☐ Love, thanks, kindness and support for others:
  - 1. _____   2. _____
  - 3. _____   4. _____
- ☐ Love, thanks, kindness and support for me:
  - 1. _____   2. _____
  - 3. _____   4. _____
- ☐ Good Deed/Selfless Act/Random Kindness: _____
- ☐ I gave undivided attention to: _____
- ☐ I made things better by: _____
- ☐ I experienced joy, happiness, fun and/or laughter: _____
- ☐ I smiled _____ minutes
- ☐ Meditation/Prayer _____ minutes
- ☐ Inspiration (reading, video, music): _____
- ☐ I listened to my intuition: _____
- ☐ Physical activity _____ minutes
- ☐ I was 100% honest today
- ☐ I took care of myself by: _____
- ☐ Reviewed purpose 3 times
- ☐ Reviewed intentions 3 times
- ☐ Steps toward goals, intentions and purpose
  - 1. _____   2. _____   3. _____
- ☐ Reviewed vision
- ☐ I am grateful for:
  - 1. _____   6. _____
  - 2. _____   7. _____
  - 3. _____   8. _____
  - 4. _____   9. _____
  - 5. _____   10. _____
- ☐ I am looking forward to: _____

Notes: _____
_____
_____
_____

MINDFUL LIVING WORKSHEET

M   Tu   W   Th   F   S   S   Date:_____   Rate:_____

- ☐ I am content with: _____
- ☐ I am proud of: _____
- ☐ Success review
- ☐ I love myself because: _____ ☐
- ☐ Love, thanks, kindness and support for others:
    1. _____   2. _____
    3. _____   4. _____
- ☐ Love, thanks, kindness and support for me:
    1. _____   2. _____
    3. _____   4. _____
- ☐ Good Deed/Selfless Act/Random Kindness: _____
- ☐ I gave undivided attention to: _____
- ☐ I made things better by: _____
- ☐ I experienced joy, happiness, fun and/or laughter: _____
- ☐ I smiled _____ minutes
- ☐ Meditation/Prayer _____ minutes
- ☐ Inspiration (reading, video, music): _____
- ☐ I listened to my intuition: _____
- ☐ Physical activity _____ minutes
- ☐ I was 100% honest today
- ☐ I took care of myself by: _____
- ☐ Reviewed purpose 3 times
- ☐ Reviewed intentions 3 times
- ☐ Steps toward goals, intentions and purpose
    1. _____   2. _____   3. _____
- ☐ Reviewed vision
- ☐ I am grateful for:
    1. _____   6. _____
    2. _____   7. _____
    3. _____   8. _____
    4. _____   9. _____
    5. _____   10. _____

- ☐ I am looking forward to: _____

Notes: _____
_____
_____
_____

MINDFUL LIVING WORKSHEET

M Tu W Th F S S   Date:_____   Rate:_____

- ☐ I am content with: _____
- ☐ I am proud of: _____
- ☐ Success review
- ☐ I love myself because: _____ ☐
- ☐ Love, thanks, kindness and support for others:
  - 1. _____   2. _____
  - 3. _____   4. _____
- ☐ Love, thanks, kindness and support for me:
  - 1. _____   2. _____
  - 3. _____   4. _____
- ☐ Good Deed/Selfless Act/Random Kindness: _____
- ☐ I gave undivided attention to: _____
- ☐ I made things better by: _____
- ☐ I experienced joy, happiness, fun and/or laughter: _____
- ☐ I smiled _____ minutes
- ☐ Meditation/Prayer _____ minutes
- ☐ Inspiration (reading, video, music): _____
- ☐ I listened to my intuition: _____
- ☐ Physical activity _____ minutes
- ☐ I was 100% honest today
- ☐ I took care of myself by: _____
- ☐ Reviewed purpose 3 times
- ☐ Reviewed intentions 3 times
- ☐ Steps toward goals, intentions and purpose
  - 1. _____   2. _____   3. _____
- ☐ Reviewed vision
- ☐ I am grateful for:
  - 1. _____   6. _____
  - 2. _____   7. _____
  - 3. _____   8. _____
  - 4. _____   9. _____
  - 5. _____   10. _____

- ☐ I am looking forward to: _____

Notes: _____
_____
_____
_____

MINDFUL LIVING WORKSHEET

M Tu W Th F S S   Date:_____   Rate:_____

- ☐ I am content with: _____
- ☐ I am proud of: _____
- ☐ Success review
- ☐ I love myself because: _____ ☐
- ☐ Love, thanks, kindness and support for others:
    1. _____   2. _____
    3. _____   4. _____
- ☐ Love, thanks, kindness and support for me:
    1. _____   2. _____
    3. _____   4. _____
- ☐ Good Deed/Selfless Act/Random Kindness: _____
- ☐ I gave undivided attention to: _____
- ☐ I made things better by: _____
- ☐ I experienced joy, happiness, fun and/or laughter: _____
- ☐ I smiled _____ minutes
- ☐ Meditation/Prayer _____ minutes
- ☐ Inspiration (reading, video, music): _____
- ☐ I listened to my intuition: _____
- ☐ Physical activity _____ minutes
- ☐ I was 100% honest today
- ☐ I took care of myself by: _____
- ☐ Reviewed purpose 3 times
- ☐ Reviewed intentions 3 times
- ☐ Steps toward goals, intentions and purpose
    1. _____   2. _____   3. _____
- ☐ Reviewed vision
- ☐ I am grateful for:
    1. _____   6. _____
    2. _____   7. _____
    3. _____   8. _____
    4. _____   9. _____
    5. _____   10. _____

- ☐ I am looking forward to: _____

Notes: _____
_____
_____
_____

MINDFUL LIVING WORKSHEET

M Tu W Th F S S   Date:_____   Rate:_____

- ☐ I am content with: _____
- ☐ I am proud of: _____
- ☐ Success review
- ☐ I love myself because: _____ ☐
- ☐ Love, thanks, kindness and support for others:
    - 1. _____   2. _____
    - 3. _____   4. _____
- ☐ Love, thanks, kindness and support for me:
    - 1. _____   2. _____
    - 3. _____   4. _____
- ☐ Good Deed/Selfless Act/Random Kindness: _____
- ☐ I gave undivided attention to: _____
- ☐ I made things better by: _____
- ☐ I experienced joy, happiness, fun and/or laughter: _____
- ☐ I smiled _____ minutes
- ☐ Meditation/Prayer _____ minutes
- ☐ Inspiration (reading, video, music): _____
- ☐ I listened to my intuition: _____
- ☐ Physical activity _____ minutes
- ☐ I was 100% honest today
- ☐ I took care of myself by: _____
- ☐ Reviewed purpose 3 times
- ☐ Reviewed intentions 3 times
- ☐ Steps toward goals, intentions and purpose
    - 1. _____   2. _____   3. _____
- ☐ Reviewed vision
- ☐ I am grateful for:
    - 1. _____   6. _____
    - 2. _____   7. _____
    - 3. _____   8. _____
    - 4. _____   9. _____
    - 5. _____   10. _____

- ☐ I am looking forward to: _____

Notes: _____
_____
_____

MINDFUL LIVING WORKSHEET

M Tu W Th F S S   Date:_____   Rate:_____

- ☐ I am content with: _____
- ☐ I am proud of: _____
- ☐ Success review
- ☐ I love myself because: _____ ☐
- ☐ Love, thanks, kindness and support for others:
  - 1. _____   2. _____
  - 3. _____   4. _____
- ☐ Love, thanks, kindness and support for me:
  - 1. _____   2. _____
  - 3. _____   4. _____
- ☐ Good Deed/Selfless Act/Random Kindness: _____
- ☐ I gave undivided attention to: _____
- ☐ I made things better by: _____
- ☐ I experienced joy, happiness, fun and/or laughter: _____
- ☐ I smiled _____ minutes
- ☐ Meditation/Prayer _____ minutes
- ☐ Inspiration (reading, video, music): _____
- ☐ I listened to my intuition: _____
- ☐ Physical activity _____ minutes
- ☐ I was 100% honest today
- ☐ I took care of myself by: _____
- ☐ Reviewed purpose 3 times
- ☐ Reviewed intentions 3 times
- ☐ Steps toward goals, intentions and purpose
  - 1. _____ 2. _____ 3. _____
- ☐ Reviewed vision
- ☐ I am grateful for:
  - 1. _____   6. _____
  - 2. _____   7. _____
  - 3. _____   8. _____
  - 4. _____   9. _____
  - 5. _____   10. _____

- ☐ I am looking forward to: _____

Notes: _____
_____
_____
_____

MINDFUL LIVING WORKSHEET

M   Tu   W   Th   F   S   S   Date: _____   Rate: _____

- ☐ I am content with: _____
- ☐ I am proud of: _____
- ☐ Success review
- ☐ I love myself because: _____ ☐
- ☐ Love, thanks, kindness and support for others:
    1. _____   2. _____
    3. _____   4. _____
- ☐ Love, thanks, kindness and support for me:
    1. _____   2. _____
    3. _____   4. _____
- ☐ Good Deed/Selfless Act/Random Kindness: _____
- ☐ I gave undivided attention to: _____
- ☐ I made things better by: _____
- ☐ I experienced joy, happiness, fun and/or laughter: _____
- ☐ I smiled _____ minutes
- ☐ Meditation/Prayer _____ minutes
- ☐ Inspiration (reading, video, music): _____
- ☐ I listened to my intuition: _____
- ☐ Physical activity _____ minutes
- ☐ I was 100% honest today
- ☐ I took care of myself by: _____
- ☐ Reviewed purpose 3 times
- ☐ Reviewed intentions 3 times
- ☐ Steps toward goals, intentions and purpose
    1. _____   2. _____   3. _____
- ☐ Reviewed vision
- ☐ I am grateful for:
    1. _____   6. _____
    2. _____   7. _____
    3. _____   8. _____
    4. _____   9. _____
    5. _____   10. _____

- ☐ I am looking forward to: _____

Notes: _____
_____
_____
_____

MINDFUL LIVING WORKSHEET

M   Tu   W   Th   F   S   S   Date:_____   Rate:_____

- ☐ I am content with: _____
- ☐ I am proud of: _____
- ☐ Success review
- ☐ I love myself because: _____ ☐
- ☐ Love, thanks, kindness and support for others:
    - 1. _____   2. _____
    - 3. _____   4. _____
- ☐ Love, thanks, kindness and support for me:
    - 1. _____   2. _____
    - 3. _____   4. _____
- ☐ Good Deed/Selfless Act/Random Kindness: _____
- ☐ I gave undivided attention to: _____
- ☐ I made things better by: _____
- ☐ I experienced joy, happiness, fun and/or laughter: _____
- ☐ I smiled _____ minutes
- ☐ Meditation/Prayer _____ minutes
- ☐ Inspiration (reading, video, music): _____
- ☐ I listened to my intuition: _____
- ☐ Physical activity _____ minutes
- ☐ I was 100% honest today
- ☐ I took care of myself by: _____
- ☐ Reviewed purpose 3 times
- ☐ Reviewed intentions 3 times
- ☐ Steps toward goals, intentions and purpose
    - 1. _____   2. _____   3. _____
- ☐ Reviewed vision
- ☐ I am grateful for:
    - 1. _____   6. _____
    - 2. _____   7. _____
    - 3. _____   8. _____
    - 4. _____   9. _____
    - 5. _____   10. _____

- ☐ I am looking forward to: _____

Notes: _____
_____
_____
_____

Mindful Living Worksheet

M Tu W Th F S S   Date:_____   Rate:_____

- ☐ I am content with: _____
- ☐ I am proud of: _____
- ☐ Success review
- ☐ I love myself because: _____ ☐
- ☐ Love, thanks, kindness and support for others:
    - 1. _____   2. _____
    - 3. _____   4. _____
- ☐ Love, thanks, kindness and support for me:
    - 1. _____   2. _____
    - 3. _____   4. _____
- ☐ Good Deed/Selfless Act/Random Kindness: _____
- ☐ I gave undivided attention to: _____
- ☐ I made things better by: _____
- ☐ I experienced joy, happiness, fun and/or laughter: _____
- ☐ I smiled _____ minutes
- ☐ Meditation/Prayer _____ minutes
- ☐ Inspiration (reading, video, music): _____
- ☐ I listened to my intuition: _____
- ☐ Physical activity _____ minutes
- ☐ I was 100% honest today
- ☐ I took care of myself by: _____
- ☐ Reviewed purpose 3 times
- ☐ Reviewed intentions 3 times
- ☐ Steps toward goals, intentions and purpose
    - 1. _____   2. _____   3. _____
- ☐ Reviewed vision
- ☐ I am grateful for:
    - 1. _____   6. _____
    - 2. _____   7. _____
    - 3. _____   8. _____
    - 4. _____   9. _____
    - 5. _____   10. _____

- ☐ I am looking forward to: _____

Notes: _____
_____
_____
_____

MINDFUL LIVING WORKSHEET

M   Tu   W   Th   F   S   S   Date: _____   Rate: _____

☐ I am content with: _____
☐ I am proud of: _____
☐ Success review
☐ I love myself because: _____ ☐
☐ Love, thanks, kindness and support for others:
    1. _____   2. _____
    3. _____   4. _____
☐ Love, thanks, kindness and support for me:
    1. _____   2. _____
    3. _____   4. _____
☐ Good Deed/Selfless Act/Random Kindness: _____
☐ I gave undivided attention to: _____
☐ I made things better by: _____
☐ I experienced joy, happiness, fun and/or laughter: _____
☐ I smiled _____ minutes
☐ Meditation/Prayer _____ minutes
☐ Inspiration (reading, video, music): _____
☐ I listened to my intuition: _____
☐ Physical activity _____ minutes
☐ I was 100% honest today
☐ I took care of myself by: _____
☐ Reviewed purpose 3 times
☐ Reviewed intentions 3 times
☐ Steps toward goals, intentions and purpose
    1. _____   2. _____   3. _____
☐ Reviewed vision
☐ I am grateful for:
    1. _____   6. _____
    2. _____   7. _____
    3. _____   8. _____
    4. _____   9. _____
    5. _____   10. _____

☐ I am looking forward to: _____

Notes: _____
_____
_____

Mindful Living Worksheet

M   Tu   W   Th   F   S   S   Date:_____   Rate:_____

- ☐ I am content with: _____
- ☐ I am proud of: _____
- ☐ Success review
- ☐ I love myself because: _____ ☐
- ☐ Love, thanks, kindness and support for others:
  - 1. _____   2. _____
  - 3. _____   4. _____
- ☐ Love, thanks, kindness and support for me:
  - 1. _____   2. _____
  - 3. _____   4. _____
- ☐ Good Deed/Selfless Act/Random Kindness: _____
- ☐ I gave undivided attention to: _____
- ☐ I made things better by: _____
- ☐ I experienced joy, happiness, fun and/or laughter: _____
- ☐ I smiled _____ minutes
- ☐ Meditation/Prayer _____ minutes
- ☐ Inspiration (reading, video, music): _____
- ☐ I listened to my intuition: _____
- ☐ Physical activity _____ minutes
- ☐ I was 100% honest today
- ☐ I took care of myself by: _____
- ☐ Reviewed purpose 3 times
- ☐ Reviewed intentions 3 times
- ☐ Steps toward goals, intentions and purpose
  - 1. _____   2. _____   3. _____
- ☐ Reviewed vision
- ☐ I am grateful for:
  - 1. _____   6. _____
  - 2. _____   7. _____
  - 3. _____   8. _____
  - 4. _____   9. _____
  - 5. _____   10. _____

- ☐ I am looking forward to: _____

Notes: _____
_____
_____

MINDFUL LIVING WORKSHEET

M Tu W Th F S S   Date:_____   Rate:_____

- ☐ I am content with: _____
- ☐ I am proud of: _____
- ☐ Success review
- ☐ I love myself because: _____ ☐
- ☐ Love, thanks, kindness and support for others:
    1. _____   2. _____
    3. _____   4. _____
- ☐ Love, thanks, kindness and support for me:
    1. _____   2. _____
    3. _____   4. _____
- ☐ Good Deed/Selfless Act/Random Kindness: _____
- ☐ I gave undivided attention to: _____
- ☐ I made things better by: _____
- ☐ I experienced joy, happiness, fun and/or laughter: _____
- ☐ I smiled _____ minutes
- ☐ Meditation/Prayer _____ minutes
- ☐ Inspiration (reading, video, music): _____
- ☐ I listened to my intuition: _____
- ☐ Physical activity _____ minutes
- ☐ I was 100% honest today
- ☐ I took care of myself by: _____
- ☐ Reviewed purpose 3 times
- ☐ Reviewed intentions 3 times
- ☐ Steps toward goals, intentions and purpose
    1. _____ 2. _____ 3. _____
- ☐ Reviewed vision
- ☐ I am grateful for:
    1. _____   6. _____
    2. _____   7. _____
    3. _____   8. _____
    4. _____   9. _____
    5. _____   10. _____

- ☐ I am looking forward to: _____

Notes: _____
_____
_____
_____

MINDFUL LIVING WORKSHEET

M Tu W Th F S S   Date:_____   Rate:_____

- ☐ I am content with: _____
- ☐ I am proud of: _____
- ☐ Success review
- ☐ I love myself because: _____ ☐
- ☐ Love, thanks, kindness and support for others:
    1. _____   2. _____
    3. _____   4. _____
- ☐ Love, thanks, kindness and support for me:
    1. _____   2. _____
    3. _____   4. _____
- ☐ Good Deed/Selfless Act/Random Kindness: _____
- ☐ I gave undivided attention to: _____
- ☐ I made things better by: _____
- ☐ I experienced joy, happiness, fun and/or laughter: _____
- ☐ I smiled _____ minutes
- ☐ Meditation/Prayer _____ minutes
- ☐ Inspiration (reading, video, music): _____
- ☐ I listened to my intuition: _____
- ☐ Physical activity _____ minutes
- ☐ I was 100% honest today
- ☐ I took care of myself by: _____
- ☐ Reviewed purpose 3 times
- ☐ Reviewed intentions 3 times
- ☐ Steps toward goals, intentions and purpose
    1. _____ 2. _____ 3. _____
- ☐ Reviewed vision
- ☐ I am grateful for:
    1. _____   6. _____
    2. _____   7. _____
    3. _____   8. _____
    4. _____   9. _____
    5. _____   10. _____

- ☐ I am looking forward to: _____

Notes: _____
_____
_____

MINDFUL LIVING WORKSHEET

M Tu W Th F S S   Date:_____   Rate:_____

- ☐ I am content with: _____
- ☐ I am proud of: _____
- ☐ Success review
- ☐ I love myself because: _____ ☐
- ☐ Love, thanks, kindness and support for others:
  - 1. _____   2. _____
  - 3. _____   4. _____
- ☐ Love, thanks, kindness and support for me:
  - 1. _____   2. _____
  - 3. _____   4. _____
- ☐ Good Deed/Selfless Act/Random Kindness: _____
- ☐ I gave undivided attention to: _____
- ☐ I made things better by: _____
- ☐ I experienced joy, happiness, fun and/or laughter: _____
- ☐ I smiled _____ minutes
- ☐ Meditation/Prayer _____ minutes
- ☐ Inspiration (reading, video, music): _____
- ☐ I listened to my intuition: _____
- ☐ Physical activity _____ minutes
- ☐ I was 100% honest today
- ☐ I took care of myself by: _____
- ☐ Reviewed purpose 3 times
- ☐ Reviewed intentions 3 times
- ☐ Steps toward goals, intentions and purpose
  - 1. _____ 2. _____ 3. _____
- ☐ Reviewed vision
- ☐ I am grateful for:
  - 1. _____   6. _____
  - 2. _____   7. _____
  - 3. _____   8. _____
  - 4. _____   9. _____
  - 5. _____   10. _____
- ☐ I am looking forward to: _____

Notes: _____
_____
_____
_____

MINDFUL LIVING WORKSHEET

M Tu W Th F S S   Date:_____   Rate:_____

- ☐ I am content with: _____
- ☐ I am proud of: _____
- ☐ Success review
- ☐ I love myself because: _____ ☐
- ☐ Love, thanks, kindness and support for others:
  - 1. _____   2. _____
  - 3. _____   4. _____
- ☐ Love, thanks, kindness and support for me:
  - 1. _____   2. _____
  - 3. _____   4. _____
- ☐ Good Deed/Selfless Act/Random Kindness: _____
- ☐ I gave undivided attention to: _____
- ☐ I made things better by: _____
- ☐ I experienced joy, happiness, fun and/or laughter: _____
- ☐ I smiled _____ minutes
- ☐ Meditation/Prayer _____ minutes
- ☐ Inspiration (reading, video, music): _____
- ☐ I listened to my intuition: _____
- ☐ Physical activity _____ minutes
- ☐ I was 100% honest today
- ☐ I took care of myself by: _____
- ☐ Reviewed purpose 3 times
- ☐ Reviewed intentions 3 times
- ☐ Steps toward goals, intentions and purpose
  - 1. _____   2. _____   3. _____
- ☐ Reviewed vision
- ☐ I am grateful for:
  - 1. _____   6. _____
  - 2. _____   7. _____
  - 3. _____   8. _____
  - 4. _____   9. _____
  - 5. _____   10. _____

- ☐ I am looking forward to: _____

Notes: _____
_____
_____
_____

MINDFUL LIVING WORKSHEET

M Tu W Th F S S   Date:_____   Rate:_____

- ☐ I am content with: _____
- ☐ I am proud of: _____
- ☐ Success review
- ☐ I love myself because: _____ ☐
- ☐ Love, thanks, kindness and support for others:
  - 1. _____   2. _____
  - 3. _____   4. _____
- ☐ Love, thanks, kindness and support for me:
  - 1. _____   2. _____
  - 3. _____   4. _____
- ☐ Good Deed/Selfless Act/Random Kindness: _____
- ☐ I gave undivided attention to: _____
- ☐ I made things better by: _____
- ☐ I experienced joy, happiness, fun and/or laughter: _____
- ☐ I smiled _____ minutes
- ☐ Meditation/Prayer _____ minutes
- ☐ Inspiration (reading, video, music): _____
- ☐ I listened to my intuition: _____
- ☐ Physical activity _____ minutes
- ☐ I was 100% honest today
- ☐ I took care of myself by: _____
- ☐ Reviewed purpose 3 times
- ☐ Reviewed intentions 3 times
- ☐ Steps toward goals, intentions and purpose
  - 1. _____ 2. _____ 3. _____
- ☐ Reviewed vision
- ☐ I am grateful for:
  - 1. _____   6. _____
  - 2. _____   7. _____
  - 3. _____   8. _____
  - 4. _____   9. _____
  - 5. _____   10. _____

- ☐ I am looking forward to: _____

Notes: _____
_____
_____
_____

MINDFUL LIVING WORKSHEET

M Tu W Th F S S   Date:_____   Rate:_____

- ☐ I am content with: _____
- ☐ I am proud of: _____
- ☐ Success review
- ☐ I love myself because: _____ ☐
- ☐ Love, thanks, kindness and support for others:
    - 1. _____   2. _____
    - 3. _____   4. _____
- ☐ Love, thanks, kindness and support for me:
    - 1. _____   2. _____
    - 3. _____   4. _____
- ☐ Good Deed/Selfless Act/Random Kindness: _____
- ☐ I gave undivided attention to: _____
- ☐ I made things better by: _____
- ☐ I experienced joy, happiness, fun and/or laughter: _____
- ☐ I smiled _____ minutes
- ☐ Meditation/Prayer _____ minutes
- ☐ Inspiration (reading, video, music): _____
- ☐ I listened to my intuition: _____
- ☐ Physical activity _____ minutes
- ☐ I was 100% honest today
- ☐ I took care of myself by: _____
- ☐ Reviewed purpose 3 times
- ☐ Reviewed intentions 3 times
- ☐ Steps toward goals, intentions and purpose
    - 1. _____ 2. _____ 3. _____
- ☐ Reviewed vision
- ☐ I am grateful for:
    - 1. _____   6. _____
    - 2. _____   7. _____
    - 3. _____   8. _____
    - 4. _____   9. _____
    - 5. _____   10. _____

- ☐ I am looking forward to: _____

Notes: _____
_____
_____
_____

MINDFUL LIVING WORKSHEET

M Tu W Th F S S   Date:_____   Rate:_____

☐ I am content with: _____
☐ I am proud of: _____
☐ Success review
☐ I love myself because: _____ ☐
☐ Love, thanks, kindness and support for others:
    1. _____   2. _____
    3. _____   4. _____
☐ Love, thanks, kindness and support for me:
    1. _____   2. _____
    3. _____   4. _____
☐ Good Deed/Selfless Act/Random Kindness: _____
☐ I gave undivided attention to: _____
☐ I made things better by: _____
☐ I experienced joy, happiness, fun and/or laughter: _____
☐ I smiled _____ minutes
☐ Meditation/Prayer _____ minutes
☐ Inspiration (reading, video, music): _____
☐ I listened to my intuition: _____
☐ Physical activity _____ minutes
☐ I was 100% honest today
☐ I took care of myself by: _____
☐ Reviewed purpose 3 times
☐ Reviewed intentions 3 times
☐ Steps toward goals, intentions and purpose
    1. _____ 2. _____ 3. _____
☐ Reviewed vision
☐ I am grateful for:
    1. _____   6. _____
    2. _____   7. _____
    3. _____   8. _____
    4. _____   9. _____
    5. _____   10. _____

☐ I am looking forward to: _____

Notes: _____
_____
_____
_____

Mindful Living Worksheet

M Tu W Th F S S   Date:_____   Rate:_____

- ☐ I am content with: _____
- ☐ I am proud of: _____
- ☐ Success review
- ☐ I love myself because: _____ ☐
- ☐ Love, thanks, kindness and support for others:
    - 1. _____   2. _____
    - 3. _____   4. _____
- ☐ Love, thanks, kindness and support for me:
    - 1. _____   2. _____
    - 3. _____   4. _____
- ☐ Good Deed/Selfless Act/Random Kindness: _____
- ☐ I gave undivided attention to: _____
- ☐ I made things better by: _____
- ☐ I experienced joy, happiness, fun and/or laughter: _____
- ☐ I smiled _____ minutes
- ☐ Meditation/Prayer _____ minutes
- ☐ Inspiration (reading, video, music): _____
- ☐ I listened to my intuition: _____
- ☐ Physical activity _____ minutes
- ☐ I was 100% honest today
- ☐ I took care of myself by: _____
- ☐ Reviewed purpose 3 times
- ☐ Reviewed intentions 3 times
- ☐ Steps toward goals, intentions and purpose
    - 1. _____   2. _____   3. _____
- ☐ Reviewed vision
- ☐ I am grateful for:
    - 1. _____   6. _____
    - 2. _____   7. _____
    - 3. _____   8. _____
    - 4. _____   9. _____
    - 5. _____   10. _____
- ☐ I am looking forward to: _____

Notes: _____
_____
_____
_____

Mindful Living Worksheet

M Tu W Th F S S   Date:_____   Rate:_____

- ☐ I am content with: _____
- ☐ I am proud of: _____
- ☐ Success review
- ☐ I love myself because: _____ ☐
- ☐ Love, thanks, kindness and support for others:
  - 1. _____   2. _____
  - 3. _____   4. _____
- ☐ Love, thanks, kindness and support for me:
  - 1. _____   2. _____
  - 3. _____   4. _____
- ☐ Good Deed/Selfless Act/Random Kindness: _____
- ☐ I gave undivided attention to: _____
- ☐ I made things better by: _____
- ☐ I experienced joy, happiness, fun and/or laughter: _____
- ☐ I smiled _____ minutes
- ☐ Meditation/Prayer _____ minutes
- ☐ Inspiration (reading, video, music): _____
- ☐ I listened to my intuition: _____
- ☐ Physical activity _____ minutes
- ☐ I was 100% honest today
- ☐ I took care of myself by: _____
- ☐ Reviewed purpose 3 times
- ☐ Reviewed intentions 3 times
- ☐ Steps toward goals, intentions and purpose
  - 1. _____ 2. _____ 3. _____
- ☐ Reviewed vision
- ☐ I am grateful for:
  - 1. _____   6. _____
  - 2. _____   7. _____
  - 3. _____   8. _____
  - 4. _____   9. _____
  - 5. _____   10. _____

- ☐ I am looking forward to: _____

Notes: _____
_____
_____
_____

Mindful Living Worksheet

M Tu W Th F S S   Date:_____   Rate:_____

- ☐ I am content with: _____
- ☐ I am proud of: _____
- ☐ Success review
- ☐ I love myself because: _____ ☐
- ☐ Love, thanks, kindness and support for others:
    1. _____   2. _____
    3. _____   4. _____
- ☐ Love, thanks, kindness and support for me:
    1. _____   2. _____
    3. _____   4. _____
- ☐ Good Deed/Selfless Act/Random Kindness: _____
- ☐ I gave undivided attention to: _____
- ☐ I made things better by: _____
- ☐ I experienced joy, happiness, fun and/or laughter: _____
- ☐ I smiled _____ minutes
- ☐ Meditation/Prayer _____ minutes
- ☐ Inspiration (reading, video, music): _____
- ☐ I listened to my intuition: _____
- ☐ Physical activity _____ minutes
- ☐ I was 100% honest today
- ☐ I took care of myself by: _____
- ☐ Reviewed purpose 3 times
- ☐ Reviewed intentions 3 times
- ☐ Steps toward goals, intentions and purpose
    1. _____ 2. _____ 3. _____
- ☐ Reviewed vision
- ☐ I am grateful for:
    1. _____   6. _____
    2. _____   7. _____
    3. _____   8. _____
    4. _____   9. _____
    5. _____   10. _____

- ☐ I am looking forward to: _____

Notes: _____
_____
_____
_____

MINDFUL LIVING WORKSHEET

M   Tu   W   Th   F   S   S   Date:_____   Rate:_____

☐ I am content with: _____
☐ I am proud of: _____
☐ Success review
☐ I love myself because: _____ ☐
☐ Love, thanks, kindness and support for others:
    1. _____   2. _____
    3. _____   4. _____
☐ Love, thanks, kindness and support for me:
    1. _____   2. _____
    3. _____   4. _____
☐ Good Deed/Selfless Act/Random Kindness: _____
☐ I gave undivided attention to: _____
☐ I made things better by: _____
☐ I experienced joy, happiness, fun and/or laughter: _____
☐ I smiled _____ minutes
☐ Meditation/Prayer _____ minutes
☐ Inspiration (reading, video, music): _____
☐ I listened to my intuition: _____
☐ Physical activity _____ minutes
☐ I was 100% honest today
☐ I took care of myself by: _____
☐ Reviewed purpose 3 times
☐ Reviewed intentions 3 times
☐ Steps toward goals, intentions and purpose
    1. _____   2. _____   3. _____
☐ Reviewed vision
☐ I am grateful for:
    1. _____   6. _____
    2. _____   7. _____
    3. _____   8. _____
    4. _____   9. _____
    5. _____   10. _____

☐ I am looking forward to: _____

Notes: _____
_____
_____
_____

MINDFUL LIVING WORKSHEET

M Tu W Th F S S   Date: _____   Rate: _____

- ☐ I am content with: _____
- ☐ I am proud of: _____
- ☐ Success review
- ☐ I love myself because: _____ ☐
- ☐ Love, thanks, kindness and support for others:
  - 1. _____   2. _____
  - 3. _____   4. _____
- ☐ Love, thanks, kindness and support for me:
  - 1. _____   2. _____
  - 3. _____   4. _____
- ☐ Good Deed/Selfless Act/Random Kindness: _____
- ☐ I gave undivided attention to: _____
- ☐ I made things better by: _____
- ☐ I experienced joy, happiness, fun and/or laughter: _____
- ☐ I smiled _____ minutes
- ☐ Meditation/Prayer _____ minutes
- ☐ Inspiration (reading, video, music): _____
- ☐ I listened to my intuition: _____
- ☐ Physical activity _____ minutes
- ☐ I was 100% honest today
- ☐ I took care of myself by: _____
- ☐ Reviewed purpose 3 times
- ☐ Reviewed intentions 3 times
- ☐ Steps toward goals, intentions and purpose
  - 1. _____   2. _____   3. _____
- ☐ Reviewed vision
- ☐ I am grateful for:
  - 1. _____   6. _____
  - 2. _____   7. _____
  - 3. _____   8. _____
  - 4. _____   9. _____
  - 5. _____   10. _____

- ☐ I am looking forward to: _____

Notes: _____
_____
_____
_____

MINDFUL LIVING WORKSHEET

M Tu W Th F S S   Date:_____   Rate:_____

☐ I am content with: _____
☐ I am proud of: _____
☐ Success review
☐ I love myself because: _____ ☐
☐ Love, thanks, kindness and support for others:
   1. _____   2. _____
   3. _____   4. _____
☐ Love, thanks, kindness and support for me:
   1. _____   2. _____
   3. _____   4. _____
☐ Good Deed/Selfless Act/Random Kindness: _____
☐ I gave undivided attention to: _____
☐ I made things better by: _____
☐ I experienced joy, happiness, fun and/or laughter: _____
☐ I smiled _____ minutes
☐ Meditation/Prayer _____ minutes
☐ Inspiration (reading, video, music): _____
☐ I listened to my intuition: _____
☐ Physical activity _____ minutes
☐ I was 100% honest today
☐ I took care of myself by: _____
☐ Reviewed purpose 3 times
☐ Reviewed intentions 3 times
☐ Steps toward goals, intentions and purpose
   1. _____   2. _____   3. _____
☐ Reviewed vision
☐ I am grateful for:
   1. _____   6. _____
   2. _____   7. _____
   3. _____   8. _____
   4. _____   9. _____
   5. _____   10. _____

☐ I am looking forward to: _____

Notes: _____
_____
_____
_____

Mindful Living Worksheet

M Tu W Th F S S   Date:_____   Rate:_____

- ☐ I am content with: _____
- ☐ I am proud of: _____
- ☐ Success review
- ☐ I love myself because: _____ ☐
- ☐ Love, thanks, kindness and support for others:
  - 1. _____   2. _____
  - 3. _____   4. _____
- ☐ Love, thanks, kindness and support for me:
  - 1. _____   2. _____
  - 3. _____   4. _____
- ☐ Good Deed/Selfless Act/Random Kindness: _____
- ☐ I gave undivided attention to: _____
- ☐ I made things better by: _____
- ☐ I experienced joy, happiness, fun and/or laughter: _____
- ☐ I smiled _____ minutes
- ☐ Meditation/Prayer _____ minutes
- ☐ Inspiration (reading, video, music): _____
- ☐ I listened to my intuition: _____
- ☐ Physical activity _____ minutes
- ☐ I was 100% honest today
- ☐ I took care of myself by: _____
- ☐ Reviewed purpose 3 times
- ☐ Reviewed intentions 3 times
- ☐ Steps toward goals, intentions and purpose
  - 1. _____ 2. _____ 3. _____
- ☐ Reviewed vision
- ☐ I am grateful for:
  - 1. _____   6. _____
  - 2. _____   7. _____
  - 3. _____   8. _____
  - 4. _____   9. _____
  - 5. _____   10. _____
- ☐ I am looking forward to: _____

Notes: _____
_____
_____

MINDFUL LIVING WORKSHEET

M Tu W Th F S S   Date:_____   Rate:_____

- ☐ I am content with: _____
- ☐ I am proud of: _____
- ☐ Success review
- ☐ I love myself because: _____ ☐
- ☐ Love, thanks, kindness and support for others:
  - 1. _____ 2. _____
  - 3. _____ 4. _____
- ☐ Love, thanks, kindness and support for me:
  - 1. _____ 2. _____
  - 3. _____ 4. _____
- ☐ Good Deed/Selfless Act/Random Kindness: _____
- ☐ I gave undivided attention to: _____
- ☐ I made things better by: _____
- ☐ I experienced joy, happiness, fun and/or laughter: _____
- ☐ I smiled _____ minutes
- ☐ Meditation/Prayer _____ minutes
- ☐ Inspiration (reading, video, music): _____
- ☐ I listened to my intuition: _____
- ☐ Physical activity _____ minutes
- ☐ I was 100% honest today
- ☐ I took care of myself by: _____
- ☐ Reviewed purpose 3 times
- ☐ Reviewed intentions 3 times
- ☐ Steps toward goals, intentions and purpose
  - 1. _____ 2. _____ 3. _____
- ☐ Reviewed vision
- ☐ I am grateful for:
  - 1. _____ 6. _____
  - 2. _____ 7. _____
  - 3. _____ 8. _____
  - 4. _____ 9. _____
  - 5. _____ 10. _____

- ☐ I am looking forward to: _____

Notes: _____
_____
_____
_____

Mindful Living Worksheet

M Tu W Th F S S   Date:_____   Rate:_____

- ☐ I am content with: _____
- ☐ I am proud of: _____
- ☐ Success review
- ☐ I love myself because: _____ ☐
- ☐ Love, thanks, kindness and support for others:
    1. _____   2. _____
    3. _____   4. _____
- ☐ Love, thanks, kindness and support for me:
    1. _____   2. _____
    3. _____   4. _____
- ☐ Good Deed/Selfless Act/Random Kindness: _____
- ☐ I gave undivided attention to: _____
- ☐ I made things better by: _____
- ☐ I experienced joy, happiness, fun and/or laughter: _____
- ☐ I smiled _____ minutes
- ☐ Meditation/Prayer _____ minutes
- ☐ Inspiration (reading, video, music): _____
- ☐ I listened to my intuition: _____
- ☐ Physical activity _____ minutes
- ☐ I was 100% honest today
- ☐ I took care of myself by: _____
- ☐ Reviewed purpose 3 times
- ☐ Reviewed intentions 3 times
- ☐ Steps toward goals, intentions and purpose
    1. _____   2. _____   3. _____
- ☐ Reviewed vision
- ☐ I am grateful for:
    1. _____   6. _____
    2. _____   7. _____
    3. _____   8. _____
    4. _____   9. _____
    5. _____   10. _____

- ☐ I am looking forward to: _____

Notes: _____
_____
_____
_____

MINDFUL LIVING WORKSHEET

M Tu W Th F S S   Date:_____   Rate:_____

- ☐ I am content with: _____
- ☐ I am proud of: _____
- ☐ Success review
- ☐ I love myself because: _____ ☐
- ☐ Love, thanks, kindness and support for others:
  - 1. _____   2. _____
  - 3. _____   4. _____
- ☐ Love, thanks, kindness and support for me:
  - 1. _____   2. _____
  - 3. _____   4. _____
- ☐ Good Deed/Selfless Act/Random Kindness: _____
- ☐ I gave undivided attention to: _____
- ☐ I made things better by: _____
- ☐ I experienced joy, happiness, fun and/or laughter: _____
- ☐ I smiled _____ minutes
- ☐ Meditation/Prayer _____ minutes
- ☐ Inspiration (reading, video, music): _____
- ☐ I listened to my intuition: _____
- ☐ Physical activity _____ minutes
- ☐ I was 100% honest today
- ☐ I took care of myself by: _____
- ☐ Reviewed purpose 3 times
- ☐ Reviewed intentions 3 times
- ☐ Steps toward goals, intentions and purpose
  - 1. _____ 2. _____ 3. _____
- ☐ Reviewed vision
- ☐ I am grateful for:
  - 1. _____   6. _____
  - 2. _____   7. _____
  - 3. _____   8. _____
  - 4. _____   9. _____
  - 5. _____   10. _____

- ☐ I am looking forward to: _____

Notes: _____
_____
_____

Mindful Living Worksheet

M   Tu   W   Th   F   S   S   Date:_____   Rate:_____

☐ I am content with: _____
☐ I am proud of: _____
☐ Success review
☐ I love myself because: _____ ☐
☐ Love, thanks, kindness and support for others:
     1. _____ 2. _____
     3. _____ 4. _____
☐ Love, thanks, kindness and support for me:
     1. _____ 2. _____
     3. _____ 4. _____
☐ Good Deed/Selfless Act/Random Kindness: _____
☐ I gave undivided attention to: _____
☐ I made things better by: _____
☐ I experienced joy, happiness, fun and/or laughter: _____
☐ I smiled _____ minutes
☐ Meditation/Prayer _____ minutes
☐ Inspiration (reading, video, music): _____
☐ I listened to my intuition: _____
☐ Physical activity _____ minutes
☐ I was 100% honest today
☐ I took care of myself by: _____
☐ Reviewed purpose 3 times
☐ Reviewed intentions 3 times
☐ Steps toward goals, intentions and purpose
     1. _____ 2. _____ 3. _____
☐ Reviewed vision
☐ I am grateful for:
     1. _____ 6. _____
     2. _____ 7. _____
     3. _____ 8. _____
     4. _____ 9. _____
     5. _____ 10. _____

☐ I am looking forward to: _____

Notes: _____
_____
_____
_____

MINDFUL LIVING WORKSHEET

M   Tu   W   Th   F   S   S   Date:_____   Rate:_____

- ☐ I am content with: _____
- ☐ I am proud of: _____
- ☐ Success review
- ☐ I love myself because: _____ ☐
- ☐ Love, thanks, kindness and support for others:
    - 1. _____   2. _____
    - 3. _____   4. _____
- ☐ Love, thanks, kindness and support for me:
    - 1. _____   2. _____
    - 3. _____   4. _____
- ☐ Good Deed/Selfless Act/Random Kindness: _____
- ☐ I gave undivided attention to: _____
- ☐ I made things better by: _____
- ☐ I experienced joy, happiness, fun and/or laughter: _____
- ☐ I smiled _____ minutes
- ☐ Meditation/Prayer _____ minutes
- ☐ Inspiration (reading, video, music): _____
- ☐ I listened to my intuition: _____
- ☐ Physical activity _____ minutes
- ☐ I was 100% honest today
- ☐ I took care of myself by: _____
- ☐ Reviewed purpose 3 times
- ☐ Reviewed intentions 3 times
- ☐ Steps toward goals, intentions and purpose
    - 1. _____   2. _____   3. _____
- ☐ Reviewed vision
- ☐ I am grateful for:
    - 1. _____   6. _____
    - 2. _____   7. _____
    - 3. _____   8. _____
    - 4. _____   9. _____
    - 5. _____   10. _____
- ☐ I am looking forward to: _____

Notes: _____
_____
_____

Mindful Living Worksheet

M Tu W Th F S S   Date:_____   Rate:_____

- ☐ I am content with: _____
- ☐ I am proud of: _____
- ☐ Success review
- ☐ I love myself because: _____ ☐
- ☐ Love, thanks, kindness and support for others:
  - 1. _____   2. _____
  - 3. _____   4. _____
- ☐ Love, thanks, kindness and support for me:
  - 1. _____   2. _____
  - 3. _____   4. _____
- ☐ Good Deed/Selfless Act/Random Kindness: _____
- ☐ I gave undivided attention to: _____
- ☐ I made things better by: _____
- ☐ I experienced joy, happiness, fun and/or laughter: _____
- ☐ I smiled _____ minutes
- ☐ Meditation/Prayer _____ minutes
- ☐ Inspiration (reading, video, music): _____
- ☐ I listened to my intuition: _____
- ☐ Physical activity _____ minutes
- ☐ I was 100% honest today
- ☐ I took care of myself by: _____
- ☐ Reviewed purpose 3 times
- ☐ Reviewed intentions 3 times
- ☐ Steps toward goals, intentions and purpose
  - 1. _____ 2. _____ 3. _____
- ☐ Reviewed vision
- ☐ I am grateful for:
  - 1. _____   6. _____
  - 2. _____   7. _____
  - 3. _____   8. _____
  - 4. _____   9. _____
  - 5. _____   10. _____

- ☐ I am looking forward to: _____

Notes: _____
_____
_____

Mindful Living Worksheet

M   Tu   W   Th   F   S   S   Date:_____   Rate:_____

- ☐ I am content with: _____
- ☐ I am proud of: _____
- ☐ Success review
- ☐ I love myself because: _____ ☐
- ☐ Love, thanks, kindness and support for others:
  1. _____   2. _____
  3. _____   4. _____
- ☐ Love, thanks, kindness and support for me:
  1. _____   2. _____
  3. _____   4. _____
- ☐ Good Deed/Selfless Act/Random Kindness: _____
- ☐ I gave undivided attention to: _____
- ☐ I made things better by: _____
- ☐ I experienced joy, happiness, fun and/or laughter: _____
- ☐ I smiled _____ minutes
- ☐ Meditation/Prayer _____ minutes
- ☐ Inspiration (reading, video, music): _____
- ☐ I listened to my intuition: _____
- ☐ Physical activity _____ minutes
- ☐ I was 100% honest today
- ☐ I took care of myself by: _____
- ☐ Reviewed purpose 3 times
- ☐ Reviewed intentions 3 times
- ☐ Steps toward goals, intentions and purpose
  1. _____   2. _____   3. _____
- ☐ Reviewed vision
- ☐ I am grateful for:
  1. _____   6. _____
  2. _____   7. _____
  3. _____   8. _____
  4. _____   9. _____
  5. _____   10. _____

- ☐ I am looking forward to: _____

Notes: _____

_____

_____

Mindful Living Worksheet

M Tu W Th F S S   Date:_____   Rate:_____

- ☐ I am content with: _____
- ☐ I am proud of: _____
- ☐ Success review
- ☐ I love myself because: _____ ☐
- ☐ Love, thanks, kindness and support for others:
    1. _____   2. _____
    3. _____   4. _____
- ☐ Love, thanks, kindness and support for me:
    1. _____   2. _____
    3. _____   4. _____
- ☐ Good Deed/Selfless Act/Random Kindness: _____
- ☐ I gave undivided attention to: _____
- ☐ I made things better by: _____
- ☐ I experienced joy, happiness, fun and/or laughter: _____
- ☐ I smiled _____ minutes
- ☐ Meditation/Prayer _____ minutes
- ☐ Inspiration (reading, video, music): _____
- ☐ I listened to my intuition: _____
- ☐ Physical activity _____ minutes
- ☐ I was 100% honest today
- ☐ I took care of myself by: _____
- ☐ Reviewed purpose 3 times
- ☐ Reviewed intentions 3 times
- ☐ Steps toward goals, intentions and purpose
    1. _____ 2. _____ 3. _____
- ☐ Reviewed vision
- ☐ I am grateful for:
    1. _____   6. _____
    2. _____   7. _____
    3. _____   8. _____
    4. _____   9. _____
    5. _____   10. _____

- ☐ I am looking forward to: _____

Notes: _____
_____
_____
_____

Mindful Living Worksheet

M Tu W Th F S S   Date:_____   Rate:_____

- ☐ I am content with: _____
- ☐ I am proud of: _____
- ☐ Success review
- ☐ I love myself because: _____ ☐
- ☐ Love, thanks, kindness and support for others:
  - 1. _____   2. _____
  - 3. _____   4. _____
- ☐ Love, thanks, kindness and support for me:
  - 1. _____   2. _____
  - 3. _____   4. _____
- ☐ Good Deed/Selfless Act/Random Kindness: _____
- ☐ I gave undivided attention to: _____
- ☐ I made things better by: _____
- ☐ I experienced joy, happiness, fun and/or laughter: _____
- ☐ I smiled _____ minutes
- ☐ Meditation/Prayer _____ minutes
- ☐ Inspiration (reading, video, music): _____
- ☐ I listened to my intuition: _____
- ☐ Physical activity _____ minutes
- ☐ I was 100% honest today
- ☐ I took care of myself by: _____
- ☐ Reviewed purpose 3 times
- ☐ Reviewed intentions 3 times
- ☐ Steps toward goals, intentions and purpose
  - 1. _____   2. _____   3. _____
- ☐ Reviewed vision
- ☐ I am grateful for:
  - 1. _____   6. _____
  - 2. _____   7. _____
  - 3. _____   8. _____
  - 4. _____   9. _____
  - 5. _____   10. _____

- ☐ I am looking forward to: _____

Notes: _____
_____
_____
_____

Mindful Living Worksheet

M   Tu   W   Th   F   S   S   Date:_____   Rate:_____

- ☐ I am content with: _____
- ☐ I am proud of: _____
- ☐ Success review
- ☐ I love myself because: _____ ☐
- ☐ Love, thanks, kindness and support for others:
  - 1. _____   2. _____
  - 3. _____   4. _____
- ☐ Love, thanks, kindness and support for me:
  - 1. _____   2. _____
  - 3. _____   4. _____
- ☐ Good Deed/Selfless Act/Random Kindness: _____
- ☐ I gave undivided attention to: _____
- ☐ I made things better by: _____
- ☐ I experienced joy, happiness, fun and/or laughter: _____
- ☐ I smiled _____ minutes
- ☐ Meditation/Prayer _____ minutes
- ☐ Inspiration (reading, video, music): _____
- ☐ I listened to my intuition: _____
- ☐ Physical activity _____ minutes
- ☐ I was 100% honest today
- ☐ I took care of myself by: _____
- ☐ Reviewed purpose 3 times
- ☐ Reviewed intentions 3 times
- ☐ Steps toward goals, intentions and purpose
  - 1. _____   2. _____   3. _____
- ☐ Reviewed vision
- ☐ I am grateful for:
  - 1. _____   6. _____
  - 2. _____   7. _____
  - 3. _____   8. _____
  - 4. _____   9. _____
  - 5. _____   10. _____
- ☐ I am looking forward to: _____

Notes: _____
_____
_____
_____

MINDFUL LIVING WORKSHEET

M   Tu   W   Th   F   S   S   Date:_____   Rate:_____

- ☐ I am content with: _____
- ☐ I am proud of: _____
- ☐ Success review
- ☐ I love myself because: _____ ☐
- ☐ Love, thanks, kindness and support for others:
  - 1. _____   2. _____
  - 3. _____   4. _____
- ☐ Love, thanks, kindness and support for me:
  - 1. _____   2. _____
  - 3. _____   4. _____
- ☐ Good Deed/Selfless Act/Random Kindness: _____
- ☐ I gave undivided attention to: _____
- ☐ I made things better by: _____
- ☐ I experienced joy, happiness, fun and/or laughter: _____
- ☐ I smiled _____ minutes
- ☐ Meditation/Prayer _____ minutes
- ☐ Inspiration (reading, video, music): _____
- ☐ I listened to my intuition: _____
- ☐ Physical activity _____ minutes
- ☐ I was 100% honest today
- ☐ I took care of myself by: _____
- ☐ Reviewed purpose 3 times
- ☐ Reviewed intentions 3 times
- ☐ Steps toward goals, intentions and purpose
  - 1. _____ 2. _____ 3. _____
- ☐ Reviewed vision
- ☐ I am grateful for:
  - 1. _____   6. _____
  - 2. _____   7. _____
  - 3. _____   8. _____
  - 4. _____   9. _____
  - 5. _____   10. _____

- ☐ I am looking forward to: _____

Notes: _____
_____
_____
_____

Mindful Living Worksheet

M Tu W Th F S S   Date:_____   Rate:_____

- ☐ I am content with: _____
- ☐ I am proud of: _____
- ☐ Success review
- ☐ I love myself because: _____ ☐
- ☐ Love, thanks, kindness and support for others:
    - 1. _____   2. _____
    - 3. _____   4. _____
- ☐ Love, thanks, kindness and support for me:
    - 1. _____   2. _____
    - 3. _____   4. _____
- ☐ Good Deed/Selfless Act/Random Kindness: _____
- ☐ I gave undivided attention to: _____
- ☐ I made things better by: _____
- ☐ I experienced joy, happiness, fun and/or laughter: _____
- ☐ I smiled _____ minutes
- ☐ Meditation/Prayer _____ minutes
- ☐ Inspiration (reading, video, music): _____
- ☐ I listened to my intuition: _____
- ☐ Physical activity _____ minutes
- ☐ I was 100% honest today
- ☐ I took care of myself by: _____
- ☐ Reviewed purpose 3 times
- ☐ Reviewed intentions 3 times
- ☐ Steps toward goals, intentions and purpose
    - 1. _____ 2. _____ 3. _____
- ☐ Reviewed vision
- ☐ I am grateful for:
    - 1. _____   6. _____
    - 2. _____   7. _____
    - 3. _____   8. _____
    - 4. _____   9. _____
    - 5. _____   10. _____

- ☐ I am looking forward to: _____

Notes: _____
_____
_____
_____

Mindful Living Worksheet

M Tu W Th F S S   Date:_____   Rate:_____

- ☐ I am content with: _____
- ☐ I am proud of: _____
- ☐ Success review
- ☐ I love myself because: _____ ☐
- ☐ Love, thanks, kindness and support for others:
    - 1. _____   2. _____
    - 3. _____   4. _____
- ☐ Love, thanks, kindness and support for me:
    - 1. _____   2. _____
    - 3. _____   4. _____
- ☐ Good Deed/Selfless Act/Random Kindness: _____
- ☐ I gave undivided attention to: _____
- ☐ I made things better by: _____
- ☐ I experienced joy, happiness, fun and/or laughter: _____
- ☐ I smiled _____ minutes
- ☐ Meditation/Prayer _____ minutes
- ☐ Inspiration (reading, video, music): _____
- ☐ I listened to my intuition: _____
- ☐ Physical activity _____ minutes
- ☐ I was 100% honest today
- ☐ I took care of myself by: _____
- ☐ Reviewed purpose 3 times
- ☐ Reviewed intentions 3 times
- ☐ Steps toward goals, intentions and purpose
    - 1. _____   2. _____   3. _____
- ☐ Reviewed vision
- ☐ I am grateful for:
    - 1. _____   6. _____
    - 2. _____   7. _____
    - 3. _____   8. _____
    - 4. _____   9. _____
    - 5. _____   10. _____

- ☐ I am looking forward to: _____

Notes: _____
_____
_____
_____

Mindful Living Worksheet

M   Tu   W   Th   F   S   S   Date:_____   Rate:_____

- ☐ I am content with: _____
- ☐ I am proud of: _____
- ☐ Success review
- ☐ I love myself because: _____ ☐
- ☐ Love, thanks, kindness and support for others:
    - 1. _____   2. _____
    - 3. _____   4. _____
- ☐ Love, thanks, kindness and support for me:
    - 1. _____   2. _____
    - 3. _____   4. _____
- ☐ Good Deed/Selfless Act/Random Kindness: _____
- ☐ I gave undivided attention to: _____
- ☐ I made things better by: _____
- ☐ I experienced joy, happiness, fun and/or laughter: _____
- ☐ I smiled _____ minutes
- ☐ Meditation/Prayer _____ minutes
- ☐ Inspiration (reading, video, music): _____
- ☐ I listened to my intuition: _____
- ☐ Physical activity _____ minutes
- ☐ I was 100% honest today
- ☐ I took care of myself by: _____
- ☐ Reviewed purpose 3 times
- ☐ Reviewed intentions 3 times
- ☐ Steps toward goals, intentions and purpose
    - 1. _____   2. _____   3. _____
- ☐ Reviewed vision
- ☐ I am grateful for:
    - 1. _____   6. _____
    - 2. _____   7. _____
    - 3. _____   8. _____
    - 4. _____   9. _____
    - 5. _____   10. _____
- ☐ I am looking forward to: _____

Notes: _____
_____
_____

Mindful Living Worksheet

M Tu W Th F S S   Date: _____   Rate: _____

- ☐ I am content with: _____
- ☐ I am proud of: _____
- ☐ Success review
- ☐ I love myself because: _____ ☐
- ☐ Love, thanks, kindness and support for others:
  - 1. _____   2. _____
  - 3. _____   4. _____
- ☐ Love, thanks, kindness and support for me:
  - 1. _____   2. _____
  - 3. _____   4. _____
- ☐ Good Deed/Selfless Act/Random Kindness: _____
- ☐ I gave undivided attention to: _____
- ☐ I made things better by: _____
- ☐ I experienced joy, happiness, fun and/or laughter: _____
- ☐ I smiled _____ minutes
- ☐ Meditation/Prayer _____ minutes
- ☐ Inspiration (reading, video, music): _____
- ☐ I listened to my intuition: _____
- ☐ Physical activity _____ minutes
- ☐ I was 100% honest today
- ☐ I took care of myself by: _____
- ☐ Reviewed purpose 3 times
- ☐ Reviewed intentions 3 times
- ☐ Steps toward goals, intentions and purpose
  - 1. _____ 2. _____ 3. _____
- ☐ Reviewed vision
- ☐ I am grateful for:
  - 1. _____   6. _____
  - 2. _____   7. _____
  - 3. _____   8. _____
  - 4. _____   9. _____
  - 5. _____   10. _____
- ☐ I am looking forward to: _____

Notes: _____
_____
_____

MINDFUL LIVING WORKSHEET

M   Tu   W   Th   F   S   S   Date:_____   Rate:_____

- ☐ I am content with: _____
- ☐ I am proud of: _____
- ☐ Success review
- ☐ I love myself because: _____ ☐
- ☐ Love, thanks, kindness and support for others:
    1. _____   2. _____
    3. _____   4. _____
- ☐ Love, thanks, kindness and support for me:
    1. _____   2. _____
    3. _____   4. _____
- ☐ Good Deed/Selfless Act/Random Kindness: _____
- ☐ I gave undivided attention to: _____
- ☐ I made things better by: _____
- ☐ I experienced joy, happiness, fun and/or laughter: _____
- ☐ I smiled _____ minutes
- ☐ Meditation/Prayer _____ minutes
- ☐ Inspiration (reading, video, music): _____
- ☐ I listened to my intuition: _____
- ☐ Physical activity _____ minutes
- ☐ I was 100% honest today
- ☐ I took care of myself by: _____
- ☐ Reviewed purpose 3 times
- ☐ Reviewed intentions 3 times
- ☐ Steps toward goals, intentions and purpose
    1. _____ 2. _____ 3. _____
- ☐ Reviewed vision
- ☐ I am grateful for:
    1. _____   6. _____
    2. _____   7. _____
    3. _____   8. _____
    4. _____   9. _____
    5. _____   10. _____

- ☐ I am looking forward to: _____

Notes: _____
_____
_____
_____

MINDFUL LIVING WORKSHEET

M Tu W Th F S S   Date:_____   Rate:_____

- ☐ I am content with: _____
- ☐ I am proud of: _____
- ☐ Success review
- ☐ I love myself because: _____ ☐
- ☐ Love, thanks, kindness and support for others:
    - 1. _____   2. _____
    - 3. _____   4. _____
- ☐ Love, thanks, kindness and support for me:
    - 1. _____   2. _____
    - 3. _____   4. _____
- ☐ Good Deed/Selfless Act/Random Kindness: _____
- ☐ I gave undivided attention to: _____
- ☐ I made things better by: _____
- ☐ I experienced joy, happiness, fun and/or laughter: _____
- ☐ I smiled _____ minutes
- ☐ Meditation/Prayer _____ minutes
- ☐ Inspiration (reading, video, music): _____
- ☐ I listened to my intuition: _____
- ☐ Physical activity _____ minutes
- ☐ I was 100% honest today
- ☐ I took care of myself by: _____
- ☐ Reviewed purpose 3 times
- ☐ Reviewed intentions 3 times
- ☐ Steps toward goals, intentions and purpose
    - 1. _____   2. _____   3. _____
- ☐ Reviewed vision
- ☐ I am grateful for:
    - 1. _____   6. _____
    - 2. _____   7. _____
    - 3. _____   8. _____
    - 4. _____   9. _____
    - 5. _____   10. _____

- ☐ I am looking forward to: _____

Notes: _____
_____
_____
_____

MINDFUL LIVING WORKSHEET

M   Tu   W   Th   F   S   S   Date:_____   Rate:_____

- ☐ I am content with: _____
- ☐ I am proud of: _____
- ☐ Success review
- ☐ I love myself because: _____ ☐
- ☐ Love, thanks, kindness and support for others:
  - 1. _____   2. _____
  - 3. _____   4. _____
- ☐ Love, thanks, kindness and support for me:
  - 1. _____   2. _____
  - 3. _____   4. _____
- ☐ Good Deed/Selfless Act/Random Kindness: _____
- ☐ I gave undivided attention to: _____
- ☐ I made things better by: _____
- ☐ I experienced joy, happiness, fun and/or laughter: _____
- ☐ I smiled _____ minutes
- ☐ Meditation/Prayer _____ minutes
- ☐ Inspiration (reading, video, music): _____
- ☐ I listened to my intuition: _____
- ☐ Physical activity _____ minutes
- ☐ I was 100% honest today
- ☐ I took care of myself by: _____
- ☐ Reviewed purpose 3 times
- ☐ Reviewed intentions 3 times
- ☐ Steps toward goals, intentions and purpose
  - 1. _____   2. _____   3. _____
- ☐ Reviewed vision
- ☐ I am grateful for:
  - 1. _____   6. _____
  - 2. _____   7. _____
  - 3. _____   8. _____
  - 4. _____   9. _____
  - 5. _____   10. _____

- ☐ I am looking forward to: _____

Notes: _____
_____
_____
_____

MINDFUL LIVING WORKSHEET

M Tu W Th F S S   Date:_____   Rate:_____

- ☐ I am content with: _____
- ☐ I am proud of: _____
- ☐ Success review
- ☐ I love myself because: _____ ☐
- ☐ Love, thanks, kindness and support for others:
  - 1. _____   2. _____
  - 3. _____   4. _____
- ☐ Love, thanks, kindness and support for me:
  - 1. _____   2. _____
  - 3. _____   4. _____
- ☐ Good Deed/Selfless Act/Random Kindness: _____
- ☐ I gave undivided attention to: _____
- ☐ I made things better by: _____
- ☐ I experienced joy, happiness, fun and/or laughter: _____
- ☐ I smiled _____ minutes
- ☐ Meditation/Prayer _____ minutes
- ☐ Inspiration (reading, video, music): _____
- ☐ I listened to my intuition: _____
- ☐ Physical activity _____ minutes
- ☐ I was 100% honest today
- ☐ I took care of myself by: _____
- ☐ Reviewed purpose 3 times
- ☐ Reviewed intentions 3 times
- ☐ Steps toward goals, intentions and purpose
  - 1. _____   2. _____   3. _____
- ☐ Reviewed vision
- ☐ I am grateful for:
  - 1. _____   6. _____
  - 2. _____   7. _____
  - 3. _____   8. _____
  - 4. _____   9. _____
  - 5. _____   10. _____

- ☐ I am looking forward to: _____

Notes: _____
_____
_____
_____

MINDFUL LIVING WORKSHEET

M Tu W Th F S S   Date:_____   Rate:_____

- ☐ I am content with: _____
- ☐ I am proud of: _____
- ☐ Success review
- ☐ I love myself because: _____ ☐
- ☐ Love, thanks, kindness and support for others:
  - 1. _____   2. _____
  - 3. _____   4. _____
- ☐ Love, thanks, kindness and support for me:
  - 1. _____   2. _____
  - 3. _____   4. _____
- ☐ Good Deed/Selfless Act/Random Kindness: _____
- ☐ I gave undivided attention to: _____
- ☐ I made things better by: _____
- ☐ I experienced joy, happiness, fun and/or laughter: _____
- ☐ I smiled _____ minutes
- ☐ Meditation/Prayer _____ minutes
- ☐ Inspiration (reading, video, music): _____
- ☐ I listened to my intuition: _____
- ☐ Physical activity _____ minutes
- ☐ I was 100% honest today
- ☐ I took care of myself by: _____
- ☐ Reviewed purpose 3 times
- ☐ Reviewed intentions 3 times
- ☐ Steps toward goals, intentions and purpose
  - 1. _____   2. _____   3. _____
- ☐ Reviewed vision
- ☐ I am grateful for:
  - 1. _____   6. _____
  - 2. _____   7. _____
  - 3. _____   8. _____
  - 4. _____   9. _____
  - 5. _____   10. _____

- ☐ I am looking forward to: _____

Notes: _____
_____
_____
_____

MINDFUL LIVING WORKSHEET

M Tu W Th F S S   Date:_____   Rate:_____

- ☐ I am content with: _____
- ☐ I am proud of: _____
- ☐ Success review
- ☐ I love myself because: _____ ☐
- ☐ Love, thanks, kindness and support for others:
    - 1. _____   2. _____
    - 3. _____   4. _____
- ☐ Love, thanks, kindness and support for me:
    - 1. _____   2. _____
    - 3. _____   4. _____
- ☐ Good Deed/Selfless Act/Random Kindness: _____
- ☐ I gave undivided attention to: _____
- ☐ I made things better by: _____
- ☐ I experienced joy, happiness, fun and/or laughter: _____
- ☐ I smiled _____ minutes
- ☐ Meditation/Prayer _____ minutes
- ☐ Inspiration (reading, video, music): _____
- ☐ I listened to my intuition: _____
- ☐ Physical activity _____ minutes
- ☐ I was 100% honest today
- ☐ I took care of myself by: _____
- ☐ Reviewed purpose 3 times
- ☐ Reviewed intentions 3 times
- ☐ Steps toward goals, intentions and purpose
    - 1. _____   2. _____   3. _____
- ☐ Reviewed vision
- ☐ I am grateful for:
    - 1. _____   6. _____
    - 2. _____   7. _____
    - 3. _____   8. _____
    - 4. _____   9. _____
    - 5. _____   10. _____

- ☐ I am looking forward to: _____

Notes: _____
_____
_____
_____

MINDFUL LIVING WORKSHEET

M Tu W Th F S S   Date:_____   Rate:_____

☐ I am content with: _____
☐ I am proud of: _____
☐ Success review
☐ I love myself because: _____ ☐
☐ Love, thanks, kindness and support for others:
   1. _____   2. _____
   3. _____   4. _____
☐ Love, thanks, kindness and support for me:
   1. _____   2. _____
   3. _____   4. _____
☐ Good Deed/Selfless Act/Random Kindness: _____
☐ I gave undivided attention to: _____
☐ I made things better by: _____
☐ I experienced joy, happiness, fun and/or laughter: _____
☐ I smiled _____ minutes
☐ Meditation/Prayer _____ minutes
☐ Inspiration (reading, video, music): _____
☐ I listened to my intuition: _____
☐ Physical activity _____ minutes
☐ I was 100% honest today
☐ I took care of myself by: _____
☐ Reviewed purpose 3 times
☐ Reviewed intentions 3 times
☐ Steps toward goals, intentions and purpose
   1. _____ 2. _____ 3. _____
☐ Reviewed vision
☐ I am grateful for:
   1. _____   6. _____
   2. _____   7. _____
   3. _____   8. _____
   4. _____   9. _____
   5. _____   10. _____

☐ I am looking forward to: _____

Notes: _____
_____
_____

MINDFUL LIVING WORKSHEET

M Tu W Th F S S   Date:_____   Rate:_____

☐ I am content with: _____
☐ I am proud of: _____
☐ Success review
☐ I love myself because: _____ ☐
☐ Love, thanks, kindness and support for others:
    1. _____   2. _____
    3. _____   4. _____
☐ Love, thanks, kindness and support for me:
    1. _____   2. _____
    3. _____   4. _____
☐ Good Deed/Selfless Act/Random Kindness: _____
☐ I gave undivided attention to: _____
☐ I made things better by: _____
☐ I experienced joy, happiness, fun and/or laughter: _____
☐ I smiled _____ minutes
☐ Meditation/Prayer _____ minutes
☐ Inspiration (reading, video, music): _____
☐ I listened to my intuition: _____
☐ Physical activity _____ minutes
☐ I was 100% honest today
☐ I took care of myself by: _____
☐ Reviewed purpose 3 times
☐ Reviewed intentions 3 times
☐ Steps toward goals, intentions and purpose
    1. _____ 2. _____ 3. _____
☐ Reviewed vision
☐ I am grateful for:
    1. _____   6. _____
    2. _____   7. _____
    3. _____   8. _____
    4. _____   9. _____
    5. _____   10. _____

☐ I am looking forward to: _____

Notes: _____
_____
_____
_____

Mindful Living Worksheet

M Tu W Th F S S   Date:_____   Rate:_____

- ☐ I am content with: _____
- ☐ I am proud of: _____
- ☐ Success review
- ☐ I love myself because: _____ ☐
- ☐ Love, thanks, kindness and support for others:
  - 1. _____ 2. _____
  - 3. _____ 4. _____
- ☐ Love, thanks, kindness and support for me:
  - 1. _____ 2. _____
  - 3. _____ 4. _____
- ☐ Good Deed/Selfless Act/Random Kindness: _____
- ☐ I gave undivided attention to: _____
- ☐ I made things better by: _____
- ☐ I experienced joy, happiness, fun and/or laughter: _____
- ☐ I smiled _____ minutes
- ☐ Meditation/Prayer _____ minutes
- ☐ Inspiration (reading, video, music): _____
- ☐ I listened to my intuition: _____
- ☐ Physical activity _____ minutes
- ☐ I was 100% honest today
- ☐ I took care of myself by: _____
- ☐ Reviewed purpose 3 times
- ☐ Reviewed intentions 3 times
- ☐ Steps toward goals, intentions and purpose
  - 1. _____ 2. _____ 3. _____
- ☐ Reviewed vision
- ☐ I am grateful for:
  - 1. _____ 6. _____
  - 2. _____ 7. _____
  - 3. _____ 8. _____
  - 4. _____ 9. _____
  - 5. _____ 10. _____

- ☐ I am looking forward to: _____

Notes: _____
_____
_____

Mindful Living Worksheet

M   Tu   W   Th   F   S   S   Date: _____   Rate: _____

- ☐ I am content with: _____
- ☐ I am proud of: _____
- ☐ Success review
- ☐ I love myself because: _____ ☐
- ☐ Love, thanks, kindness and support for others:
    1. _____   2. _____
    3. _____   4. _____
- ☐ Love, thanks, kindness and support for me:
    1. _____   2. _____
    3. _____   4. _____
- ☐ Good Deed/Selfless Act/Random Kindness: _____
- ☐ I gave undivided attention to: _____
- ☐ I made things better by: _____
- ☐ I experienced joy, happiness, fun and/or laughter: _____
- ☐ I smiled _____ minutes
- ☐ Meditation/Prayer _____ minutes
- ☐ Inspiration (reading, video, music): _____
- ☐ I listened to my intuition: _____
- ☐ Physical activity _____ minutes
- ☐ I was 100% honest today
- ☐ I took care of myself by: _____
- ☐ Reviewed purpose 3 times
- ☐ Reviewed intentions 3 times
- ☐ Steps toward goals, intentions and purpose
    1. _____   2. _____   3. _____
- ☐ Reviewed vision
- ☐ I am grateful for:
    1. _____   6. _____
    2. _____   7. _____
    3. _____   8. _____
    4. _____   9. _____
    5. _____   10. _____

- ☐ I am looking forward to: _____

Notes: _____
_____
_____
_____

MINDFUL LIVING WORKSHEET

M Tu W Th F S S   Date:_____   Rate:_____

- ☐ I am content with: _____
- ☐ I am proud of: _____
- ☐ Success review
- ☐ I love myself because: _____ ☐
- ☐ Love, thanks, kindness and support for others:
    - 1. _____   2. _____
    - 3. _____   4. _____
- ☐ Love, thanks, kindness and support for me:
    - 1. _____   2. _____
    - 3. _____   4. _____
- ☐ Good Deed/Selfless Act/Random Kindness: _____
- ☐ I gave undivided attention to: _____
- ☐ I made things better by: _____
- ☐ I experienced joy, happiness, fun and/or laughter: _____
- ☐ I smiled _____ minutes
- ☐ Meditation/Prayer _____ minutes
- ☐ Inspiration (reading, video, music): _____
- ☐ I listened to my intuition: _____
- ☐ Physical activity _____ minutes
- ☐ I was 100% honest today
- ☐ I took care of myself by: _____
- ☐ Reviewed purpose 3 times
- ☐ Reviewed intentions 3 times
- ☐ Steps toward goals, intentions and purpose
    - 1. _____   2. _____   3. _____
- ☐ Reviewed vision
- ☐ I am grateful for:
    - 1. _____   6. _____
    - 2. _____   7. _____
    - 3. _____   8. _____
    - 4. _____   9. _____
    - 5. _____   10. _____

- ☐ I am looking forward to: _____

Notes: _____
_____
_____
_____

MINDFUL LIVING WORKSHEET

M Tu W Th F S S   Date:_____   Rate:_____

- ☐ I am content with: _____
- ☐ I am proud of: _____
- ☐ Success review
- ☐ I love myself because: _____ ☐
- ☐ Love, thanks, kindness and support for others:
    1. _____   2. _____
    3. _____   4. _____
- ☐ Love, thanks, kindness and support for me:
    1. _____   2. _____
    3. _____   4. _____
- ☐ Good Deed/Selfless Act/Random Kindness: _____
- ☐ I gave undivided attention to: _____
- ☐ I made things better by: _____
- ☐ I experienced joy, happiness, fun and/or laughter: _____
- ☐ I smiled _____ minutes
- ☐ Meditation/Prayer _____ minutes
- ☐ Inspiration (reading, video, music): _____
- ☐ I listened to my intuition: _____
- ☐ Physical activity _____ minutes
- ☐ I was 100% honest today
- ☐ I took care of myself by: _____
- ☐ Reviewed purpose 3 times
- ☐ Reviewed intentions 3 times
- ☐ Steps toward goals, intentions and purpose
    1. _____ 2. _____ 3. _____
- ☐ Reviewed vision
- ☐ I am grateful for:
    1. _____   6. _____
    2. _____   7. _____
    3. _____   8. _____
    4. _____   9. _____
    5. _____   10. _____

- ☐ I am looking forward to: _____

Notes: _____
_____
_____
_____

MINDFUL LIVING WORKSHEET

M Tu W Th F S S   Date:_____   Rate:_____

- ☐ I am content with: _____
- ☐ I am proud of: _____
- ☐ Success review
- ☐ I love myself because: _____ ☐
- ☐ Love, thanks, kindness and support for others:
    1. _____   2. _____
    3. _____   4. _____
- ☐ Love, thanks, kindness and support for me:
    1. _____   2. _____
    3. _____   4. _____
- ☐ Good Deed/Selfless Act/Random Kindness: _____
- ☐ I gave undivided attention to: _____
- ☐ I made things better by: _____
- ☐ I experienced joy, happiness, fun and/or laughter: _____
- ☐ I smiled _____ minutes
- ☐ Meditation/Prayer _____ minutes
- ☐ Inspiration (reading, video, music): _____
- ☐ I listened to my intuition: _____
- ☐ Physical activity _____ minutes
- ☐ I was 100% honest today
- ☐ I took care of myself by: _____
- ☐ Reviewed purpose 3 times
- ☐ Reviewed intentions 3 times
- ☐ Steps toward goals, intentions and purpose
    1. _____ 2. _____ 3. _____
- ☐ Reviewed vision
- ☐ I am grateful for:
    1. _____   6. _____
    2. _____   7. _____
    3. _____   8. _____
    4. _____   9. _____
    5. _____   10. _____

- ☐ I am looking forward to: _____

Notes: _____
_____
_____

MINDFUL LIVING WORKSHEET

M   Tu   W   Th   F   S   S   Date:_____   Rate:_____

- ☐ I am content with: _____
- ☐ I am proud of: _____
- ☐ Success review
- ☐ I love myself because: _____ ☐
- ☐ Love, thanks, kindness and support for others:
    1. _____   2. _____
    3. _____   4. _____
- ☐ Love, thanks, kindness and support for me:
    1. _____   2. _____
    3. _____   4. _____
- ☐ Good Deed/Selfless Act/Random Kindness: _____
- ☐ I gave undivided attention to: _____
- ☐ I made things better by: _____
- ☐ I experienced joy, happiness, fun and/or laughter: _____
- ☐ I smiled _____ minutes
- ☐ Meditation/Prayer _____ minutes
- ☐ Inspiration (reading, video, music): _____
- ☐ I listened to my intuition: _____
- ☐ Physical activity _____ minutes
- ☐ I was 100% honest today
- ☐ I took care of myself by: _____
- ☐ Reviewed purpose 3 times
- ☐ Reviewed intentions 3 times
- ☐ Steps toward goals, intentions and purpose
    1. _____ 2. _____ 3. _____
- ☐ Reviewed vision
- ☐ I am grateful for:
    1. _____   6. _____
    2. _____   7. _____
    3. _____   8. _____
    4. _____   9. _____
    5. _____   10. _____

- ☐ I am looking forward to: _____

Notes: _____
_____
_____
_____

MINDFUL LIVING WORKSHEET

M Tu W Th F S S   Date:_____   Rate:_____

- ☐ I am content with: _____
- ☐ I am proud of: _____
- ☐ Success review
- ☐ I love myself because: _____ ☐
- ☐ Love, thanks, kindness and support for others:
  - 1. _____   2. _____
  - 3. _____   4. _____
- ☐ Love, thanks, kindness and support for me:
  - 1. _____   2. _____
  - 3. _____   4. _____
- ☐ Good Deed/Selfless Act/Random Kindness: _____
- ☐ I gave undivided attention to: _____
- ☐ I made things better by: _____
- ☐ I experienced joy, happiness, fun and/or laughter: _____
- ☐ I smiled _____ minutes
- ☐ Meditation/Prayer _____ minutes
- ☐ Inspiration (reading, video, music): _____
- ☐ I listened to my intuition: _____
- ☐ Physical activity _____ minutes
- ☐ I was 100% honest today
- ☐ I took care of myself by: _____
- ☐ Reviewed purpose 3 times
- ☐ Reviewed intentions 3 times
- ☐ Steps toward goals, intentions and purpose
  - 1. _____   2. _____   3. _____
- ☐ Reviewed vision
- ☐ I am grateful for:
  - 1. _____   6. _____
  - 2. _____   7. _____
  - 3. _____   8. _____
  - 4. _____   9. _____
  - 5. _____   10. _____
- ☐ I am looking forward to: _____

Notes: _____
_____
_____

MINDFUL LIVING WORKSHEET

M   Tu   W   Th   F   S   S   Date:_____   Rate:_____

- ☐ I am content with: _____
- ☐ I am proud of: _____
- ☐ Success review
- ☐ I love myself because: _____ ☐
- ☐ Love, thanks, kindness and support for others:
  - 1. _____ 2. _____
  - 3. _____ 4. _____
- ☐ Love, thanks, kindness and support for me:
  - 1. _____ 2. _____
  - 3. _____ 4. _____
- ☐ Good Deed/Selfless Act/Random Kindness: _____
- ☐ I gave undivided attention to: _____
- ☐ I made things better by: _____
- ☐ I experienced joy, happiness, fun and/or laughter: _____
- ☐ I smiled _____ minutes
- ☐ Meditation/Prayer _____ minutes
- ☐ Inspiration (reading, video, music): _____
- ☐ I listened to my intuition: _____
- ☐ Physical activity _____ minutes
- ☐ I was 100% honest today
- ☐ I took care of myself by: _____
- ☐ Reviewed purpose 3 times
- ☐ Reviewed intentions 3 times
- ☐ Steps toward goals, intentions and purpose
  - 1. _____ 2. _____ 3. _____
- ☐ Reviewed vision
- ☐ I am grateful for:
  - 1. _____ 6. _____
  - 2. _____ 7. _____
  - 3. _____ 8. _____
  - 4. _____ 9. _____
  - 5. _____ 10. _____
- ☐ I am looking forward to: _____

Notes: _____
_____
_____
_____

Mindful Living Worksheet

M Tu W Th F S S   Date:_____   Rate:_____

- ☐ I am content with: _____
- ☐ I am proud of: _____
- ☐ Success review
- ☐ I love myself because: _____ ☐
- ☐ Love, thanks, kindness and support for others:
  - 1. _____   2. _____
  - 3. _____   4. _____
- ☐ Love, thanks, kindness and support for me:
  - 1. _____   2. _____
  - 3. _____   4. _____
- ☐ Good Deed/Selfless Act/Random Kindness: _____
- ☐ I gave undivided attention to: _____
- ☐ I made things better by: _____
- ☐ I experienced joy, happiness, fun and/or laughter: _____
- ☐ I smiled _____ minutes
- ☐ Meditation/Prayer _____ minutes
- ☐ Inspiration (reading, video, music): _____
- ☐ I listened to my intuition: _____
- ☐ Physical activity _____ minutes
- ☐ I was 100% honest today
- ☐ I took care of myself by: _____
- ☐ Reviewed purpose 3 times
- ☐ Reviewed intentions 3 times
- ☐ Steps toward goals, intentions and purpose
  - 1. _____   2. _____   3. _____
- ☐ Reviewed vision
- ☐ I am grateful for:
  - 1. _____   6. _____
  - 2. _____   7. _____
  - 3. _____   8. _____
  - 4. _____   9. _____
  - 5. _____   10. _____

- ☐ I am looking forward to: _____

Notes: _____
_____
_____

MINDFUL LIVING WORKSHEET

M Tu W Th F S S   Date:_____   Rate:_____

☐ I am content with: _____
☐ I am proud of: _____
☐ Success review
☐ I love myself because: _____ ☐
☐ Love, thanks, kindness and support for others:
    1. _____ 2. _____
    3. _____ 4. _____
☐ Love, thanks, kindness and support for me:
    1. _____ 2. _____
    3. _____ 4. _____
☐ Good Deed/Selfless Act/Random Kindness: _____
☐ I gave undivided attention to: _____
☐ I made things better by: _____
☐ I experienced joy, happiness, fun and/or laughter: _____
☐ I smiled _____ minutes
☐ Meditation/Prayer _____ minutes
☐ Inspiration (reading, video, music): _____
☐ I listened to my intuition: _____
☐ Physical activity _____ minutes
☐ I was 100% honest today
☐ I took care of myself by: _____
☐ Reviewed purpose 3 times
☐ Reviewed intentions 3 times
☐ Steps toward goals, intentions and purpose
    1. _____ 2. _____ 3. _____
☐ Reviewed vision
☐ I am grateful for:
    1. _____ 6. _____
    2. _____ 7. _____
    3. _____ 8. _____
    4. _____ 9. _____
    5. _____ 10. _____

☐ I am looking forward to: _____

Notes: _____
_____
_____

MINDFUL LIVING WORKSHEET

M Tu W Th F S S   Date:_____   Rate:_____

- ☐ I am content with: _____
- ☐ I am proud of: _____
- ☐ Success review
- ☐ I love myself because: _____ ☐
- ☐ Love, thanks, kindness and support for others:
    - 1. _____   2. _____
    - 3. _____   4. _____
- ☐ Love, thanks, kindness and support for me:
    - 1. _____   2. _____
    - 3. _____   4. _____
- ☐ Good Deed/Selfless Act/Random Kindness: _____
- ☐ I gave undivided attention to: _____
- ☐ I made things better by: _____
- ☐ I experienced joy, happiness, fun and/or laughter: _____
- ☐ I smiled _____ minutes
- ☐ Meditation/Prayer _____ minutes
- ☐ Inspiration (reading, video, music): _____
- ☐ I listened to my intuition: _____
- ☐ Physical activity _____ minutes
- ☐ I was 100% honest today
- ☐ I took care of myself by: _____
- ☐ Reviewed purpose 3 times
- ☐ Reviewed intentions 3 times
- ☐ Steps toward goals, intentions and purpose
    - 1. _____ 2. _____ 3. _____
- ☐ Reviewed vision
- ☐ I am grateful for:
    - 1. _____   6. _____
    - 2. _____   7. _____
    - 3. _____   8. _____
    - 4. _____   9. _____
    - 5. _____   10. _____

- ☐ I am looking forward to: _____

Notes: _____
_____
_____

MINDFUL LIVING WORKSHEET

M Tu W Th F S S   Date:_____   Rate:_____

- ☐ I am content with: _____
- ☐ I am proud of: _____
- ☐ Success review
- ☐ I love myself because: _____ ☐
- ☐ Love, thanks, kindness and support for others:
  - 1. _____ 2. _____
  - 3. _____ 4. _____
- ☐ Love, thanks, kindness and support for me:
  - 1. _____ 2. _____
  - 3. _____ 4. _____
- ☐ Good Deed/Selfless Act/Random Kindness: _____
- ☐ I gave undivided attention to: _____
- ☐ I made things better by: _____
- ☐ I experienced joy, happiness, fun and/or laughter: _____
- ☐ I smiled _____ minutes
- ☐ Meditation/Prayer _____ minutes
- ☐ Inspiration (reading, video, music): _____
- ☐ I listened to my intuition: _____
- ☐ Physical activity _____ minutes
- ☐ I was 100% honest today
- ☐ I took care of myself by: _____
- ☐ Reviewed purpose 3 times
- ☐ Reviewed intentions 3 times
- ☐ Steps toward goals, intentions and purpose
  - 1. _____ 2. _____ 3. _____
- ☐ Reviewed vision
- ☐ I am grateful for:
  - 1. _____ 6. _____
  - 2. _____ 7. _____
  - 3. _____ 8. _____
  - 4. _____ 9. _____
  - 5. _____ 10. _____
- ☐ I am looking forward to: _____

Notes: _____
_____
_____

Mindful Living Worksheet

M Tu W Th F S S   Date:_____   Rate:_____

- ☐ I am content with: _____
- ☐ I am proud of: _____
- ☐ Success review
- ☐ I love myself because: _____ ☐
- ☐ Love, thanks, kindness and support for others:
  - 1. _____   2. _____
  - 3. _____   4. _____
- ☐ Love, thanks, kindness and support for me:
  - 1. _____   2. _____
  - 3. _____   4. _____
- ☐ Good Deed/Selfless Act/Random Kindness: _____
- ☐ I gave undivided attention to: _____
- ☐ I made things better by: _____
- ☐ I experienced joy, happiness, fun and/or laughter: _____
- ☐ I smiled _____ minutes
- ☐ Meditation/Prayer _____ minutes
- ☐ Inspiration (reading, video, music): _____
- ☐ I listened to my intuition: _____
- ☐ Physical activity _____ minutes
- ☐ I was 100% honest today
- ☐ I took care of myself by: _____
- ☐ Reviewed purpose 3 times
- ☐ Reviewed intentions 3 times
- ☐ Steps toward goals, intentions and purpose
  - 1. _____   2. _____   3. _____
- ☐ Reviewed vision
- ☐ I am grateful for:
  - 1. _____   6. _____
  - 2. _____   7. _____
  - 3. _____   8. _____
  - 4. _____   9. _____
  - 5. _____   10. _____

- ☐ I am looking forward to: _____

Notes: _____
_____
_____

Mindful Living Worksheet

M Tu W Th F S S   Date:_____   Rate:_____

- ☐ I am content with: _____
- ☐ I am proud of: _____
- ☐ Success review
- ☐ I love myself because: _____ ☐
- ☐ Love, thanks, kindness and support for others:
  - 1. _____   2. _____
  - 3. _____   4. _____
- ☐ Love, thanks, kindness and support for me:
  - 1. _____   2. _____
  - 3. _____   4. _____
- ☐ Good Deed/Selfless Act/Random Kindness: _____
- ☐ I gave undivided attention to: _____
- ☐ I made things better by: _____
- ☐ I experienced joy, happiness, fun and/or laughter: _____
- ☐ I smiled _____ minutes
- ☐ Meditation/Prayer _____ minutes
- ☐ Inspiration (reading, video, music): _____
- ☐ I listened to my intuition: _____
- ☐ Physical activity _____ minutes
- ☐ I was 100% honest today
- ☐ I took care of myself by: _____
- ☐ Reviewed purpose 3 times
- ☐ Reviewed intentions 3 times
- ☐ Steps toward goals, intentions and purpose
  - 1. _____ 2. _____ 3. _____
- ☐ Reviewed vision
- ☐ I am grateful for:
  - 1. _____   6. _____
  - 2. _____   7. _____
  - 3. _____   8. _____
  - 4. _____   9. _____
  - 5. _____   10. _____
- ☐ I am looking forward to: _____

Notes: _____
_____
_____
_____

Mindful Living Worksheet

M Tu W Th F S S   Date:_____   Rate:_____

☐ I am content with: _____
☐ I am proud of: _____
☐ Success review
☐ I love myself because: _____ ☐
☐ Love, thanks, kindness and support for others:
    1. _____   2. _____
    3. _____   4. _____
☐ Love, thanks, kindness and support for me:
    1. _____   2. _____
    3. _____   4. _____
☐ Good Deed/Selfless Act/Random Kindness: _____
☐ I gave undivided attention to: _____
☐ I made things better by: _____
☐ I experienced joy, happiness, fun and/or laughter: _____
☐ I smiled _____ minutes
☐ Meditation/Prayer _____ minutes
☐ Inspiration (reading, video, music): _____
☐ I listened to my intuition: _____
☐ Physical activity _____ minutes
☐ I was 100% honest today
☐ I took care of myself by: _____
☐ Reviewed purpose 3 times
☐ Reviewed intentions 3 times
☐ Steps toward goals, intentions and purpose
    1. _____ 2. _____ 3. _____
☐ Reviewed vision
☐ I am grateful for:
    1. _____   6. _____
    2. _____   7. _____
    3. _____   8. _____
    4. _____   9. _____
    5. _____   10. _____

☐ I am looking forward to: _____

Notes: _____
_____
_____
_____

MINDFUL LIVING WORKSHEET

M Tu W Th F S S   Date:_____   Rate:_____

- ☐ I am content with: _____
- ☐ I am proud of: _____
- ☐ Success review
- ☐ I love myself because: _____ ☐
- ☐ Love, thanks, kindness and support for others:
  - 1. _____   2. _____
  - 3. _____   4. _____
- ☐ Love, thanks, kindness and support for me:
  - 1. _____   2. _____
  - 3. _____   4. _____
- ☐ Good Deed/Selfless Act/Random Kindness: _____
- ☐ I gave undivided attention to: _____
- ☐ I made things better by: _____
- ☐ I experienced joy, happiness, fun and/or laughter: _____
- ☐ I smiled _____ minutes
- ☐ Meditation/Prayer _____ minutes
- ☐ Inspiration (reading, video, music): _____
- ☐ I listened to my intuition: _____
- ☐ Physical activity _____ minutes
- ☐ I was 100% honest today
- ☐ I took care of myself by: _____
- ☐ Reviewed purpose 3 times
- ☐ Reviewed intentions 3 times
- ☐ Steps toward goals, intentions and purpose
  - 1. _____ 2. _____ 3. _____
- ☐ Reviewed vision
- ☐ I am grateful for:
  - 1. _____   6. _____
  - 2. _____   7. _____
  - 3. _____   8. _____
  - 4. _____   9. _____
  - 5. _____   10. _____

- ☐ I am looking forward to: _____

Notes: _____
_____
_____
_____

Mindful Living Worksheet

M Tu W Th F S S   Date:_____   Rate:_____

- ☐ I am content with: _____
- ☐ I am proud of: _____
- ☐ Success review
- ☐ I love myself because: _____ ☐
- ☐ Love, thanks, kindness and support for others:
    1. _____   2. _____
    3. _____   4. _____
- ☐ Love, thanks, kindness and support for me:
    1. _____   2. _____
    3. _____   4. _____
- ☐ Good Deed/Selfless Act/Random Kindness: _____
- ☐ I gave undivided attention to: _____
- ☐ I made things better by: _____
- ☐ I experienced joy, happiness, fun and/or laughter: _____
- ☐ I smiled _____ minutes
- ☐ Meditation/Prayer _____ minutes
- ☐ Inspiration (reading, video, music): _____
- ☐ I listened to my intuition: _____
- ☐ Physical activity _____ minutes
- ☐ I was 100% honest today
- ☐ I took care of myself by: _____
- ☐ Reviewed purpose 3 times
- ☐ Reviewed intentions 3 times
- ☐ Steps toward goals, intentions and purpose
    1. _____ 2. _____ 3. _____
- ☐ Reviewed vision
- ☐ I am grateful for:
    1. _____   6. _____
    2. _____   7. _____
    3. _____   8. _____
    4. _____   9. _____
    5. _____   10. _____

- ☐ I am looking forward to: _____

Notes: _____
_____
_____
_____

Mindful Living Worksheet

M Tu W Th F S S   Date:_____   Rate:_____

- ☐ I am content with: _____
- ☐ I am proud of: _____
- ☐ Success review
- ☐ I love myself because: _____ ☐
- ☐ Love, thanks, kindness and support for others:
    - 1. _____   2. _____
    - 3. _____   4. _____
- ☐ Love, thanks, kindness and support for me:
    - 1. _____   2. _____
    - 3. _____   4. _____
- ☐ Good Deed/Selfless Act/Random Kindness: _____
- ☐ I gave undivided attention to: _____
- ☐ I made things better by: _____
- ☐ I experienced joy, happiness, fun and/or laughter: _____
- ☐ I smiled _____ minutes
- ☐ Meditation/Prayer _____ minutes
- ☐ Inspiration (reading, video, music): _____
- ☐ I listened to my intuition: _____
- ☐ Physical activity _____ minutes
- ☐ I was 100% honest today
- ☐ I took care of myself by: _____
- ☐ Reviewed purpose 3 times
- ☐ Reviewed intentions 3 times
- ☐ Steps toward goals, intentions and purpose
    - 1. _____   2. _____   3. _____
- ☐ Reviewed vision
- ☐ I am grateful for:
    - 1. _____   6. _____
    - 2. _____   7. _____
    - 3. _____   8. _____
    - 4. _____   9. _____
    - 5. _____   10. _____

- ☐ I am looking forward to: _____

Notes: _____
_____
_____
_____

Mindful Living Worksheet

M   Tu   W   Th   F   S   S   Date: _____   Rate: _____

☐ I am content with: _____
☐ I am proud of: _____
☐ Success review
☐ I love myself because: _____ ☐
☐ Love, thanks, kindness and support for others:
    1. _____ 2. _____
    3. _____ 4. _____
☐ Love, thanks, kindness and support for me:
    1. _____ 2. _____
    3. _____ 4. _____
☐ Good Deed/Selfless Act/Random Kindness: _____
☐ I gave undivided attention to: _____
☐ I made things better by: _____
☐ I experienced joy, happiness, fun and/or laughter: _____
☐ I smiled _____ minutes
☐ Meditation/Prayer _____ minutes
☐ Inspiration (reading, video, music): _____
☐ I listened to my intuition: _____
☐ Physical activity _____ minutes
☐ I was 100% honest today
☐ I took care of myself by: _____
☐ Reviewed purpose 3 times
☐ Reviewed intentions 3 times
☐ Steps toward goals, intentions and purpose
    1. _____ 2. _____ 3. _____
☐ Reviewed vision
☐ I am grateful for:
    1. _____ 6. _____
    2. _____ 7. _____
    3. _____ 8. _____
    4. _____ 9. _____
    5. _____ 10. _____

☐ I am looking forward to: _____

Notes: _____
_____
_____
_____

Mindful Living Worksheet

M Tu W Th F S S   Date:_____   Rate:_____

- ☐ I am content with: _____
- ☐ I am proud of: _____
- ☐ Success review
- ☐ I love myself because: _____ ☐
- ☐ Love, thanks, kindness and support for others:
  - 1. _____   2. _____
  - 3. _____   4. _____
- ☐ Love, thanks, kindness and support for me:
  - 1. _____   2. _____
  - 3. _____   4. _____
- ☐ Good Deed/Selfless Act/Random Kindness: _____
- ☐ I gave undivided attention to: _____
- ☐ I made things better by: _____
- ☐ I experienced joy, happiness, fun and/or laughter: _____
- ☐ I smiled _____ minutes
- ☐ Meditation/Prayer _____ minutes
- ☐ Inspiration (reading, video, music): _____
- ☐ I listened to my intuition: _____
- ☐ Physical activity _____ minutes
- ☐ I was 100% honest today
- ☐ I took care of myself by: _____
- ☐ Reviewed purpose 3 times
- ☐ Reviewed intentions 3 times
- ☐ Steps toward goals, intentions and purpose
  - 1. _____   2. _____   3. _____
- ☐ Reviewed vision
- ☐ I am grateful for:
  - 1. _____   6. _____
  - 2. _____   7. _____
  - 3. _____   8. _____
  - 4. _____   9. _____
  - 5. _____   10. _____

- ☐ I am looking forward to: _____

Notes: _____
_____
_____
_____

Mindful Living Worksheet

M Tu W Th F S S   Date:_____   Rate:_____

- ☐ I am content with: _____
- ☐ I am proud of: _____
- ☐ Success review
- ☐ I love myself because: _____ ☐
- ☐ Love, thanks, kindness and support for others:
    1. _____   2. _____
    3. _____   4. _____
- ☐ Love, thanks, kindness and support for me:
    1. _____   2. _____
    3. _____   4. _____
- ☐ Good Deed/Selfless Act/Random Kindness: _____
- ☐ I gave undivided attention to: _____
- ☐ I made things better by: _____
- ☐ I experienced joy, happiness, fun and/or laughter: _____
- ☐ I smiled _____ minutes
- ☐ Meditation/Prayer _____ minutes
- ☐ Inspiration (reading, video, music): _____
- ☐ I listened to my intuition: _____
- ☐ Physical activity _____ minutes
- ☐ I was 100% honest today
- ☐ I took care of myself by: _____
- ☐ Reviewed purpose 3 times
- ☐ Reviewed intentions 3 times
- ☐ Steps toward goals, intentions and purpose
    1. _____ 2. _____ 3. _____
- ☐ Reviewed vision
- ☐ I am grateful for:
    1. _____   6. _____
    2. _____   7. _____
    3. _____   8. _____
    4. _____   9. _____
    5. _____   10. _____

- ☐ I am looking forward to: _____

Notes: _____
_____
_____
_____

Mindful Living Worksheet

M Tu W Th F S S   Date:_____   Rate:_____

- ☐ I am content with: _____
- ☐ I am proud of: _____
- ☐ Success review
- ☐ I love myself because: _____ ☐
- ☐ Love, thanks, kindness and support for others:
  - 1. _____   2. _____
  - 3. _____   4. _____
- ☐ Love, thanks, kindness and support for me:
  - 1. _____   2. _____
  - 3. _____   4. _____
- ☐ Good Deed/Selfless Act/Random Kindness: _____
- ☐ I gave undivided attention to: _____
- ☐ I made things better by: _____
- ☐ I experienced joy, happiness, fun and/or laughter: _____
- ☐ I smiled _____ minutes
- ☐ Meditation/Prayer _____ minutes
- ☐ Inspiration (reading, video, music): _____
- ☐ I listened to my intuition: _____
- ☐ Physical activity _____ minutes
- ☐ I was 100% honest today
- ☐ I took care of myself by: _____
- ☐ Reviewed purpose 3 times
- ☐ Reviewed intentions 3 times
- ☐ Steps toward goals, intentions and purpose
  - 1. _____   2. _____   3. _____
- ☐ Reviewed vision
- ☐ I am grateful for:
  - 1. _____   6. _____
  - 2. _____   7. _____
  - 3. _____   8. _____
  - 4. _____   9. _____
  - 5. _____   10. _____

- ☐ I am looking forward to: _____

Notes: _____
_____
_____

MINDFUL LIVING WORKSHEET

M Tu W Th F S S   Date:_____   Rate:_____

- ☐ I am content with: _____
- ☐ I am proud of: _____
- ☐ Success review
- ☐ I love myself because: _____ ☐
- ☐ Love, thanks, kindness and support for others:
    - 1. _____   2. _____
    - 3. _____   4. _____
- ☐ Love, thanks, kindness and support for me:
    - 1. _____   2. _____
    - 3. _____   4. _____
- ☐ Good Deed/Selfless Act/Random Kindness: _____
- ☐ I gave undivided attention to: _____
- ☐ I made things better by: _____
- ☐ I experienced joy, happiness, fun and/or laughter: _____
- ☐ I smiled _____ minutes
- ☐ Meditation/Prayer _____ minutes
- ☐ Inspiration (reading, video, music): _____
- ☐ I listened to my intuition: _____
- ☐ Physical activity _____ minutes
- ☐ I was 100% honest today
- ☐ I took care of myself by: _____
- ☐ Reviewed purpose 3 times
- ☐ Reviewed intentions 3 times
- ☐ Steps toward goals, intentions and purpose
    - 1. _____   2. _____   3. _____
- ☐ Reviewed vision
- ☐ I am grateful for:
    - 1. _____   6. _____
    - 2. _____   7. _____
    - 3. _____   8. _____
    - 4. _____   9. _____
    - 5. _____   10. _____

- ☐ I am looking forward to: _____

Notes: _____
_____
_____
_____

Mindful Living Worksheet

M   Tu   W   Th   F   S   S   Date:_____   Rate:_____

☐ I am content with: _____
☐ I am proud of: _____
☐ Success review
☐ I love myself because: _____ ☐
☐ Love, thanks, kindness and support for others:
      1. _____   2. _____
      3. _____   4. _____
☐ Love, thanks, kindness and support for me:
      1. _____   2. _____
      3. _____   4. _____
☐ Good Deed/Selfless Act/Random Kindness: _____
☐ I gave undivided attention to: _____
☐ I made things better by: _____
☐ I experienced joy, happiness, fun and/or laughter: _____
☐ I smiled _____ minutes
☐ Meditation/Prayer _____ minutes
☐ Inspiration (reading, video, music): _____
☐ I listened to my intuition: _____
☐ Physical activity _____ minutes
☐ I was 100% honest today
☐ I took care of myself by: _____
☐ Reviewed purpose 3 times
☐ Reviewed intentions 3 times
☐ Steps toward goals, intentions and purpose
   1. _____   2. _____   3. _____
☐ Reviewed vision
☐ I am grateful for:
      1. _____   6. _____
      2. _____   7. _____
      3. _____   8. _____
      4. _____   9. _____
      5. _____   10. _____

☐ I am looking forward to: _____

Notes: _____
_____
_____
_____

MINDFUL LIVING WORKSHEET

M   Tu   W   Th   F   S   S   Date:_____   Rate:_____

- ☐ I am content with: _____
- ☐ I am proud of: _____
- ☐ Success review
- ☐ I love myself because: _____ ☐
- ☐ Love, thanks, kindness and support for others:
    1. _____   2. _____
    3. _____   4. _____
- ☐ Love, thanks, kindness and support for me:
    1. _____   2. _____
    3. _____   4. _____
- ☐ Good Deed/Selfless Act/Random Kindness: _____
- ☐ I gave undivided attention to: _____
- ☐ I made things better by: _____
- ☐ I experienced joy, happiness, fun and/or laughter: _____
- ☐ I smiled _____ minutes
- ☐ Meditation/Prayer _____ minutes
- ☐ Inspiration (reading, video, music): _____
- ☐ I listened to my intuition: _____
- ☐ Physical activity _____ minutes
- ☐ I was 100% honest today
- ☐ I took care of myself by: _____
- ☐ Reviewed purpose 3 times
- ☐ Reviewed intentions 3 times
- ☐ Steps toward goals, intentions and purpose
    1. _____   2. _____   3. _____
- ☐ Reviewed vision
- ☐ I am grateful for:
    1. _____   6. _____
    2. _____   7. _____
    3. _____   8. _____
    4. _____   9. _____
    5. _____   10. _____

- ☐ I am looking forward to: _____

Notes: _____
_____
_____
_____

MINDFUL LIVING WORKSHEET

M Tu W Th F S S   Date:_____   Rate:_____

- ☐ I am content with: _____
- ☐ I am proud of: _____
- ☐ Success review
- ☐ I love myself because: _____ ☐
- ☐ Love, thanks, kindness and support for others:
    1. _____   2. _____
    3. _____   4. _____
- ☐ Love, thanks, kindness and support for me:
    1. _____   2. _____
    3. _____   4. _____
- ☐ Good Deed/Selfless Act/Random Kindness: _____
- ☐ I gave undivided attention to: _____
- ☐ I made things better by: _____
- ☐ I experienced joy, happiness, fun and/or laughter: _____
- ☐ I smiled _____ minutes
- ☐ Meditation/Prayer _____ minutes
- ☐ Inspiration (reading, video, music): _____
- ☐ I listened to my intuition: _____
- ☐ Physical activity _____ minutes
- ☐ I was 100% honest today
- ☐ I took care of myself by: _____
- ☐ Reviewed purpose 3 times
- ☐ Reviewed intentions 3 times
- ☐ Steps toward goals, intentions and purpose
    1. _____   2. _____   3. _____
- ☐ Reviewed vision
- ☐ I am grateful for:
    1. _____   6. _____
    2. _____   7. _____
    3. _____   8. _____
    4. _____   9. _____
    5. _____   10. _____

- ☐ I am looking forward to: _____

Notes: _____
_____
_____
_____

MINDFUL LIVING WORKSHEET

M Tu W Th F S S   Date:_____   Rate:_____

- ☐ I am content with: _____
- ☐ I am proud of: _____
- ☐ Success review
- ☐ I love myself because: _____ ☐
- ☐ Love, thanks, kindness and support for others:
    1. _____   2. _____
    3. _____   4. _____
- ☐ Love, thanks, kindness and support for me:
    1. _____   2. _____
    3. _____   4. _____
- ☐ Good Deed/Selfless Act/Random Kindness: _____
- ☐ I gave undivided attention to: _____
- ☐ I made things better by: _____
- ☐ I experienced joy, happiness, fun and/or laughter: _____
- ☐ I smiled _____ minutes
- ☐ Meditation/Prayer _____ minutes
- ☐ Inspiration (reading, video, music): _____
- ☐ I listened to my intuition: _____
- ☐ Physical activity _____ minutes
- ☐ I was 100% honest today
- ☐ I took care of myself by: _____
- ☐ Reviewed purpose 3 times
- ☐ Reviewed intentions 3 times
- ☐ Steps toward goals, intentions and purpose
    1. _____   2. _____   3. _____
- ☐ Reviewed vision
- ☐ I am grateful for:
    1. _____   6. _____
    2. _____   7. _____
    3. _____   8. _____
    4. _____   9. _____
    5. _____   10. _____

- ☐ I am looking forward to: _____

Notes: _____
_____
_____
_____

Mindful Living Worksheet

M Tu W Th F S S   Date:_____   Rate:_____

- ☐ I am content with: _____
- ☐ I am proud of: _____
- ☐ Success review
- ☐ I love myself because: _____ ☐
- ☐ Love, thanks, kindness and support for others:
    - 1. _____   2. _____
    - 3. _____   4. _____
- ☐ Love, thanks, kindness and support for me:
    - 1. _____   2. _____
    - 3. _____   4. _____
- ☐ Good Deed/Selfless Act/Random Kindness: _____
- ☐ I gave undivided attention to: _____
- ☐ I made things better by: _____
- ☐ I experienced joy, happiness, fun and/or laughter: _____
- ☐ I smiled _____ minutes
- ☐ Meditation/Prayer _____ minutes
- ☐ Inspiration (reading, video, music): _____
- ☐ I listened to my intuition: _____
- ☐ Physical activity _____ minutes
- ☐ I was 100% honest today
- ☐ I took care of myself by: _____
- ☐ Reviewed purpose 3 times
- ☐ Reviewed intentions 3 times
- ☐ Steps toward goals, intentions and purpose
    - 1. _____   2. _____   3. _____
- ☐ Reviewed vision
- ☐ I am grateful for:
    - 1. _____   6. _____
    - 2. _____   7. _____
    - 3. _____   8. _____
    - 4. _____   9. _____
    - 5. _____   10. _____

- ☐ I am looking forward to: _____

Notes: _____
_____
_____

Mindful Living Worksheet

M Tu W Th F S S   Date: _____   Rate: _____

- ☐ I am content with: _____
- ☐ I am proud of: _____
- ☐ Success review
- ☐ I love myself because: _____ ☐
- ☐ Love, thanks, kindness and support for others:
    1. _____   2. _____
    3. _____   4. _____
- ☐ Love, thanks, kindness and support for me:
    1. _____   2. _____
    3. _____   4. _____
- ☐ Good Deed/Selfless Act/Random Kindness: _____
- ☐ I gave undivided attention to: _____
- ☐ I made things better by: _____
- ☐ I experienced joy, happiness, fun and/or laughter: _____
- ☐ I smiled _____ minutes
- ☐ Meditation/Prayer _____ minutes
- ☐ Inspiration (reading, video, music): _____
- ☐ I listened to my intuition: _____
- ☐ Physical activity _____ minutes
- ☐ I was 100% honest today
- ☐ I took care of myself by: _____
- ☐ Reviewed purpose 3 times
- ☐ Reviewed intentions 3 times
- ☐ Steps toward goals, intentions and purpose
    1. _____ 2. _____ 3. _____
- ☐ Reviewed vision
- ☐ I am grateful for:
    1. _____   6. _____
    2. _____   7. _____
    3. _____   8. _____
    4. _____   9. _____
    5. _____   10. _____

- ☐ I am looking forward to: _____

Notes: _____
_____
_____
_____

MINDFUL LIVING WORKSHEET

M   Tu   W   Th   F   S   S   Date:_____   Rate:_____

- ☐ I am content with: _____
- ☐ I am proud of: _____
- ☐ Success review
- ☐ I love myself because: _____ ☐
- ☐ Love, thanks, kindness and support for others:
  - 1. _____   2. _____
  - 3. _____   4. _____
- ☐ Love, thanks, kindness and support for me:
  - 1. _____   2. _____
  - 3. _____   4. _____
- ☐ Good Deed/Selfless Act/Random Kindness: _____
- ☐ I gave undivided attention to: _____
- ☐ I made things better by: _____
- ☐ I experienced joy, happiness, fun and/or laughter: _____
- ☐ I smiled _____ minutes
- ☐ Meditation/Prayer _____ minutes
- ☐ Inspiration (reading, video, music): _____
- ☐ I listened to my intuition: _____
- ☐ Physical activity _____ minutes
- ☐ I was 100% honest today
- ☐ I took care of myself by: _____
- ☐ Reviewed purpose 3 times
- ☐ Reviewed intentions 3 times
- ☐ Steps toward goals, intentions and purpose
  - 1. _____   2. _____   3. _____
- ☐ Reviewed vision
- ☐ I am grateful for:
  - 1. _____   6. _____
  - 2. _____   7. _____
  - 3. _____   8. _____
  - 4. _____   9. _____
  - 5. _____   10. _____

- ☐ I am looking forward to: _____

Notes: _____
_____
_____
_____

Mindful Living Worksheet

M Tu W Th F S S   Date:_____   Rate:_____

- ☐ I am content with: _____
- ☐ I am proud of: _____
- ☐ Success review
- ☐ I love myself because: _____ ☐
- ☐ Love, thanks, kindness and support for others:
  - 1. _____   2. _____
  - 3. _____   4. _____
- ☐ Love, thanks, kindness and support for me:
  - 1. _____   2. _____
  - 3. _____   4. _____
- ☐ Good Deed/Selfless Act/Random Kindness: _____
- ☐ I gave undivided attention to: _____
- ☐ I made things better by: _____
- ☐ I experienced joy, happiness, fun and/or laughter: _____
- ☐ I smiled _____ minutes
- ☐ Meditation/Prayer _____ minutes
- ☐ Inspiration (reading, video, music): _____
- ☐ I listened to my intuition: _____
- ☐ Physical activity _____ minutes
- ☐ I was 100% honest today
- ☐ I took care of myself by: _____
- ☐ Reviewed purpose 3 times
- ☐ Reviewed intentions 3 times
- ☐ Steps toward goals, intentions and purpose
  - 1. _____   2. _____   3. _____
- ☐ Reviewed vision
- ☐ I am grateful for:
  - 1. _____   6. _____
  - 2. _____   7. _____
  - 3. _____   8. _____
  - 4. _____   9. _____
  - 5. _____   10. _____

- ☐ I am looking forward to: _____

Notes: _____
_____
_____
_____

MINDFUL LIVING WORKSHEET

M Tu W Th F S S   Date:_____   Rate:_____

☐ I am content with: _____
☐ I am proud of: _____
☐ Success review
☐ I love myself because: _____ ☐
☐ Love, thanks, kindness and support for others:
    1. _____   2. _____
    3. _____   4. _____
☐ Love, thanks, kindness and support for me:
    1. _____   2. _____
    3. _____   4. _____
☐ Good Deed/Selfless Act/Random Kindness: _____
☐ I gave undivided attention to: _____
☐ I made things better by: _____
☐ I experienced joy, happiness, fun and/or laughter: _____
☐ I smiled _____ minutes
☐ Meditation/Prayer _____ minutes
☐ Inspiration (reading, video, music): _____
☐ I listened to my intuition: _____
☐ Physical activity _____ minutes
☐ I was 100% honest today
☐ I took care of myself by: _____
☐ Reviewed purpose 3 times
☐ Reviewed intentions 3 times
☐ Steps toward goals, intentions and purpose
    1. _____ 2. _____ 3. _____
☐ Reviewed vision
☐ I am grateful for:
    1. _____   6. _____
    2. _____   7. _____
    3. _____   8. _____
    4. _____   9. _____
    5. _____   10. _____

☐ I am looking forward to: _____

Notes: _____
_____
_____
_____

MINDFUL LIVING WORKSHEET

M Tu W Th F S S   Date:_____   Rate:_____

- ☐ I am content with: _____
- ☐ I am proud of: _____
- ☐ Success review
- ☐ I love myself because: _____ ☐
- ☐ Love, thanks, kindness and support for others:
    - 1. _____   2. _____
    - 3. _____   4. _____
- ☐ Love, thanks, kindness and support for me:
    - 1. _____   2. _____
    - 3. _____   4. _____
- ☐ Good Deed/Selfless Act/Random Kindness: _____
- ☐ I gave undivided attention to: _____
- ☐ I made things better by: _____
- ☐ I experienced joy, happiness, fun and/or laughter: _____
- ☐ I smiled _____ minutes
- ☐ Meditation/Prayer _____ minutes
- ☐ Inspiration (reading, video, music): _____
- ☐ I listened to my intuition: _____
- ☐ Physical activity _____ minutes
- ☐ I was 100% honest today
- ☐ I took care of myself by: _____
- ☐ Reviewed purpose 3 times
- ☐ Reviewed intentions 3 times
- ☐ Steps toward goals, intentions and purpose
    - 1. _____ 2. _____ 3. _____
- ☐ Reviewed vision
- ☐ I am grateful for:
    - 1. _____   6. _____
    - 2. _____   7. _____
    - 3. _____   8. _____
    - 4. _____   9. _____
    - 5. _____   10. _____

- ☐ I am looking forward to: _____

Notes: _____
_____
_____

MINDFUL LIVING WORKSHEET

M Tu W Th F S S   Date:_____   Rate:_____

- ☐ I am content with: _____
- ☐ I am proud of: _____
- ☐ Success review
- ☐ I love myself because: _____ ☐
- ☐ Love, thanks, kindness and support for others:
    1. _____   2. _____
    3. _____   4. _____
- ☐ Love, thanks, kindness and support for me:
    1. _____   2. _____
    3. _____   4. _____
- ☐ Good Deed/Selfless Act/Random Kindness: _____
- ☐ I gave undivided attention to: _____
- ☐ I made things better by: _____
- ☐ I experienced joy, happiness, fun and/or laughter: _____
- ☐ I smiled _____ minutes
- ☐ Meditation/Prayer _____ minutes
- ☐ Inspiration (reading, video, music): _____
- ☐ I listened to my intuition: _____
- ☐ Physical activity _____ minutes
- ☐ I was 100% honest today
- ☐ I took care of myself by: _____
- ☐ Reviewed purpose 3 times
- ☐ Reviewed intentions 3 times
- ☐ Steps toward goals, intentions and purpose
    1. _____ 2. _____ 3. _____
- ☐ Reviewed vision
- ☐ I am grateful for:
    1. _____   6. _____
    2. _____   7. _____
    3. _____   8. _____
    4. _____   9. _____
    5. _____   10. _____

- ☐ I am looking forward to: _____

Notes: _____
_____
_____
_____

Mindful Living Worksheet

M Tu W Th F S S   Date:_____   Rate:_____

- ☐ I am content with: _____
- ☐ I am proud of: _____
- ☐ Success review
- ☐ I love myself because: _____ ☐
- ☐ Love, thanks, kindness and support for others:
    1. _____   2. _____
    3. _____   4. _____
- ☐ Love, thanks, kindness and support for me:
    1. _____   2. _____
    3. _____   4. _____
- ☐ Good Deed/Selfless Act/Random Kindness: _____
- ☐ I gave undivided attention to: _____
- ☐ I made things better by: _____
- ☐ I experienced joy, happiness, fun and/or laughter: _____
- ☐ I smiled _____ minutes
- ☐ Meditation/Prayer _____ minutes
- ☐ Inspiration (reading, video, music): _____
- ☐ I listened to my intuition: _____
- ☐ Physical activity _____ minutes
- ☐ I was 100% honest today
- ☐ I took care of myself by: _____
- ☐ Reviewed purpose 3 times
- ☐ Reviewed intentions 3 times
- ☐ Steps toward goals, intentions and purpose
    1. _____ 2. _____ 3. _____
- ☐ Reviewed vision
- ☐ I am grateful for:
    1. _____   6. _____
    2. _____   7. _____
    3. _____   8. _____
    4. _____   9. _____
    5. _____   10. _____

- ☐ I am looking forward to: _____

Notes: _____
_____
_____
_____

MINDFUL LIVING WORKSHEET

M Tu W Th F S S   Date:_____   Rate:_____

☐ I am content with: _____
☐ I am proud of: _____
☐ Success review
☐ I love myself because: _____ ☐
☐ Love, thanks, kindness and support for others:
    1. _____   2. _____
    3. _____   4. _____
☐ Love, thanks, kindness and support for me:
    1. _____   2. _____
    3. _____   4. _____
☐ Good Deed/Selfless Act/Random Kindness: _____
☐ I gave undivided attention to: _____
☐ I made things better by: _____
☐ I experienced joy, happiness, fun and/or laughter: _____
☐ I smiled _____ minutes
☐ Meditation/Prayer _____ minutes
☐ Inspiration (reading, video, music): _____
☐ I listened to my intuition: _____
☐ Physical activity _____ minutes
☐ I was 100% honest today
☐ I took care of myself by: _____
☐ Reviewed purpose 3 times
☐ Reviewed intentions 3 times
☐ Steps toward goals, intentions and purpose
    1. _____   2. _____   3. _____
☐ Reviewed vision
☐ I am grateful for:
    1. _____   6. _____
    2. _____   7. _____
    3. _____   8. _____
    4. _____   9. _____
    5. _____   10. _____

☐ I am looking forward to: _____

Notes: _____
_____
_____

Mindful Living Worksheet

M Tu W Th F S S   Date:_____   Rate:_____

- ☐ I am content with: _____
- ☐ I am proud of: _____
- ☐ Success review
- ☐ I love myself because: _____ ☐
- ☐ Love, thanks, kindness and support for others:
  - 1. _____   2. _____
  - 3. _____   4. _____
- ☐ Love, thanks, kindness and support for me:
  - 1. _____   2. _____
  - 3. _____   4. _____
- ☐ Good Deed/Selfless Act/Random Kindness: _____
- ☐ I gave undivided attention to: _____
- ☐ I made things better by: _____
- ☐ I experienced joy, happiness, fun and/or laughter: _____
- ☐ I smiled _____ minutes
- ☐ Meditation/Prayer _____ minutes
- ☐ Inspiration (reading, video, music): _____
- ☐ I listened to my intuition: _____
- ☐ Physical activity _____ minutes
- ☐ I was 100% honest today
- ☐ I took care of myself by: _____
- ☐ Reviewed purpose 3 times
- ☐ Reviewed intentions 3 times
- ☐ Steps toward goals, intentions and purpose
  - 1. _____   2. _____   3. _____
- ☐ Reviewed vision
- ☐ I am grateful for:
  - 1. _____   6. _____
  - 2. _____   7. _____
  - 3. _____   8. _____
  - 4. _____   9. _____
  - 5. _____   10. _____

- ☐ I am looking forward to: _____

Notes: _____
_____
_____
_____

MINDFUL LIVING WORKSHEET

M Tu W Th F S S   Date:_____   Rate:_____

- ☐ I am content with: _____
- ☐ I am proud of: _____
- ☐ Success review
- ☐ I love myself because: _____ ☐
- ☐ Love, thanks, kindness and support for others:
    - 1. _____   2. _____
    - 3. _____   4. _____
- ☐ Love, thanks, kindness and support for me:
    - 1. _____   2. _____
    - 3. _____   4. _____
- ☐ Good Deed/Selfless Act/Random Kindness: _____
- ☐ I gave undivided attention to: _____
- ☐ I made things better by: _____
- ☐ I experienced joy, happiness, fun and/or laughter: _____
- ☐ I smiled _____ minutes
- ☐ Meditation/Prayer _____ minutes
- ☐ Inspiration (reading, video, music): _____
- ☐ I listened to my intuition: _____
- ☐ Physical activity _____ minutes
- ☐ I was 100% honest today
- ☐ I took care of myself by: _____
- ☐ Reviewed purpose 3 times
- ☐ Reviewed intentions 3 times
- ☐ Steps toward goals, intentions and purpose
    - 1. _____   2. _____   3. _____
- ☐ Reviewed vision
- ☐ I am grateful for:
    - 1. _____   6. _____
    - 2. _____   7. _____
    - 3. _____   8. _____
    - 4. _____   9. _____
    - 5. _____   10. _____
- ☐ I am looking forward to: _____

Notes: _____
_____
_____
_____

Mindful Living Worksheet

M Tu W Th F S S   Date:_____   Rate:_____

- ☐ I am content with: _____
- ☐ I am proud of: _____
- ☐ Success review
- ☐ I love myself because: _____ ☐
- ☐ Love, thanks, kindness and support for others:
  - 1. _____   2. _____
  - 3. _____   4. _____
- ☐ Love, thanks, kindness and support for me:
  - 1. _____   2. _____
  - 3. _____   4. _____
- ☐ Good Deed/Selfless Act/Random Kindness: _____
- ☐ I gave undivided attention to: _____
- ☐ I made things better by: _____
- ☐ I experienced joy, happiness, fun and/or laughter: _____
- ☐ I smiled _____ minutes
- ☐ Meditation/Prayer _____ minutes
- ☐ Inspiration (reading, video, music): _____
- ☐ I listened to my intuition: _____
- ☐ Physical activity _____ minutes
- ☐ I was 100% honest today
- ☐ I took care of myself by: _____
- ☐ Reviewed purpose 3 times
- ☐ Reviewed intentions 3 times
- ☐ Steps toward goals, intentions and purpose
  - 1. _____ 2. _____ 3. _____
- ☐ Reviewed vision
- ☐ I am grateful for:
  - 1. _____   6. _____
  - 2. _____   7. _____
  - 3. _____   8. _____
  - 4. _____   9. _____
  - 5. _____   10. _____
- ☐ I am looking forward to: _____

Notes: _____
_____
_____

MINDFUL LIVING WORKSHEET

M   Tu   W   Th   F   S   S   Date:_____   Rate:_____

- ☐ I am content with: _____
- ☐ I am proud of: _____
- ☐ Success review
- ☐ I love myself because: _____ ☐
- ☐ Love, thanks, kindness and support for others:
    - 1. _____   2. _____
    - 3. _____   4. _____
- ☐ Love, thanks, kindness and support for me:
    - 1. _____   2. _____
    - 3. _____   4. _____
- ☐ Good Deed/Selfless Act/Random Kindness: _____
- ☐ I gave undivided attention to: _____
- ☐ I made things better by: _____
- ☐ I experienced joy, happiness, fun and/or laughter: _____
- ☐ I smiled _____ minutes
- ☐ Meditation/Prayer _____ minutes
- ☐ Inspiration (reading, video, music): _____
- ☐ I listened to my intuition: _____
- ☐ Physical activity _____ minutes
- ☐ I was 100% honest today
- ☐ I took care of myself by: _____
- ☐ Reviewed purpose 3 times
- ☐ Reviewed intentions 3 times
- ☐ Steps toward goals, intentions and purpose
    - 1. _____ 2. _____ 3. _____
- ☐ Reviewed vision
- ☐ I am grateful for:
    - 1. _____   6. _____
    - 2. _____   7. _____
    - 3. _____   8. _____
    - 4. _____   9. _____
    - 5. _____   10. _____
- ☐ I am looking forward to: _____

Notes: _____
_____
_____
_____

Mindful Living Worksheet

M Tu W Th F S S   Date:_____   Rate:_____

- ☐ I am content with: _____
- ☐ I am proud of: _____
- ☐ Success review
- ☐ I love myself because: _____ ☐
- ☐ Love, thanks, kindness and support for others:
  - 1. _____   2. _____
  - 3. _____   4. _____
- ☐ Love, thanks, kindness and support for me:
  - 1. _____   2. _____
  - 3. _____   4. _____
- ☐ Good Deed/Selfless Act/Random Kindness: _____
- ☐ I gave undivided attention to: _____
- ☐ I made things better by: _____
- ☐ I experienced joy, happiness, fun and/or laughter: _____
- ☐ I smiled _____ minutes
- ☐ Meditation/Prayer _____ minutes
- ☐ Inspiration (reading, video, music): _____
- ☐ I listened to my intuition: _____
- ☐ Physical activity _____ minutes
- ☐ I was 100% honest today
- ☐ I took care of myself by: _____
- ☐ Reviewed purpose 3 times
- ☐ Reviewed intentions 3 times
- ☐ Steps toward goals, intentions and purpose
  - 1. _____   2. _____   3. _____
- ☐ Reviewed vision
- ☐ I am grateful for:
  - 1. _____   6. _____
  - 2. _____   7. _____
  - 3. _____   8. _____
  - 4. _____   9. _____
  - 5. _____   10. _____
- ☐ I am looking forward to: _____

Notes: _____
_____
_____
_____

MINDFUL LIVING WORKSHEET

M   Tu   W   Th   F   S   S   Date:_____   Rate:_____

- ☐ I am content with: _____
- ☐ I am proud of: _____
- ☐ Success review
- ☐ I love myself because: _____ ☐
- ☐ Love, thanks, kindness and support for others:
    1. _____   2. _____
    3. _____   4. _____
- ☐ Love, thanks, kindness and support for me:
    1. _____   2. _____
    3. _____   4. _____
- ☐ Good Deed/Selfless Act/Random Kindness: _____
- ☐ I gave undivided attention to: _____
- ☐ I made things better by: _____
- ☐ I experienced joy, happiness, fun and/or laughter: _____
- ☐ I smiled _____ minutes
- ☐ Meditation/Prayer _____ minutes
- ☐ Inspiration (reading, video, music): _____
- ☐ I listened to my intuition: _____
- ☐ Physical activity _____ minutes
- ☐ I was 100% honest today
- ☐ I took care of myself by: _____
- ☐ Reviewed purpose 3 times
- ☐ Reviewed intentions 3 times
- ☐ Steps toward goals, intentions and purpose
    1. _____   2. _____   3. _____
- ☐ Reviewed vision
- ☐ I am grateful for:
    1. _____   6. _____
    2. _____   7. _____
    3. _____   8. _____
    4. _____   9. _____
    5. _____   10. _____

- ☐ I am looking forward to: _____

Notes: _____
_____
_____
_____

Mindful Living Worksheet

M Tu W Th F S S   Date:_____   Rate:_____

- ☐ I am content with: _____
- ☐ I am proud of: _____
- ☐ Success review
- ☐ I love myself because: _____ ☐
- ☐ Love, thanks, kindness and support for others:
  - 1. _____ 2. _____
  - 3. _____ 4. _____
- ☐ Love, thanks, kindness and support for me:
  - 1. _____ 2. _____
  - 3. _____ 4. _____
- ☐ Good Deed/Selfless Act/Random Kindness: _____
- ☐ I gave undivided attention to: _____
- ☐ I made things better by: _____
- ☐ I experienced joy, happiness, fun and/or laughter: _____
- ☐ I smiled _____ minutes
- ☐ Meditation/Prayer _____ minutes
- ☐ Inspiration (reading, video, music): _____
- ☐ I listened to my intuition: _____
- ☐ Physical activity _____ minutes
- ☐ I was 100% honest today
- ☐ I took care of myself by: _____
- ☐ Reviewed purpose 3 times
- ☐ Reviewed intentions 3 times
- ☐ Steps toward goals, intentions and purpose
  - 1. _____ 2. _____ 3. _____
- ☐ Reviewed vision
- ☐ I am grateful for:
  - 1. _____ 6. _____
  - 2. _____ 7. _____
  - 3. _____ 8. _____
  - 4. _____ 9. _____
  - 5. _____ 10. _____

- ☐ I am looking forward to: _____

Notes: _____
_____
_____

MINDFUL LIVING WORKSHEET

M   Tu   W   Th   F   S   S   Date:_____   Rate:_____

- ☐ I am content with: _____
- ☐ I am proud of: _____
- ☐ Success review
- ☐ I love myself because: _____ ☐
- ☐ Love, thanks, kindness and support for others:
    1. _____   2. _____
    3. _____   4. _____
- ☐ Love, thanks, kindness and support for me:
    1. _____   2. _____
    3. _____   4. _____
- ☐ Good Deed/Selfless Act/Random Kindness: _____
- ☐ I gave undivided attention to: _____
- ☐ I made things better by: _____
- ☐ I experienced joy, happiness, fun and/or laughter: _____
- ☐ I smiled _____ minutes
- ☐ Meditation/Prayer _____ minutes
- ☐ Inspiration (reading, video, music): _____
- ☐ I listened to my intuition: _____
- ☐ Physical activity _____ minutes
- ☐ I was 100% honest today
- ☐ I took care of myself by: _____
- ☐ Reviewed purpose 3 times
- ☐ Reviewed intentions 3 times
- ☐ Steps toward goals, intentions and purpose
    1. _____ 2. _____ 3. _____
- ☐ Reviewed vision
- ☐ I am grateful for:
    1. _____   6. _____
    2. _____   7. _____
    3. _____   8. _____
    4. _____   9. _____
    5. _____   10. _____

- ☐ I am looking forward to: _____

Notes: _____
_____
_____
_____

MINDFUL LIVING WORKSHEET

M Tu W Th F S S   Date:_____   Rate:_____

- ☐ I am content with: _____
- ☐ I am proud of: _____
- ☐ Success review
- ☐ I love myself because: _____ ☐
- ☐ Love, thanks, kindness and support for others:
    1. _____   2. _____
    3. _____   4. _____
- ☐ Love, thanks, kindness and support for me:
    1. _____   2. _____
    3. _____   4. _____
- ☐ Good Deed/Selfless Act/Random Kindness: _____
- ☐ I gave undivided attention to: _____
- ☐ I made things better by: _____
- ☐ I experienced joy, happiness, fun and/or laughter: _____
- ☐ I smiled _____ minutes
- ☐ Meditation/Prayer _____ minutes
- ☐ Inspiration (reading, video, music): _____
- ☐ I listened to my intuition: _____
- ☐ Physical activity _____ minutes
- ☐ I was 100% honest today
- ☐ I took care of myself by: _____
- ☐ Reviewed purpose 3 times
- ☐ Reviewed intentions 3 times
- ☐ Steps toward goals, intentions and purpose
    1. _____ 2. _____ 3. _____
- ☐ Reviewed vision
- ☐ I am grateful for:
    1. _____   6. _____
    2. _____   7. _____
    3. _____   8. _____
    4. _____   9. _____
    5. _____   10. _____

- ☐ I am looking forward to: _____

Notes: _____
_____
_____
_____

MINDFUL LIVING WORKSHEET

M   Tu   W   Th   F   S   S   Date:_____   Rate:_____

- ☐ I am content with: _____
- ☐ I am proud of: _____
- ☐ Success review
- ☐ I love myself because: _____ ☐
- ☐ Love, thanks, kindness and support for others:
    - 1. _____   2. _____
    - 3. _____   4. _____
- ☐ Love, thanks, kindness and support for me:
    - 1. _____   2. _____
    - 3. _____   4. _____
- ☐ Good Deed/Selfless Act/Random Kindness: _____
- ☐ I gave undivided attention to: _____
- ☐ I made things better by: _____
- ☐ I experienced joy, happiness, fun and/or laughter: _____
- ☐ I smiled _____ minutes
- ☐ Meditation/Prayer _____ minutes
- ☐ Inspiration (reading, video, music): _____
- ☐ I listened to my intuition: _____
- ☐ Physical activity _____ minutes
- ☐ I was 100% honest today
- ☐ I took care of myself by: _____
- ☐ Reviewed purpose 3 times
- ☐ Reviewed intentions 3 times
- ☐ Steps toward goals, intentions and purpose
    - 1. _____   2. _____   3. _____
- ☐ Reviewed vision
- ☐ I am grateful for:
    - 1. _____   6. _____
    - 2. _____   7. _____
    - 3. _____   8. _____
    - 4. _____   9. _____
    - 5. _____   10. _____

- ☐ I am looking forward to: _____

Notes: _____
_____
_____
_____

MINDFUL LIVING WORKSHEET

M Tu W Th F S S   Date:_____   Rate:_____

- ☐ I am content with: _____
- ☐ I am proud of: _____
- ☐ Success review
- ☐ I love myself because: _____ ☐
- ☐ Love, thanks, kindness and support for others:
    - 1. _____   2. _____
    - 3. _____   4. _____
- ☐ Love, thanks, kindness and support for me:
    - 1. _____   2. _____
    - 3. _____   4. _____
- ☐ Good Deed/Selfless Act/Random Kindness: _____
- ☐ I gave undivided attention to: _____
- ☐ I made things better by: _____
- ☐ I experienced joy, happiness, fun and/or laughter: _____
- ☐ I smiled _____ minutes
- ☐ Meditation/Prayer _____ minutes
- ☐ Inspiration (reading, video, music): _____
- ☐ I listened to my intuition: _____
- ☐ Physical activity _____ minutes
- ☐ I was 100% honest today
- ☐ I took care of myself by: _____
- ☐ Reviewed purpose 3 times
- ☐ Reviewed intentions 3 times
- ☐ Steps toward goals, intentions and purpose
    - 1. _____   2. _____   3. _____
- ☐ Reviewed vision
- ☐ I am grateful for:
    - 1. _____   6. _____
    - 2. _____   7. _____
    - 3. _____   8. _____
    - 4. _____   9. _____
    - 5. _____   10. _____

- ☐ I am looking forward to: _____

Notes: _____
_____
_____
_____

MINDFUL LIVING WORKSHEET

M Tu W Th F S S   Date: _____   Rate: _____

- ☐ I am content with: _____
- ☐ I am proud of: _____
- ☐ Success review
- ☐ I love myself because: _____ ☐
- ☐ Love, thanks, kindness and support for others:
    1. _____   2. _____
    3. _____   4. _____
- ☐ Love, thanks, kindness and support for me:
    1. _____   2. _____
    3. _____   4. _____
- ☐ Good Deed/Selfless Act/Random Kindness: _____
- ☐ I gave undivided attention to: _____
- ☐ I made things better by: _____
- ☐ I experienced joy, happiness, fun and/or laughter: _____
- ☐ I smiled _____ minutes
- ☐ Meditation/Prayer _____ minutes
- ☐ Inspiration (reading, video, music): _____
- ☐ I listened to my intuition: _____
- ☐ Physical activity _____ minutes
- ☐ I was 100% honest today
- ☐ I took care of myself by: _____
- ☐ Reviewed purpose 3 times
- ☐ Reviewed intentions 3 times
- ☐ Steps toward goals, intentions and purpose
    1. _____   2. _____   3. _____
- ☐ Reviewed vision
- ☐ I am grateful for:
    1. _____   6. _____
    2. _____   7. _____
    3. _____   8. _____
    4. _____   9. _____
    5. _____   10. _____

- ☐ I am looking forward to: _____

Notes: _____
_____
_____
_____

Mindful Living Worksheet

M Tu W Th F S S   Date: _____   Rate: _____

- ☐ I am content with: _____
- ☐ I am proud of: _____
- ☐ Success review
- ☐ I love myself because: _____ ☐
- ☐ Love, thanks, kindness and support for others:
  - 1. _____   2. _____
  - 3. _____   4. _____
- ☐ Love, thanks, kindness and support for me:
  - 1. _____   2. _____
  - 3. _____   4. _____
- ☐ Good Deed/Selfless Act/Random Kindness: _____
- ☐ I gave undivided attention to: _____
- ☐ I made things better by: _____
- ☐ I experienced joy, happiness, fun and/or laughter: _____
- ☐ I smiled _____ minutes
- ☐ Meditation/Prayer _____ minutes
- ☐ Inspiration (reading, video, music): _____
- ☐ I listened to my intuition: _____
- ☐ Physical activity _____ minutes
- ☐ I was 100% honest today
- ☐ I took care of myself by: _____
- ☐ Reviewed purpose 3 times
- ☐ Reviewed intentions 3 times
- ☐ Steps toward goals, intentions and purpose
  - 1. _____ 2. _____ 3. _____
- ☐ Reviewed vision
- ☐ I am grateful for:
  - 1. _____   6. _____
  - 2. _____   7. _____
  - 3. _____   8. _____
  - 4. _____   9. _____
  - 5. _____   10. _____

- ☐ I am looking forward to: _____

Notes: _____
_____
_____

Mindful Living Worksheet

M   Tu   W   Th   F   S   S   Date:_____   Rate:_____

- ☐ I am content with: _____
- ☐ I am proud of: _____
- ☐ Success review
- ☐ I love myself because: _____ ☐
- ☐ Love, thanks, kindness and support for others:
  - 1. _____   2. _____
  - 3. _____   4. _____
- ☐ Love, thanks, kindness and support for me:
  - 1. _____   2. _____
  - 3. _____   4. _____
- ☐ Good Deed/Selfless Act/Random Kindness: _____
- ☐ I gave undivided attention to: _____
- ☐ I made things better by: _____
- ☐ I experienced joy, happiness, fun and/or laughter: _____
- ☐ I smiled _____ minutes
- ☐ Meditation/Prayer _____ minutes
- ☐ Inspiration (reading, video, music): _____
- ☐ I listened to my intuition: _____
- ☐ Physical activity _____ minutes
- ☐ I was 100% honest today
- ☐ I took care of myself by: _____
- ☐ Reviewed purpose 3 times
- ☐ Reviewed intentions 3 times
- ☐ Steps toward goals, intentions and purpose
  - 1. _____   2. _____   3. _____
- ☐ Reviewed vision
- ☐ I am grateful for:
  - 1. _____   6. _____
  - 2. _____   7. _____
  - 3. _____   8. _____
  - 4. _____   9. _____
  - 5. _____   10. _____

- ☐ I am looking forward to: _____

Notes: _____
_____
_____
_____

Mindful Living Worksheet

M   Tu   W   Th   F   S   S   Date: _____   Rate: _____

- ☐ I am content with: _____
- ☐ I am proud of: _____
- ☐ Success review
- ☐ I love myself because: _____ ☐
- ☐ Love, thanks, kindness and support for others:
    1. _____   2. _____
    3. _____   4. _____
- ☐ Love, thanks, kindness and support for me:
    1. _____   2. _____
    3. _____   4. _____
- ☐ Good Deed/Selfless Act/Random Kindness: _____
- ☐ I gave undivided attention to: _____
- ☐ I made things better by: _____
- ☐ I experienced joy, happiness, fun and/or laughter: _____
- ☐ I smiled _____ minutes
- ☐ Meditation/Prayer _____ minutes
- ☐ Inspiration (reading, video, music): _____
- ☐ I listened to my intuition: _____
- ☐ Physical activity _____ minutes
- ☐ I was 100% honest today
- ☐ I took care of myself by: _____
- ☐ Reviewed purpose 3 times
- ☐ Reviewed intentions 3 times
- ☐ Steps toward goals, intentions and purpose
    1. _____   2. _____   3. _____
- ☐ Reviewed vision
- ☐ I am grateful for:
    1. _____   6. _____
    2. _____   7. _____
    3. _____   8. _____
    4. _____   9. _____
    5. _____   10. _____
- ☐ I am looking forward to: _____

Notes: _____
_____
_____

MINDFUL LIVING WORKSHEET

M Tu W Th F S S   Date:_____   Rate:_____

- ☐ I am content with: _____
- ☐ I am proud of: _____
- ☐ Success review
- ☐ I love myself because: _____ ☐
- ☐ Love, thanks, kindness and support for others:
  - 1. _____   2. _____
  - 3. _____   4. _____
- ☐ Love, thanks, kindness and support for me:
  - 1. _____   2. _____
  - 3. _____   4. _____
- ☐ Good Deed/Selfless Act/Random Kindness: _____
- ☐ I gave undivided attention to: _____
- ☐ I made things better by: _____
- ☐ I experienced joy, happiness, fun and/or laughter: _____
- ☐ I smiled _____ minutes
- ☐ Meditation/Prayer _____ minutes
- ☐ Inspiration (reading, video, music): _____
- ☐ I listened to my intuition: _____
- ☐ Physical activity _____ minutes
- ☐ I was 100% honest today
- ☐ I took care of myself by: _____
- ☐ Reviewed purpose 3 times
- ☐ Reviewed intentions 3 times
- ☐ Steps toward goals, intentions and purpose
  - 1. _____   2. _____   3. _____
- ☐ Reviewed vision
- ☐ I am grateful for:
  - 1. _____   6. _____
  - 2. _____   7. _____
  - 3. _____   8. _____
  - 4. _____   9. _____
  - 5. _____   10. _____
- ☐ I am looking forward to: _____

Notes: _____
_____
_____
_____

Mindful Living Worksheet

M Tu W Th F S S   Date:_____   Rate:_____

- ☐ I am content with: _____
- ☐ I am proud of: _____
- ☐ Success review
- ☐ I love myself because: _____ ☐
- ☐ Love, thanks, kindness and support for others:
  - 1. _____   2. _____
  - 3. _____   4. _____
- ☐ Love, thanks, kindness and support for me:
  - 1. _____   2. _____
  - 3. _____   4. _____
- ☐ Good Deed/Selfless Act/Random Kindness: _____
- ☐ I gave undivided attention to: _____
- ☐ I made things better by: _____
- ☐ I experienced joy, happiness, fun and/or laughter: _____
- ☐ I smiled _____ minutes
- ☐ Meditation/Prayer _____ minutes
- ☐ Inspiration (reading, video, music): _____
- ☐ I listened to my intuition: _____
- ☐ Physical activity _____ minutes
- ☐ I was 100% honest today
- ☐ I took care of myself by: _____
- ☐ Reviewed purpose 3 times
- ☐ Reviewed intentions 3 times
- ☐ Steps toward goals, intentions and purpose
  - 1. _____   2. _____   3. _____
- ☐ Reviewed vision
- ☐ I am grateful for:
  - 1. _____   6. _____
  - 2. _____   7. _____
  - 3. _____   8. _____
  - 4. _____   9. _____
  - 5. _____   10. _____

- ☐ I am looking forward to: _____

Notes: _____
_____
_____
_____

MINDFUL LIVING WORKSHEET

M Tu W Th F S S   Date:_____   Rate:_____

☐ I am content with: _____
☐ I am proud of: _____
☐ Success review
☐ I love myself because: _____ ☐
☐ Love, thanks, kindness and support for others:
    1. _____   2. _____
    3. _____   4. _____
☐ Love, thanks, kindness and support for me:
    1. _____   2. _____
    3. _____   4. _____
☐ Good Deed/Selfless Act/Random Kindness: _____
☐ I gave undivided attention to: _____
☐ I made things better by: _____
☐ I experienced joy, happiness, fun and/or laughter: _____
☐ I smiled _____ minutes
☐ Meditation/Prayer _____ minutes
☐ Inspiration (reading, video, music): _____
☐ I listened to my intuition: _____
☐ Physical activity _____ minutes
☐ I was 100% honest today
☐ I took care of myself by: _____
☐ Reviewed purpose 3 times
☐ Reviewed intentions 3 times
☐ Steps toward goals, intentions and purpose
    1. _____ 2. _____ 3. _____
☐ Reviewed vision
☐ I am grateful for:
    1. _____   6. _____
    2. _____   7. _____
    3. _____   8. _____
    4. _____   9. _____
    5. _____   10. _____

☐ I am looking forward to: _____

Notes: _____
_____
_____
_____

Mindful Living Worksheet

M Tu W Th F S S   Date:_____   Rate:_____

- ☐ I am content with: _____
- ☐ I am proud of: _____
- ☐ Success review
- ☐ I love myself because: _____ ☐
- ☐ Love, thanks, kindness and support for others:
    1. _____   2. _____
    3. _____   4. _____
- ☐ Love, thanks, kindness and support for me:
    1. _____   2. _____
    3. _____   4. _____
- ☐ Good Deed/Selfless Act/Random Kindness: _____
- ☐ I gave undivided attention to: _____
- ☐ I made things better by: _____
- ☐ I experienced joy, happiness, fun and/or laughter: _____
- ☐ I smiled _____ minutes
- ☐ Meditation/Prayer _____ minutes
- ☐ Inspiration (reading, video, music): _____
- ☐ I listened to my intuition: _____
- ☐ Physical activity _____ minutes
- ☐ I was 100% honest today
- ☐ I took care of myself by: _____
- ☐ Reviewed purpose 3 times
- ☐ Reviewed intentions 3 times
- ☐ Steps toward goals, intentions and purpose
    1. _____ 2. _____ 3. _____
- ☐ Reviewed vision
- ☐ I am grateful for:
    1. _____   6. _____
    2. _____   7. _____
    3. _____   8. _____
    4. _____   9. _____
    5. _____   10. _____

- ☐ I am looking forward to: _____

Notes: _____
_____
_____
_____

MINDFUL LIVING WORKSHEET

M Tu W Th F S S   Date:_____   Rate:_____

- ☐ I am content with: _____
- ☐ I am proud of: _____
- ☐ Success review
- ☐ I love myself because: _____ ☐
- ☐ Love, thanks, kindness and support for others:
  - 1. _____   2. _____
  - 3. _____   4. _____
- ☐ Love, thanks, kindness and support for me:
  - 1. _____   2. _____
  - 3. _____   4. _____
- ☐ Good Deed/Selfless Act/Random Kindness: _____
- ☐ I gave undivided attention to: _____
- ☐ I made things better by: _____
- ☐ I experienced joy, happiness, fun and/or laughter: _____
- ☐ I smiled _____ minutes
- ☐ Meditation/Prayer _____ minutes
- ☐ Inspiration (reading, video, music): _____
- ☐ I listened to my intuition: _____
- ☐ Physical activity _____ minutes
- ☐ I was 100% honest today
- ☐ I took care of myself by: _____
- ☐ Reviewed purpose 3 times
- ☐ Reviewed intentions 3 times
- ☐ Steps toward goals, intentions and purpose
  - 1. _____   2. _____   3. _____
- ☐ Reviewed vision
- ☐ I am grateful for:
  - 1. _____   6. _____
  - 2. _____   7. _____
  - 3. _____   8. _____
  - 4. _____   9. _____
  - 5. _____   10. _____

- ☐ I am looking forward to: _____

Notes: _____
_____
_____

MINDFUL LIVING WORKSHEET

M   Tu   W   Th   F   S   S   Date:_____   Rate:_____

- ☐ I am content with: _____
- ☐ I am proud of: _____
- ☐ Success review
- ☐ I love myself because: _____ ☐
- ☐ Love, thanks, kindness and support for others:
  - 1. _____   2. _____
  - 3. _____   4. _____
- ☐ Love, thanks, kindness and support for me:
  - 1. _____   2. _____
  - 3. _____   4. _____
- ☐ Good Deed/Selfless Act/Random Kindness: _____
- ☐ I gave undivided attention to: _____
- ☐ I made things better by: _____
- ☐ I experienced joy, happiness, fun and/or laughter: _____
- ☐ I smiled _____ minutes
- ☐ Meditation/Prayer _____ minutes
- ☐ Inspiration (reading, video, music): _____
- ☐ I listened to my intuition: _____
- ☐ Physical activity _____ minutes
- ☐ I was 100% honest today
- ☐ I took care of myself by: _____
- ☐ Reviewed purpose 3 times
- ☐ Reviewed intentions 3 times
- ☐ Steps toward goals, intentions and purpose
  - 1. _____   2. _____   3. _____
- ☐ Reviewed vision
- ☐ I am grateful for:
  - 1. _____   6. _____
  - 2. _____   7. _____
  - 3. _____   8. _____
  - 4. _____   9. _____
  - 5. _____   10. _____

- ☐ I am looking forward to: _____

Notes: _____
_____
_____
_____

MINDFUL LIVING WORKSHEET

M Tu W Th F S S   Date:_____   Rate:_____

- ☐ I am content with: _____
- ☐ I am proud of: _____
- ☐ Success review
- ☐ I love myself because: _____ ☐
- ☐ Love, thanks, kindness and support for others:
  - 1. _____   2. _____
  - 3. _____   4. _____
- ☐ Love, thanks, kindness and support for me:
  - 1. _____   2. _____
  - 3. _____   4. _____
- ☐ Good Deed/Selfless Act/Random Kindness: _____
- ☐ I gave undivided attention to: _____
- ☐ I made things better by: _____
- ☐ I experienced joy, happiness, fun and/or laughter: _____
- ☐ I smiled _____ minutes
- ☐ Meditation/Prayer _____ minutes
- ☐ Inspiration (reading, video, music): _____
- ☐ I listened to my intuition: _____
- ☐ Physical activity _____ minutes
- ☐ I was 100% honest today
- ☐ I took care of myself by: _____
- ☐ Reviewed purpose 3 times
- ☐ Reviewed intentions 3 times
- ☐ Steps toward goals, intentions and purpose
  - 1. _____ 2. _____ 3. _____
- ☐ Reviewed vision
- ☐ I am grateful for:
  - 1. _____   6. _____
  - 2. _____   7. _____
  - 3. _____   8. _____
  - 4. _____   9. _____
  - 5. _____   10. _____
- ☐ I am looking forward to: _____

Notes: _____
_____
_____
_____

Mindful Living Worksheet

M Tu W Th F S S   Date:_____   Rate:_____

☐ I am content with: _____
☐ I am proud of: _____
☐ Success review
☐ I love myself because: _____ ☐
☐ Love, thanks, kindness and support for others:
      1. _____   2. _____
      3. _____   4. _____
☐ Love, thanks, kindness and support for me:
      1. _____   2. _____
      3. _____   4. _____
☐ Good Deed/Selfless Act/Random Kindness: _____
☐ I gave undivided attention to: _____
☐ I made things better by: _____
☐ I experienced joy, happiness, fun and/or laughter: _____
☐ I smiled _____ minutes
☐ Meditation/Prayer _____ minutes
☐ Inspiration (reading, video, music): _____
☐ I listened to my intuition: _____
☐ Physical activity _____ minutes
☐ I was 100% honest today
☐ I took care of myself by: _____
☐ Reviewed purpose 3 times
☐ Reviewed intentions 3 times
☐ Steps toward goals, intentions and purpose
    1. _____ 2. _____ 3. _____
☐ Reviewed vision
☐ I am grateful for:
      1. _____   6. _____
      2. _____   7. _____
      3. _____   8. _____
      4. _____   9. _____
      5. _____   10. _____

☐ I am looking forward to: _____

Notes: _____
_____
_____

Mindful Living Worksheet

M Tu W Th F S S   Date:_____   Rate:_____

- ☐ I am content with: _____
- ☐ I am proud of: _____
- ☐ Success review
- ☐ I love myself because: _____ ☐
- ☐ Love, thanks, kindness and support for others:
  - 1. _____   2. _____
  - 3. _____   4. _____
- ☐ Love, thanks, kindness and support for me:
  - 1. _____   2. _____
  - 3. _____   4. _____
- ☐ Good Deed/Selfless Act/Random Kindness: _____
- ☐ I gave undivided attention to: _____
- ☐ I made things better by: _____
- ☐ I experienced joy, happiness, fun and/or laughter: _____
- ☐ I smiled _____ minutes
- ☐ Meditation/Prayer _____ minutes
- ☐ Inspiration (reading, video, music): _____
- ☐ I listened to my intuition: _____
- ☐ Physical activity _____ minutes
- ☐ I was 100% honest today
- ☐ I took care of myself by: _____
- ☐ Reviewed purpose 3 times
- ☐ Reviewed intentions 3 times
- ☐ Steps toward goals, intentions and purpose
  - 1. _____ 2. _____ 3. _____
- ☐ Reviewed vision
- ☐ I am grateful for:
  - 1. _____   6. _____
  - 2. _____   7. _____
  - 3. _____   8. _____
  - 4. _____   9. _____
  - 5. _____   10. _____
- ☐ I am looking forward to: _____

Notes: _____
_____
_____
_____

Mindful Living Worksheet

M   Tu   W   Th   F   S   S   Date:_____   Rate:_____

☐ I am content with: _____
☐ I am proud of: _____
☐ Success review
☐ I love myself because: _____ ☐
☐ Love, thanks, kindness and support for others:
    1. _____ 2. _____
    3. _____ 4. _____
☐ Love, thanks, kindness and support for me:
    1. _____ 2. _____
    3. _____ 4. _____
☐ Good Deed/Selfless Act/Random Kindness: _____
☐ I gave undivided attention to: _____
☐ I made things better by: _____
☐ I experienced joy, happiness, fun and/or laughter: _____
☐ I smiled _____ minutes
☐ Meditation/Prayer _____ minutes
☐ Inspiration (reading, video, music): _____
☐ I listened to my intuition: _____
☐ Physical activity _____ minutes
☐ I was 100% honest today
☐ I took care of myself by: _____
☐ Reviewed purpose 3 times
☐ Reviewed intentions 3 times
☐ Steps toward goals, intentions and purpose
    1. _____ 2. _____ 3. _____
☐ Reviewed vision
☐ I am grateful for:
    1. _____ 6. _____
    2. _____ 7. _____
    3. _____ 8. _____
    4. _____ 9. _____
    5. _____ 10. _____

☐ I am looking forward to: _____

Notes: _____
_____
_____

MINDFUL LIVING WORKSHEET

M Tu W Th F S S   Date:_____   Rate:_____

- ☐ I am content with: _____
- ☐ I am proud of: _____
- ☐ Success review
- ☐ I love myself because: _____ ☐
- ☐ Love, thanks, kindness and support for others:
    1. _____   2. _____
    3. _____   4. _____
- ☐ Love, thanks, kindness and support for me:
    1. _____   2. _____
    3. _____   4. _____
- ☐ Good Deed/Selfless Act/Random Kindness: _____
- ☐ I gave undivided attention to: _____
- ☐ I made things better by: _____
- ☐ I experienced joy, happiness, fun and/or laughter: _____
- ☐ I smiled _____ minutes
- ☐ Meditation/Prayer _____ minutes
- ☐ Inspiration (reading, video, music): _____
- ☐ I listened to my intuition: _____
- ☐ Physical activity _____ minutes
- ☐ I was 100% honest today
- ☐ I took care of myself by: _____
- ☐ Reviewed purpose 3 times
- ☐ Reviewed intentions 3 times
- ☐ Steps toward goals, intentions and purpose
    1. _____ 2. _____ 3. _____
- ☐ Reviewed vision
- ☐ I am grateful for:
    1. _____   6. _____
    2. _____   7. _____
    3. _____   8. _____
    4. _____   9. _____
    5. _____   10. _____

- ☐ I am looking forward to: _____

Notes: _____
_____
_____

Made in the USA
Middletown, DE
31 January 2018